We Are Not One People

We Are Not One People

Secession and Separatism in American Politics Since 1776

MICHAEL J. LEE AND
R. JARROD ATCHISON

OXFORD
UNIVERSITY PRESS

Oxford University Press is a department of the University of Oxford. It furthers the University's objective of excellence in research, scholarship, and education by publishing worldwide. Oxford is a registered trade mark of Oxford University Press in the UK and certain other countries.

Published in the United States of America by Oxford University Press 198 Madison Avenue, New York, NY 10016, United States of America.

© Oxford University Press 2022

All rights reserved. No part of this publication may be reproduced, stored in a retrieval system, or transmitted, in any form or by any means, without the prior permission in writing of Oxford University Press, or as expressly permitted by law, by license, or under terms agreed with the appropriate reproduction rights organization. Inquiries concerning reproduction outside the scope of the above should be sent to the Rights Department, Oxford University Press, at the address above.

You must not circulate this work in any other form and you must impose this same condition on any acquirer.

Library of Congress Cataloging-in-Publication Data
Names: Lee, Michael J., 1979– author. | Atchison, R. Jarrod (Robert Jarrod), 1979– author.
Title: We are not one people : secession and separatism in American politics since 1776 / Michael J. Lee & R. Jarrod Atchison.
Description: New York, NY : Oxford University Press, [2022] | Includes bibliographical references and index.
Identifiers: LCCN 2021036248 (print) | LCCN 2021036249 (ebook) | ISBN 9780190876500 (hardback) | ISBN 9780190876517 (paperback) | ISBN 9780190876531 (epub)
Subjects: LCSH: Secession—United States—History. | Separatist movements. | National characteristics, American. | Political culture—United States. | United States—Politics and government. | United States—History—Autonomy and independence movements.
Classification: LCC E183 .L38 2022 (print) | LCC E183 (ebook) | DDC 973—dc23
LC record available at https://lccn.loc.gov/2021036248
LC ebook record available at https://lccn.loc.gov/2021036249

DOI: 10.1093/oso/9780190876500.001.0001

1 3 5 7 9 8 6 4 2

Paperback printed by Lakeside Book Company, United States of America
Hardback printed by Bridgeport National Bindery, Inc., United States of America

This book is dedicated to the policy debate community, who gave us opportunities to learn in ways we never imagined were possible

Epigraph

We must also remember what our service personnel know better than anyone: that we are one people, with one home and one glorious American destiny. We come from all different walks of life, but we all share the same dream: to live in peace and safety, to work with honor and dignity, and to build a better future for those we love.

—Donald Trump, 2017

The pundits like to slice-and-dice our country into Red States and Blue States; Red States for Republicans, Blue States for Democrats. But I've got news for them, too. We worship an awesome God in the Blue States, and we don't like federal agents poking around our libraries in the Red States. We coach Little League in the Blue States and have gay friends in the Red States. There are patriots who opposed the war in Iraq and patriots who supported it. We are one people, all of us pledging allegiance to the stars and stripes, all of us defending the United States of America.

—Barack Obama, 2004

This has been an extraordinary election. But in one of God's unforeseen paths, this belatedly broken impasse can point us all to a new common ground, for its very closeness can serve to remind us that we are one people with a shared history and a shared destiny. Indeed, that history gives us many examples of contests as hotly debated, as fiercely fought, with their own challenges to the popular will. Other disputes have dragged on for weeks before reaching resolution. And each time, both the victor and the vanquished have accepted the result peacefully and in a spirit of reconciliation. So let it be with us.

—Al Gore, 2000

A nation derives its soul, strength, and character from the sum of the creative efforts of all its citizens. While we are a nation of more than 230 million individuals, we are one people—interdependent on each other for our accomplishments and our future.

—Ronald Reagan, 1982

America still is going through an agony of transition. It takes time for old myths to give way to new awareness. It takes time to erase the old stereotypes. But the point is that we are moving forward, and moving rapidly, toward what the riot commission refers to as a "single society"— one nation, one people, one common ideal, in which each person is measured as an individual, and in which legal rights are fleshed out with actual opportunities. We must do more. But if progress is to be made, the first essential now is order.

—Richard Nixon, 1968

The federal Government ought to be, and is, solicitous for the welfare of every one of its inhabitants, every one of its business activities, whether they be small or great. This is one country; we are one people united by common interests. There should be no favorites and no outcasts; no race or religious prejudices in government. America opposes special privilege for anybody, and favors equal opportunity for everybody. It has adopted these principles because they are the logical conclusions of our ideals of freedom.

—Calvin Coolidge, 1924

viii EPIGRAPH

In this "land of the free" we are burned, tortured, and denied a fair trial, murdered for any imaginary wrong conceived in the brain of the negro-hating white man. There is no redress for us from a government which promised to protect all under its flag. It seems a mystery to me. They say, "One flag, one nation, one country indivisible." Is this true? Can we say this truthfully, when one race is allowed to burn, hang, and inflict the most horrible torture weekly, monthly, on another? No, we cannot sing "My country, 'tis of thee, Sweet land of Liberty!" It is hollow mockery.

—Susie King Taylor, 1902

We are two peoples, essentially different in all that makes a people.

—Robert Barnwell Rhett, 1860

We are not one people. We are two peoples. We are a people for Freedom and a people for Slavery. Between the two, conflict is inevitable.

—Horace Greeley, 1855

We must remember, it is the most difficult process in the world to make two people of one.

—John C. Calhoun, 1838

The people of the United States formed the Constitution, acting through the State legislatures in making the compact, to meet and discuss its provisions, and acting in separate conventions when they ratified those provisions; but the terms used in its construction show it to be a Government in which the people of all the States, collectively, are represented. We are one people in the choice of President and Vice-President.

—Andrew Jackson, 1832

The unity of government which constitutes you one people is also now dear to you. It is justly so, for it is a main pillar in the edifice of your real independence, the support of your tranquility at home, your peace abroad; of your safety; of your prosperity; of that very liberty which you so highly prize. But as it is easy to foresee that, from different causes and from different quarters, much pains will be taken, many artifices employed to weaken in your minds the conviction of this truth.

—George Washington, 1796

Contents

Acknowledgments		xiii
Prologue		1
1.	Bands, Bonds, and Affections	15
2.	Secession All the Way Down: Libertarians Opt Out	47
3.	"A Slave Republic": Secession and Southern Slavery	75
4.	White Devils and Black Separatists	105
5.	"Dykes First": Lesbian Separatism in America	141
6.	Secession in Exodus: Achieving God's Terrestrial Kingdom	169
7.	Conclusion	195
Notes		211
Index		285

Acknowledgments

This project began in a series of conversations in graduate school at the University of Georgia. Nearly twenty years later, as it nears completion, the intellectual debts we have accumulated are incalculable. So many people helped us hone our arguments, offered texts for consideration, suggested historical instances to discuss, sent us articles, and generally tolerated our ongoing obsession with secession and separation.

We would not have been able to complete this project without the love of our families. Our partners, Erin Benson and Becca Atchison, created space for us to read, research, and write, and they provided untold amounts of intellectual comradery, thoughtful recommendations, and badly needed encouragement. Our extended families, including our parents and in-laws, also provided essential support, and we thank them profusely. Our children provided perspective, encouragement, and comic relief, which we needed from start to finish.

Our academic institutions have been essential partners in this research. The College of Charleston supported us through the dean's discretionary fund, a faculty research and development grant, membership in the faculty liberal arts and sciences colloquium, sponsored writing retreats, and support in two first-year experience seminars on the subject. Wake Forest University provided research funds, an opportunity to present in the New Ideas series, and the Reinsch/Pierce Family Fellowship. We completed writing this book during a pandemic, and our library staffs were miracle workers; they found loans and copies of obscure book chapters while most of the nation was in total lockdown. Our departmental colleagues and chairs also supported our work. Anyone familiar with higher education knows that department administrative support is the only reason anything gets done. Toward that end, we would like to thank Mary Jones, Candice Burris, Janice Jennings, and Jo Lowe for everything they do day in and day out. Our classroom conversations were vital as we generated and road-tested ideas, and we would like to thank our graduate and undergraduate students. Beyond our current institutions, we benefited greatly from the opportunity to return to the University of Georgia to present drafts of our chapters to the Communication Studies colloquium series.

This project has benefited immensely from conversations with a brilliant set of friends and colleagues. We would like to thank the following people for their intellectual support and camaraderie: Paul Achter, Andrew Alwine, Daryl Burch, Tim Cochran, Nate Cohn, Matthew Cressler, Julia Eichelberger, Sam Flores, Seth Gannon, Cagney Gentry, Steve Giles, Becca Gill, Justin and Sarah Green, Michael Hyde, Kelly Jakes, Lisa Jasinski, Paul Johnson, Patrick Keating, Casey Kelly, Amber Kelsi, Jennie Keohane, John Llewellyn, Allan Louden, Calum Matheson, Kristen McCauliff, John and Megan Medica, Ryan Milner, David and Leigh Moscowitz, John Murphy, Len and Rachel Neighbors, Ed Panetta, David Parisi, Catherine Riley, Ken Rufo, Alison Shermeta, Drew Shermeta, Ross Smith, Gordon Stables, Ken Strange, Ron and Alessandra Von Burg, Eric Watts, Kirt Wilson, and Meg Zulick.

Finally, we are deeply grateful for the support, guidance, and patience that Oxford University Press, especially Meredith Keffer, has given us.

Prologue

Alexander Hamilton coined the name "Whiskey Rebellion" to suggest that the Pennsylvanians revolting against federal authority in 1794 were a confederacy of drunkards. Thomas Jefferson called it "Hamilton's insurrection," suggesting that his fellow founder distorted the ordinary grievances of frontier farmers into an existential threat to get his political wish: federal authority.[1] Hamilton's name stuck, but not because it was more accurate than Jefferson's. The Whiskey Rebellion was about whiskey in the same sense that the American Revolution was about tea.

The land west of the Alleghenies had been the frontier since long before the Revolutionary War. Pittsburgh had just a thousand residents in 1794; gold and silver coins were rare. Since whiskey had supplanted rum and brandy as Americans' drink of choice, it held a consistent value for many small farmers who produced it at community stills. Whiskey became liquid currency; landlords accepted whiskey as rent, and laborers accepted grain used to make whiskey as wages. The entire community ran on whiskey. One-fourth of the nation's stills operated there, and the strong rye whiskey distilled in the region's rounded hills carried brand recognition as far away as New Orleans.[2]

An excise tax is a tax on a specific good, but western Pennsylvanians experienced the whiskey tax that Hamilton championed in 1791 as an existence tax. The tax, moreover, had to be paid in coin, and if the tax went unpaid or an unregistered still was discovered, tax collectors were authorized to seize the whiskey and the still, both property and currency.[3] Frontier Pennsylvanians began revolting against federal authority immediately after its passage. Gangs dressed as Native Americans, enslaved people, and women tortured collectors of the excise tax. This resistance in western Pennsylvania had been flaring for three years when local irregulars tried to kill one tax collector and burned down another's house.

We Are Not One People. Michael J. Lee and R. Jarrod Atchison, Oxford University Press. © Oxford University Press 2022. DOI: 10.1093/oso/9780190876500.003.0001

2   WE ARE NOT ONE PEOPLE

Between 1791 and the fall of 1794, these spasmodic attacks on tax collectors coalesced into something more organized, more coherent: a maturing secession movement. Rebels adopted a totemic flag with six stripes to symbolize the number of counties in active rebellion. These Whiskey Rebels, many of whom were veterans of the Revolution, were loosely organized near where the Allegheny and Monongahela joined, forming the Ohio River. In August 1794, six thousand rebels gathered at Braddock's Field, where, in 1755, British troops, despite the considerable battlefield daring of the twenty-three-year-old George Washington, had been massacred by French and Native American guerillas. This frontier crowd heard speakers encourage the seizure of a local federal armory and, emulating the revolutionaries in France, the creation of a committee of public safety and the assembly of guillotines.[4] These Pennsylvania rebels, of course, opposed the disparate impact of the whiskey tax, but their brief revolt fundamentally disturbed both the theory and practice of American democracy's untested ideals: liberty, self-determination, sovereignty, federalism, popular rule, the rule of law, minority rights, the limits of protest, presidential power, and whether one people's folkways must submit to We the People's commercial civilization.

The bourgeoning American commercial civilization needed money. The new country had war debts to pay, and, at the time, the excise tax was pivotal to federal financial solvency.[5] Hamilton thought that taxing spirits would, as he outlined in *Federalist* 12, both tamp down a "national extravagance" and "furnish a considerable revenue."[6] Hamilton was not alone in worrying about both federal coffers and laws. Washington also wrote that the whiskey crisis could end the American experiment: "If the laws are to be trampled upon with impunity, and a minority is to dictate to the majority, there is an end put at one stroke to republican government."[7] Both feared that the whiskey revolt was already spreading to other states.[8] But, as Ron Chernow has rendered him, Hamilton, scarred by dreadful childhood hardships, was "haunted by the hobgoblins of disorder."[9] He urged Washington to assert federal authority definitively, especially in the hinterlands. Washington agreed.

Seven years after Pennsylvania became the first large state to ratify the Constitution, it became the first state of any size to revolt against

PROLOGUE 3

it. With the capital in Philadelphia, a conflict between eastern and western Pennsylvania was both provincial and national. Washington called up thirteen thousand militia troops from several states. Henry Knox, then secretary of war, was unavailable to command this ad hoc force; his rash investment in one million acres in Maine had gone south, and he was away from the capital tending to personal business.[10] Instead, Washington named Henry "Light Horse Harry" Lee III, then governor of Virginia, major general. Washington set Carlisle, Pennsylvania, two hundred miles east of Pittsburgh, as a rendezvous point with the counterinsurgency troops, and he and Hamilton set off to war down Market Street in a shared carriage.[11]

As an uprising, the Whiskey Rebellion was trivial. Threatened by thirteen thousand organized soldiers descending the Alleghenies' western edge, the Pennsylvania freedom fighters scattered before any combat commenced. Many fled the region entirely. Only two rebel leaders were formally convicted of treason and scheduled for the gallows. Washington, exercising this power of the office for the first time, pardoned them both, over Hamilton's objections.[12] "This business must not be skimmed over," Hamilton urged unsuccessfully. "The political putrefaction of Pennsylvania is greater than I had any idea of."[13]

As a dramatic display of the ever-present tensions of disunion that dogged the evolving American nation, the Whiskey Rebellion was both momentous and portentous. First, the battle may have been a non-event, but federal troops occupied the area nonetheless. Washington, in ill health, traveled back to Philadelphia after the Carlisle meet-up. He gave Hamilton and Lee, essentially dual commanders, explicit instructions that troops were to conduct an occupation without acting as occupiers. Conflicts over spirits aside, this was, after all, an American army interacting with other Americans.[14] Washington knew that frontier submission to federal law would be especially unlikely after wholesale slaughter or the creation of martyrs.[15] The extent to which Hamilton and Lee followed the first president's advice is debatable. Lee amnestied, over Hamilton's objections yet again, all but the most violent rebels, but American troops did, at bayonet point, round up, imprison, interrogate, and torture hundreds of American citizens.[16]

4   WE ARE NOT ONE PEOPLE

Second, the lives and legacies, both personal and familial, of Washington, Hamilton, and Lee highlight the enduring difficulty of balancing federalism and anti-federalism, of harmonizing liberty and union, calibrating individuality and community, reconciling local and national, pairing disagreement and order. This was neither the trio's first campaign together nor their first brush with revolutionary secession. They had played an opposite role in that first campaign, however. Nearly two decades prior, Washington, Hamilton, and Lee had agitated on behalf of disaffected, backwoods colonies against an overbearing state. Hamilton had been Washington's trusted aide-de-camp during the Revolution; Lee was his ruthless guerilla commander. In 1777, Hamilton and Lee, anticipating a British assault on Philadelphia, executed a bold scorched-earth maneuver together when Washington ordered them to torch flour mills on the Schuylkill River before the British could seize them; Hamilton was nearly killed.[17]

Much of Hamilton's career as a post-Revolutionary statesman was devoted to preventing the country from fracturing. His "overwhelming passion" was the "strength and stability of the union." His death, in fact, was a unionist act. His duel with Aaron Burr, of course, was prompted by Burr's accusation that Hamilton had slandered him. Nevertheless, New England Federalists worried about the expansion of slavery and southern slave power and talked openly of secession if Thomas Jefferson won the 1804 election. Burr, Jefferson's sitting vice president, knew he would be dropped from the reelection ticket; for his next act, he hoped to become New York's governor and lead the state into this New England splinter group. Hamilton fretted about Burr and this "breakaway confederacy." The night before the Weehawken duel, Hamilton wrote a friend in Massachusetts of the self-destructive threat secession posed. Secession occupied his mind immediately after the duel, on his final night, as well. As Hamilton succumbed to Burr's bullet, some of his last recorded words were, "If they break this union, they will break my heart."[18]

Hamilton and Washington occupied two different points on a large spectrum between liberty and union. At times in his life, Lee occupied various points on this spectrum; at others, he took more radical positions, leaning toward anarchy or toward tyranny. He won glory as the commander of a nimble light infantry force during the

PROLOGUE 5

Revolutionary War, but he was excessive, even medieval, in his punishment of deserters, and he butchered loyalist civilians, fellow colonials. He was court-martialed twice, though acquitted both times.[19] As a war hero, he brought tremendous recognition to his family, but he also managed to be written out of two wills, his first wife's and his father's. In one historian's estimation, Lee was a "patriot and scoundrel, upright citizen and confidence man, benefactor and deceiver."[20] Assessing his hunger for power, ruthlessness, and opportunism, Hamilton saw "Julius Caesar or Cromwell" in Lee.[21]

Lee is a cautionary tale for both freedom run amok and unity pursued unmercifully. He was a promoter of common fealty to a central authority while also a selfish flouter of familial, social, and political norms. Lee favored a strong federal government while serving in the Continental Congress, then whipsawed in the other direction, allegedly due to a rebuke from Hamilton when Lee requested advance knowledge of a ruling on local and national currencies, textbook insider trading. His adoption of anti-federalism was convincing enough for the Virginia state legislature to appoint him governor, a largely ceremonial job.[22] Curiously, Lee advocated changing "We, the people" to "We, the states" during the ratification debates.[23] Befitting his erratic politics, Lee even began to negotiate a generalship in the revolutionary French army in 1792, only to be talked down by Washington and others. Once the Whiskey Rebellion began, Lee cherished his new title of major general title and, a Federalist once more, warned of unruly mobs.[24]

He would not find glory, martial or otherwise, again. In 1794, Lee left Pennsylvania without a fight but returned to Virginia to find he was without a job.[25] He had been ousted from office in absentia. Shifting from amassing public glory to accumulating private wealth, Lee tried to become a proper American baron instead. He invested in more than a hundred thousand acres of land scattered from Georgia to Pennsylvania. It all failed, and Lee spent two years in debtor's prison beginning in 1808.[26] After being disfigured and nearly killed by, oddly enough, a Baltimore mob of pro-war rioters in 1812, Lee abandoned his family, his country, and his remaining debtors. He wandered the Caribbean for five years. In failing health, he tried to return to Virginia but did not make it, dying on Cumberland Island off the Georgia coast

6   WE ARE NOT ONE PEOPLE

in 1818. One of his children, Henry "Black Horse Harry" Lee IV, would contribute to the enduring argument over the union of these United States as John C. Calhoun's speechwriter. Four decades later, Light Horse Harry's youngest son, Robert Edward, fought in earnest to ensure that the Union perished from the earth. Professional and amateur historians have speculated, some quite wildly, about the psychological impact Harry Lee's public and private indiscretions had on Robert Edward, who was eleven when his derelict father died.[27]

A Divisible Nation

E pluribus unum was suggested for the national seal by Pierre Eugène du Simitière in 1776. We argue that this notion of national oneness has been haunted by its twin, *E pluribus pluria*, ever since. American schism was not some wrenching national growing pain that ended in an Appomattox courthouse.[28] The Civil War wiped out the armies of secession, not the prominence of separatism in American political culture. *We Are Not One People* is a broad examination of the disunionists who have unmade the nation since seventy-four Constitutional Conventioneers designed a "more perfect union." The persistence of American separatist rhetoric reveals as much about the nation's politics as it does the would-be separatists. That is, great swaths of Americans of every ideological stripe, in good times and bad, in and beyond the South, disputed the nation's oneness and its indivisibility. Separatist rhetoric has shaped Americans' experience of what it means to be an American.

To show that they never felt what James Madison named "the chords of affection," to prove that what he called "kindred blood" flowed in fewer veins, Americans have warred to leave the nation; aiming to become a new people in departure, they have also just left.[29] Inveighing against the nation's oppression of their people, they have fled to found "Godly Republics," green kingdoms, or, in one case, "an opt-in society, ultimately outside the United States, run by technology."[30] They have also pledged disallegiance in off-the-grid enclaves to escape national oversight. They have sought their own spaces to live in racial solidarity, to achieve oneness in gender, to prepare for the end times, to revel in

PROLOGUE 7

Stone Age simplicity in "rewilding" compounds.[31] They have forsworn the "disappointing world of human affairs" and gravitated toward "the succor" of the natural world, "its promise of reprieve" preferable to "the grime of the present."[32] They have sojourned into the wild, disengaged from mass culture, beyond juridical oversight, where they "carry weapons," "think of themselves as warriors," and "refuse to acknowledge any allegiance to the devices of what we fondly call our democracy."[33] They have walled themselves off, both literally and figuratively, to experiment in utopian living.

They have also built decidedly on-the-grid citadels of separatism. In what one writer called "the quiet wave" of school secession, scores of wealthy white communities, particularly in the South, have left integrated schools by creating new districts, even new towns such as Gardendale, Alabama.[34] Severing their ties to American cities, many white Americans after the 1960s thought and spoke in decidedly "secessionist" terms, defending their "freedom of association" as they emigrated to "the spatially and socially removed lands of suburbia."[35] Parents of the counterculture Left and the religious Right have opted for homeschooling rather than public schools.[36] Selecting certain states, such as New Hampshire or Utah or Kansas, as strategic staging grounds, they have migrated internally to live among the like-minded in some semblance of "territorial autonomy."[37] Others have opted for seclusion solidarity in urban quarters where they frequented maverick bars, bookstores, music vendors, coffeehouses, and clubs in distinct neighborhoods a world apart yet a stone's throw from millions of other city dwellers. They have sued for exemptions to federal laws; they have set up parallel public institutions including hospitals, banks, and more.[38] The wealthy, Robert Reich lamented in 1991, have withdrawn their money from public use and built gates around themselves to live in "open secession" in networked private health spas, elite schools, beaches, islands, and resorts with revealing names like Secession Golf Club in coastal South Carolina.[39] Some separatists did not go anywhere but, as one libertarian secessionist suggested, stayed put: "Secession really begins at home, with the actions we all take in our everyday lives to distance and remove ourselves from state authority—quietly, nonviolently, inexorably."[40] For the electronically inclined, the possibility of online freedom where cyber-seceders' "virtual selves" could become

8 WE ARE NOT ONE PEOPLE

"immune" to national power held real promise.[41] Still other separatists have focused their efforts even further internally, guarding "the realm of the psyche" against cultural incursions.[42] "Black is a country," Amiri Baraka wrote.[43]

Various writers have diagnosed the country's "slumbering secession obsession," the grip of its "secession fever," the resonance of its "secessionist ethos," the "extraordinarily privileged position" of "exit" in the nation's political traditions.[44] "Disunion," Richard Kreitner notes in *Break It Up* (2020), is one of the nation's "only truly national ideas."[45] *We Are Not One People*, however, is a novel take on the symbolic resonance of separatism, secession, and a family of disintegrative concepts across varied groups throughout the nation's history. Valuable studies of specific separatists abound—histories of the forty "Separatists" who landed in Cape Cod aboard the *Mayflower* in 1620 or chronicles of southern secession—but these are limited to specific groups in particular eras.[46] Separatism's power in America is symbolic; its purchase is cultural.[47] Secession is likely "the most serious constitutional question ever to arise in America," in one scholar's judgment, but separatism's multicentury, intergroup, transideological influence cannot be accounted for solely by attending to questions of legality or illegality.[48] In this book, we treat separatism as a political language. Separatism is spoken, written, and performed to entice audiences to exit the nation in one way or another; its speakers blend their group's particular patois with iconic American narratives to achieve disaggregating ends.

We Are Not One People is about groups of Americans, some eccentric, some thoughtful, some reckless, all audacious, from 1776 to the present who gave up, moved on, and opted out, people who tried to bring forth on this continent or another a new nation. Groups both marginal and mainstream, wielders of and aliens from political power, have used a common political language to withdraw from American laws, American politics, American culture, and the American public and whatever subjugation, norms, practices, obligations, customs, or laws they thought citizenship entailed. Nevertheless, since they cited the hallmark moments and national heroes of the nation's history, they withdrew as Americans. They cited the nation to undo it.

We Are Not One People joins a growing number of books about American disunity, disintegration, fragmentation, and unraveling, chronicles of a splintered public sphere in which, as Ira Glass, host of *This American Life*, said half in jest, "everyone in the country hates everyone else all the time."[49] Aiming to understand how American democracy has simultaneously aided and been threatened by many types of separatist withdrawal, we are theorizing the concept by historicizing it, or, more simply, exploring the political theory and actual practice of American separatism at the same time.[50] Polarization and separatism increase in tandem: as political opponents look less like rivals and more like monsters, the "psychic appeal" of ignoring them, nullifying their laws, moving away from them, or splintering off entirely is potent. Cutting ties appears simpler than winning elections and mobilizing majorities; separation seems easier than suasion.[51] Separation is seductive, especially but not exclusively in polarized times, because no government needs to be overthrown and no prevailing order needs to be overturned; the disaffected group just opts out.

In an 1838 speech in Springfield, Illinois, twenty-eight-year-old Abraham Lincoln hoped that a "reverence for the laws" would become the nation's "political religion" practiced by "the old and the young, the rich and the poor, the grave and the gay, of all sexes and tongues, and colors and conditions."[52] We are tracing a different kind of American reverence, how all colors and conditions have piously worshipped their divisibility. Many Americans have thought of their "union" not, as George Washington urged in his Farewell Address, as the "main prop" of their "liberty" but, by contrast, as the opposite. Instead of focusing on those who would reform or transform that union, we concentrate on those who depart.[53] To that end, we are interested in the variety of ways in which scattered American communities have achieved de facto secession by adopting separatist strategies, by taking leave rather than taking over. Secession's broad appeal as a symbolic action comes into full view when it is considered not singularly but as the endpoint of a spectrum of political disengagement. What we call the separatist spectrum spans targeted, temporary, and issue-specific acts of political exit all the way to the total, formal, and public political withdrawal of one group from a larger group. Other, softer strategies stop short of strict secession but allow communities to divorce themselves meaningfully from the American demos; these include geographic separation, in which seclusion enables countergovernmental or countercultural

10   WE ARE NOT ONE PEOPLE

practices, and acts of legal resistance such as interposition, in which local governments serve as a kind of roadblock between the citizenry and national laws, and nullification, in which local governments explicitly invalidate or supersede federal law.[54] We reimagine separatism as a horizon of potent rebukes of national authority rather than a determinative event.

After the Civil War, no state or group has again attempted such a grand-scale, violent secession, but that did not mean that secessionist dreams have ceased; the means became in some cases more creative and in others more clandestine. The Civil War's deterrent effect was far from total.[55] Since 1865, many groups have voiced separatist appeals and accomplished secessionist ends through strategic acts of geographical distancing and legal noncompliance, including both interposition and nullification, strategies adopted by many southern states soon after the Civil War ended.[56] Secession and separatism hold primary positions in the nation's history among disparate groups of people spread widely over two and a half centuries, tremendous geographical terrain, extreme power differences, and vast ideological territory. "American history from its inception," one historian argues, "consists of the stories of many separatist movements."[57] Withdrawing from America, while explicitly un-American, is also, paradoxically, the mythological core of American national identity. Americanness is substantially self-negating because moving on from and refusing comity with other Americans is a pretty American thing to do. The nation names military bases after officers in secessionist armies; its citizens routinely encounter shrines to seceders along federal highways. It is strangely easy to imagine the governor of an American state threatening secession and stranger and easier still to imagine an American president acting like or praising secessionists, at least some of them. As one Vermont secessionist quipped, secession is as American "as apple pie."[58]

Separatism, after all, was stressed in America's founding documents. The Declaration of Independence did not merely recommend separation; it required it. Separation is exalted in cherished cultural myths wherein the biblical story of exodus transforms into a flexible American tale of exit. Separation is narrated in familiar American historical stories: of Pilgrims escaping religious oppression, of colonists

PROLOGUE 11

starting anew in the New World, of enslaved people's flight to freedom, of citizens staking a claim out west, of the Civil War's violent romance, of the indomitable last Mohican or Lakota or Apache. Separation is dramatized in popular American media in which the main characters, nearly ensnared over and again, finally gaze at an open, unpeopled frontier of infinite freedom and blissful peace and quiet. Separation is philosophically authorized in American political doctrines: in self-determination, in federalism, in states' rights, in local control, in home rule, in the consent of the governed, in the self-reliant anti-conformity of Ralph Waldo Emerson, in the defiant solitude of Henry David Thoreau. Separation is intimated in America's national watchwords: we the people, the American dream, Manifest Destiny, rags to riches, power to the people, liberty or death, don't tread on me, live free or die, land of the free and home of the brave. It is implied in everyday American idioms: getting away from it all, getting out of Dodge, striking out on your own, being your own boss, working for yourself, riding off into the sunset, going back to the land, going it alone, looking for some space to breathe, starting over, a fresh start, finding a home where the buffalo roam. Separation is affirmed in America's cultural heroes: cowboys, outlaws, outsiders on the open road, wayfaring dreamers, untethered rebels riding the rails. Trumpeted in American myths, mottos, mantras, maxims, movies, stories, and songs, separation is omnipresent in American political culture.

Our book tells the story of separatism in America by narrating how five specific groups (libertarians, Confederates, Black nationalists, lesbian separatists, and Latter-day Saints) across American history have interpreted and rhetorically practiced it. Each of these five groups exemplifies a distinct type of visceral solidarity against national identity. For libertarian separatists (Chapter 2), the democratic public was a collection of sovereign citizens, each of whom risked everything if absorbed into an indivisible American mass. The Confederate demos (Chapter 3) hinged on racial hierarchy generally and slavery specifically, and the nation threatened that foundation of their caste-based peoplehood. For Black nationalists (Chapter 4), America was irrevocably white and racist; separation was both an act of self-preservation and self-discovery for a people robbed of their ancestry. For lesbian separatists (Chapter 5), biological sex and sexual practice were

12   WE ARE NOT ONE PEOPLE

emblems of peoplehood; women could never be treated justly while living among males in a male-dominated nation. For the Latter-day Saints (Chapter 6), nations should be grounded in a higher law, and the Kingdom of God was unachievable in a sinful, oppressive country. In the conclusion (Chapter 7), we theorize the democratic tensions inherent in a nation whose citizens have consistently admired separatists. The ferocity with which scattered groups have defended their right to withdraw challenges critics, theorists, activists, and anyone invested in a future where Americans owe other Americans something by dint of their shared nationality. Toward that end, we conclude by reflecting on the public value of the separatist language versus other American political languages of mutual obligation and national belonging.

To draw conclusions about these group's separatist philosophies and practices, we have relied on close readings of their sacred texts, the documents these communities canonized, circulated, studied, and memorized. Some of these texts are among the most influential in American history; others are obscure. Some are dense tracts of separatist political theory; some are incendiary. Regardless, each chapter considers a separatist community and a collection of texts they have treated as vital resources of self-definition. Moreover, we used four dialectics to parse similarities and differences in each group's separatism. First, we tracked how each group framed their demos, their "real" peoplehood, versus those coded as irredeemably different: the Other, foreigners, barbarians, interlopers, and traitors.[59] How did the separating community make sense of itself as a pure group with clear boundaries? A people exist "in rhetoric," not "in some neutral history devoid of human interpretation."[60] To be cast as a member of a people is to be given a "narrative," to acquire "history, motives, and a *telos*."[61] Since "we" are not "them," "we" must limit or eliminate a shared collective life with "them."[62] There are so many "negative reference points" between the people and their enemies that separation is logically necessary.[63] With every definition of a different people, there is an argument for separation, an argument for a new nation.[64] A people might see themselves as "belonging to an ethnic, cultural, civic, socio-political, diasporic, multisocietal or multiterritorial" group.[65] Regardless of the specific source of their peoplehood, such as a shared language,

PROLOGUE 13

religion, or geography, separatists often practice an exclusionary politics of identity at the end of the line.

Second, we explored how each group depicted its future Canaan. We looked at how separatist groups envisioned their land of milk and honey: In some specific, sacred homeland, or in any space that could be called home? Within America's physical boundaries, national identity, or dominant culture, or beyond them?

Third, we charted secrecy and publicity in separatist rhetoric. Separation is not a public process if it is unspoken, but the need for some publicity has not made all separatists skywriters. How, then, have separatists rhetorically accomplished their withdrawal? Have they withdrawn by declaring open war against their oppressors? Have they recruited comrades without attempting to offend the wider culture? Have they, in an attempt to practice self-government in peace, retreated to safety in relative secrecy? Finally, we tracked whether separatists characterized themselves as radicals or restorers. Did the withdrawing group imagine itself as bringing forth an unprecedented era that began the world anew, or did it restore some lost promise or reclaim some historical glory in the act of separation?

Our reconceptualization of separatism as a symbolic spectrum is broader than the case studies we use to prove it. We have chosen groups as exemplars, focusing on the different ways in which groups might define themselves as beyond the nation from within the nation. We created case studies to represent specific strains of national withdrawal, separate justifications for separating. Each case study explores a group separating from some fundamental aspect of the nation: from its legal institutions, its national economy, its mainstream culture, its religious hierarchy, and/or its race and gender norms.

We Are Not One People is a big project in history and scope, both empirically and conceptually. This breadth is both an advantage and a disadvantage. The case studies we offer exemplify without exhausting American separation's symbolic range. Our choice of case studies is open to objections that we have overlooked or excluded this group's desire to get out of America or that type of separation. We have surely missed key groups, and although we cover several categories of separation, our limited case studies do not show variety within these categories. At the risk of parochialism, this book is an attempt to understand

14   WE ARE NOT ONE PEOPLE

separatism's place in American political and cultural history.[66] We do not cover Quebec or Kurdistan, Catalonia or Katanga. Instead, we have taken up Alexis de Tocqueville's suggestion from 1835: "If there is a single country in the world where the true value of the sovereignty of the people can hope to be appreciated, where its application to the affairs of society can be studied and where its advantages and dangers can be judged, that country is assuredly America."[67] In the end, we hope that these potential drawbacks reaffirm our central point: nations are imagined, but they are also unimagined and reimagined, and we can learn much about the durable appeal and enduring fragility of the American figment from those who tried to leave it.

1

Bands, Bonds, and Affections

"To secede" comes from the Latin word *secedere*. Secession as a splintering act is evident in the roots of the term: *se-* for "apart" and *cedere* for "to go."[1] In ancient Rome, *secessio* referred to the mass exodus of plebes from the city. The exact number of plebian secessions is unclear, but on several occasions the poor dramatically demonstrated their value by leaving the city. Without a servant class, patricians were left to prepare food, move goods, tend animals, care for themselves, and keep up with civilization's drudgeries.[2] Until the eighteenth century, secession referred to a variety of withdrawals, many of which were apolitical: the secession of a soul from a body, a person seceding from one room to another, or a group seceding from a social gathering. During the Enlightenment era, secession began to refer to religious schisms as well. Democratic reformers, "seceders," broke away from the Church of Scotland to form the Original Secession Church in 1732.[3]

The idea of secession, like the notion of a nation, is an ancient one, but it acquired new meanings as powerful nation-states emerged in the eighteenth and nineteenth centuries and began delineating boundaries and citizenship more meticulously.[4] The Enlightenment notion that rational individuals should have the democratic power to govern themselves upset traditional forms of feudal, aristocratic, theocratic, and monarchic rule. Notions of hereditary rule, the rule of the wise, the rule of the powerful, or the rule of the pious had "dominated political thought" for millennia.[5] The Declaration of Independence and the Declaration of the Rights of Man and of the Citizen of the late Enlightenment made revolutionary universal claims that all people had the undeniable right to self-rule.[6] Sovereignty came from the sacred power of citizens; citizens did not exist at the whims of a sacred sovereign. "Self-determination," one scholar wrote, meant "that the people should determine the content and course of their government."[7]

We Are Not One People. Michael J. Lee and R. Jarrod Atchison, Oxford University Press. © Oxford University Press 2022. DOI: 10.1093/oso/9780190876500.003.0002

16 WE ARE NOT ONE PEOPLE

Self-government was an old idea—the Greek roots of the word "democracy" were *demos* and *kratia*, meaning "people rule" or "rule by the people"—taking new shape as the world sorted into nations.[8] Secession and revolution seemed corollary rights; if the people had the right to rise up against a tyrannical government, they also had the right to split off if revolution was unworkable.[9] To secede was to self-determine, and self-determination required the right of secession.[10] Although secession and separatism remain thorny concepts to define, as the era of revolutionary nationalism began, secession started to denote a people and a place, a demos attached to a space, a group leaving a nation and taking part of it with them.[11] To cede meant to give over territory and jurisdiction over the inhabitants of the territory.[12] To secede meant to detach from a nation-state. Nearly as soon as human societies began organizing themselves in nations, they adopted a word to describe getting out of them.

America was the first modern nation "born of secession," and the Declaration of Independence, the nation's birth announcement, "became a template for hundreds of similar separatist movements."[13] The logic of political separation in the Declaration was lucid; the newly seceded nation, however, was—like Thomas Jefferson, the principal author of its birth announcement—a paradox. The nation was "conceived in liberty," but many of its inhabitants were enslaved. The nation was founded as an exercise in self-government, but most people could not participate. The nation was founded in opposition to colonial oppression, but it colonized and exterminated the original inhabitants of the land that would come to be known as America.

The question of national identity was perplexing even among those who could participate in their new government. In some places around the world, peoplehood, a sense of collective identity, arises "over tens of centuries, the product of generations of common kinship, common language, common myths and a shared history, and the collective ties of tradition."[14] Early Americans had charters, covenants, agreements, and a powerful negative reference; they were no longer English subjects. Beyond that, however, questions of togetherness persisted. Were they united by "inclusive yet abstract political ideas," "a strong moral code," or "some other, more visceral, tie of affinity?"[15] Their national bond was also a simple numbers question. After the American

Revolution, were they members of one nation or thirteen? Moreover, if they were members of one nation, did they have to stay that way? The "true nature" of the American republic was "very much in dispute" both during and after the founding.[16]

Early Americans, one historian argues, "felt great anxiety" about the durability of their "political institutions" as well as "whether they were one people who could live together as one nation."[17] Some worried that the new country was just too big; it would "fly apart sooner or later."[18] Opposing the new Constitution in 1787, the pseudonymous Brutus (likely Robert Yates) wrote, "In a republic, the manners, sentiments, and interests of the people should be similar. If this be not the case, there will be a constant clashing of opinions; and the representatives of one part will be continually striving against those of the other. This will retard the operations of government, and prevent such conclusions as will promote the public good. If we apply this remark to the condition of the United States, we shall be convinced that it forbids that we should be one government."[19] Contemporaries worried that the country was really two nations, a slave society and a commercial society, that had been sutured together. Many thinkers of the period held that nationality emerged from shared geography, and the new nation included at least three peoples: one up north, another down south, and still another out west. When Alexis de Tocqueville toured the twenty-four states of the country in the 1830s, he famously found a nation of joiners, of spontaneous voluntary associations. He also found "twenty-four small sovereign nations," as he put it, "that together form the great body of the Union."[20]

There may have been many countries hiding in the United States; perhaps the nation also had two points of origin. As one scholar termed it, there were "Two Foundings," an Anti-Federalist beginning of separate and independent states stretching from the Declaration of Independence to the Articles of Confederation (1776–1781) and a Federalist restart during the composition and ratification of the national Constitution (1787–1789).[21] The Articles of Confederation bound the states, however loosely, to a "perpetual" union, but that did not stop states from threatening to bolt.[22] The Constitution committed the states to a new national union but was silent on secession and perpetuity. The text contains a federal supremacy clause (Article VI), an

18   WE ARE NOT ONE PEOPLE

amendment affirming state jurisdiction over matters "not delegated" to the federal government (the Tenth Amendment), and no endorsement or prohibition of secession whatsoever; the words "nation" and "national" do not appear either.[23] Curiously, the issue of divisibility was discussed only sporadically during the ratification debates.[24]

Secession was warned against but not explicitly taken up as a constitutional question in *The Federalist Papers* either. Hamilton, Madison, Jay, and many other founders nevertheless were quite concerned by the prospect of disintegration. Hamilton wrote in *Federalist* 8 that "the airy phantoms that flit before the distempered imaginations" of the Constitution's enemies would pale compared to the "real, certain, and formidable" dangers of genuine disunion. "A firm Union," he predicted, guarded against "perpetual vibration."[25] In *Federalist* 9, he worried that loose confederations would become monarchies or split "into an infinity of little jealous, clashing, tumultuous commonwealths, the wretched nurseries of unceasing discord, and the miserable objects of universal pity or contempt."[26]

In 1798, Vice President Thomas Jefferson, seldom aligned with Hamilton, employed different metaphors to propose a similar idea. The "central government" was a "common Sun" around which the states, like "planets," revolved. The "respective weights & balances" that made the American constitutional equilibrium possible was "unexampled but in the planetary system itself."[27] Jefferson enacted this view during his presidency when he took a hard line against separatist plots, which he saw as "threats to majority rule and to the legitimate powers granted to the national state."[28] The beauty of American harmony, he thought, was that eventually another majority could emerge, win elections, and work peacefully through the constitutional system to govern as they saw fit.

Taking up the matter of secession directly, Jefferson explained in a letter to John Taylor, who proposed that North Carolina and Virginia form a separate nation, that the evils of "scission" were unpredictable. Exit might seem attractive to anyone out of power, Jefferson counseled Taylor, but the act of detachment not only would destroy the American equilibrium but also would put the newly separated nation on a slippery slope; secessionists would start seceding from other secessionists ad infinitum.[29] "A little patience," he cautioned, "and we shall see the reign of witches pass over, their spells dissolved, and the people recovering their true sight, restoring their government to its true principles."[30]

Jefferson was not always patient with witches, however. Many historians reflexively presume that he would have taken the secessionist side in the Civil War.[31] Had he been alive during the secession winter of 1860–1861, one historian suggests, "Jefferson would have gone with the Confederacy."[32] His Kentucky Resolution of 1798 and James Madison's Virginia Resolution of 1799 were public threats by two states to nullify the Alien and Sedition Acts. In a letter to James Madison, Jefferson said that he intended their resolutions as protests "against the principle & the precedent" of the acts, as affirmations of "our warm attachment to union with our sister-states" in the "federal compact," and as clarifications that they did not intend to "make every measure of error or wrong a cause of scission." Nevertheless, Jefferson insisted on the right "to sever ourselves from that union we so much value, rather than give up the rights of self government which we have reserved, & in which alone we see liberty, safety & happiness."[33] As president, he wrote in 1803 that the union of eastern and western states might be "good" but separate confederations might "be better."[34] In 1816, he wrote that he would greet any state's desire to leave the union by saying "Let us separate."[35] These later letters show a "radical edge" in Jefferson's states' rights thinking that was not evinced in his leery 1798 letter to Taylor. Jefferson, in fact, flirted with secessionism for decades, an attraction from which Madison "tried to pull his neighbor at Monticello, who was more prone to impulsive statements, back to a more prudent position."[36]

In the 1830s, Madison, in direct contrast to Jefferson, was at pains to save his eighteenth-century writings, the Virginia Resolution in particular, from John C. Calhoun and the nineteenth-century nullifiers. Nullification was both an alternative history of the nation and a theory of its proper governance. Since the states ratified the Constitution, they could, therefore, void laws they viewed as unconstitutional; the states were the enactors and protectors of the people's will, and the national government was merely a product of their power, created for the convenience of their people. It might be easy in hindsight to view the nullification crisis, pitting Calhoun and South Carolina against Andrew

20   WE ARE NOT ONE PEOPLE

Jackson, Congress, and the might of the federal government, as a narrow dispute over economics or the limits of government power. It was much bigger than that; the crisis concerned "the very nature—and even the very existence—of an 'American' people."[37] Madison saw this existential threat and declared nullification a "strange" doctrine to be "deplored" and "dreaded."[38] He worried to Henry Clay that nullification "captivated so many honest minds" despite "its hideous aspect & fatal tendency."[39] Aghast that Calhoun cited his work, Madison warned that nullification put "powder under the Constitution & Union" and gave a "match" to "every party." It was the death of majority rule.[40] Madison saw nullification as the first step before "secession" and "a farewell separation," the destruction of a "more beautiful China vase than the British Empire ever was."[41]

In several *Federalist* essays, Madison characterized federalism as a system that avoided the risks of splinter by splitting, rather than concentrating, government power. "Multiple independent levels of government could legitimately exist within a single polity," he thought, and "such an arrangement was not a defect to be lamented but a virtue to be celebrated."[42] He wrote in *Federalist* 39 that the Constitution was not "national" or "federal" but "a composition of both."[43] Calhoun, however, found nullification amply justified in Madison's and Jefferson's writings and built a robust theory of home rule—the nation would be governed by competing "concurrent majorities," each of which could veto national policy—with their work as primary source material. In Calhoun's rendering, the Constitution was a compact between the states, the states were sovereign, the states were the ultimate judges of the limits of constitutional power, and the states could, at the very least, nullify federal law.[44] To him, South Carolina's nullification of the socalled Tariff of Abominations was little different from Kentucky and Virginia's reaction to the Alien and Sedition Acts.[45]

Although Jefferson's 1798 Kentucky Resolution, tellingly, gave Calhoun more ammunition, Calhoun's reading of Madison's Virginia Resolution was mostly faithful. Madison's Virginia Resolution asserted a "most sincere affection" for citizens of other states and a commitment to "perpetuating the union of all," but it also unilaterally declared a federal law unconstitutional and interposed between Virginians and the federal government.[46] In his nullification-era writings of the

1830s, Madison insisted that he had merely hoped to mobilize a multistate protest of an odious law; he was not licensing state supremacy.[47] "Collectively," one scholar notes of Madison's later rebukes of nullification, "these writings of his last years constitute something approaching a revised version of his contributions to *The Federalist*, with the new emphasis decidedly more on the national features of the Constitution and less on the surviving aspects of state sovereignty."[48] Madison was attempting a redo to deny states the right to nullify or secede.

Separatism in American History

Separatism, both in practice and in imagination, has been conspicuous in the American national experience. Its prominence, however, is often overlooked, ignored, or pigeonholed in studies of American history and political culture. Specifically, separatism is discounted as a through-line in American history in at least six ways. First, many studies of American history treat secession like a genie's lamp that was dropped in 1865 and never rubbed again.[49] A "conventional piece of constitutional wisdom" holds that the Civil War ended this back-and-forth over state sovereignty and the perpetuity of the Union.[50] As historian Eric Foner argued, "In a sense, the Constitution and national political system had failed in the difficult task of creating a nation—only the Civil War itself would accomplish it."[51] According to this theory of decisive warfare, the Civil War violently clarified that the Constitution created a people living in a nation, not peoples living in separate states. Before the Civil War, Garry Wills argues, the nation was spoken of as a plural noun; after the Civil War, the nation became singular. The United States "are" became the United States "is."[52] In the 1820s and 1830s, Americans spoke of the nation in terms suggesting a convenient partnership: "the states United," "the united States," and "a league of sovereign states."[53]

The Civil War is treated as the volatile young nation's final fusion, its permanent melding. According to this view, the Civil War resolved American disunity militarily and legally. Secession's fate, one scholar asserts, was "decided at Appomattox Court House."[54] Envisioning a farcical film plot in which Maine seceded to join Canada, a screenwriter

22   WE ARE NOT ONE PEOPLE

actually wrote to every Supreme Court justice in 2006 to inquire about the legality of secession. Antonin Scalia wrote back. "If there was any constitutional issue resolved by the Civil War," he reasoned in his reply, "it is that there is no right to secede."[55] For Scalia, the Constitution was unclear about secession, and the divided country adjudicated the matter in blood.

Other scholars, like Akhil Amar, think the Constitution was actually transparent on secession. They endorse Abraham Lincoln and Andrew Jackson's view that the "text, structure, and enactment history" of the Constitution clearly prohibited secession before 1861.[56] By this view, the Civil War was a particularly bloody attempt to enforce federal law. Regardless of whether the secession question was ambiguous in 1861, both views frame the legal matter of secession as closed by 1865. The legal scholar Cass Sunstein put the matter categorically: "No serious scholar or politician now argues that a right to secede exists under United States constitutional law."[57]

The legality of secession, in 1861, 1865, or now, has been more of an open question than clear-cut conclusions acknowledge.[58] The legal case against secession was far from "ironclad" before the Civil War, and many other historians have not had nearly as much surety about the legal lessons of the founding or the Civil War.[59] Some prominent scholars have even examined the historical arguments for and against a right to secession in American law, thrown their hands up, shrugged, and concluded, "I don't know."[60] Even those who lived through the Civil War were dubious that a "trial by battle" could "lend the imprimatur of a legal action to the violent turmoil of war."[61] As George Ticknor Curtis wrote in 1875, "It might seem strange, in the abstract, somewhat paradoxical to suppose that such a question could definitely be settled by fighting."[62] At best, the legal battle over secession was quasi-legally half-decided by what one law professor called "the case of *Grant v. Lee*."[63] Put differently, the debate over the lawfulness of secession was not refereed by "the constitutional experts on Missionary Ridge."[64] Secession's legality, furthermore, is related only loosely, if at all, to its resilient cultural popularity. As the historian David Blight explained, since the Civil War "generation after generation" of Americans have learned how many people "never fully accepted the verdicts of Appomattox."[65]

The post–Civil War Fourteenth Amendment arguably precluded secession by tying citizenship to the federal government rather than any given state, but none of the Reconstruction amendments ended the matter forcefully.[66] Some Reconstruction-era legislators feared that declaring secession to be illegal in a post–Civil War amendment would somehow afford post hoc legitimacy to pre–Civil War secessionists.[67] For similar reasons, Jefferson Davis never faced treason charges, but not because national courts were trying to send a magnanimous, forgiving message to prodigal southerners; Davis's federal prosecutors thought they might lose. It would have taken only one juror to acquit the Confederacy's former president. After years of continuances, the treason case against Davis was dropped, and the head of a fallen renegade nation was set free.[68]

The Supreme Court weighed in on secession, albeit indirectly, in *Texas v. White* (1869). Salmon Chase described the American nation as "indissoluble" in his opinion, which read like the nationalist arguments of Lincoln, Jackson, Daniel Webster, Joseph Story, John Marshall, and Alexander Hamilton. The nation preceded the states.[69] The nation was perpetual; secession violated the basic principles of majority-rules democracy. The technical issue, nevertheless, in *Texas v. White* was the state's sale of federal bonds to fund the Confederacy. Texas's Reconstruction-era government argued that the state's previous Confederate government could not have legally sold federal bonds to underwrite disunion. The bonds' buyers, of course, replied that they acquired the bonds not from the semi-sovereign state of Texas but from a fully sovereign nation-state called Texas, so the sale was final. In a narrowly worded decision that some scholars deem "fundamentally incoherent," the Supreme Court ruled 5–3 that Texas had never legally seceded and could get its bonds back.[70] *Texas v. White* was "more a lecture about who won the Civil War" than a pronouncement regarding state secession, the Constitution, and national sovereignty.[71]

Second, just as secession is treated as a concern settled by the Civil War, the matter is also set aside as an exclusively southern issue. Before South Carolina and Mississippi began the cascade of seceding southern states in late 1860, however, several other states considered the same new start: California, Oregon, and New Jersey. New York City did as well.[72] To be sure, the story of the American South is essential

24   WE ARE NOT ONE PEOPLE

to the history of secession, but the conceptual history of American secession is not exclusively a southern tale. Georgia's early intransigence prompted two Supreme Court cases: *Chisholm v. Georgia* (1793) and *Worcester v. Georgia* (1832). South Carolina, of course, took the nation's first formal step toward secession on December 20, 1860, but proto-Confederates like John C. Calhoun had been threatening secession and practicing nullification for decades by that point.[73] Six other states followed South Carolina out of the Union by the time Davis was elected president of the Confederate States of America in February 1861. Lincoln appealed to the "better angels of our nature" that March, but any "chorus of Union" was overwhelmed by the fusillade at Fort Sumter roughly a month later. Eleven states seceded in all, presaging a four-year war that ended 750,000 lives.[74]

The South launched the most consequential secession in the nation's history, but the notion that secession only sprouts under Spanish moss is another way its persistent, formative role in American history has been pigeonholed. Historical specters of secession and related ghosts, nullification and interposition, appear throughout American history. At various points in his public life, Jefferson endorsed separatism, but during his presidency he agonized that Aaron Burr was buying up western land, recruiting a militia, threatening to capture New Orleans, and stoking fears of a war with Spain with the ultimate aim of trying to do the Whiskey Rebels one better: to sever the entirety of the West from the East. By seizing New Orleans, Burr could control western trade and split the union down its Appalachian "back bone."[75] According to widely held fears, Burr was testing the young country's coherence; he was put on trial and formally accused of treason, of "fomenting the separatism" that early Americans feared.[76] The jury could not find evidence that Burr had committed a direct act of war against the United States, and he was set free.

Northerners were also enamored with secession in the early republic. A group of prominent New England Federalists dubbed the "Essex Junto" plotted three secession attempts in the first two decades of the nineteenth century: in 1804, in opposition to the Louisiana Purchase and motivated by fears that Jefferson's massive new land deal would tilt the nation's political balance toward southern slaveowners; in 1807, when the Embargo Act threatened New England shipping interests; and, yet again, at the Hartford Convention of 1814–1815 over the War of 1812.[77] This convention, including delegates from Rhode Island, Connecticut, Massachusetts, Connecticut, and breakaway counties in New Hampshire and Vermont, threatened to secede if seven constitutional amendments were not passed. Several New England states restricted their militias from participating in the War of 1812, and these states also discouraged New England financiers from funding the domestic war effort.[78] They even considered entering into bilateral negotiations between New England and England. "There is," Timothy Pickering, a prominent New England Federalist and the nation's second secretary of war, intoned, "no magic in the sound of Union."[79]

Much nineteenth-century disunionism was motivated by the vexing question of slavery. Pierce Butler, a South Carolina planter, slave owner, and senator, had been living in Philadelphia with an enslaved person named Ben for six months in 1804 when he was served a writ of habeas corpus declaring that Ben was free according to local statutes. Butler replied tersely: "I am a citizen of South Carolina. The laws of Pennsylvania have nothing to do with me."[80]

Butler's response maps onto modern conceptions of the slave-owning, states'-rights-promoting southerner, but the reverse is also true. The Pennsylvania anti-slavery ordinance, like similar ones in Ohio, New York, Wisconsin, and elsewhere above the Mason-Dixon, were among the "most aggressive states' rights arguments" of the era.[81] In the first half of the nineteenth century, the free states of the North adopted a wide range of "personal liberty" laws to stop or slow the enforcement of federal fugitive slave codes. Textbook examples of interposition and nullification, such laws afforded jury trials to fugitive slaves, granted freedom to slaves once they had resided in a state for a specified period, and prohibited public employees from aiding in the capture or return of runaways.

Wisconsin's Supreme Court even nullified the Fugitive Slave Act, prompting the U.S. Supreme Court, in *Ableman v. Booth* (1859), to rule that state courts had no such jurisdiction. In *Prigg v. Pennsylvania* (1842), the Supreme Court also held that personal liberty laws were unconstitutional but that states could not be compelled to assist in the enforcement of federal slavery statutes.[82] States could not nullify

26   WE ARE NOT ONE PEOPLE

slavery statutes, but they could withhold cooperation. Summarizing the *Prigg* ruling, Henry Clay, the compromise merchant who settled the Missouri crisis in 1820, the South Carolina nullification crisis in 1832, and the California crisis of 1850, noted, "Laws of impediment are unconstitutional."[83]

William Lloyd Garrison thought southern slavery could not survive without national support and demanded that "ye idolators of the Union" recognize that the Constitution, which he publicly burned in 1854, was "a Covenant with Death and an Agreement with Hell."[84] The delegates to the Constitutional Convention acceded to southern pro-slavery demands and, in so doing, perpetrated a moral giveaway to keep slaveholders in the Union. Secession had become an indispensable aspect of Garrisonian abolitionism by 1843.[85] His magazine, *The Liberator*, was regularly emblazoned with disunionist rallying cries, and he called for the "immediate dissolution" of the Union in public speeches.[86] "No Union with Slaveholders!" should be the "watchword of every uncompromising abolitionist, of every friend of God and liberty," he wrote in 1845.[87] Abolition and national disintegration were permanently yoked for Garrison. As he put it in an 1850 letter, "I am for the abolition of slavery, and therefore for the dissolution of the Union."[88]

Garrison hoped the American Union, "drenched" in the "blood" of slaves, would meet "the fate of Rome and Carthage, of Babylon and Tyre."[89] He also hoped that the dissolution of the Union would end southern slavery. The seceded free states of the North could starve slavers from the outside through coordinated boycotts, and the existence of a shelter of freedom immediately to the north might destabilize the South.[90] But the real power of Garrison's disunionist arguments was not pragmatic; Garrison framed northern secession as a moral repudiation of the South and a path to purification, a "prelude to a national rebirth."[91] Garrison "became the prophet at the gate, warning people to leave the corrupt city or face destruction."[92] He urged anyone disturbed by slavery to follow a higher law than the Constitution and "come out" of a slave society. He borrowed the language from Revelation 18:4: "And I heard another voice from heaven, saying, Come out of her, my people, that ye be not partakers of her sins, and that ye receive not of her plagues." Coming out was a total act of

BANDS, BONDS, AND AFFECTIONS 27

separation; even the ballot box was, to Garrison, a "pro-slavery argument."[93] When faced with the great moral evil of slavery, secession was the only morally defensible position.

Garrison aimed to "shame" freedom-espousing Americans into recognizing their complicity with slavery, to force a reckoning with the illusion that some Americans were separate from and therefore not responsible for slavery, to "dispel the comforting idea that one could oppose slavery yet still be in political or spiritual fellowship with slaveholders."[94]

Other abolitionists shared Garrison's secessionist views. Wendell Phillips warned of two separate and distinct nations, one slave and one free, as early as 1837.[95] In 1842, John Quincy Adams presented to Congress an anti-slavery petition signed by forty-six people in Haverhill, Massachusetts, each of whom prayed for the Union's "dissolution."[96] Thomas Wentworth Higginson, a pastor and women's suffrage advocate who financially supported John Brown, helped organize a Disunion Convention in Worcester in 1857 after James Buchanan's victory over John Frémont in the 1856 presidential election.[97] Hoping the Harpers Ferry raid would yield a weapons stockpile, John Brown planned to found a half-nation, half-citadel in the Appalachians, a safe haven from which additional abolitionist raids could be staged.[98] As historian Elizabeth Varon writes, "Brown was inspired both by guerilla resistance to Napoleon in Europe and by slave and Indian resistance in the Americas; indeed, he hoped to create his own 'maroon' stronghold, of blacks and whites, in the mountains."[99]

Obscure examples of secession talk in Worcester, Hartford, and Haverhill, arcane names of lost disunionist plots (the Blount Conspiracy in Tennessee, the Spanish Conspiracy in Kentucky, Indian Stream in New Hampshire, the State of Franklin in the Appalachians), and forgotten disunionists (the Tertium Quids) might suggest a third way to miss the enduring importance of national fracture in American history: that separatism is a quaint relic of a distant American past, the argumentative equivalent of a powdered wig. The nineteenth-century fascination with communal living—at least eighty utopian experimental communities were founded in the 1840s alone—can give the modern era a veneer of connected coherence.[100] The early republic's spasms over federal authority can make the era resemble a bygone "impetuous

28 WE ARE NOT ONE PEOPLE

marriage in which the partners kept having second thoughts."[101] It can be tempting to view post–Civil War politics as a serene, stable relationship by comparison; the nation, after all, survived these early rows, and no American blood has been spilled in secessionist wars since. A quick perusal of maps of the country's borders ostensibly confirms narratives of national stabilization: America has expanded but not contracted. Everyone has stayed, and no groups have left.

Separatism, however, has figured prominently in every era of American politics in an "unbroken link of secessionist threats emanating from the country's earliest days."[102] Since World War II, to give one prominent example, every point on the separatist scale including interposition, nullification, and full-on secession have been hallmarks of American conservative thought. In practice, conservatives have leaned on an absolutist interpretation of the Tenth Amendment to nullify federal laws. State-level rebukes of national authority were most prevalent during the South's "massive resistance" to civil rights laws and the Supreme Court's desegregation cases when four states declared *Brown v. Board* (1954) null and void and eight others passed interposition measures.[103] Such resistance prompted the Supreme Court to declare in *Cooper v. Aaron* (1958) that the integration of public schools "can neither be nullified openly and directly by the state legislators or state executive or judicial officers, nor nullified indirectly by them through evasive schemes for segregation whether attempted 'ingeniously or ingenuously.' "[104]

Conservatives in and beyond the South and on issues including but not limited to race, however, have also suggested, endorsed, and implemented nullification schemes in response to federal voting rights statutes, federal health care mandates, federal marriage equality rulings, abortion rights, and federal gun laws (erecting "gun sanctuaries").[105] Many conservatives' antipathy toward wearing masks during pandemics coheres with this nullificationist spirit.[106] Conservatives have practiced nullification so broadly that one writer termed it their "form of governance—or, more accurately, anti-governance."[107] Whether invoked by right-wing militias or members of Congress, the notion that the nation's seizure by un-American elites hostile to the Constitution requires legal and extralegal resistance has become a "dominant rhetoric across the conservative spectrum."[108]

Many canonical texts of the Right, like Barry Goldwater's *The Conscience of a Conservative* (1960) or Russell Kirk's *The Conservative Mind* (1953), developed theories of conservatism resting on the atomized separation of people, communities, towns, states, and nations.[109] The core beliefs of different types of traditionalist, religious, and libertarian conservatives—in individualism, in local control, in tradition and traditional authority, or in the sanctity of communities—align symmetrically with separatism. Conservatives of various sorts have held that "things are not connected to other things, that people are not connected to other people, and that they are all better off unconnected."[110] As Douglas MacKinnon declared in *The Secessionist States of America* (2014), "Freedom-loving and Traditional Values-espousing people anywhere—be they in Canada or the United States—should always have the *legal option*" to form their own nation.[111] As a respite from liberals, especially "the homosexual lobby," he proposed that conservatives should separate and form a new nation named Reagan helmed by a government that was simultaneously theocratic and limited.[112]

Even those conservative thinkers who claimed to fear how secessionist threats, emerging from polarized sects of Americans, might tear the country apart defend adjacent concepts. In *American Secession* (2020), F. H. Buckley recommends "federalism on steroids," beefed-up "home rule," as the way to stave off the need for secession.[113] The conservative writer David French arrived at a similar conclusion in *Divided We Fall* (2020). Skipping past Madison's late-in-life worries of a nation fractured by nullification, he writes, "To go forward, we have to go back—to the principles of Federalist No. 10."[114] Separatism, they argue, can mitigate the risk of secession. There is scant difference, however, between the federalism they theorize, supercharged state sovereignty, and the actual practice of nullification and interposition.

The concentric circles of advocates of secession, nullification, and interposition on the one hand and slavery and segregation on the other might be mistaken as proof of a fourth way to dismiss separatism's importance: that the concept is exclusively right-wing or reactionary. Some conservative ideologists may be drawn to separation, but separatism is extra-ideological.[115] The American secession story features an ensemble of southern and conservative characters, but they are far

30　WE ARE NOT ONE PEOPLE

from the only ones in the cast. In some cases, conservatives have been quick to tar blue states as Confederates when they defy local or federal police powers or drug, immigration, or education laws.[116]

Public support for separatism is so widespread that it defies easy red-state/blue-state categorization. Surveying the many attempts by localities across the political spectrum to skirt, shirk, or skate around unpalatable laws, one legal scholar noted "a nullificationist (and even secessionist) impulse coursing through" every part of modern America.[117] One 2018 poll found that nearly 40 percent of all Americans supported secession in theory.[118] Some polls late in Barack Obama's presidency found that nearly a quarter of all Americans wanted their state to declare independence.[119] The cause of separatism can attract strange bedfellows; the League of the South, a southern na-tionalist organization, and the Middlebury Institute, founded in op-position to the Iraq War and American imperialism, even co-hosted a secession conference.[120]

The 2020 presidential election prompted secessionist threats from both sides of the aisle. Within days of Trump's loss, Rush Limbaugh, Glenn Beck, and many other high-profile conservatives mused about what Republican secession might look like.[121] One 2020 poll found that half of the Republican electorate favored withdrawing from Joe Biden's America.[122] Interestingly, much of the deadly Capitol riot on January 6, 2021, was planned on a closed Facebook group called Red State Secession.[123] Even after their 2020 victory, some Democrats, despondent about their prospects of actually governing, clamored for secession. Faced with achieving a supermajority in the Senate to pass legislation, worried about the future of a gerrymandered House, fearful of an ideologically titled Supreme Court, and incensed by voter suppression efforts in many states, one writer suggested a "serious blue-state threat to secede" to force conservative concessions.[124]

Although extremely polarized, the 2020 election was not the only contest this century to spark secession threats. Reviving the 150-year-old dream of a Bear Republic, some Californians threatened seces-sion, a "Calexit," days after Donald Trump's 2016 election.[125] Others devised plots to cleave a liberal, populous blue archipelago from the conservative, underpopulated red American expanse, a "Bluexit."[126] After Obama's reelection in 2012, residents of more than forty states filed secession petitions with nearly one million signatures.[127] One economist gained notoriety in 2008 by calling for Vermont to reclaim its independence, which it held from 1777 to 1791, "to provide a kinder, gentler model for a nation obsessed with money, power, size, speed, greed, and fear of terrorism."[128] Active, organized secessionists held town hall meetings, distributed separatist literature, circulated petitions, and raised money in numerous states during George W. Bush's presidency. An editorialist's anguish over the disputed 2000 presidential election was, in fact, a plausible recap of how many groups have felt about their American citizenship generally: "If at first you don't secede . . ."[129]

Fifth, some writers treat would-be secessionists not just as people drawn to malodorous, long-dead causes but also as fringe blowhards, representatives of a wacky rabble.[130] "In today's United States," Andrew Delbanco declares, "a call for secession is a crank call."[131] This dismissal makes some sense given that the South's rabid defense of and paranoia about slavery precipitated their secession. As one historian clarifies, "The most important secession movement in the nineteenth century was inextricably connected to the issue of slavery, and as such, arguments for a right of secession in the United States—for long, the world's largest and most successful liberal democracy—were largely discredited by association with the evils of slavery."[132] There are many other examples of secession beyond southern nationalism, more quirky than calamitous—instances that might provoke eye-rolling dismissals of presumably kooky eccentrics. The lead character in Bill McKibben's *Radio Free Vermont* (2017), Vern Barclay, a fed-up seventy-two-year-old radio host who thinks a free, small nation of Vermont would be "Finland with fall colors," perfectly captures this quirkiness.[133]

Of course, it is easy to find peculiar nonfiction examples of idiosyncratic separatists. In 1900, a group of Delaware Single Taxers, followers of Henry George who wanted to abolish all taxes except for one on land, set up their own town to achieve what they could not at the ballot box. They founded Arden, an unincorporated anarchist enclave, a "private town," a "double experiment in communalism and privatization"—a place where, as one resident put it in 2017, there was more than "a wingnut or two." Arden residents adopted the single tax voluntarily.[134]

32   WE ARE NOT ONE PEOPLE

A handwritten sign outside the village of Oyotunji, near Beaufort, South Carolina, tells visitors that they are "leaving the U.S." and entering "the Yoruba kingdom." A few dozen people resided in Oyotunji in the late 2010s, down from more than a hundred in its 1970s heyday.[135] The Republic of Molossia, an eleven-acre micronation in northern Nevada, is another illustrative example. Tourists drawn to this nation-as-roadside-attraction can have their passport stamped and enjoy a guided tour by the president and founder, Kevin Baugh. Tourists can also trade their dollars for Molossia's currency, poker chips, in case they want to buy national swag. They cannot, however, apply for citizenship; all citizens are members of the Baugh family.[136] Molossia sprang from the same "idea that kids often have" when "they declare their bedroom to be an independent country," Baugh told a Nevada reporter. "We've sort of taken that to the nth degree."[137]

"Deep down," Ralph Ellison wrote, "the American condition is a state of unease."[138] Secession may seem to some a fringe part of American life and some secessionists part of an eccentric, isolated rabble, but when reconceptualized as a spectrum of symbolically potent withdrawals along a separatist spectrum, of scaled refusals made by individuals and communities, secession moves out of the periphery and closer to the center. To put it bluntly, many Americans have never seen a cause that was not worth seceding over. Visionaries have dreamed of a Second Vermont Republic, a Third Palmetto Republic in South Carolina, an independent Alaska, a dissociated Utah, and a sovereign Hawaii.[139] Texas's case to regain its independence, held from 1836 to 1845, has been ceaseless.[140]

Separatism, therefore, is hard to box; it is not over, not southern, not marginal, not ideologically limited, and irreducible to legal questions. It is also not easily mapped. Secessionists have not always tied their demands to the existing boundaries of existing states. The pious believers of many flocks have practiced geographical separation in places like Ruby Ridge, Waco, and many other locales that never drew the FBI's attention.[141] Some Indigenous Peoples activists have urged the creation of a new Republic of Lakotah centered around the Black Hills.[142] Some doomsday preppers have gathered in and around Idaho and call this fortified land the American Redoubt, a new nation they hope would survive America's cataclysmic end.[143] Still further west,

BANDS, BONDS, AND AFFECTIONS   33

activists have sought the creation of Cascadia along the mountainous Pacific shores stretching from Oregon well into Canada. Back east, other nation-builders wanted to turn New England into New Acadia. New York City has hosted a periodic free-city movement.[144]

Upstate, the firefighters in Town Line, New York, wore Confederate emblems on their uniforms until 2011 because their city seceded in solidarity with the Confederacy in 1861; it did not officially rejoin the Union until the Truman administration. The long delay was not due to strident determination; most people had just forgotten that Town Line seceded in the first place.[145]

Sixth, perhaps the greatest drawback of analyses of separatism or secession is that they only consider one or the other, not a spectrum of separatist political action. Separatists say that there are certain people to whom national laws and norms do not apply, and there are certain areas where laws and norms have no force. Secession is separatist logic at the end of the line. "Secession," philosopher Allen Buchanan points out, "is the most extreme form of political separation, and there are modes of self-determination short of it."[146] All secession is separatist; all separatism suggests secession. The difference in practice between secession, geographic separatism, nullification, and interposition is often immaterial. There can be many functionally different nations in the same country at the same time without any formal secession declaration. "Nullification," Anna Ella Carroll wrote to Edward Everett in 1861, "is the application to one or more of the acts of the agent, within its territorial limits. Secession is to arrest all the acts, and dismiss the agent altogether!"[147] In the United States, "talk of secession had almost invariably accompanied talk of nullification."[148]

Formal, legal secession is only one means of national withdrawal in the same sense that breaking up is only one way to end a relationship. The spectrum in between committed, cooperative partnership and official, mutually recognized dissolution yawns. An exclusive focus on straightforward secession assumes that secession is all or nothing; there are secessionists, and then there is everyone else.[149] Secession, moreover, is especially difficult to consider in a vacuum because "most secessionist movements try to foster some ambiguity about their aims."[150] Secessionist inclinations have been rebranded and enshrined in law as "states' rights," "local control," "home rule," and "right to

34 WE ARE NOT ONE PEOPLE

work," each of which allowed individuals and states to exempt themselves from laws they disliked.[151] In a spate of cases in the 2010s, the Supreme Court even legalized separatist practices by carving out "religious liberty" exemptions to federal anti-discrimination laws in cases like *Hosanna-Tabor Evangelical Lutheran Church and School v. EEOC* (2011), *Burwell v. Hobby Lobby, Inc.* (2014), *Masterpiece Cakeshop v. Colorado Civil Rights Commission* (2018), and *Roman Catholic Diocese of Brooklyn v. Cuomo* (2020).[152]

Few but the most diehard advocates push for full secession at every turn. Purist, radical secessionists, like William Lloyd Garrison, regarded voting and paying taxes as acts of infidelity to the sacred cause of separation, but half- and hybrid acts of separation thrive. Radical secession can portend immediate, wholesale life changes, but cherry-picked separatism avoids confrontations, legal, armed, and otherwise, with sovereign powers and does not require abandoning the nation or modernity. The whiskey tax was, after all, difficult to collect even after the demise of the Whiskey Rebellion. Rebels continued to disrupt law enforcement and threaten tax collectors, but, one historian notes, "mainly there was sneakiness and recalcitrance, smuggling and moonshining." Federal authority was "eluded" rather than directly "challenged."[153] The Whiskey Rebellion went underground. Southern fire-eaters, moreover, were situational secessionists; whenever possible, they wielded national political power, especially fugitive slave codes, to serve their interests; otherwise, they threatened to nullify federal law or secede entirely.

National Resources of Separatism

Separatists have not dreamed of the same new nation, and they all certainly did not conceive all of these new nations in liberty. The similarities in how these dispersed advocates developed, framed, and made the case for withdrawal, however, are striking. *We Are Not One People* examines separatism as a durable, flexible, adaptable, and modular political language.[154] A specific political language, as distinguished from an era or nation's language of politics, is a storehouse of narratives, standard references and citations, idioms, god and devil terms, tropes, and lines of argument.[155] If a group's goal is to withdraw from some legal jurisdiction, a political convention, or a cultural norm, they typically invoke a stable set of keywords.

Some political languages, like conservatism or Communism, are concentrated; their speakers largely accept a common term of political identity. When considered as a political language, separatism is quite different. It is scattered; its speakers belong to different communities, each employing a similar vocabulary in pursuit of different objectives. We approach separatism as a diffuse, widely available public language that has been employed and adjusted by dissimilar ideological groups or, often, groups within groups: Black nationalists among Black activists or separatist theocrats among religious activists. Unlike the key words ("law and order," for example) and common stories employed by members of the same political identity, diffuse political languages are often used by groups across the political landscape. Such languages are, to offer a different metaphor, an original song covered widely by different artists across musical genres for different audiences; we are interested in both the original and the covers.

On the whole, separatism is a political language of peculiar, contradictory, parentage. It is simultaneously a centrifugal and centripetal language, one of nationalism and denationalization, of integration and disintegration, of sameness and difference, of pessimism and hope. It is a language that refuses the possibility of togetherness among one people while reaffirming another people's inherent bonds. The political language of separatism is, in short, an amalgam. Its speakers gather rhetorical resources from several political traditions, some international, many distinctly American.

The Icons of American Exit

America began in secession; its first word was, in essence, "goodbye."[156] Albert O. Hirschman argued that the American political tradition has replicated this founding departure over and over again. Opposed to "voice," meaning patient reform, the American preference for the "neatness of exit" has been persistent "throughout our national history." Political dissatisfaction compelled many Americans to choose

36 WE ARE NOT ONE PEOPLE

flight over fight.[157] The "aim" of the American Revolution, as Benedict Anderson identified it, "was not to have New London succeed, overthrow, or destroy Old London, but rather to safeguard their continuing parallelism."[158] The Revolution was not, as another scholar put it, Whiggish, Lockean, or Jacobin; it did not restore an older order, overthrow the monarchy, or transform English society from the ground up. Americans merely pressed to limit England's jurisdiction and, thereby, "to be let alone."[159]

In his classic book on American political culture, *The Liberal Tradition in America* (1955), Louis Hartz made a similar point. That the American revolutionaries revolted in "flight" was not a "minor fact: for it is one thing to stay at home and fight the 'canon and feudal law,' and it is another to leave it far behind." "Physical flight," he argued, "is the American substitute for the European experience of social revolution."[160]

This separatist tradition of flight in North America preceded the American Revolution; much of the early colonial experience consisted of "secessions and withdrawals, separations and dissolutions."[161] The Pilgrims arrived in the New World only after an initial separation from England to the Netherlands. They are just one of many influential colonial groups whose legacy to generations of Americans has been, in part, to connect separation, isolation, and freedom. Leaders like Roger Williams, Anne Hutchison, and William Penn and groups like the Puritans and Quakers endorsed then-radical notions that authentic experiences of the divine were possible, even likely, outside the auspices of established churches.[162]

American separatists have employed the secular, rebellious resources of the Enlightenment, but they have also cast themselves as persecuted but pious, true believers punished for being faithful. Separatism is a political language infused with sacred, religious narratives, especially its stark dichotomies: Babylon and the promised land, apostates and apostles, the coming apocalypse and the redemptive promise of solidarity. The quest for "purity through separation" has been a hallmark of American religious activity since the Puritans and Quakers sought to create a New World. As Sean Wilentz suggests, "Even before the outbreak of the English Civil War, religious sectarians who preferred flight to New England to life under Tudor monarchy

BANDS, BONDS, AND AFFECTIONS   37

established at least a nominal conception of self-rule by compact, to which some dissenters (such as a group of four Rhode Island towns in 1647) attached the word 'democracy.'" The "radicalism" of English plebes of the mid-seventeenth century "crossed the Atlantic and survived to help inspire the American revolutionaries and frighten their opponents over a century later."[163]

Additionally, the Balkanization of religious denominations like the Baptists or Methodists provided the secular world a sacred, sectarian template for a community breaking away to achieve, or revive, holiness. "Religious purists," G. Jeffrey MacDonald writes, "have the Bible to guide their quest; secessionists look to the Constitution and the Declaration of Independence."[164] Secessionists become Pilgrims at Plymouth with different aims, separating to live on their own, by their own rules, in a new world.

Some of the deists and atheists at the forefront of the American Revolution did not view the natural or political world as the Puritans did, but they developed a similar line of argument: freedom was found in departure. Although many newly minted American citizens— "Revolutionary War veterans, school teachers, gentlemen historians, partisan newspaper editors, and professional politicians"—began teaching the Revolution as a national fable as soon as the war ended, the anti-authoritarian language of exit at the center of the story made for a "pliable" tale.[165] American citizens learned that their country was founded "as a missionary republic committed to liberty and opposed to tyranny."[166] They would also soon learn that these principles— freedom, independence, popular government, the consent of the governed, and the distinctiveness of peoples—could justify a populist absolutism and make and unmake nations.[167]

Americans began using these founding words to split their new nation apart almost immediately. The "Framers' revolutionary rhetoric" of the people's sovereignty "created as many fresh problems as it solved" in the nation's earliest days.[168] Early Americans broadly supported the people's sovereignty; they just were not sure which people that meant or how that sovereignty could be legitimately expressed.[169] Some peoples in America were bent on discovering the limits of their newfound power, and they practiced sovereignty through relatively frequent acts of exit. Vermont seceded from New York and New Hampshire.

38   WE ARE NOT ONE PEOPLE

Kentucky seceded from Virginia. (West Virginia, decades later, did as well.) Maine seceded from Massachusetts. Texas seceded from Mexico and then the United States.

Other settlement movements, attempts at self-government that never became fully fledged states, occurred up and down the new country's western frontiers: Westsylvania, Transylvania, Franklin, the Wyoming Valley, the Cumberland Valley, and the Watauga Valley.[170] These separatist movements phrased their claims for local control, for independence, in the cherished rhetoric of the American Revolution. The citizens of each of these new settlements were an identifiable people, and each of these peoples gave their consent to form a new government to faithfully represent their interests; they did not need the permission of existing state governments or the federal government any more than the American Founders needed George III's permission. "The shoe," one scholar explains, "was now on the other foot: for many revolutionary leaders, maintaining the status quo of newly established American governments was a more pressing concern than extending the logic of the Revolution's principles that might challenge those governments." Revolutionary War veterans who had become local and state officials were put in an awkward, ironic position: they had to defend the territorial possessions of existing states.[171]

Although separatists are often, but not exclusively, alienated minority groups who pursue exit because direct revolutionary actions would be suicidal and building a majority coalition was numerically unlikely, the legacy of the American Revolution has given them one argumentative advantage: the icons of the founding and the language of freedom fighting. Since Americans "seceded from Britain," in one writer's estimation, "the right of secession lies at the heart of our country's legitimacy." To deny the right of secession is to "reject the American founding."[172] Revolutionary republicanism lent early separatist calls "extra potency."[173]

George Washington is an illustrative case. Although he first served and then fought against the crown, laudatory American accounts of his military career in the colonial and Continental armies brand him a brave patriot, an honorable revolutionary, not a low traitor. "Win a war for independence," one historian points out, "and the leaders become founding fathers after whom cities, mountains, and holidays

BANDS, BONDS, AND AFFECTIONS 39

are named; lose the fight, and they might well be branded traitors and rebels and end with their heads on pikes as a warning to others."[174] Benedict Arnold was a turncoat; Washington was not. The nation's first president achieved national heroism by leading a violent separation and, as such, casts two shadows: one as a national unifier, another as a just divider. Separatists have used the nation's hallowed words to justify their exit, and they have enlisted Washington in their cause.

Few have done so as dramatically as John C. Calhoun did in 1850 during the last speech of his long career. "Washington," Calhoun emphasized before the Senate, "was born and grew up" under another "Union"—that of the colonies with England. He found "distinction" serving the crown, and, in Calhoun's story, "he was devotedly attached to it." But his attachment was pragmatic, not permanent. He protected England until England oppressed the colonists and then, Calhoun warned ominously, "he did not hesitate to draw his sword." Washington helmed "the great movement by which that union was forever severed, and the independence of these States established." If there was a lesson that subsequent generations of Americans should learn from Washington, it was this "crowning glory of his life" transmitted perpetually "to the latest posterity" by those who might retell of the honor he achieved in rupture.[175] Southerners, in Calhoun's telling, brandished Washington's sword against an imperial power.

Calhoun's rendition of Washington's legacy, fealty to section over nation, was typical among southern nationalists of the era. "It was hardly coincidental," one scholar remarks, "that those who designed and endorsed the official seal of the new Southern Confederacy sought to appropriate the metaphorical father of the United States, George Washington—the first U.S. president as well as commander of the Continental Army that had won independence from Great Britain—as the personal symbol of the Confederacy's claim to national independence."[176]

Calhoun's celebration of Washington certainly was tailored to a specific context: sectional crisis over the admission of California in 1850. Nevertheless, Calhoun's encomium mirrored the argumentative structure of the ur-text of American separatism: the Declaration of Independence. In his telling, Washington was the living embodiment of the principles Jefferson drafted; just government was based on the

40   WE ARE NOT ONE PEOPLE

consent of the governed, and consent can be withdrawn when government becomes tyrannical. But the line of argument that Calhoun aped is just one of several possible arguments for separatism that are succinctly developed in the Declaration. The Declaration, all told, was a catalog of possible justifications for separation. Motivated readers of the Declaration can find three distinct licenses for separation in the first few paragraphs: separation based on just cause, separation based on free choice, and separation based on fundamental differences between peoples.[177]

First, the Declaration's opening two paragraphs set up one specific condition for a just departure: the consistent denial of basic human rights. Oppression was a requirement to sever the ties of nationality. Sometimes "one people" must "dissolve the political bands which have connected them with another." Jefferson and the drafters of the Declaration did not mean that one people could be banded to another by coercion. Bands could not be established by servitude or serfdom. Bands were established benevolently by mutual affection between social creatures, and government merely formalized and protected their affections.[178]

Such bands, moreover, could not be broken capriciously. Over and again in the first three hundred words of the Declaration, before the litany of allegations of misconduct against George III, Jefferson accentuated the colonists' careful deliberations, the "patient sufferance" that preceded their final act. The colonies, he stressed, were not acting rashly.

People had the right to "alter or abolish" governments, the Declaration read, that were "destructive" of "life, liberty, and the pursuit of happiness." Separation was, therefore, conditional. The would-be separatists must prove that their basic rights were insecure. Such insecurity, moreover, should not be confined to a moment in time; "governments long established" deserve some patience on the part of the governed. They should not be altered or abolished for "light and transient causes." Instead, the just case for separation rested on proving "a long train of abuses and usurpations," on showing government to be an "absolute despotism." "Independence," one scholar summarizes, "was a remedy of last resort to the prolonged abuse of basic human rights."[179] Jefferson repeats this argument of necessity twice in the first

BANDS, BONDS, AND AFFECTIONS 41

three hundred words for precisely this reason: to substantiate a just cause. Per the standard he established, the people must show that there was no other way except to find a way out.

The second paragraph of the Declaration sketched an atomized ideal: individuals with protected rights freely pursuing their happiness. If a political arrangement was unsatisfactory, individuals should be free to opt out. Jefferson's logic has become a kind of commonsense nationalism and permits a second, far broader argument for separation. If people were free to assemble communities based on mutually held goodwill, then they should be free to disassemble them when that will lapsed and the community became a seething mass of resentments.[180] In other words, "If a subunit no longer wants to stay within the nation, why should it have to do so?"[181] This second separatist argument, stemming from the claim that the "just powers" of government come only from the "consent of the governed," valorized unconditional, unrestricted freedom of choice. Groups should be able to leave if they want to; there should be no heavy burden of proof. Several leaders of the American Revolution worried about the disorder that could erupt from an overly literal interpretation of this section of the Declaration, of sovereignty resting solely on the people's fickle consent.[182]

The theory that individuals should be able to exercise their freedoms rationally even when choosing governments was one of the main currents of democratic thought during the Enlightenment. Democratic thinkers of the Enlightenment did not theorize secession thoroughly or consistently, but they developed concepts like individual self-ownership, the social contract, popular sovereignty, natural rights, and the consent of the governed (all of which influenced Jefferson) to stake claims against tyranny.

All of these concepts can, when read by a particular light, justify secession.[183] Thomas Paine's idea in *The Rights of Man* that "individuals themselves, each in his own personal and sovereign right, entered into a compact with each other to produce a government" was easily extended to mean that individuals can leave that arrangement when government becomes unsatisfactory.[184] The social contract, in short, implied the secession of the contractors. The process, as one scholar explains, by which a people band together to form a government to

42 WE ARE NOT ONE PEOPLE

suit their ends should also work in reverse if the people's freedom of choice is a paramount value: "A political philosophy that places a pre-eminent value on liberty and autonomy, that highly values diversity, or that holds that legitimate political authority in some sense rests on consent must either acknowledge a right to secede or supply weighty arguments to show why a presumption in favor of such a right is rebutted."[185]

The language of democracy is often the language of secession.[186] As Abraham Lincoln, then a first-year member of the House of Representatives, said of the 1848 Texan revolt against Mexico: "Any people anywhere, being inclined and having the power, have the right to rise up, and shake off the existing government, and form a new one that suits them better. This is a most valuable—a most sacred right—a right, which we hope and believe, is to liberate the world."[187] What mattered was not whether some group of people, whether a minority or majority in a given area, could meet the high threshold of a "long train of abuses" to prove a just cause; what mattered was a people's desire to associate or dissociate. The freedom that this second, more capacious argument for secession enshrined was the freedom to associate with others based on choice and, just as important, to choose to end associations.[188]

Self-determination is democracy's basis, but it is also its riddle. Once sovereignty has been seized from kings or churches, once the right to self-determination against any and all coercion is sanctified, then every community, perhaps every person, is equally justified to rule or to retreat from the rule of others to live unbeholden.[189] Each person searching for a Walden Pond of their own to live out their days unconnected to others, unbothered by others' desires, uninterested in others' ideas, might seem a refusal of any social tapestry of reciprocal and mutual obligation. John Stuart Mill's conception of self-determination and individual freedom of choice is both the bedrock of classical liberalism and a challenge to coalition-building in diverse political communities: "The only freedom which deserves the name, is that of pursuing our own good in our own way, so long as we do not attempt to deprive others of theirs, or impede their efforts to obtain it." For Mill, the "greater" gain came from leaving others alone to live as they saw fit rather than "compelling each to live as seems good to the rest."[190] Separatists have agreed wholeheartedly; let us live apart rather than constrain one another together.

Nations, for Jefferson, were composed of individuals. More specifically, nations were made by feelings, by shared sentiments between individuals. The American Revolution was, therefore, a "matter of shattered affections."[191] Hamilton, arguing more than a decade later for a new federal constitution to secure his new nation, worried these affections might shatter again. He hoped that the "sacred knot which binds the people of America together" would survive "ambition," "avarice," "jealousy," and "misrepresentation."[192] He knew that if nations were built on feeling, then sustained animus, quite common in democracies both large and small, could justify dissolution.

Lincoln, who once credited Jefferson with inspiring his political thought as well, employed similar binding metaphors in his first inaugural address as he tried to revive the "bonds of affection" that southerners, some citing Jefferson, had declared dead. Lincoln ridiculed secessionists by comparing their view of society to a flimsy "free-love arrangement," not "anything like a regular marriage."[193] For him, secession was anarchy.[194] Francis Lieber, the influential nineteenth-century political theorist, chose a different metaphor to demean southern arguments for secession in 1850. "Should we," he asked sardonically in a speech in the secessionist hotbed of South Carolina, treat government "as a sort of political picnic" to which guests may come and go as they please?[195]

Nations, following Jefferson's bands and affections line of thought, were not built on blood or soil; they were civic associations of feeling, not ethnic associations of kind. There is, however, a third separatist argument lurking in the Declaration, one not at all rooted in the liberal individualism of either the just-cause or free-choice arguments for separation. Nations can be defined by "subjective" characteristics such as "self-awareness, the sense of solidarity, loyalty, a common will or a sentiment of belonging," but they can also be delineated by seemingly "objective" factors like "language, religion, territory, ancestry or kinship, and culture."[196] People, in other words, were banded together not just because they liked one another or because they had a shared

44   WE ARE NOT ONE PEOPLE

experience; they were banded together whether they knew one another or not; they were banded together by something more permanent than mutual affection, something visual or visceral.

This third claim for separation motivated by racial or cultural difference is implied by a more absolutist interpretation of "one people" moving on from another in the Declaration's first lines. Jefferson did not directly pursue in the Declaration the idea that one people must separate from another because their differences were so vast, but he included an adjacent idea in the rough draft of the document. Buried in the voluminous charges against George III in Jefferson's first draft was an allegation that the king had prosecuted a "cruel war against human nature itself." The king's mercenaries, Jefferson charged, spread slavery through the colonies and, in so doing, violated the "most sacred rights" of a "distant people." Then, Jefferson continued, the king encouraged those "very people" to revolt in the colonies, pitting two different peoples against one another.[197]

Jefferson, of course, owned more than six hundred enslaved people in his lifetime, and his hypocrisy here is striking.[198] Voided by his fellow southern slave owners, Jefferson's anti-slavery lines did not make the final document.[199] Nevertheless, Jefferson defended a view of the world where nations were found in nature, where some differences between people could not be overcome; some people, that is, did not belong with other people. Different peoples, moreover, could not be made into one people, a claim that was not lost on some who read the Declaration through the lens of race.[200]

Jefferson developed a science of white supremacy in *Notes on the State of Virginia*, but he did not deny the right of self-rule to free Black people.[201] What he did deny was their right to self-rule in America. He signed on to a deportation scheme to remove people of African descent from America so that, in Garry Wills's words, they might have "a *separate* station, for that to become an *equal* one."[202] He felt similarly about Indigenous Peoples. He professed a sympathetic admiration, "but it never entered his head that they could become part of the white man's government."[203] If they and presumably many other American peoples wanted self-determination, they would have to write their own Declarations of Independence. They have.[204]

Conclusion

Questions about the boundaries of national union, about the consent to be governed, about the limits of freedom, and about remedies to polarization sprout in every democracy. But, we argue, they are given particular shape in the keywords, narratives, lines of argument, shared histories, vaunted heroes, fallen villains, and nation-defining acts of particular political cultures. From Pilgrims to the American Revolution to Manifest Destiny to People Power, exit narratives of getting out and starting over are endemic to America.

Separatists have used distinctly American symbols to unmake the nation. The "Don't Tread on Me" Gadsden flag and Patrick Henry's "Live free or die" motto may have particular historical associations, but each is remarkably adaptable to different causes. American separatists have been enchanted by a packed roster of legendary self-starters as they charted a course to a city on a hill or a thousand miles from nowhere. This narrative's resonance and wide circulation are matched only by its flexibility. The hero of this quest can be of any shape or stripe, represent any cause or creed, and shirk any set of rules. The narrative works so long as the hero or heroic community betrays the designs of others for a self-determined quest. "The prospect," Richard Tsai writes, of a new start was, for many Americans, "exhilarating, no matter how bleak one's circumstances."[205]

This do-it-yourself ethos has been reflected in famous works of American political thought like Emerson's "Self-Reliance." Emerson framed "society" as a "conspiracy" against "every one of its members" and identified "the great man" as one "who in the midst of the crowd keeps with perfect sweetness the independence of solitude."[206] The sociologist Robert Bellah and his colleagues found Emerson's notion "common" in many different American social and political traditions. They wrote, "What, if not self-reliant, were the Puritans, many of whom, like John Winthrop, left wealth and comfort to set out in small ships on a dangerous 'errand into the wilderness'?"[207]

Much of the mythology of the American West is bound up in a dynamic of a new kind of sovereignty, escaping a world controlled by others for a self-controlled world. Rooted in the imaginary history of a wide-open West, Rebecca Solnit identifies "the cowboy" as

46   WE ARE NOT ONE PEOPLE

the "embodiment" of an "ideology of isolation."[208] Separatists, as such, have also adapted and extended the tradition of the celebrated American renegade, outlaws with no use for the opinions of others or rule of the masses, as they crafted their reasons for withdrawal. The American separatist tradition is, in this sense, a natural extension of the nation's "romance of the outsider."[209] Hunter S. Thompson recognized and slyly critiqued this narrative of the self-contained rebel in the epigraph to *Hell's Angels*: "In my own country I am in a far-off land / I am strong but have no force or power / I win all yet remain a loser / At break of day I say goodnight / When I lie down I have a great fear / Of Falling."[210]

2

Secession All the Way Down

Libertarians Opt Out

By the time he reached his late thirties, Mike Oliver had lived an accomplished, if atypical, life. Born in Lithuania in 1928, Oliver survived imprisonment in two Nazi concentration camps. He immigrated to America after World War II and spent five years in the Air Force. Eventually he landed in the West, first as a technical writer in California, then as a land developer and coin dealer in Nevada. He made a fortune developing subdivisions. But his life's passion really began when he started reading libertarian classics by Ayn Rand, Ludwig von Mises, and Andrew Galambos. He took his builder's eye to their libertarian utopias and began constructing, both literally and figuratively, the raw materials for a brand-new libertarian nation.[1] A 1980 *People* profile of Oliver hyped this goal as homegrown Americana: "Only in America, so the saying goes, can anyone grow up to be president. For Michael Oliver, a Carson City, Nevada businessman, that wasn't enough. He wanted his own country."[2]

The polymathic Oliver even wrote a book on nation-building. His *A New Constitution for a New Country* (1968) was a how-to guide for libertarian nationalists, including suggested laws to partition the government and economy. He started writing, he said, because the United States was vulnerable to "Nazi Storm Troopers," or people who claimed to want freedom but actually sowed violence. He dreamed of a nation where "everyone" possessed the "maximum amount of freedom."[3]

Government would offer some basic services, and citizens could pay "voluntary premiums" to subscribe. Only judicial subscribers could file claims in court, for example. Government had no taxation power whatsoever; it was, instead, a "private agency hired for the sole function of protecting against force and fraud." Defense against invasion and police protection against violence would be free to all. Otherwise,

We Are Not One People. Michael J. Lee and R. Jarrod Atchison, Oxford University Press. © Oxford University Press 2022. DOI: 10.1093/oso/9780190876500.003.0003

48   WE ARE NOT ONE PEOPLE

there would be "no free schools, no social security, no government welfare."[4] The economy would bustle with transnational corporations flocking to a deregulated nation without taxes, labor laws, and pesky questions about money sources or client activities.[5] He saw himself as a modern Benjamin Franklin.[6]

Oliver was more practitioner than theorist; he dedicated his time and considerable financial resources to what he named the New Country Project. The project's trite name concealed some extravagant, arguably harebrained, national ploys. Minerva, for example, was to have been a "sea city" for thirty thousand inhabitants built upon pilings in shallow South Pacific waters. Minerva took its name from its location, and the Minerva Reefs presented quite the development challenge. Since it was submerged four feet under water at high tide with only three feet of reef above water at low tide, engineers would have to work like mad when the tide ebbed. Starting in 1972, they did, and they managed to build a stone tower and lay some concrete foundations atop pilings lodged in the reef for the future sea city.

The king of Tonga, however, was resistant to sovereignty claims on the Minerva Reefs. Having no Tongan navy, he conscripted five convicts as a landing party; a four-piece band played inspirational Tongan music from the deck of the king's yacht while the convicts practiced Operation Overlord in miniature in what was basically open water. Minerva was unoccupied when the convicts landed. The Tongan king came ashore to read a declaration of sovereignty, but only after waiting out the tide. The convicts razed Minerva.[7]

Undeterred, Oliver made many other nation-building attempts in New Caledonia, Curaçao, Turks, Caicos, Tortuga (adjacent to Haiti), and other spots in Africa and elsewhere. A home-rule effort to liberate the island of Abaco from the greater Bahamas was inspired by his work.[8] Perhaps the closest he came to inventing a nation was in the late 1970s in New Hebrides (now Vanuatu), then an Anglo-French-ruled Pacific island chain.[9] There, amid the *South Pacific* setting, Oliver became both an ideological and material sponsor to a secessionist movement led by the roguish Jimmy Stevens, the area's "self-styled Moses." Their idea was to convert one island, Espiritu Santo, into a new nation, Vemerana, governed according to Oliver's libertarian nationalist playbook.[10] "They were the most disciplined people I have ever seen," Oliver said of the islanders, "not like those hippies in Berkeley."[11]

Stevens and his compatriots, armed with bows and arrows, even occupied government offices.[12] The type of arms they brandished, whether bows or bazookas, did not matter to the colonial British government; a small peacekeeping force was dispatched. Eventually, allied troops from Papua New Guinea put down the rebellion and confiscated caches of bows and arrows.[13] Oliver ended his nation-building efforts in the 1990s when he could not lure investors to Oceania, yet another floating state.[14]

Libertarians have a rich tradition of nation-building. Ayn Rand's Galt's Gulch, the fictional secluded mountain town from which John Galt directed the strike of owner-producers against a confiscatory culture in *Atlas Shrugged* (1957), is the most influential, if not the original, vision of a totally voluntary society.[15] Rand's fictional Gulch has inspired real Gulches, one of which, a self-reliant community tucked in the Chilean Andes, failed in 2014 as its American founders accused "one another of being drunks, liars, and sociopaths."[16]

Remarkably, Oliver was not the only libertarian seeking water states of either the floating or island variety. Such "seasteading" gained real purchase among well-heeled, imaginative libertarians after Oliver.[17] Dreamers of a new Atlantis included Patri Friedman, son of David, grandson of Rose and Milton, and Peter Thiel, PayPal founder and billionaire venture capitalist.[18] Thiel supported seasteading, he wrote, because "politics" was not the art of the possible. Echoing Albert Jay Nock's pathbreaking *Our Enemy, the State* (1935), Thiel argued that politics restricted the possible, and only by finding "an escape from politics in all forms" could libertarians avoid being party to "totalitarian and fundamentalist catastrophes."[19] The sea offered just such an escape; there, they could live apolitically.

Other libertarians have sought refuge, but they framed their escapes as explicitly political retreats from central authority. The Free State Project has, since 2001, been persuading libertarians to move to New Hampshire to join forces and change the politics of a single American state. The Granite State, with its "Live free or die" motto, won an online vote among some libertarians as the best destination because it had no state sales or income taxes, a low population, a low citizen-to-legislator

50   WE ARE NOT ONE PEOPLE

ratio, and lax gun and knife laws.[20] The original target number of pledged migrants was twenty thousand, a number the Free State Project surpassed in early 2016.[21] One Free Stater refrain boasted that "married gay couples" could reach for their "guns to defend their marijuana plants" in New Hampshire.[22]

Beyond winning local and state elections, New Hampshire's culture has been altered by this growing concentration of libertarians.[23] In towns like Keene and Nashua, libertarians occasionally staged defiant stunts like refusing to remove their hats in court or giving a manicure without a state-issued cosmetology license.[24] Every summer, about fifteen hundred people gather in the northern New Hampshire woods for the Porcupine Freedom Festival, or Porc Fest. They attend this "backwoods Burning Man" to camp, shoot guns, listen to lectures on Ayn Rand and polyamory and political strategy, and buy meats off the FDA's radar with hard money or cryptocurrency.[25] Free Staters were called "Porcs" after their prickly mascot, which, a Porc Fest organizer stressed, was far less aggressive or "militia-y" than the coiled snake emblazoned on the "Don't Tread on Me" Gadsden flag.[26]

The Free State idea came from Jason Sorens, a Yale political science graduate student when he hatched the single-state scheme in the early 2000s. Sorens hoped to gather dispersed libertarians in one place where they could become an active, local voting bloc pushing for deregulation. He was inspired by the migration and concentration of Mormons in Utah.[27] They made a state in their own image; perhaps libertarians could, too. "Once we've taken over the state government," he wrote in the original Free State siren call, "we can slash state and local budgets, which make up a sizeable portion of the tax and regulatory burden we face every day."

Once Free Staters were entrenched in the Granite State, Sorens then suggested a bigger gambit: secession, both as a feint to bargain for greater concessions from the federal government and to attract non-libertarians to the cause of independence. "Of course," he surmised, "once secession is achieved, libertarianism is the likely outcome if we've concentrated our forces."[28] Sorens later regretted his emphasis on secession in that foundational essay. "Some Free Staters," he hedged, "support independence for New Hampshire. Others do not. Independence is not my objective."[29]

The Free State Project was fashioned as an alternative to what Sorens termed a "lone wolf lifestyle" of moving on, dropping out, and living apart; some libertarian fellow travelers, however, have taken to such a hermitic life as the only viable freedom.[30] One such lone wolf in New Hampshire told a reporter that he did odd jobs to make rent but ate only what he grew or killed. "I am about as free as I can be in this country," he remarked.[31]

Then there is Eustace Conway, who nearly got away from it all in the North Carolina mountains. Holed up on a thousand acres of Appalachian land Conway called, nodding to Indigenous Peoples' legends, Turtle Island, he practiced frontier life in late modernity: skinning deer, sewing clothes, plowing, clearing land, gardening, tending some animals, and making shelter, all by himself. Untethered to others in near-total "cultural isolation" every single day, he rewound the clock to another century. "I sometimes feel like a man without a country," he admitted. His bucolic retreat, according to a *GQ* profile, was Conway's own "small, self-sufficient planet."[32] "I want to tell the world," Conway announced in a 2010 interview, "that you are not handcuffed to your culture." Everyone could "return to the woods."[33] But even Conway, a lone wolf seemingly out to undo most modern comforts and relationships, courted personal, public connections in magazine interviews, in speaking gigs, even in a recurring role on *Mountain Men*, a reality television show about roughing it.[34] For him, there was likely no solitude in celebrity, but there was some celebrity in solitude.

Liberty, Coercion, and Withdrawal

Libertarians are, both nominally and philosophically, committed to preserving liberty. Free choice should be maximized; restraints on choice should be minimized. An antipathy for authority, especially the authority of a centralized government, follows these precepts. Ranging from classical liberal "minarchist" believers in Robert Nozick's "night watchman state" to anarchists delighted by literal lawlessness, libertarians champion individuals who rebuke, neighborhoods that ignore, towns that rebuff, and states that say no to the state.[35]

52   WE ARE NOT ONE PEOPLE

Libertarians have always been reluctant Americans insofar as America, both as a national identity and a legal institution, can run roughshod over individual Americans. In fact, libertarians have been trying to secede since before there were people called libertarians and before there was something called the United States. If the nation-state is, always and forever, a criminal enterprise, bands of violent thieves with badges, then opting out of its authority is, always and forever, a valiant act of self-preservation. As one nineteenth-century individualist-anarchist explained in 1890, government invades and aggresses; resisters merely defend and protect.[36]

As the Minervans, Free Staters, and lone wolves show, vexing questions await just one step beyond this hostility toward central authority. How and why should people live together in the first place? What is the proper locus of authority when people band together? Can anyone for any reason ever be justly compelled to do something by this authority (assuming, of course, that this seat of proper authority is not sovereign, self-owning individuals in the first place)? What is a law if it only applies to people when they want it to? Finally, is libertarian nationalism an oxymoron?

Although American libertarians, both in theory and in practice, have answered these big questions quite differently, the models of voluntary, non-aggressive communities they have envisioned and attempted have all been premised on rehabilitating secession—libertarian literature uses the word frequently—as a legal and moral act. For them, secession is both a starting point and an endpoint; what happens after secession is more secession. Any problems caused by the secession of one group from another group can be, in turn, solved by the further secession of yet another group. Secession solved public problems, and secession cured the ills of secession.

Secession is a true expression of individual liberty, and liberty is the end result of secession. For libertarians, secession was not some far-flung possibility to be sought after tectonic shifts in national politics. Secession was an everyday act. We should all secede, all of the time, and, in so doing, destroy government power, the so-called public interest, collective goods, society, criminality, and every collective noun that erased individuality. The land of milk and honey that libertarians described was, in sum, a society of secessionists.[37]

These libertarian national imaginings—Mike Oliver's, the Free Staters', and the lone wolves'—resemble a reverse pyramid, with nation-builders designing large societies atop the inverted base, smaller congregations of anti-authoritarians in communes or short-lived conventions in the tapered middle of the pyramid, and then tight bands of off-the-gridders, perhaps just one person glorifying freedom in the boondocks, at the pyramid's point. These and many other individual libertarian acts, like jury nullification or tax shelters, are united in secession from American legal, cultural, and economic norms. Where they differ is in the amount of secession; for some, it's secession all the way down.

American libertarianism is both an ideology and an identity of separation. That collective identity is, of course, one that favors "me" over "we." Secession, one libertarian declared, was a "defining principle of classical liberalism."[38] "If freedom is the greatest political good" in classical liberalism, then how can any nation that lauds freedom deny the right of secession?[39] In this chapter, we show how libertarians litigated the social contract generally and the American social contract specifically. We examine the key thinkers and core texts of American libertarianism to explore how two rhetorical resources, natural rights philosophy and early American legal and cultural history, have enabled the libertarian case for ignoring the state. They pulled from global examples of statist oppression and Enlightenment-inspired language of first principles—"Absolute power corrupts absolutely"—but they also brought these analogies and commonplaces to bear domestically with endless citations of Thomas Jefferson and the Anti-Federalists, data-mining regarding the ratification and meaning of the Constitution, and reproaches of a thick roster of American autocrats like Alexander Hamilton, Abraham Lincoln, Justices John Marshall and Joseph Story, Daniel Webster—basically any influential "federal supremacist."[40] American libertarians used both arguments for majority rules as well as arguments for minority rights to justify secession, and they employed the language of America's founding to unsettle national foundations.

The Natural Right to Secede

Many of the terms some libertarians have used to distinguish themselves from other libertarians—the Austrian School, the Chicago School, classical liberalism, market fundamentalism, objectivism,

54   WE ARE NOT ONE PEOPLE

voluntaryism, contractarianism, anarcho-capitalism—overlap; nevertheless, each of these terms denoted meaningful differences in the nature of markets, the moral status of individuals, and how much, if any, government, each imagined as a necessary evil to protect a group of people from each other and themselves.

Secession, however, united libertarians. Classical liberals, like Friedrich Hayek for example, believed in a vital role for government in protecting the sanctity of markets and the rational choices of individuals.[41] Some libertarians, Charles Murray explained, "present a logic of individual liberty that is purer and more uncompromising" than he defended. He cleaved these dogmatic "Libertarians" from his and Hayek's camp, mere "libertarians" in a lower key.[42] More radical Libertarians, especially those of the anarcho-capitalist tradition or taught by the influential Austrian economist Ludwig von Mises (excluding Hayek), wanted to eliminate the idea of governmentally protected public goods altogether.[43] Whatever masqueraded as a public good—parks, roads, health care, sanitation services, even the police and military—would be privatized; "sell the schools" and "sell the streets."[44] Austrians and anarchists considered individual secession as a first principle, but that did not mean that secession faded into the background for classical liberals.

This is a crude spectrum of a complicated group of thinkers, but the ultimate goal of Libertarians and libertarians alike was liberty; when liberty was couched as a natural right of all human beings, the secession of groups or individuals from a centralized government was both a basic human impulse and a pragmatic protection. A philosophy of individual secession gushed from nearly every natural rights concept, like liberty, self-government, and nationalism, cited by many prominent American libertarians. As former Libertarian Party presidential candidate John Hospers put it, "For many libertarians, anarchists and believers in limited government alike, the principal question to be put to any view of the State is the right of secession.[45] "Secession," another wrote, was "surely the crux of federalism."[46]

Democracy is a variable concept. No democracy—"social, liberal, radical, republican, representative, authoritarian, direct, participatory, deliberative, plebiscite"—looks the same as any other.[47] But part of every democratic tradition is a duality, a balancing act between easily opposed traditions: a concern for and a fear of individual choices. Put differently, democracies weigh liberty and equality, individuality and community, minority rights and majoritarian rule, local and national priorities, and publicity and privacy. Convinced that balancing acts were cop-outs, libertarians have lobbed grenades at these tightrope walkers. They styled secessionists as the true democrats and adapted different interpretations of liberty to justify secession from republican, majoritarian, and democracies with minority rights protections.[48] Individuality and community were not coequal traditions, different values that brought out the best in the other; they were mortal enemies. Liberty was a natural right; community was a dangerous social fiction employed to trammel individual liberty.

Murray Rothbard, the Austrian School economist turned Chamber of Commerce advisor, thought that most libertarians believed in natural rights.[49] They believed that everything on earth had essential qualities, which humans could investigate through "sense perception and mental faculties." To interact successfully with the world around them, people must choose the proper means and ends to attain knowledge. They had to cultivate individual reasoning to learn for themselves. Curious reason was humanity's default mental setting; "to interfere and cripple this process," especially through violence, was unnatural.[50] Artificial restrictions on any person's ability to learn about or move in the world denied an essential need. Liberty was essential to a scientific approach to life: "Individuals had the absolute right to own their own bodies, to choose where their bodies went, to choose the work their bodies did, to choose how they used their bodies."[51] Violence against another was wrong because it violated another's right to self-control.[52] "Liberty," Isabel Paterson, who along with Rand and Rose Wilder Lane was one of libertarianism's three midcentury "mothers," agreed. Liberty "is a truly natural condition," she concluded. There was no life without "independent action" because creatures "subjected to absolute restraint" perish.[53]

Although theories of inalienable natural rights far predate him, Herbert Spencer, the nineteenth-century English academic, was among the most influential progenitors of the idea that naturally derived liberties were the bedrock of anti-government politics and anti-statist secession.[54] He wrote in *Social Statics* (1851) that freedom

56   WE ARE NOT ONE PEOPLE

meant exercising one's own choices to the fullest without limiting the "equal freedom" of others.[55] Spencer was developing Locke's concept of self-ownership from the *Second Treatise of Government* (1689). Locke held that "every man has a property in his own person."[56] He used this principle to build a case against tyranny. Like later libertarians, Spencer took this Enlightenment precept to equate majoritarian decision-making with majoritarian tyranny. Any majority compelling any minority automatically used despotism to do so, even if the issue in question was put to a vote. For Spencer, there was an inviolable sphere around each person; people were sovereign entities. As such, they should be free to opt into and out of personal, social, legal, or political communities as they wished.

When the real world stopped short of that Shangri-La, people should practice "voluntary outlawry." Do not pay taxes; do not acknowledge the authority of the law, the police, or the court system; do not show up for jury duty. Individuals should be, in short, free to secede. He wrote, "If every man has freedom to do all that he wills, provided he infringes not the equal freedom of any other man, then he is free to drop connection with the state—to relinquish its protection, and to refuse paying towards its support." The state should be ignored to preserve individual freedom, and all should have the right to ignore the state.[57]

The Spencerian "law of equal freedom"—live freely, and let others do the same—was replicated widely among later libertarians.[58] Self-ownership gave libertarians robust arguments not just against state control or violence but also against coercion, compulsion, or force of any kind beyond interpersonal persuasion. Nevertheless, even the least outwardly restrictive of laws, like jaywalking codes, were considered "aggression," invasions upon the "person or property of another." Libertarians claimed that such laws, even those passed by elected representatives or decided on directly by popular referendum, were assaults on free will enforced by "bayonet point," prison, or both.[59] When David Friedman, Milton's son whose politics were more radical than his well-connected father's, posited that "the central idea of libertarianism is that people should be permitted to run their own lives as they wish," he got to both the spirit and letter of this ethic of cutting loose of social hindrances on individual conduct. The only "enforceable claim" that anyone had against anyone else beyond freely chosen contracts was to be "left alone."[60] Adapting this logic, Friedman deduced, "A man who prevents me from taking heroin coerces me; a man who prevents me from shooting him does not."[61]

The assertion of a sphere of inviolability around each self-owning citizen and the definition of liberty as absolute freedom from restraint enabled libertarians to crowbar liberty from democracy. They exploited the tension inherent in the balance of liberty, equality, and the consent of the governed. Albert Jay Nock distinguished between "government" and "the State," with the former only restraining force and fraud and the latter a conquest of natural rights by state-based rights.[62] If a person believed their liberty to be in jeopardy or if a community concluded that it was, then separation, whether a limited act of withdrawal or a more complete secession, was merely an expression of the consent to be governed. But they leveled this critique against the legal acts of a popularly chosen legislature or a popularly chosen president, not George III; as such, natural-rights-possessing individuals had no more duty to obey the results of a popular vote than they did the whims of a despot.

For the most radical of libertarians, the difference between a tyrant and a president was a matter of degree anyway. As Nock insisted, all government was a "*coup d'état*."[63] This line of libertarian argument put natural rights squarely at odds with majority-rules democracy and encouraged those who did not like a law or support the result of an election to opt out. One law professor and activist called secession a "god given right" that no government, court, or voting majority could ever usurp. "I don't care," he clamored, "if every single judge or jurist in this country said 'well, this question is settled.' No, it's not."[64]

The right of individuals to reconsider their assent to be governed was unimpeachable. This right of reconsideration superseded any right of a democratic majority to govern, even a landslide majority. Rothbard explained, "The government does not in any accurate sense 'represent' the majority of the people, but even if it did, even if 90 percent of the people decided to murder or enslave the other 10 percent, this would *still* be murder and slavery. . . . There is nothing sacrosanct about the majority; the lynch mob, too, is the majority in its own domain."[65] Americans, after all, would not exist if the Revolution had been put to a vote in 1776. What mattered was the "principle of justice,"

58   WE ARE NOT ONE PEOPLE

not any collection of opinions.[66] What was right was decided individually, not socially. Paterson put it more succinctly: "Liberty and democracy," she announced, were "incompatible."[67]

In *Nation, State, and Economy* (1919) and *Liberalism* (1927), Mises looked at Europe tearing itself apart and wondered if the solution was to reassert the sanctity of the individual against dangerous fictions of nations. Mises rethought nationalism from a strident individualist position. "The essence of nationality" emerged in the aggregate, from individuals banding together.[68] Countering nationalist theorists of the nineteenth century like Herder and Fichte, Mises argued that nations were not based on the fundamental characteristics of distinct races or ethnicities.[69] Nor were nations merely the byproducts of shared languages. Nations were individually self-determined expressions of the desire to be free from subjugation; nationality was a tool individuals used in concert with others to oppose the "rule" of "tyrants."[70] Mises employed far-reaching, history-spanning examples in support of his empirical theory of nationalism. The French became "a nation" when they broke "the despotism of the Bourbons," and "Germans and Italians became self-conscious nations because foreign princes, joined in the Holy Alliance, hindered them from the establishing a free state."[71]

Mises's vision was a world bursting at the seams with new self-determining states, each competing to attract the freely floating individuals who moved between them as more advantageous circumstances arose elsewhere. In his utopia, the world was a great grocery store of nation-states, and citizens constantly shopped for better deals in new national homes. The market for new nations was theoretically unlimited; they came in all shapes and sizes. There were no size criteria to be eligible for secession. A "single village," or "district," or "a series of adjacent districts"—Mises even supported the self-determination of individuals if feasible—could exit and "form an independent state" or "attach themselves to some other state."[72]

Whereas some libertarians built a natural-rights argument for secession, Rothbard also developed a majoritarian argument. If a majority of, to use an example of his, the residents of Deep Falls, Wyoming, decided to secede from their state or nation, they should be able to.[73] Those Deep Falls residents who found the notion of a Deep Falls nation-state foolish would be free to remain Americans, of course; the

SECESSION ALL THE WAY DOWN   59

Deep Falls majority would have no claim to take unwilling nationalists with them. Nevertheless, depending on the boundaries of a given community or the voting rules in a given plebiscite, if a Deep Falls majority wanted out, then they would no longer be part of the American demos or polity.[74]

Rothbard cited the "tuath," the "basic political unit of ancient Ireland," which consisted of the property owners and workers of a given area, as a precedent for communities of unrestricted secession.[75] If nationality was determined of the people, by the people, and for the people again and again, then close-quarters, multiethnic conflicts like that in the former Yugoslavia would be mitigated by "decomposing the swollen central nation-state" into independent, less combustible nations.[76] Rothbard wanted to transform countries into "nations of consent" in which every "group" or "nationalist" was allowed "to secede" and "join any other" welcoming country. The global spread of nations of consent would, he predicted, dissolve the "brutal and repressive state" and transform the globe into a "harmonious and increasingly prosperous social order."[77]

Beyond Rothbard, Mises's other numerous and influential acolytes have reiterated and expounded upon his secessionist theories of majoritarian self-determination for decades. Several American institutions founded by and dedicated to thinkers in this circle of libertarians, especially those who were of the Austrian School or inspired by it, have become geysers of secessionist literature since World War II. Institutions like the Foundation of Economic Education (FEE), the Cato Institute, and the Mises Institute at Auburn University published prolifically about American secession, international secessionist movements, and political theories of secession. Lines like "three cheers for secession" (from a Cato writer) were typical toasts.[78] Beyond citations and invocations, libertarian redoubts like the Liberty Fund or the Mises Institute made many canonical and semi-canonical libertarian works freely available, sponsored learning seminars, and hosted semi-regular conferences devoted to the topic.

Mises and a few thinkers of his or earlier eras, like Spencer or even Mill, loomed large as modern writers cited them to argue that "secession" and "free trade" would usher in international "peace."[79] The more nations that competed for citizens by offering low taxes or

60 WE ARE NOT ONE PEOPLE

"preferable conditions," a FEE writer speculated, the more "everyone's living conditions improve" through competition. "Freedom for all" was possible with "secessionist movements around the world."[80] According to these writers, Mises and others were sages of secessionism, and secessionists were the peacemakers.[81] Whatever conflicts that occurred between peoples resulted from the "political denial of the right of self-determination," an unnatural imposition on the natural order of liberty.[82]

Jefferson and Individual Sovereignty

As a lot, libertarian citation patterns span centuries, even millennia, stretching to the Magna Carta, the Jewish exodus, the Theban revolt, Melos, and the Athenian League.[83] Paterson wrote about libertarian principles in physics; Mises wrote about Poles, Finns, Latvians, and Germans in Schleswig-Holstein, Slavs under Hapsburg rule, and other peoples all the way back to Rome. Many American libertarians, including Nock, Rothbard, and scores of others, wrote obsessively about America.[84] They have built a transhistorical case for individual liberty by leaning on the most individualist thinkers of the European Enlightenment, like Locke, David Hume, and others.[85] Nevertheless, they dwell on American politics between the Revolutionary and Civil Wars. They grieve the triumph of a "Unionist," "nationalist" theory, what one writer called a "noble lie," of the American founding.[86] They lament Americans' "lost and stolen heritage of states' rights."[87]

Modern libertarians continue the perpetually unsettled debates between Hamilton and Jefferson specifically and the Federalists and Anti-Federalists generally.[88] The resources to make a case for limited, local, or no government were readily evident in Jefferson, the Anti-Federalists, Thomas Paine, and virtually any writer of the era who was suspicious of concentrated authority. They mined major events of early American history as well as the minutia and marginalia of the period to prove that the nation's individualist, secessionist essence was lost, perhaps at Appomattox, when, declared Lew Rockwell, founder of the Mises Institute, "the modern American state emerged out of the violent suppression of the attempted secession of eleven states."[89] American

SECESSION ALL THE WAY DOWN   61

libertarians have engaged in a massive historical excavation of "the real union of sovereign states founded by our forefathers."[90]

They have collectively uncovered "the compact *fact* of the Constitution," John Marshall and Joseph Story's judicial usurpation, secessionist plots in the North (like the time Oliver Ellsworth and Rufus King pressed for secession in 1794, or the Essex Junto, or the secessionist Hartford Convention in 1814), William Lloyd Garrison's "No Union with Slaveholders," Wisconsin's defiance of fugitive slave laws, the question of whether Lincoln supported the right of secession before conveniently changing his mind during his presidency and just parroted Daniel Webster, New York City's brief flirtation with city-state status in 1861, and much else in the antebellum period. They recited these episodes not just for argumentative inspiration but also to reinterpret the nation's founding, its political design, and its social history as favoring the individual over the state, society, or any so-called public good.[91] "Whether they called themselves anti-Federalists, Tertium Quids, or simply states' rights men," the historian Eric Walther wrote, many early Americans "feared that through one usurpation of power after another, naive or even sinister forces encouraged the growth of federal power."[92]

Much of this historical recitation and reinterpretation was premised on rehabilitating and defending secession as both a natural right and a specifically American political right. Donald Livingston, founder of the Abbeville Institute, argued, "A right of secession was not written into the U.S. Constitution, but the *authority* of the Constitution consists solely in acts of ratification by sovereign states. In writing into their ordinances of ratification the right to withdraw those powers delegated to the central government, Virginia, New York, and Rhode Island may be said to have framed a right of secession in the constitutional compact."[93] When libertarians have, either strategically or expediently, stopped short of a forthright defense of secession, they reread early America, like Tenth Amendment jurisprudence or the Articles of Confederation, to support adjacent ideas on the separatist spectrum: nullification, interposition, and subsidiarity.

Nullification, the idea that communities or states should be able to invalidate federal law at the local level, has been a core feature of American libertarian thought even if John C. Calhoun, nullification's

62 WE ARE NOT ONE PEOPLE

chief exponent, has not regularly been recognized as a libertarian saint. Calhoun, a reformed nationalist, began developing the theory of nullification—he initially called it "interposition"—during the crisis over the "tariff of Abominations" in the late 1820s and early 1830s. John Niven, a Calhoun biographer, explained that nullification was intended as a state's shield against specific federal incursion.

But Calhoun did not stop there; he thought states should also have an enhanced right to secede from a government that repeatedly offends.[94] Following Calhoun's leadership in public documents like the "Exposition and Protest" and the Fort Hill address, South Carolina sponsored a nullification convention in 1832 over the tariff and began recruiting a state militia of twenty thousand soldiers. Andrew Jackson replied forcefully; the states, he corrected, were part of, and subservient to, the nation. But he was not content to upbraid his former vice president; he also threatened force and promised a military occupation of South Carolina.

Henry Clay brokered a compromise wherein Congress lowered the tariff and South Carolina backed off.[95] From a certain vantage point, Calhoun's theorizing and activism look like a quintessential libertarian celebration of localism and smaller government against nationalism and larger government. Calhoun's idea of nullification, however, was bound up in a larger idea that has repulsed libertarians: the concurrent majority. Rather than tallying votes to determining a course of action, every powerful "interest" in a given society should be granted a veto power. If, he reasoned, a numerical majority knew they faced a state's, region's, or interest's veto—Calhoun was cagey about what constituted an interest—they would be forced to the bargaining table to hammer out a solution that worked for everyone. The concurrent majority ran riot over individual preferences as well as majoritarian rule.[96] Calhoun thought interests made individuals, not the other way around.[97] Unlike libertarians, Calhoun had no goal to preserve the liberties of the great mass of individuals, only the influence of a particular class of men in his section. An estimated seventy to eighty enslaved people toiled in bondage on Calhoun's Fort Hill Plantation in South Carolina as Calhoun venerated slavery as a "positive good."[98]

Calhoun has received scant praise in the libertarian literature, but the concepts he espoused, minus the idea of the concurrent majority, have not. Libertarians defended nullification differently, not as the protection of "interests" whose authority is absolute or even as the necessary right of a state but as essential to the protection of local freedom. Subsidiarity, the broader principle undergirding nullification, meant that local and individual decisions held greater weight than national ones; put differently, government that governed closest governed best. Thus, resistance to federal oversight might not require full, unequivocal secession; subsidiarity guaranteed local communities' right to revoke or withhold their consent to be governed without any formal severance of national ties.[99] Nock called this bottom-up structure of authority "the principle of lodging final authority in the smallest unit rather than the largest."[100]

Libertarians were far from univocal on early American history, especially on whether the Constitution recognized or violated subsidiarity.[101] Some, like Nock, saw the Constitutional Convention as an "unscrupulous and dishonourable" coup that tossed "the Articles of Confederation into the waste-basket."[102] Others claimed the Constitution as an expression of libertarian governing principles, including the right of secession.[103] Federal powers expressed in the Constitution were given, one writer noted, "by the states, which implies that the states were prior and superior to the federal government."[104]

Although the Tenth Amendment was the clearest example of subsidiarity in the Constitution, the Second Amendment, another said, was the most important legal principle to aid a state's withdrawal from the American polity; mass gun ownership was the "enforcement mechanism" of secession.[105] Ultimately, half-secessions like nullification or broad-based subsidiarity were only partial indicators of a free society. "Our ultimate defense against the federal government," Joseph Sobran claimed, "is the right of secession."[106]

Aside from their intramural disputes about the Constitution, libertarians shared a broad consensus on three important claims about early America. First, Americans, by nature, have always been anti-government and, thereby, pro-secession. Distrusting government was in "America's DNA," David Boaz argued.[107] Lincoln's phrasing "of the people, by the people, for the people" in the Gettysburg Address "was probably the most effective single stroke of propaganda ever made in behalf of Republican State prestige."[108] Second, individual states were, at the very

64 WE ARE NOT ONE PEOPLE

least, free and independent nations before 1789 if not after it as well; revolutionary America was thirteen nations, not one. Third, as libertarians describe him, the patron saint of American secession was Thomas Jefferson, and the Declaration of Independence was his holy writ.[109]

This last move is vital because it has allowed libertarians to assign the nation an original essence and bypass any or all knotted political and legal debates. America was enacted in secession from England and devised by the pen of a secessionist. With such parentage, how could future Americans be denied this foundational act? For libertarians, "the Declaration of Independence is the most famous act of secession in our history." Jefferson wrote a "legal brief in international law justifying the secession of thirteen self-proclaimed states from the British Empire."[110] By modern libertarian eyes, the cause of this original American "act of secession" was big government.[111] King George III imposed "economic controls" on colonists that "limited their freedom." The Crown trapped otherwise enterprising colonists in "a spider's web of regulations and restrictions" that controlled the production and limited the flow of goods.[112] This critique of British control of the colonies differed little from libertarian takedowns of the New Deal or the Great Society. George III made the same mistakes that all arrogant central planners do.

But libertarians also found some deeper truth in the Lockean notion of self-ownership. The Declaration, one writer argued, insisted "that each man should be considered as owning himself, and not be viewed as the property of the state to be manipulated by either king or Parliament."[113] "Self-ownership," another asserted, "is unalienable, to borrow a word from the Declaration of Independence—a person cannot sell himself, any more than he can sell his rights to life, liberty, and the pursuit of happiness."[114]

"Jefferson and Lincoln," Garry Wills holds, "are the twinned saints of our politics."[115] Modern libertarians venerated a "Jeffersonian" view of American law and history with localized sovereignty, as opposed to a "Lincolnian" view where the sovereignty of the "national will" was expressed through national government. But the Declaration of Independence was not their only canonical text written by Jefferson.

The larger body of Jefferson's work has been read as a defense of all just political society as necessitating the "consent of equals" minus any element of "coercion." Specifically, his Kentucky Resolutions of 1798 and 1799 (as well as James Madison's nearly simultaneous Virginia Resolution) should, Donald Livingston urged, be commemorated "in a little book" about nullification.[116] Jefferson's Kentucky Resolutions reaffirmed the state's commitment to the "union," but it called that union a "compact" between separate states.[117] These "sovereign and independent" states were empowered as judges of Congress's legal authority. Nullification remedied Congress's violations of the Constitution.

Liberty and Race

To some, despite the machinations of the Hamiltons, Marshalls, Websters, and Federalist worshipers of national authority, these "principles of '98" made pre–Civil War America the land of the free.[118] Between the Revolution and 1861, one influential libertarian asserted, "Americans arguably enjoyed more individual and political liberty than any people in the world, before or since" excepting, of course, Indigenous Peoples and Black Americans, who were "not considered part of the polity."[119] Nullification was "the Jeffersonian brake" that preserved this Eden of freedom.[120] Even Jefferson had to face down "extreme states' rights" members of his own party who wanted to pull the brake. John Randolph, John Taylor, and Nathaniel Macon (the Tertium Quids) were powerful members of Congress who professed a loyalty to the vision of the nation in the Kentucky and Virginia Resolutions. They used these documents to build an "intricate philosophy of state sovereignty" including "the right of secession."[121] But they used the Jeffersonian brake to preserve privilege at the expense of freedom. When northern legislators attempted to end the intercoastal trade of enslaved people in addition to the importation of enslaved people in 1807, they "threatened disunion."[122]

It is easy to read the defenses of local freedom or individual rights by slave owners like Jefferson and the Quids as hollow; their pronouncements of universal equality were not universally applied. After all, Jefferson did not practice equality, and he certainly alienated many people from their lives, their liberty, and their happiness. Shortly before drafting the Declaration, Jefferson drafted a shorter document

66   WE ARE NOT ONE PEOPLE

that was quite the opposite: a reward offer for a fugitive enslaved person whom he described as "artful and knavish."[123]

Along the same lines, it is especially easy to read subsequent warnings against government intrusion, many also penned by white southerners and used to spread the Lost Cause myth of knightly secessionists in the nineteenth century and justify segregation in the twentieth century, in this Jeffersonian tradition as hollow as well.[124] These southern arguments for liberty of some sort (individualism, local control, or states' rights) have been racist camouflage. Samuel Johnson, the English author who opposed the American Revolution, saw through the smokescreen in 1775: "How is it that we hear the loudest yelps for liberty among the drivers of Negroes?"[125]

James J. Kilpatrick, the prominent mid-twentieth-century columnist and author of *The Sovereign States* (1957), is a telling case.[126] Kilpatrick's writings in the 1950s leaned heavily on Jefferson and Jefferson's language. "If our strength be in union," Kilpatrick intoned, recalling Jefferson's fondness for separatism, "it lies first in apartness."[127] He routinely quoted or reprinted the works of states' rights eminences like Calhoun or Randolph, but Jefferson, in particular, provided this case for southern interposition of federal civil rights laws an "authenticity and a cover of respectability."[128] Kilpatrick cut words like "nation" and "national" from his public work and, lest his proper nouns be nationalized, he even stopped including the article "the" before "United States." He stoked southern "massive resistance" to desegregation by popularizing interposition and nullification and notions of America as an interstate compact where states could do as they pleased. Pro-segregation advocates and state legislators followed Kilpatrick's lead and railed against civil rights in these founding formulations alongside racial diatribes.[129]

Kilpatrick believed in the right of secession, but he concentrated on justifying more limited acts of withdrawal for pragmatic reasons. He told another conservative writer, "Life is short, honest to God it is, and life is too short to waste it in vain and abortive causes that offer no conceivable hope of advantage anywhere. I don't mind taking up lost causes—it is the fate of every Southerner—but I want to be a little selective in the lost causes I take up."[130] A quick look just beneath the surface of Kilpatrick's writing revealed his lost cause to be less a fiery anti-imperialism and more rock-ribbed racism. He admitted to libertarian luminary Frank Chodorov that southern resistance was motivated by fears of a "mixed society." He spent some twenty pages in the original draft of *The Sovereign States* on his theories of white racial superiority, but the editorial staff at Regnery, the premier publisher of conservatives in post–World War II America, convinced Kilpatrick to cut most, though not all, of the speculation about a biological hierarchy of racial capability.[131] Nullification was equivocation; it was far easier to gain a big audience by praising an American secular saint like Jefferson than to howl about a multiracial science classroom.

In the end, however, the ploys of Kilpatrick and many others—Jefferson Davis's inaugural address and his memoirs were just such ruses[132]—exhibited the same stealth maneuver that Jefferson had.[133] The policies enabled by mostly race-neutral rhetoric preserved an explicitly race-conscious hierarchy from which each, especially in the case of slave owners like Jefferson, Calhoun, and Davis, personally benefited. In these stealth strategies, keywords like "liberty" and "local control" meant the freedom and dominance of white businesses, white communities, and white-controlled towns and states.

The on-and-off coalition with southern conservatives within and beyond the Republican Party has made libertarians susceptible to charges of racism. Furthermore, elements of limited-government libertarianism have become indistinguishable from mainstream conservatism.[134] Justifying secession is incontrovertibly libertarian, but defending the secession of slavers was easily contested as a maneuver that yielded less liberty on balance. Nevertheless, not every individualist dressed racism up in rights talk; not every American anti-government treatise was, in effect, an argument for southern nationalism or Jim Crow. Anti-*Brown* or anti-busing forces concealed fears of race-mixing with arguments against government control, but not all arguments against government control camouflaged bigotry. Pro-slavery and anti-civil-rights forces have sullied without entirely subsuming the libertarian defense of secession.

Some self-reflective libertarians have been acutely aware of the racially disparate impact their treasured words have had. As Rockwell claimed, "Every libertarian worthy of the name opposes any government support for slavery, centralization, inflation, conscription,

68   WE ARE NOT ONE PEOPLE

taxation, or the suppression of speech and press."[135] Libertarian advocates aimed to remove the Civil War "stigma that secession has," the "zombie" linkage between slavery and secession.[136] As one Foundation for Economic Education writer hoped, "The best we can do today is understand what really happened and work to rehabilitate the bedrock American principles of limited, decentralized government and the natural right of secession, good ideas given a bad name by Lincoln and the Confederates alike."[137]

Their quest to decouple secession from southern nationalism and libertarianism from racism has been reinforced considerably by a rich, if somewhat obscure, tradition of American abolitionist, anarchist, and socially progressive individualists spanning the nineteenth century who all supported secession. The term "libertarian" had not caught on yet, and thinkers like Josiah Warren, Lysander Spooner, Benjamin Tucker, and a few others also called themselves socialists and anarchists. Some of their collective work reads like modern libertarianism, however.[138] Twentieth-century libertarians, especially in Rothbard's, Rand's, and Hayek's intellectual circles, regularly invoked these writers.[139] These nineteenth-century thinkers have been essential resources as modern libertarians built a consistent, historically thorough case for American individualism and secession dissociated from slavery or the interests of slaveholders. This tradition allowed, for example, Rothbard to quilt together an assortment of American libertarian forebearers: "Libertarians are the only genuine current heirs of Jefferson, Paine, Jackson, and the abolitionists."[140]

Antebellum sons of Massachusetts were particularly well represented in modern libertarian literature. The most famous of these, Henry David Thoreau, also penned one of the most widely cited essays of the era.[141] "Civil Disobedience" (1849) did not encourage readers to become "libertarians" or "anarchists" specifically, but it made a forceful case for outlawry, especially insofar as government aided the enslavement of human beings. Some "injustice," Thoreau argued, is "part of the necessary friction of the machine of government." But some laws, like fugitive slave laws, which enlisted citizens to commit injustices against others, were made to be broken. "Let your life," Thoreau counseled, "be a counter-friction to stop the machine."[142]

Although Thoreau asked individuals to withdraw from state enforcement of slavery, he also praised those who lived "aloof" from the

SECESSION ALL THE WAY DOWN 69

state, not necessarily by an idyllic pond, and those who "fulfilled all the duties of neighbors" without "meddling" with or being "embraced by" government.[143] This approach, abolitionist on one hand but broadly separatist on the other, characterized the work of three other Massachusetts scions, all rough contemporaries of Thoreau's.

Much about Josiah Warren's early years are unknown, but he was born in Boston in 1798, and the historical record suggests that he was well educated; he turned up in Cincinnati with a young family after his twentieth birthday. He taught music and led an orchestra, and he even patented a lard-fueled lamp.[144] Warren met his calling, however, after he heard a lecture by Robert Owen, the socialist-communalist. Enamored with Owen, Warren became, in turn, fascinated by withdrawing from the rules and strictures of the mass public and into self-selected, self-governing communities.[145] Warren moved his family to New Harmony, where they lived from 1825 to 1827. Owen's philosophical system was dedicated to achieving human equality, but over time Warren broke with Owen over philosophical differences about individualism and personal freedom.[146] He tried to correct this failed New Harmony stint by founding several communes of his own: a twenty-five-person settlement in Tuscarawas County, Ohio, in 1835, another called Utopia on the Ohio River eleven years later, and a more durable one on Long Island dubbed Modern Times.[147] True believers as well as a host of nineteenth-century eccentrics, ranging from nudists to legume dieters, made a home there. One of Modern Times' most prominent members, Stephen Pearl Andrews, inventor of his own language and his own science (called Universology), became an influential popularizer and interpreter of Warren's.[148]

Warren's three communal experiments were libertarian communities of voluntary, cooperative associations, not capitalist laboratories. "Personal sovereignty," Warren wrote in *True Civilization* (1869), should be the foremost social and political organizing principle.[149] Beyond his endeavors in off-the-grid communities, Warren's major contribution to anarcho-libertarianism was his gloss on Locke: "self-sovereignty."[150] Locke thought that each person held inviolable property in themselves, but Warren did him one better. A self-owning person could still join with other self-owning persons to form a collective nation. Locke allowed for greater civic authority beyond the individual to which the individual might submit, a polis in which an

70   WE ARE NOT ONE PEOPLE

individual might participate. Warren elevated individuals on par with nations; for him, there was no greater authority except God.[151] John Stuart Mill was influenced by Warren's concept of self-sovereignty as he wrote *Essays on Liberty*.[152]

Warren's belief in the sovereignty of individuals was not racially restricted; he was a fervent abolitionist. But Warren, like William Lloyd Garrison, did not think of the sectional crisis as saints in the North and slavers in the South; he believed that the federal government was fundamentally complicit in slavery. When South Carolina threatened to nullify federal tariffs during Jackson's presidency, Warren sided with the nullifiers. Rather than adopt coercive or violent measures, Warren preferred a policy of respecting "the liberty of others to differ from us."[153] If southerners could not "exercise their inalienable liberty" without harming the interests of other sections, then the rational answer was "disconnection."[154]

Lysander Spooner did not create upstart communities, but he was, like Warren, both a practitioner and a theorist of separating from government and civil society. He was profoundly influenced by Warren's idea of individual sovereignty. Born on his family's Athol, Massachusetts, farm in 1808, he apprenticed under two prominent lawyers before beginning a legal practice. But Spooner was more of a legal activist by nature, carrying forth the Enlightenment tradition of systematically examining any and all institutions or practices that did not meet a basic test of rational justification.[155] Spooner's anarchism, as well as his abolitionism, stemmed from the same premise as did Warren's: individual sovereignty. Spooner practically invented a form of individual secession called jury nullification in *Trial by Jury* (1852). Jurists, he said, were not exercising their judgment as free citizens unless they could assess not just the facts of a case but whether the law in question was worth upholding as well. If a juror thought that a defendant was indeed guilty of trespassing but did not agree that the trespassing statute was just, then the juror should let the defendant walk.[156] "Constitutions," Spooner wrote, were "utterly worthless" in restraining government without the active resistance of people.[157]

Spooner's enduring contribution to libertarian theories of secession came from his abolitionist activism. He was uncompromising; he may have even been involved in a plot to kidnap the governor of

SECESSION ALL THE WAY DOWN   71

Virginia after John Brown was captured. Spooner held that slavery had never been legal in America; it had been forced by some, tolerated by many, but was never legal.[158] In a series of essays in the 1860s collectively called *No Treason*, Spooner reasoned that a government of free people could never be coercive. Allegiance was always based on voluntary loyalty, not force. It was contradictory to say that opting out of a voluntary relationship was either disloyal or treasonous. This preference for explicit consent to be governed put far more than present legal practices up for scrutiny. Allegiance must be freely given by individuals who were party to a contract whose terms they were fully aware of. How, then, could citizens of the 1860s be bound to a federal contract written and voted on seventy years prior? The Constitution, therefore, applied only to those who had written and ratified it, and they were long dead. The Framers possessed no mystical power to command future generations.[159]

These abolitionist premises led Spooner, like Warren, to side with southerners on the question of secession; anyone subjected to government they did not want was a political slave.[160] The right to withdraw, Spooner held, was true regardless of whether Lincoln (or Webster or Story) or Jefferson was right about the nature of the American federation. If "We, the People" enacted the Constitution, the people, obviously, should have a say in their Constitution.[161] If, however, the states adopted the Constitution, then "it necessarily follows that they had the right to secede at pleasure."[162]

Spooner's work offered libertarians an argument against Lincoln, an argument against slavery, an individualist account of the American Revolution, and broadsides against government robbery; his work has remained consistently influential among them.[163] "Every libertarian," Rockwell declared, "acknowledges the greatness and importance" of this "avowed secessionist."[164] The same has been true of Benjamin Tucker, another nineteenth-century denizen of Massachusetts.[165] Born in 1854, Tucker was a child when Modern Times, Warren's last communal venture, folded, but he was an acolyte of Warren's nevertheless; he saw the light of individual sovereignty after reading *True Civilization*.[166] He had been exposed to Warren, Spooner, and other prominent libertarian-anarchists like William B. Greene at an 1872 Free Labor convention. Greene, who had lived at Modern Times, later

72   WE ARE NOT ONE PEOPLE

introduced Tucker to the work of Pierre-Joseph Proudhon, the French anarchist philosopher, and Tucker translated Proudhon's corpus in its entirety into English for publication in *Radical Review*, a journal he created. Tucker founded a far more influential journal, *Liberty*, in 1881. The libertarian anarchism of *Liberty* was strident, infectious, and all-consuming.[167] It was for Progressive-era individualists what *National Review* was for post–World War II conservatives.[168]

Tucker's main enemies were monopolies on land and credit and economic institutions that kept goods and capital from circulating freely. He also thought monopolies were propped up by the state. Tucker fumed about all concentrated and arbitrary power that stifled individual choice, including majoritarian democracy. Americans might elect their representatives, but those representatives manipulated Americans' choices.[169] True freedom, real democracy, and just government meant the informed consent of every individual. America failed that repeatedly. Women, he wrote in 1882, had always been "denied representation," as had enslaved people, so "the number permitted to express consent or dissent was in the aggregate cut down to less than one-tenth of the people." The "glittering generalities" about equality from Jefferson had been rendered farcical by such race- and gender-based discrimination.[170] "The Anarchists," he announced in 1888, were "unterrified Jeffersonian Democrats" who believed "that 'the best government is that which governs least,' and that that which governs least is no government at all."[171]

Tucker's individualism was distinguished by his penchant for indirect activism. Contrary to the typical image of the anarchist revolutionary, Tucker thought that engaging Leviathan in conventional warfare or even clandestine violence was foolish at best, suicidal at worst.[172] Instead of combating tax collectors or making a show of refusing to pay taxes, citizens should engage in quieter acts to withhold cooperation and neglecting payments. If great numbers of people followed this quiet separatism, he reasoned, "it would cost more to collect their taxes, or to try to collect hem, than the other four-fifths would consent to pay into the treasury." This kind of passive resistance was the only feasible resistance against the state's massive power to imprison or kill. Passive resistance, as practiced by an "inoffensive people who do not even gather in the streets," was a third way beyond the

SECESSION ALL THE WAY DOWN   73

"ballot" or the "bayonet."[173] Liberty could be preserved through tacit refusals that might save the resister from harm or death.

Conclusion

A leitmotif in libertarian debates about resisting any authority impeding an individual or local decision has been a tactical dispute between overt secession and covert separation, between direct state or local nullification and implicit interposition by individuals. Explicit threats of nullification and secession have certainly not been driven underground because the libertarian cry for these maneuvers as legal instruments never really stopped, at least since World War II. Citing California's resistance to federal marijuana laws, one well-placed libertarian insisted in 2016 that "nullification can work today" on issues like "abortion, school prayer, education, law enforcement, and a hundred other reserved powers the central government has usurped from the states."[174]

Over time, however, these direct threats to national sovereignty have acquired sly cousins. The number of mechanisms libertarians have employed and the avenues they have pursued to withdraw from, resist, or simply ignore federal law or public obligations have multiplied as overt attempts at secession and nullification have been denied. There were lots of ways to secede, the *Washington Post* reported from a libertarian conference on secession in 2015, including home schooling, avoiding mainstream colleges, ignoring mainstream media outlets, buying gold, and hoarding cash, guns, and fuel.[175] Secession was not a singular, collective act, one conference speaker suggested; secession happened through the everyday ways in which citizens withdrew "consent" and walked "away from DC." Individual acts of secession could be conventional regularities, like death and not paying taxes.[176]

Two centuries of libertarian activists would applaud how libertarian legal activists advanced separatist cases without having to resort to violence, risk jail time, finance lengthy legal battles over sovereignty and jurisdiction, pay enormous fines, or upset day-to-day life. Organizations like the Tenth Amendment Center, for instance, nullified laws "in effect" through strategic legal actions designed to end

74   WE ARE NOT ONE PEOPLE

state and local cooperation with the federal government. They have normalized state separatism. Virtually every federal law, program, or agency ranging from gun laws to health care to the FDA, DEA, and even NSA surveillance, one attorney for the Tenth Amendment Center argued, required either state cooperation or state resources. Both of these can be refused. States can say no; they can refuse to expend any resources whatsoever on federal priorities they do not support. If national laws cannot be enforced, it does not matter if they were formally nullified; if individuals and communities are living beyond enforceable obligations to other individuals or communities, it does not matter if they formally seceded.[177]

State separatism may have become typical, but there is nothing commonplace about libertarian Silicon Valley billionaires' plans to escape doomsday by "launching electric cars into space," colonize Mars, or otherwise design an ark for the libertarian elite.[178] Back on earth, there is nothing normal about the baroque hideaways the rich have created for themselves in destinations like Kohanaiki, Hawaii, or Jackson Hole, Wyoming, posh locales where they can relax in VIP opulence or escape mass public life during disease outbreaks.[179] There is even nothing regular about the scale of "economic secession" of American money being "sheltered" from taxation in "havens."[180] In so many ways— in luxe travel, in neighborhood choice, in schooling, in private club membership, in self-care privileges, in food prerogatives, in health care options, in tax avoidance, in legal influence, in access to power—the rich, as Robert Reich concluded, have orchestrated a massive "secession from the rest of the population" and slipped "the bonds of national allegiance."[181] After all, as Lysander Spooner argued in the 1860s, is it unreasonable to hide property from thieves?

Looked at another way, although these kinds of escapes may be the dominion of the uber-rich, although they may occur in thin, rarefied Vail air, they are also routine for the rich. Mobility in America is just "evolutionary individualism."[182] That is, in its American context, success has not just been about wealth but the acquisition of the privileges of secession. The narrative of success in America has always included exit, of getting away with it, of moving out, on, up, and apart from everyone else.

3

"A Slave Republic"

Secession and Southern Slavery

In the last days of 1865's spring, Edmund Ruffin, a long-haired, long-in-the-tooth Virginia planter, obsessed over ancient Jews. Hiding at his son's modest farmhouse, the only one of the Ruffin family properties to escape Union pillaging, he pored over thick historical records of ancient Judea. Ruffin was searching, not studying; he scoured for a holy precedent, divine permission, some religious justification. At seventy-one, he knew his best days had passed.

Ruffin was a failed planter until his middle years, when he amassed significant wealth cultivate marl fertilizer. This pastoral existence was merely a prelude to a political one, a barnstorming public career devoted to what he called "the one great idea of my life": southern secession.[1] Bankrolled by his new fertilizer fortune, Ruffin became a fire-eating *philosophe*. As a prime mover in the secessionist movement, he orated indefatigably about the wisdom of political separation throughout the South during the tumultuous 1850s.[2] "The interest I feel for political affairs, & the Southern Confederation," he journaled on Valentine's Day, 1861, "absorbs every other."[3]

Ruffin was a radical's radical, among the hungriest of the fire-eaters. He was schooled in the Virginia states' rights tradition of John Randolph, John Taylor, and the Tertium Quids. But Ruffin came to outright southern nationalism later than some of his fellow fire-eaters, like Robert Barnwell Rhett, the so-called father of secession, who had been preaching southern independence since the 1820s.[4] Late or not, Ruffin adopted an "extreme and unyielding" pose even when measured against like-minded, slave-owning, gentry Jacobins of the age such as Rhett, Louis Wigfall, William Lowndes Yancey, and a few others.[5] Ruffin had been so enraged by John Brown's violent abolitionism that he journeyed to Harpers Ferry to watch the raider hang.[6]

We Are Not One People. Michael J. Lee and R. Jarrod Atchison, Oxford University Press. © Oxford University Press 2022. DOI: 10.1093/oso/9780190876500.003.0004

76   WE ARE NOT ONE PEOPLE

As a firebrand, Ruffin had been a minor newsmaker before the Civil War, but he did a real star turn during the first year of the conflict, its first moments in particular. He personally witnessed South Carolina's birth as a "free & independent community" at its December 1860 secession convention. "Every man waved or threw up his hat, & every lady waved her handkerchief," Ruffin exalted.[7] Shortly thereafter, he addressed the Florida secession convention, attended North Carolina's convention, and howled at his native Virginia's delay to secede before Abraham Lincoln was inaugurated on March 3, 1861: "I, at least, will become a citizen of the seceded Confederate States, & will not again reside in my native state, nor enter it except to make visits to my children, until Va shall also secede, & become a member of the Southern Confederacy."[8] Ruffin made sure to get to his beloved Charleston by the time Lincoln delivered his first inaugural address. The new president's speech, per Ruffin's interpretation, was a Unionist call to arms, a final signal "that there must be war."[9]

If war was coming, then Ruffin wanted to fight. After stationing himself with southern paramilitaries, many of whom were teenagers, in General P. T. Beauregard's Palmetto Guard at Fort Johnson outside Charleston, the old upstart, sporting a homemade uniform and blue cockaded hat, was given the honor of firing the first shot at Fort Sumter on April 12, 1861.[10] Ruffin was sixty-seven.[11] He certainly did not cause the Civil War, but he did commence it. Ruffin would spend the next few months as a celebrity combatant for a cause that was not yet lost.

His was not a long tour of duty, but it was not a one-shot commission either. Ruffin camped, ate, and dug trenches with his Confederate comrades at Bull Run and then marched and retreated in the battle.[12] The aging orator's health was failing, however, and he could not keep up with the demands of war. He left to tend to his Virginia plantations, but civilian life between Richmond and Petersburg during the Civil War was also a violent maelstrom. Thousands of fallen soldiers lay unburied where they fell at places like Manassas and Mechanicsville; Ruffin saw and smelled these ad hoc graveyards.[13] The war, moreover, was total. At the direction of generals like William Tecumseh Sherman and Philip Sheridan, farm fields, like battlefields, were scenes of devastation. Ruffin imagined that plundering southern property gave Yankees a "malignant gratification."[14]

"A SLAVE REPUBLIC" 77

Ruffin's estate was ruined by the war. George McClellan's troops tore his plantations apart; fences and furniture became firewood, food stores were exhausted, fields were trampled, and Ruffin's libraries were looted. Two hundred people he enslaved, people Ruffin believed held no desire for freedom and no attachment to their families, escaped. By the war's end, Ruffin had no income whatsoever and lived with his surviving family's support.[15] But the war had taken a devastating toll on them as well. Ruffin lost a grandson at the Battle of Seven Pines in 1862 as well as a son, Julian, at Drewry's Bluff in 1864. (Julian had honored his father's resolute devotion by naming one of his children Edmund Sumter.)[16] When he learned of Julian's death, Ruffin wrote that his affections had "dried up" and his heart had "hardened."[17]

Ruffin may have struggled to grieve, but he was gripped by fear. His world had been turned completely upside down. The slaver now dreaded captivity; he and his southern people were, he despaired, "slaves to the Yankee power."[18] He projected a free-for-all against white southerners by free Black people and Yankees.[19] Ruffin had also become convinced that he was a wanted man. One Union soldier correctly identified his Beechwood mansion and wrote a message to its owner on the wall: "You did fire the first gun on Sumter, you traitor son of a bitch."[20] Despondent with the doubt that self-determination for white "masters" in southern states was ending, Ruffin was determined to decide his fate.[21]

He wanted God's blessing to kill himself. Writing just months after Lee's Appomattox surrender, Ruffin transposed the world of ancient Judea onto his newly postbellum South. Their rebellion had failed, but ancient Jews still maintained their faith; they were physically but not psychologically conquered; they could accept their Roman occupation or they could register one final protest. Stalwart ancient believers, Ruffin concluded, "committed suicide in preference to being made prisoners."[22] Atop Mount Masada, "thousands" chose death over dishonor; "fanatically obedient" Jews, Ruffin wrote reverentially, had made the same choice during the Crusades.[23] Ruffin composed his penultimate diary entry, a seven-thousand-word treatise on the theological status of suicide in the Judeo-Christian tradition, over several days.[24]

78 WE ARE NOT ONE PEOPLE

On June 17, 1865, Ruffin excused himself after a family breakfast, wrote one last time of his hatred of "Yankee rule" and "the Yankee race," and shot himself just after noon.[25] "Death," one biographer suggested, "was his means of ultimate withdrawal, the revenge and punishment he would inflict on an unappreciative, ungrateful public."[26] Mourning the Civil War's outcome, later generations of southerners transformed Ruffin into a "mythic figure of the defeated South."[27] Some of these mythmakers said Ruffin draped himself in the Confederate battle flag before achieving martyrdom, but no evidence has ever placed the potent totem at his macabre death scene.[28]

A Nation for Masters

Antebellum southerners were not a homogeneous lot.[29] Rhetts and Ruffins did not populate the entire region. Differences of class, geography, and local politics frustrate attempts to generalize about the South. Even the fire-eaters were not univocal.[30] Some clamored for a new southern republic as an agrarian paradise, while others foresaw independence as a gateway to southern modernization.

In fact, over the span of the early republic, select groups of southern slave owners exhausted seemingly every argument they could to justify secession, nullification, and interposition. Southern "discontent," John C. Calhoun said, opposing California's entry into the Union as a free state in 1850, was partially the fault of northern abolitionists, but, he insisted, "the great and primary cause" was not the trampled rights of states but "the equilibrium between the two sections in the Government."[31] Secession, others held, was justified as an act of each state's sovereignty.[32] Jefferson Davis developed this argument in his 1861 inaugural address.[33]

Southerners also consistently made the opposite case: that secession was merited because of the North's nullification of pro-slavery laws. The federal government, they harangued, did not aggressively punish northern states and northern citizens who exercised local control, passed state abolitionist ordinances, upheld "personal liberty" laws, and refused to capture and return runaway slaves. Southerners were incensed over northern nullification and interposition. Northern states,

"A SLAVE REPUBLIC" 79

one fire-eater fumed, "continually nullified" both the Constitution and federal fugitive slave statutes and "faithlessly disregarded" southern slaveholders.[34] "The rights of the master of the slave," two other fire-eaters co-wrote in 1861, had been vitiated; the abolitionist mob had "overthrown the Constitution and the Law"; "the people of the South" were excluded from the rest of the country.[35] "I can go to England or France, or any other country in Europe with my slave, without molestation or violating any law," Robert Toombs told the Georgia legislature in 1860, but "here alone am I stigmatized as a felon," cast as "an outlaw," without recourse against "organized governments" or "the assassin who burns my dwelling or takes my life or those of my wife and children."[36]

In "one of American history's wonderful ironies," right up until the war broke out, many southerners pressed for federal supremacy while many northern communities fought for local control and practical nullification of national laws.[37] From the *Prigg* (1842) decision, a predecessor to *Dred Scott* (1857), to the attack on Fort Sumter, in one historian's judgment, "if the choice involved expanded property rights or expanded states' rights, the South chose property rights every time."[38] The Confederate constitution continued this nationalization of slavery at the expense of local freedoms and, of course, human rights. "With respect to slavery," one historian summarizes, "the Confederacy was a unitary, consolidated, national state, denying to each of its allegedly sovereign members any sort of local autonomy."[39]

Southern secessionists, in sum, employed states'-rights and anti-states'-rights justifications.[40] They kitchen-sinked the cause of secession.[41] That was by design, at least in part. As Alabama agitator William Lowndes Yancey strategized, positioning the 1861 South as the 1776 colonists, "One thing will catch our eye here and determine our hearts; another thing elsewhere; all united, may yet produce enough spirit to lead us forward, to call forth a Lexington, to fight a Bunker's Hill."[42] As a result of such an indiscriminate case, there are dozens of inconsistencies, contradictions, and disagreements, both tacit and explicit, in southern secessionist rhetoric. Simultaneous fights for "sectional balance" in Congress, shrewd maneuvers to make the national Democratic Party unconditionally pro-slavery, and demands for new pro-slavery amendments to the Constitution were

80 WE ARE NOT ONE PEOPLE

combined with "secession threats" into a southern political cocktail prior to the Civil War. By late 1860, every ingredient but the last one had been eliminated.[43]

Although they lacked total "cohesion," radicals like Rhett and Ruffin put aside their differences and devoted themselves to proving one argument: a slave society was better than a free society. The latter's threat to the former provoked secession.[44] The numbers tell the story. South Carolina, where almost half the white population belonged to a slave-owning family, was the first to go after Lincoln's election. Mississippi, with a similar ratio, immediately followed. The seven southern states with the highest proportion of enslaved people left before Lincoln was sworn in. The states of the Upper South, with far fewer enslaved people and far less money invested in slave labor, held out until the Fort Sumter attack created a sectional rallying effect.[45]

But these figures, while illustrative, can make secession looked fated. Instead, the South's status in the Union was a matter of much debate for decades before the war began. South Carolina's audacious attempt to nullify federal tariffs between 1828 and 1832 was not supported by any other southern state. As the 1850s began, Unionist candidates often beat fire-eating ones in local elections in every southern state except South Carolina and Mississippi.[46] When the League of the United South organized a southern convention in Nashville in 1850 to promote secession, the public response was tepid at best. Its organizers "had underestimated not only the enduring strength of partisan divisions but also the general mood of the region."[47] Some historians have suggested that many southerners "remained emotionally attached to the Union" through 1860.[48]

In this chapter, we wade through volumes of antebellum southern secession rhetoric—southern strategizing at the Constitutional Convention, the major speeches of John C. Calhoun, and, especially, a broad swath of the fire-eaters' speeches and pamphlets—to answer two simple questions: how did southern secessionists from the 1780s through 1861 describe the South as a place and southerners as a people, and why did that characterization necessitate separation? We recover the rhetorical spadework that southerners did for decades prior to the Civil War and the resonant vision of racial dominance in a separate nation they portrayed to convert the conflicted South into

"A SLAVE REPUBLIC" 81

a rebellious South where, by the war's eve, "a commitment to the idea that southerners constituted a separate political community was already becoming its own justification."[49]

To some extent, all secessionists claim victimization; they yearn for a separate, safe space to practice a religion, to affirm an idea, to be themselves. Their imagined separate nations, these lesbian or libertarian Zions, are purified spaces. Their group departure is a cleansing; they leave a polyglot polity where they are oppressed for a purer body politic. They build on an existing sense of alienation and answer forced segregation with proactive separation. Southern secessionists are both the quintessential and most consequential case of American separatism and, oddly enough, atypical. They pursued group power but not through social purity.

The core of the southern secessionist claim to a separate peoplehood was racial, and not just some visceral attachment to white withdrawal. America, they thought, was founded as a racially hierarchical republic; if the abolitionists' zeal had successfully convinced fickle bureaucrats otherwise, then the southern states would restore the racial promise of the American Revolution through another revolution. Their departure was grounded in dominance, on saving "the white race," but not through racial isolation; it aimed at cementing white mastery and Black slavery forever.[50]

There was no privilege without persecution, no winner without a loser, no victory in racial solitude. White antebellum southerners were not interested in a white ethnostate as were some later white nationalists, a sanguine Anglo-Saxon space where they could live exclusively among the master race.[51] They were not, in fact, even angling to live in a majority-white nation. They seceded to preserve a relationship, not a singular identity. They seceded to make their world safe for slavery.

Although they coveted an expanded slave population, southern secessionists did not clamor to expand slavery to other, presumably inferior, races. Fire-eaters depicted the system of antebellum southern slavery as the apotheosis of a perpetual institution, the ideal form of all human attempts to enslave others. As one historian summarizes, "Rather than enjoining slaveholders to fulfill their Christian responsibilities as masters or condemning the harshest, most dehumanizing

82   WE ARE NOT ONE PEOPLE

features of the institution, the fire-eaters portrayed slavery as an absolute good."[52] They glorified a civilization whose social, material, political, economic, and familial relationships, they said repeatedly, rested on the "positive good" of "African slavery."

The phrase was a rhetorical trend that had been spreading around the South since the 1830s.[53] Calhoun voiced the "positive good" mantra most prominently in an 1837 speech where he argued that southerners should stop being defensive about slavery. To Calhoun, southerners deserved to be proud and protective of slavery because in every "wealthy and civilized society" the world had ever known, "one portion of the community" lived "on the labor of the other."[54] The fire-eaters made the "positive good" line their maxim in the 1850s. For them, there was no southern way of life without African slavery, no southern people without African slavery, no south without African slavery.

In the fire-eaters' political worldview, there were no pure people, no separate sphere where one faction might live among themselves completely apart from other factions. Nations were inherently heterogeneous, and political relationships within nations were always hierarchical; some group was always enslaved by or beholden to some other, more dominant group. Until the middle of the nineteenth century, although the Rhetts and Ruffins believed otherwise, southern planters sat atop southern society and American politics. By 1860, in what the fire-eaters portrayed as the dog-eat-dog world of zero-sum American political relationships, it was either the status quo, coded as inevitable white southern slavery to northern and Black masters, or secession, coded as freedom from northern abolitionists to perpetuate African slavery. The options were submission to and enslavement by the "hostile, irresponsible, and insurmountable political power of the North" or secession to protect the racial subjection at the core of southern society.[55]

Seceding Since the Beginning

The Rhetts and Ruffins of the 1850s were just the latest iterations of a type of agitator who had bedeviled the American Union since the founding: the separatist southern slaveholder. Members of this cohort shaped the Constitution by threatening to bolt from the young

"A SLAVE REPUBLIC" 83

country. John Rutledge, for instance, was a forceful presence at the Constitutional Convention, where he said the issue of slavery in the Constitution should be assessed financially, not morally; he grew up in South Carolina with two hundred enslaved persons.[56] The "Southern States," he promised, would not automatically join a new union. If "Northern States" look to their "interest," he suggested, they "will not oppose the increase of slaves which will increase the commodities of which they will become the carriers." Rutledge's South Carolina compatriots Charles Pinckney and Charles Cotesworth Pinckney adopted similar bargaining positions at the convention, as did North Carolina's William Davie.[57] Several constitutional compromises—the Three-Fifths Clause, the Fugitive Slave Clause, and the prohibition of regulation of the slave trade until 1808—were negotiated under the threat of southern secession.[58] It was not the last time that southern secession threats led to northern "appeasement."[59]

Historians have long debated whether Rutledge and others bluffed to extract greater constitutional concessions. Was secession a posture or a political program? Some fellow founders certainly found their threats credible. Gouverneur Morris, foreshadowing William Lloyd Garrison's later reading of the Constitution as "an agreement with Hell," suggested letting southerners go establish a separate slave nation.[60] "Let us at once take a friendly leave of each other," the Pennsylvanian said.[61] Rufus King, by contrast, urged his fellow northern delegates to press southerners on their seriousness.[62] Most founders disagreed with both Morris's and King's positions. Roger Sherman's sentiment was more common. "It was better," the Connecticut statesman stipulated, "to let the southern states import slaves than to part with them, if they made that a sine qua non."[63] James Madison attributed the different interests of the different states at the convention to one factor: "having or not having slaves."[64] In a Constitutional Convention postscript, Madison told Thomas Jefferson that southerners were "inflexible on the point of the slaves."[65] Elsewhere, Madison called the foreign slave trade "evil" but calculated that the "dismemberment of the union would be worse."[66]

Southern withdrawal threats were not idle.[67] Convention delegates knew that "a Constitution that struck a serious blow at slavery" would not be ratified down south.[68] Moreover, if southerners sensed the Constitution was even tacitly anti-slavery, the records of state

84   WE ARE NOT ONE PEOPLE

ratification debates throughout the South would read quite differently. Instead, as historian Michael Klarman summarizes, "in South Carolina and Georgia, which were the states most strongly committed to the indefinite perpetuation of slavery, very few voices criticized the Constitution as insufficiently protective of the institution."[69] Lowcountry planters of South Carolina knew they had gotten a great deal. Charles Cotesworth Pinckney boasted to a Charleston audience, "We have obtained a right to recover our slaves in whatever part of America they may take refuge."[70] Georgia ratified the Constitution by a unanimous vote.[71]

Southern slaveholders successfully threatened secession and won significant constitutional advantages as a result. They again vowed secession during the 1820 debates over the admission of Missouri as a slave state and the broader issue of slavery's expansion into the territories.[72] Jefferson called the crisis over Missouri's admission as a slave state a "firebell in the night."[73] A charged conversation of the era typified the national risk that Jefferson felt the nation faced. In February of that year, secretary of war John C. Calhoun told secretary of state John Quincy Adams that southerners had thought through the secession chess match. If the admission of Missouri set off a "dissolution" of the Union, the South would ally with Great Britain. Adams, recalling two recent wars with England, was astounded by Calhoun's flirtation with treason. Calhoun replied the South's hand would be forced into creating such an alliance.[74]

From the Missouri crisis on, one of Calhoun's consistent rhetorical flourishes, unlike his "ultra" in-state rivals like Rhett, doctrinaires single-mindedly pleading for secession, was a conditional, if-then, horse-trading rhetoric of southern loyalty.[75] If they got what they wanted, all of it, and all of the time, southerners were nationalists. If their aims were thwarted, they threatened exit.[76]

In his home state, Calhoun found himself exploring the fraught space between Unionists and nullifiers before and after he wrote the "South Carolina Exposition and Protest" in 1828.[77] At points in the showdown with Andrew Jackson over federal tariffs, Calhoun sided with the Unionists, noting that if other states did not back South Carolina's tariff defiance, the state should "give it up" rather than secede on its own.[78] In his Fort Hill address of 1831, Calhoun shrewdly redefined South Carolina's position on the "Tariff of Abominations" as one of interposition, not the more directly insubordinate nullification.[79] He characterized the state veto concept he had developed as a tool to preserve, not divide, the constituent parts of the Union to stave off full disintegration. Explaining that he was personally invested in serving "the Union," Calhoun attributed "whatever public reputation" he enjoyed as "indissolubly identified with it."[80] Regardless of his ideological gloss and feints toward Unionism, Calhoun's nullification birthed the "perpetual paradox of a state being in and out of the Union at the same time."[81]

Whether it was termed interposition or nullification, Calhoun's basic idea was that states, not the Supreme Court, were the primary interpreters of the Constitution, and could invalidate federal laws they found unconstitutional. The voiding state could then appeal to other states to change the law; if the state's objections were not addressed, the state could secede.[82] Although his fondness for secession as a program grew in the 1830s and 1840s, Calhoun, in his late-career speeches following the Mexican cession, honed his Union-saving persona, the sane, reasonable middle between unreasonable abolitionists and fanatical fire-eaters.[83] But these speeches were both a reflection of and a contributor to an increasingly polarizing, toxifying political climate in which sectional violence loomed.

Calhoun's ultimate sympathies were not in doubt. He predicted, not recommended, secession if there were no additional federal concessions on slavery. These predictions, however, covered clever ultimatums. If Congress amended the Constitution to declare definitively that enslaved persons were property, then, as he put it, the "peace of the Union" could be "preserved." However, as a "Southern man and a slaveholder," Calhoun would rather, he boomed, "meet any extremity upon earth than give up one inch of our equality."[84] Calhoun foresaw southerners severing "all political ties" rather than sinking "down into abject submission."[85]

The admission of California in 1850, which occasioned the final speech of Calhoun's career, concerned combustible questions of slavery's expansion, growing abolitionism, federal enforcement of the fugitive slave codes, and the sectional balance of power. Rumor had it that the White House had been the scene of a shouting match just

86 WE ARE NOT ONE PEOPLE

days prior as Representative Robert Toombs and Senator Alexander Stephens, both Georgians, told President Zachary Taylor that some southerners were considering seceding if California entered as a free state. Taylor threatened to execute any traitors.[86]

Aided into the Senate chamber and stricken by pneumonia, Calhoun listened, shivering under blankets, as Virginia's James Mason read Calhoun's speech, the last lines of his career.[87] The "harmony and fraternal feelings between the sections" that proliferated before "the Missouri agitation" in 1820 could proliferate yet again if the North acceded. If guarantees for the national property rights of slave owners were impossible, "say so; and let the States we both represent agree to separate and part in peace." Calhoun ended in his imagined middle, where he remained a conscientious triangulator of Unionism and sectionalism. "Having faithfully done my duty to the best of my ability, both to the Union and my section," he wiped his hands clean of whatever conflict was to come.[88] Framed copies of this speech, printed on satin, were displayed around southern cities like Charleston.[89]

The Fire-Eaters' Demos

By one measure, southern slaveholders, like a romantic partner constantly threatening a breakup, began secessionist agitation when the nation began, regularly renewed these threats through the nation's infancy, then made good on these threats by seceding and inciting the Civil War. The southern secessionism that had been simmering since 1789 simply boiled over in the middle of the nineteenth century. By another measure, the South genuinely radicalized in the nineteenth century's middle decades; a *"rage militaire,"* a "war fever," swept the region.[90]

The origin point of southern radicalization, when the fire-eaters gained strength and moved to the center of southern political life, is the object of much debate. Some historians prefer a longer view, dating the origin around 1820, preceding the Missouri Compromise of 1828 and the ensuing Nullification Crisis. Others locate this growth of southern extremism after 1846 in reaction to the Wilmot Proviso, after 1848 in conflict over the legal status of the Mexican Cession, in the California dispute of 1850, or at other flashpoints—Bleeding Kansas, *Dred Scott*,

"A SLAVE REPUBLIC" 87

Harpers Ferry—in the 1850s.[91] "Southern demands in the 1850s," one historian summarizes, "*were* extreme, and they grew *more* extreme as the decade progressed."[92]

Regardless of the exact date, we are interested in tracking southern secession's rhetorical movement in the mid-nineteenth century. Always a part of southern national political strategy, secession sped from being an occasional threat from the fire-eating fringes to the center of southern politics. "Opinions develop fast in this age," the Republican George Templeton Strong recorded in his diary.[93] The fire-eaters' chauvinist words, including their promise of a utopian society for slave owners, illustrate the real growth of what southerners called "the great excitement" before the Civil War.[94]

"Fire-eater," a term denoting the most militant pro-slavery and pro-secession southerners, was first used in the early 1850s; it "carried connotations of violence and bitterness, if not also of showmanship."[95] The crux of the fire-eaters' case is best observed in several types of public texts from the era: the transcripts of each southern state's secession convention, the speeches and letters of each state's secession commissioners who encouraged other southern states to secede, widely attended speeches at commercial and political conventions throughout the 1850s South, secessionist screeds in prominent southern papers like *The Charleston Mercury* and *De Bow's Review*, and pro-secession pamphlets printed and circulated the South by the hundreds of thousands by the well-heeled propagandists of Charleston's 1860 Association.[96]

By the beginning of 1861, the rhetorical force of the fire-eaters' case was even evident in Calhoun's ideological heirs, crafty politicians like Alexander Stephens and a few others who, throughout the 1850s, sounded Unionist themes to some and disunionist notes to others but, by late 1860, sounded like Rhett and Ruffin.[97]

To the fire-eaters, the true southerner was, put simply, a slaver. Several southern states' official secession declarations cited slavery as the single factor influencing their departure. Mississippi's secession declaration stated unequivocally, "Our position is thoroughly identified with the institution of slavery—the greatest material interest of the world."[98] Georgia began its declaration of secession by highlighting the state's "numerous and serious causes of complaint against our

88　WE ARE NOT ONE PEOPLE

non-slave-holding confederate States with reference to the subject of African slavery."[99] Texas's declaration praised the "servitude of the African race as mutually beneficial to both bond and free."[100] Virginia, the scene of a contentious statewide abolition debate in the early 1830s, offered the same rationale. "African slavery," the declaration read, was both a "vital part of the social system" of slave states and the sole legal province of those states, not "the federal authority" or any people of any other state.[101]

These official secession declarations, in part, proclaimed fealty to slavery so straightforwardly because they were the expressions of virulently pro-slavery positions of the winning side in southern debates about the wisdom, timing, and strategy of secession; the immediatist delegates who favored the quick secession of separate states after Lincoln's election won the day and got to make their case. Speaking to crowded secession conventions in southern state capitals, these speakers thundered about the imminent threat that Lincoln, the Republican Party, abolitionists, and the North generally posed to slavery. This threat to slavery was the sharp edge of a larger threat to white supremacy. William Harris, a Georgia-born judge practicing in Mississippi, told a divided Georgia secession convention where Unionist sentiments were strong, "Our fathers made this a government for the white man, rejecting the negro, as an ignorant, inferior, barbarian race, incapable of self-government, and not, therefore, entitled to be associated with the white man upon terms of civil, political, or social equality." Staying in the Union meant that racial hierarchy would be struck down in favor of "the universal equality of the black and white races."[102]

Another speaker at Georgia's secession convention, Thomas R. R. Cobb, put the point similarly as he, too, wrapped himself in the Constitution. America was founded on white supremacy: "This Constitution was made for white men, and for the protection and happiness of their race." When the Constitution was written, "we were all slaveholding States—a homogenous people, having a common origin, common memories—a common cause, common hopes—a common future, a common destiny."[103]

Fire-eaters depicted themselves as the unwitting victims of a great constitutional bait-and-switch. Their forebearers seceded from

England as slave owners; their forefathers signed the Constitution because it protected slavery; their forefathers enjoyed a political arrangement wherein the South, despite its lower population, wielded comparatively outsized political power; their forefathers stayed in the Union for the better part of a century because the institution of slavery had not been seriously threatened and the status of "Africans" in America had not improved. But the North had grown intolerant. Garrison and his abolitionist hordes rallied northern mobs and peppered the South with anti-slavery propaganda; the fevered swamp they created spawned violent slave revolts, a murderous rampage in Kansas, and another at Harpers Ferry. Even worse, fire-eaters alleged, abolitionists now had their own political party, the Republicans, and their own president in Lincoln. Addressing the Virginia secession convention in February 1861, Georgia's Henry Benning plainly explained his state's "deep conviction" that "a separation from the North was the only thing that could prevent the abolition of her slavery." Secession solved "the fugitive slave evil" and, in an allusion to the expansion of slavery, "the territory evil," but those were ancillary to the "first conviction," legally protecting slavery in the South.[104]

Determined not to be tricked into false protections for slavery again, the fire-eaters spoke forcefully in the cherished terms of the American Revolution. The keystone words of the American founding, the French Revolution, and other democratic revolutions were actually the bedrock concepts of their white supremacist state. "Our peculiar institution," Stephens said in Savannah in 1861, is both "the immediate cause of the late rupture and present revolution" as well as the "corner-stone" of the new Confederacy. Stephens's new country, he said, enshrined natural rights—"great principles," he called them—of the Magna Carta and the American Constitution: "life," "liberty," "property," and religious freedom. But, Stephens clarified, the new Confederacy was founded on natural facts that circumscribed these natural rights; "the negro is not equal to the white man," and "subordination to the superior race is his natural and normal condition."[105]

Words like "liberty" and "property" had a particular, peculiar meaning to slave owners. Freedom to own human property, the unrestricted ability to practice master race status, was paramount.[106] One South Carolina pamphlet completely reversed Patrick Henry: "Give us

90 WE ARE NOT ONE PEOPLE

slavery or give us death."[107] That is, these terms, keywords of a democratic and, often, a separatist vocabulary, were stripped of any power-expanding meaning where they might apply to all people fighting unaccountable, unresponsive authority. These were not the words that Enlightenment-era philosophers and revolutionaries had used to rationally, rigorously question tyrannical power or protect the powerless; these words affirmed such power and ensured the rights of the powerful against the powerless.[108] As one historian explained, "Any government that could threaten individual property rights, guaranteed by the Fifth Amendment and including state-recognized property in human beings, could pose a despotic threat to individual liberty among the white citizenry, to state sovereignty as a bulwark of those liberties, and to a southern way of life inseparable from black chattel slavery as a system of benevolent racial control and respectable private property."[109] Southern secessionists appropriated these and other terms of democratic critique, equality, independence, self-determination, local control, constitutionalism, natural rights, and even justice to defend racial dominance and take broadsides against majoritarian democracy. They turned these terms "inside out."[110]

Equality

The fire-eaters, of course, were not the first to make fascism sound like freedom. Patrick Henry himself, a Virginia slaveholder, opposed the Constitution, fearing that it promised freedom to enslaved persons.[111] In fact, the fire-eaters paid consistent homage to the American founders as creators of a white supremacist democracy that protected slavery absolutely; one called them "Revolutionary sires,"[112] another called them "noble revolutionary fathers."[113] As historian Adam Goodheart writes, "Indeed, the Founding Fathers—led by Virginia's immortal Washington, Jefferson, and Henry, slaveholders all—had established the very principles on which the Confederate states based their own claim to independence."[114]

But theirs was not an entirely faithful devotion. A revealing thread in mid-nineteenth-century fire-eater rhetoric was a frontal attack on part of the foundational text of American separatism: the

"A SLAVE REPUBLIC" 91

Declaration of Independence. One line, in particular, stoked their ire. The Declaration was quite useful to southern secessionists on the whole because it developed several flexible arguments for exit; the notion, however, that one people should separate from another in order to secure the self-evident truth of human equality and inalienable rights threatened the entire southern enterprise. Jefferson's direct repudiations of the slave trade, in an apparent pacification of, in Jefferson's words, "Georgia and South Carolina," were struck from the rough draft of the Declaration, but that did not make "all men are created equal" much less perilous.[115]

The fire-eaters' case for secession was premised on the opposite belief: in inequality. The course of American events, by their eyes, made it necessary for southerners to dissolve the political bands that had connected them with northerners, and their declaration of causes of separation was grounded in hierarchy. Their self-evident truth was that the races were created unequal, that they were endowed by their creator with inalienable and divergent capabilities. Among Anglo-Saxon capabilities were life, liberty, happiness, and social dominance. Among African capabilities were service and subservience. "Natural rights," historian William Freehling summarizes, "were unnatural." "Men were created unequal. Black bondage was blessed."[116] Southerners largely exalted the American Revolution, but they would outdo their revolutionary forebearers one better by correcting the core flaw in their charter. As historian Sean Wilentz put it, "The new slaveholders' republic would stand as a living refutation of Jefferson's harebrained egalitarian doctrines, and of the anarchic vulgarities that had emanated from them and degraded the North."[117]

Southern life in the middle decades of the nineteenth century was full of panegyrics to inequality. Samuel A. Cartwright, a physician whose claim to fame was diagnosing "drapetomania," the supposed mental disorder that caused happy slaves to run away, wrote in De Bow's Review in 1851 that "our Declaration of Independence" was written when "negroes were scarcely considered human beings." Anyone of sound mind, quite obviously, could not support "the false dogma that all mankind possess the same mental, physiological and anatomical organization."[118] Stephens, quite similarly, lambasted Jefferson and other founders' "assumption of the equality of the races."[119]

92   WE ARE NOT ONE PEOPLE

Calhoun, yet again, provided much of this source material. Calling human equality "the most false and dangerous of all political errors," Calhoun voiced lines of fire-eaters' later attack in a Senate speech in 1848.[120] He picked apart every word in the "all men are created equal" clause. The Declaration, Calhoun chided, "asserts that 'all men are created equal,'" but only two people were "created" by God; the rest were born. More important than these semantic criticisms were his historical ones. The equality line "was inserted in our Declaration of Independence without any necessity." Equality was neither essential nor helpful "to the cause of revolutionary independence; it was irrelevant to the breach of our chartered privileges, and lawless encroachment on our acknowledged and well-established rights by the parent country." Jefferson and other Enlightenment-descended liberals got these bogus ideas from "Locke and Sydney," who were also mistaken about human nature and ability. Liberty was not a natural right, and all people were certainly not created equally capable of practicing liberty. Liberty was a "reward," not a right. It was earned by those of certain "mental and moral development" in "favorable circumstances."[121] It was a privilege of race and class.

Calhoun then applied this general rebuke of human equality to Jefferson's "utterly false view of the subordinate relation of the black to the white race in the South."[122] Jefferson, in Calhoun's words, saw depriving Black southerners of "liberty and equality" as "unjust and immoral." Calhoun labeled Black people "utterly unqualified." Jefferson's error, Calhoun alleged, was historically and politically significant. Calhoun suggested that the exclusion of slavery from the Northwest Territory in 1787, an original regulatory sin to him, was ultimately Jefferson's fault; without his guidance, Congress never would have treated slavery as something sinful to be contained. The sectional fight over slavery's regulation that began in 1787 "now threatens," Calhoun predicted in 1848, "to ingulf, and will certainly ingulf, if not speedily settled, our political institutions, and involve the country in countless woes."[123]

Beyond Jefferson's equality offense, ambiguous constitutional language about slavery consistently worried southern slave owners. The framers, preferring euphemisms, did not mention "slaves" or "slavery," a purposeful omission so that the Constitution, as Madison journaled,

"A SLAVE REPUBLIC" 93

would not affirm "the idea that there could be property in men"[124] These circumlocutions opened the door for new threats to slavery, and mendacious northerners, "a majority trained from infancy to hate our people and our institutions," crashed through.[125]

The fire-eaters exalted that their new Confederacy felt no such conflict about slavery and would protect its legal status explicitly. After Alabama's secession, Stephen Hale was appointed by the governor to convince his home state of Kentucky to follow along. Hale did not mince words about the connection between the institution of slavery and the political community that constituted the core of southern national identity: "It is upon this gigantic interest, this peculiar institution of the South . . . an institution with which is bound up not only the wealth and prosperity of the Southern people, but their very existence as a political community."[126] Hale and others went far further than suggesting that southerners shared an ideological commitment to white supremacy. To them, that much was obvious; they stressed that slavery was the heart of southern personal, social, political, theological, and economic life. Their language is galling to modern eyes, but in their estimation, such clarity of purpose was essential to bind the new southern demos together in common cause during the secession winter of 1860–1861.

The People's Institution

Southerners, as a demos, did not exist without slavery and, these fire-eaters feared, slavery as an institution would not exist without the separation of the southern demos. In a pamphlet that circulated throughout the prewar South, New Orleans–based pastor Benjamin Palmer blessed secession as a holy act.[127] He viewed the relationship between the South, slavery, and secession as a priori. Slavery was, he preached in this "Thanksgiving Sermon," "interwoven with our entire social fabric." Palmer was blunt; the institution "fashioned our modes of life," "determined all our habits of thought and feeling," and built "our civilization." To alter it would alter "our existence," he concluded.[128] Another popular southern pamphlet by noted publisher J. D. B. De Bow even involved non-slave-owning southern whites in its ode to slavery. Slave ownership was an aspiration of all southern white people, evidence they had made it. Every white man wanted to become a slave owner "as soon as his savings will admit" in order to "relieve his wife from the necessities of the kitchen and laundry" and to save "his children from the labors of the field."[129]

Slave ownership was the top rung on the white southern ladder. It was also, De Bow maintained, a privilege for non-slave-owning whites to live in a white supremacist society. They enjoyed a "status" above the "inferior or dependent" by virtue of racial hierarchy even without enslaved people of their own.[130] Without the institution, poor white southerners would be subject to mistreatment based on class or race. De Bow and others, like Georgia's Joseph Brown, encouraged white southerners of all classes to see their fates as inextricably bound up in slavery. Poor white workers will "never take the negro's place; God forbid." "We all," Brown enjoined, "poor and rich, have a common interest, a common destiny."[131]

Slavery was the South's tide; every white person's political, social, and material status rose and fell with it. The fire-eaters kept an exacting account on this point. When Hale encouraged Kentucky's secession, he assessed that "African slavery" was easily "the most valuable species" of southern property, "according to recent estimates, not less than $4,000,000,000." Slavery was, he described succinctly, "the basis upon which rests the prosperity and wealth of most of these States."[132]

Isham Garrott and Robert H. Smith, two Alabama lawyers, wrote to their native North Carolina arguing that the present value of slaves and slave labor was no guarantee of future value. In fact, if slavery was restricted to its 1860 limits across southern counties, future southern population growth would not be sustainable, and the South's political power would be confined. Drawing on figures from Alabama, Garrott and Smith reasoned, "If the slaves now in Alabama are to be restricted within her present limits, doubling as they do once in less than thirty years, the children are now born who will be compelled to flee from the land of their birth, and from the slaves their parents have toiled to acquire as an inheritance for them."[133] Southerners could only continue to cull the maximum value from slaves by forcing them to labor in additional territories.

"A SLAVE REPUBLIC" 95

In his influential pamphlet "The Doom of Slavery in the Union: Its Safety Out of It," the Edisto Island plantation owner John Townsend offered a similarly brutal, bloodless analysis of slavery's economic importance to white southerners. He predicted that the regulation of slavery would destroy all agricultural production in the South where crops needed "regular, steady, *continuous labor*" all year long "year after year." Abolitionists erred tremendously in thinking that "agriculture, at the South, can be carried on as well with *hired* (and therefore irregular) labor, as with *compulsory* labor."[134] Southern crops needed slave labor. Townsend cited deteriorating economic conditions in the British West Indies and Peru to prove that forced labor was required to develop and extend commercial agriculture. Southerners would not prosper without widely available food, and slavery protected food supplies: "It is undoubtedly true, then, that the abolition of slavery at the South means the annihilation of all negro labor, and with the loss of that labor, the end of all crops—and with loss of crops, the end of all income to the planters."[135]

James Hammond, a South Carolina planter and political grandee, built a material case for secession's desirability, but he focused on exports, not internal food supplies. By his estimation, U.S. exports in 1857 totaled "$279,000,000," of which the South produced "$158,000,000." These figures did not count the "$30,000,000" in cotton the South sent to the North or "$7 or $8,000,000 worth of tobacco" they also shipped. The North, to Hammond, was economically weak compared to the South's titanic economy. The North was the South's economic charity case, its ward: "Suppose we were to discharge you; suppose we were to take our business out of your hands; we should consign you to anarchy and poverty." Even more, an independent South would be even wealthier after cutting off its expensive northern dependents: "With an export of $220,000,000 under the present tariff, the South organized separately would have $40,000,000 of revenue."[136]

Hammond equated the South's size, some 850,000 square miles, with "Great Britain, France, Austria, Prussia, and Spain." Plus, the region boasted the "finest soil" and "most delightful climate." Hammond's 1858 speech, however, became known for three words, "cotton is king," not its numbers or plaudits. But beyond this pithy alliteration, the address was a statistically thick argument for the South's viability, even

96 WE ARE NOT ONE PEOPLE

prosperity, as a separate country. No "sane nation" would "make war on cotton," he claimed. The South's stranglehold on cotton made the world its hostage: "Without firing a gun, without drawing a sword, should they make war on us we could bring the whole world to our feet."[137]

Hammond misattributed enslaved people's productivity to happiness, but he was not overestimating their productivity. As historian Edward Baptist concludes, "The crop of cotton in 1859 was astonishing—almost 2 billion pounds of clean fiber in 4 million bales. Slavery's productivity was higher than ever—some 700 pounds per enslaved man, woman, and child in the cotton country, twenty-two times the rate in 1790."[138] Just prior to the Civil War, the region provided 70 percent of the world's cotton. The South made up only one-third of the nation's population but accounted for two-thirds of Americans with a net worth of $100,000 or more.[139] With a market value of over a billion dollars, the slave population that Hammond said were thrilled with their condition represented roughly one-fifth of the nation's entire wealth, more than every bank, factory, and railroad combined in 1850s America.[140]

There was an inflationary logic at work in the fire-eaters' positive-good arguments; if the institution as a whole was good, then every person of African descent who was enslaved in the South increased the aggregate total of positive goods. After all, as Hammond held, "Southern slaves are black, of another and inferior race. . . . They are elevated from the condition in which God first created them, by being made our slaves. . . . They are happy, content, unaspiring, and utterly incapable, from intellectual weakness, ever to give us any trouble by their aspirations."[141] This logic applied to the slave trade as well. The nation banned the importation of slaves in 1808 per the Constitution's slave trade clause, but if slavery was good for Africans and profoundly beneficial to southern whites, then banning the importation of slaves was both immoral and imprudent.

Rhett, one of the few ex-Confederates to continue to admit after the Civil War that slavery was the sole cause of secession, thought the prohibition on the slave trade was a cowardly admission that slavery was "evil." The opposite was true; slavery was "a blessing to the African Race and a system of labor appointed by God."[142]

"A SLAVE REPUBLIC" 97

In speeches around the South as well as his newspaper, *The Charleston Standard*, Leonidas Spratt became another leading advocate for reopening the slave trade. Spratt urged importing more enslaved persons from Africa at gatherings like the Savannah Commercial Convention in 1856 as well as annual meetings of the Southern Convention where he spoke alongside fire-eating luminaries like De Bow and Yancey.[143]

In a popular 1861 pamphlet, Spratt emphasized, "The South is now in the formation of a *Slave* Republic." It was plainly ridiculous for a new country based on slavery to continue the slave trade ban. The North and South were "two forms of society," with the former "composed of one race" and "the other of two races." The North was a "pure democracy," while the South was "a social aristocracy." "African slavery" was forbidden by nature up north, but "Southern civilization cannot exist without African slavery." White people, to Spratt, simply could not live down south without slavery. Without "involuntary labor," white southerners would have to depart southern climates in droves for their original "latitudes."[144] Other fire-eaters employed similar language, arguing that the science of racial adaptability and physical capability created natural conditions for a slave society composed of white masters and Black servants across the American South.[145]

Spratt departed from other fire-eaters as well as those of Calhoun's middle position who revered the Constitution as a pro-slavery document. To him, it was southern delegates who had made an agreement with Hell. Southerners at the Constitutional Convention should never have agreed to limit the foreign slave trade. Their weakness allowed two "lobsters" to uncomfortably inhabit a "single shell." In 1861, the South now had the chance to reverse the "blunder of 1789." Spratt urged southern secessionists to recognize their common raison d'être in slavery, to make sure that each state joining the Confederacy did so with open eyes and sturdy loyalty. Any state that hesitantly joined the Confederacy would create new "tests of faith" in the future; after some time, the Confederacy would, like America in 1861, be "again divided into antagonist societies" between whom "the irrepressible conflict is again commenced." Alternatively, if each seceding state agreed to join a Confederate republic with a singular mission, a slavers' paradise could be built with a greatly expanded slave population and a greatly

98 WE ARE NOT ONE PEOPLE

enlarged territory—perhaps in Cuba, perhaps in Mexico—for slavery's further expansion.[146]

"I truly think we want more slaves," Spratt emphasized. He assessed Europe's population density and figured that South Carolina alone could eventually hold the entire population of the southern states as it stood in 1861; Texas could support three times the entire population of the whole Union in 1861. The white South, in short, could grow massively. Spratt cited biological pseudoscience, ancient slave practices in Greece and Rome, and the low ratio of masters to enslaved people in South Carolina's rice fields to suggest further that the slave population could skyrocket even without a corresponding increase in the white population. Spratt projected the ideal population of southern slaves at forty million people; the 1860 census counted four million American slaves.[147]

Seceding Until the End

The fire-eaters persuaded with fear. Apocalyptic images of racial revenge extended through their discourse like, in one historian's phrase, "a scarlet thread."[148] These were graphic scenes of southern submission, vivid Miltonian depictions of "utter ruin,"[149] images of "torture and plunder,"[150] nightmares of "despised and degraded" landscapes,[151] and phantasms of subjugated southerners debased "to a position far lower than that of Mexico or of St. Domingo" by newly ascendant Africans and newly dominant northerners, Republicans, and abolitionists.[152]

Secession preserved slavery and saved white southerners from enslavement. It saved them from a Black world with "black governors, black judges, black legislators, black juries, black witnesses, everything black," a wicked world where white men were "exterminated or expelled" and white women suffered a fate "too horrible to contemplate."[153] One historian interpreted these nightmares as evidence of the region-wide power of a "psychosexual fear."[154] Secession saved southern "wives and daughters" from, one fire-eater hoped, "the lust of half-civilized Africans" and saved them all from "an eternal war of races, desolating the land with blood, and utterly wasting and

"A SLAVE REPUBLIC" 99

destroying all the resources of the country."[155] White southerners, in sum, said secession rescued them from mass immolation "in one common funeral pile."[156]

Horrifying as these images of racial reprisal were in the white slave-holding South, the fire-eaters' view of political life was never about racial purity. As Sam Houston, a secession opponent, said, "Our people are going to war to perpetuate slavery, and the first gun fired in the war will be the knell of slavery."[157] For southern secessionists, distinct groups were always mixed up in political life, and between them, there was nothing but cutthroat competition. Theirs was a dark, survival-of-the-fittest realpolitik; one group always submitted to another; one group always ruled another, dominated another. Equality was a lie, a cover for dominance, a complete misunderstanding of the high-stakes reality of political relationships between sections, states, and races. It was either them or us, they said.

In the 1850s, the fire-eaters spoke to "sharpen" sectional conflict, "the sharper the better."[158] This turgid prose looks almost willfully designed to frustrate later attempts to rewrite southern motivations. At points, it seems as if these radicals had an eye toward posterity and wanted to speak directly to future generations who might wonder why rich, powerful southerners risked so much to break from their native land. In candid thoughts about slavery and racial inferiority that are seemingly impossible to decontextualize, in exclusive statements about their absolute aim to protect slavery, in statements about the single-mindedness of their devotion to white supremacy, in punchy language designed to clear up any misconception, the fire-eaters revered slavery so hyperbolically that later attempts to rewrite southern motivations look flatly audacious.

The near-total saturation of southern life in 1860 with polarized possibilities—separation or northern domination, slavery or abolition—may have been a unique feature of the "secession mania" that gripped the region.[159] As we have shown, however, southern secession to secure slavery had been on the table since 1776, as were a host of other types of withdrawal toward the same white supremacist end.[160] The spectrum of southern disunion, the full range of options southerners availed themselves of to refuse majority rule and abandon national norms, actually disappeared during the Civil War when

100   WE ARE NOT ONE PEOPLE

secessionist slaveholders "fulfilled the historical mission they had been rehearsing for years."[161] In other words, one of the few clear instances in American history when southern powerbrokers were not embracing or threatening disunion of all kinds was when they actually left the Union.

The threat of southern secession began with their objection to Jefferson's rough draft of the Declaration of Independence, hung over the Constitutional Convention, reappeared during debates limiting the slave trade in 1807, and matured during the Missouri crisis in 1820. The threat of southerners snubbing national law through nullification or interposition began with Calhoun and South Carolina's resistance to federal tariffs in the late 1820s, but it certainly did not stop when Jackson threatened to occupy Charleston and Congress reduced the tariff.[162] James Petigru, the influential South Carolina Unionist, wrote at the time, "Nullification has done its work. It has prepared the minds of men for a separation of the states—and when the question is moved again it will be distinctly union or disunion."[163]

The question was moved again quickly. When abolitionists began distributing anti-slavery tracts through the federal mail in the 1830s, southern postmasters often refused delivery. These employees, federal employees like Charleston's Alfred Huger, for instance, sided with local prejudice over federal law. In some cases, southern communities, fearful that abolitionist literature would create more Denmark Veseys, seized and burned these mailings. Almost immediately after the Nullification Crisis, Jackson was again faced with intransigent southerners preserving racial hierarchy, but the president was no friend of abolitionism. He officially reaffirmed federal supremacy, but in practice he looked the other way while southerners in thrall to slavery effectively nullified federal law by losing, hiding, or destroying mail they did not like.[164]

The full scale of southern cultural, political, and legal disunion condensed into the most radical form of exit, secession, during the fervor of the 1850s. But the full disunionist repertoire that southerners developed over the course of antebellum America was not forgotten when the last musket went silent in 1865. The varied means of that resistance is a principal theme of southern history, and, minus formal, violent secession, it continued after the Civil War.

"A SLAVE REPUBLIC" 101

Adelbert Ames, the last of Mississippi's Radical Republican governors during Reconstruction, recounted the militant resistance of the white Democrats he faced in office. To them, foreign tyrants "had filled their state with mourning, beggared them, freed their slaves and as a last insult and injury made the enslaved a political equal." They resisted in acts of "intimidation, violence, and murder."[165]

The post–Civil War violence of guerrilla groups who canvassed "the countryside, harassing, threatening, and killing Unionists and African Americans" was not in direct service of the fallen Confederacy but was instead intended, one historian suggests, "to rebalance the white South's oppressive racial hierarchy and political oligarchy within the new postwar Union."[166] Ku Klux Klan activity was so pervasive that in 1871 President Grant even declared nine upstate South Carolina counties to be in a state of lawless rebellion. Federal troops made hundreds of arrests, and "perhaps 2,000 Klansmen fled the state."[167]

But Grant's aggressive enforcement of Reconstruction protocols like what became known as the Ku Klux Klan Act was an exception. By and large, "Southern white public opinion" would not acquiesce to "the rule of law."[168] As historian Philip Dray concludes, "The Klan's blatant misbehavior had forced the government's hand, and whites in the South recognized that future efforts to restore white rule would likely fare better if pursued with greater subtlety. There was no need to confront Reconstruction directly; better to nibble at its advances, harass its flanks, and wait out its collapse."[169]

White southerners also aimed to reclaim the practice of separatist white supremacy through legal machinations. The Fifteenth Amendment, ratified in 1870, was intended to protect the right to vote for men of all colors. White-controlled southern communities found so many ways—unfair literacy tests, impromptu poll taxes, registration shenanigans—to frustrate Black voting that, by 1920, the amendment had "no real force."[170]

The course of this postwar white southern "redemption" was, another historian argues, "neither smooth nor straight," and the basic facts were that the Civil War ended slavery and secured the Union's indivisibility. But even histories of Reconstruction that emphasize its triumphs must also note the successes of its resisters: "The last twilight of what had seemed once a promising day of equal rights reached its final

102   WE ARE NOT ONE PEOPLE

darkening only in the 1890s with the passage of Jim Crow laws formalizing separate facilities from streetcars to libraries to hotel elevators and legal barriers to the black vote in the cotton South."[171]

The white South may have lost the war, but they were determined to win the peace. White southerners defined the terms of their American reentry through Klan violence, Jim Crow, voter suppression, and resistance to civil rights. In *Cooper v. Aaron* (1958), the Supreme Court did what Andrew Jackson demurred doing during the 1830s mail crisis and reasserted federal supremacy. The Little Rock school board, citing hostile "massive resistance" stoked by national leaders like James J. Kilpatrick as well as community doyens, including the state's governor, hoped to delay the "deliberate speed" of integration demanded by *Brown v. Board* (1954).

But *Cooper* was not, of course, some final bell signaling the end of the contest between the federal government and the South over race. "Segregation academies," cost-effective private schools for white families fleeing integrated schooling, sprang up all over the South.[172] Scores of those schools were operational decades later even as many affluent white communities, heavily concentrated in the South, also began using local acts of secession to create new public school districts, even entirely new towns, to resegregate public schools.[173] As one analyst wrote, "School secessions, at least in the South, trace their roots to the arsenal of tools that white communities deployed to resist the desegregation mandate of the *Brown* ruling."[174]

Southern communities have used these tools on far more than schools. The Supreme Court, in *Shelby Co. v. Holder* (2013), decided that nine mostly southern states no longer had to seek federal approval to change their election laws, as had been mandated since the Voting Rights Act in 1965. Chief Justice John Roberts summarized the majority's reasoning: "Our country has changed."[175] Such race-conscious voting protections were outdated. Alabama began requiring photo identification to vote within hours of the ruling, and nearly every other southern state followed Alabama's lead.[176]

White southerners asserted control of the historical narrative as well. In "one of the most consequential acts of falsification in American history," Edward Pollard, Jefferson Davis, Alexander Stephens, and other ex-Confederates and sympathizers created the Lost Cause, stripping slavery from the story of southern secession.[177] Decades later, residents of towns like Abbeville, South Carolina, Calhoun's birthplace, waxed nostalgic about their hopes of southern restoration: "The world shall yet decide, in truth's clear, far-off light, that the soldiers who wore the gray and died with Lee were in the right."[178]

Several intellectual founders of post–World War II American conservatism were schooled in this revanchist tradition. Richard Weaver cast the antebellum South as Thermopylae, a besieged premodern civilization holding the line against the flattening horde of scientific modernity.[179] M. E. Bradford, quite similarly, "worshipped reverent, gray-clad soldiers and the pious officers who led them."[180] In the 1970s, he gathered dozens of young conservative college students for screenings of *Birth of a Nation*; he dramatically performed the silent film's captions for his enraptured audience.[181] "The legitimacy of secession," one scholar concludes, "was at the heart of the Lost Cause and remains a potent symbol today for those seeking to deny the centrality of slavery to secession."[182]

It would be an oversimplification to say that these conservatives specifically or most southerners generally have always resisted any national threat to regional white dominance by doing anything up to and including seceding. Nevertheless, just as resisting civil rights and romanticizing the antebellum South have been recurring themes among southern conservatives of the twentieth century, a southern "penchant for resistance" to racial equality has been evident in every period of American history.[183] William Tecumseh Sherman's prediction about the recalcitrance of conquered southerners was better and broader than he could have known: "We cannot change the hearts of those people of the South, but we can make war so terrible . . . that generations would pass away before they would again appeal to it."[184]

Contemporary organizations like the League of the South promoted southern nationalism in publications, conferences, and chapter meetings hoping to reconvince a new generation of southerners that, under "the cover of multiculturalism," the federal government would "destroy Western civilization generally and Southern culture specifically."[185] In the service of white dominance, some powerful southerners have been, as one scholar put it, "in search of another country" since the nation began.[186]

4

White Devils and Black Separatists

Born into and escaped from slavery, witness to and object of personal, routine, and institutional violence for two decades of bondage, Frederick Douglass nevertheless thought America could change. In 1845, it took $700 from English donors to buy his legal freedom, yet Douglass continued to look for political freedom within, not beyond, America. He was no naïf with a hard head and a rosy outlook; he believed that the same society that coddled his slavers and supported his enslavement could become one where races coexisted in relative, genuine peace. Americans, he thought, were better than their worst instincts. Douglass's politics were patient and forgiving.

Douglass's estimation of what was possible in mid-nineteenth-century America grew from his larger theory of nations. Nations, he thought, were composites of their inhabitants, including but not limited to their legal citizens. Nationality did not flow in blood; it was not buried in soil. Nations emerged in people's shared practices. Douglass's ideal demos was "raceless."[1] No racial group owned the national identity of "American."

Douglass was acerbic about and critical of his country, to be sure; he famously painted a "dark picture" of national hypocrisy in his 1852 speech "What to the Slave Is the Fourth of July?" Nevertheless, Douglass professed an abiding faith that America was an inclusive idea, especially the aspirational nation developed in the Declaration of Independence.[2] "He remembered when," one historian recounts, "as a boy clandestinely teaching himself to read, he had pored over a book of political oratory from the Revolution, deciphering the stirring words one letter at a time."[3] "Nations," Douglass said as he closed his Fourth of July speech, "do not now stand in the same relation to each other that they did ages ago. No nation can now shut itself up, from the surrounding world, and trot round in the same old path of its fathers without interference." Reason, science, global commerce,

We Are Not One People. Michael J. Lee and R. Jarrod Atchison, Oxford University Press. © Oxford University Press 2022. DOI: 10.1093/oso/9780190876500.003.0005

106 WE ARE NOT ONE PEOPLE

and communication technology opened city gates, destroyed national walls, and webbed the world together; times were changing. Douglass crescendoed, "No abuse, no outrage whether in taste, sport or avarice, can now hide itself from the all-pervading light."[4]

He believed fervently that reason would guide social and political progress, that it could illuminate the "arrogant and malignant nonsense about natural repellancy and the incompatibility of races."[5] America could become, as one historian summarized Douglass's view, "truer to its ideal self."[6]

Emigration, or colonization—the proposal that former enslaved people and free Black people should move to Africa, Haiti, or some other foreign locale—had both white and Black champions in the late eighteenth century and throughout the nineteenth century.[7] White colonization advocates—Henry Clay, Daniel Webster, Abraham Lincoln, James Madison—wielded massive political power.[8] Jefferson, perhaps looking out a Monticello window onto enslaved persons, supported repatriation on grounds of individual morality and public safety. The coexistence of races, each endowed by their creator with unequal capabilities, would, he predicted, "produce convulsions which will probably never end but in the extermination of the one or the other race."[9] Some white abolitionists supported colonization because it allowed them to envision a world where abolition did not presage integration. Former enslaved people could take their newfound freedom, equality, and inalienable rights elsewhere.[10]

Denmark Vesey planned to fight his way to freedom in Haiti. His intricately planned but ultimately foiled slave revolt in Charleston in 1822 was inspired, in fact, by the Haitian example of slaves throwing off their captors to govern themselves.[11] Haiti was more than a model, however; it was also Vesey's intended destination after he and his fellow rebels raided an arsenal, torched parts of Charleston, and set out on stolen ships.[12]

As early as 1851, Douglass rejected such dreams of exodus regardless of whether the dreamers were white or Black or whether the means were peaceful or violent.[13] To him, emigration plots were far-fetched and small-minded. For all his faith in the changing times and the American multiethnic democratic experiment, however, Douglass was staggered in late 1860 and early 1861 as southern states became increasingly adamant and arrogant in their assertion of slavers' rights.

WHITE DEVILS AND BLACK SEPARATISTS   107

Douglass felt that his abolitionist colleagues were distracted by their own secessionist schemes and insufficiently focused on what should be the primary goal: ending slavery.[14]

Pro-Unionists even attacked Douglass and other Black abolitionists at Boston's Tremont Hall on December 3, 1860. Five Black men were seriously injured in the melee.[15] Later that night, an incensed Douglass broke with moral suasion and opted for a more militant path. Slavers might change, Douglass intoned at a Boston church, if they sensed "death in the air."[16] The election of 1860, which Douglass hoped might swing decidedly in favor of abolition, ended with the triangulating, milquetoast Lincoln as the victor.[17] The new president, Douglass concluded, "seemed neither strong enough to preserve the Union, nor moral enough to champion emancipation."[18] Douglass read Lincoln's first inaugural address as a declaration of indifference about slavery.[19] Its high lines about "mystic chords" and "better angels" were but supplications to slavers. Lincoln, Douglass wrote, prostrated himself "before the foul and withering curse of slavery" as he assumed the presidency.[20]

As the prospects of a multihued American democracy began to dim, Douglass found colonization and racial self-determination more attractive. He even booked passage to Haiti, then the most prominent emigration destination, on April 25, 1861, for what was planned to be a visit of "six or eight weeks." Describing the trip as a fact-finding mission, Douglass nevertheless rhapsodized about Haiti's glories before the journey, suggesting what dazzling facts he expected to find. He was elated by the thought of "standing once upon the soil of San Domingo, the theatre of many stirring events and heroic achievements, the work of a people, bone of our bone, and flesh of our flesh." In the first Black republic, he would not have to debate which tactic might best convince slavers that people were not property; he would not have to defeat theories of natural racial inferiority; he would not face the *Sturm und Drang* he saw at Tremont Hall; he would not face incredulity and disbelief even among fellow abolitionists; he would not have to risk his life as a Black abolitionist in a violent slave society. For a moment, Haiti was a refuge from and a repudiation of American racism:

> Born a slave as we were, in this boasted land of liberty, tinged with
> a hated color, despised by the rulers of the State, accustomed from

108 WE ARE NOT ONE PEOPLE

childhood to hear the colored race disparaged and denounced, their mental and moral qualities held in contempt, treated as an inferior race, incapable of self government, and of maintaining, when left to themselves, a state of civilization, set apart by the laws of our being to a condition of slavery—we, naturally enough, desire to see, as we doubtless shall see, in the free, orderly and Independent Republic of Hayti, a refutation of the slanders and disparagements of our race.

Douglass called upon the touchstone Western tale of an oppressed people seeking their promised land. Haiti was the "modern land of Canaan" to which "our people" could escape from "the rigorous bondage and oppression of our modern Egypt."[21]

Edmund Ruffin and his band of Confederate irregulars fired on Fort Sumter on April 12, 1861, just shy of two weeks before Douglass's planned Haitian voyage. Douglass was elated. Upon hearing that southerners had struck first, he cheered, "Thank God!—the slaveholders themselves have saved our cause from ruin!"[22] Douglass's essay announcing his departure had already gone to press when he learned of the attack in Charleston; he canceled the trip abruptly and let readers know why in a short coda: "The last ten days have made a tremendous revolution in all things pertaining to the possible future of the colored people of the United States. We shall stay here and watch the current of events, and serve the cause of freedom and humanity in any way that shall be open to us during the struggle now going on between the slave power and the government." Douglass hoped that war between the free North and the slave South was imminent. "At any rate," he wrote with succinct shrewdness, "this is no time for us to leave the country."[23] Americans would fight Americans to settle, maybe once and for all, what the American Revolution meant, and Douglass was not going to sit it out, even in the Canaan of the Caribbean.

In Search of Space

Self-determination is the cause to which Frederick Douglass dedicated his public life. But self-determination is tricky when multiple selves seek determination in and of the same place. Charting a new

WHITE DEVILS AND BLACK SEPARATISTS   109

course where people of a certain ilk, a *Volk*, could self-govern unencumbered without considering the competing desires of other races briefly held Douglass in thrall in early 1861. The idea of a pure Black nation, a Black demos separate from white people, a nation as both an escape from white supremacy and a place to actualize as a people, an "Afrotopia," has captivated African Americans for centuries.[24] This chapter traces the Black nationalist tradition in America as a keystone example of separatist arguments based on race or ethnicity.

The Black activist tradition often typified by Martin Luther King's integrationist dream of a multiethnic children's choir singing "free at last" also features three centuries of people who dreamed of Black choirs singing freedom songs about Black nations to Black audiences. Some scholars figure nationalism as one of four broad categories of Black activism. Integrationists fought for equal legal and social standing. Pluralists saw America as composed of legally equal but socially separate races, each marshaling resources in their own enclaves. Nationalists aspired to separation, both culturally and territorially. Revolutionaries aimed to topple the nation entirely.[25]

Although useful in outlining historical trends in Black activism, analyzing the variety of thinkers and activists in just one of these four categories can be "like trying to eat Jell-O with chopsticks." Some "roguish types," moreover, refuse neat categorization.[26] It is easy to imagine, for instance, an advocate in every one of these categories encouraging Black voters to vote for a Black sheriff. While often considered the "father of black nationalism," the multitalented nineteenth-century activist, physician, publisher, and author Martin Delaney was also a categorical rogue.[27] He helmed an "African movement" in the 1850s and sailed to Liberia in 1859 to explore the possibility of resettling freed African Americans there. After the Civil War commenced, however, he was commissioned as a major in the federal army. He was then active in Reconstruction-era Republican party politics in South Carolina before resuming his back-to-Africa advocacy.[28]

Like Delany, other individuals and organizations, like the Congress of Racial Equality or the Student Non-violent Coordinating Committee, evolved through categories. Some, like the Revolutionary Action Movement, began as staunch nationalists but ended as ardent revolutionaries.[29] The Black Panthers' 1966 ten-point program

110   WE ARE NOT ONE PEOPLE

listed both revolutionary and separatist goals before recreating the Declaration of Independence.[30] After much ideological searching, Black Panther icon Huey Newton settled on revolutionary confrontation to erase America from the earth's nations; nevertheless, he still acknowledged that Black "secession" was "perfectly justified" as a tactical goal, that fighting for specific territory had "psychological value."[31] A whole host of Black freedom activists, regardless of categorical designation, employed "some variety of separatist tactics."[32] Some elements of the Black freedom struggle are just difficult to classify. Black power, one scholar concludes, "remains an enigma."[33]

These categories can, in short, mask conceptual chaos. Some scholars now prefer the label "Black radicalism" to "nationalism" or "separatism."[34] Even the latter two terms can be troubling. The self-defense activist Robert Williams thought nationalism was a "meaningless" label implying an exclusive interest in problems faced by Black communities. He thought of himself as an "Inter-Nationalist," as did many other Black advocates of self-determination who fought the colonization of people of color.[35]

In some ways, classifying some protests as separatist puts a thumb on the historical scale. Any separation requires at least an initial integration, some first act of consenting to be governed. Part of Black nationalists' fundamental point is that violent exploitation is a dominant theme in the Black experience in America. It would be senseless to say that someone was "separated" from prison upon their release because they did not desire imprisonment in the first place. Black people, therefore, did not seek separation from America; they sought liberation.

Nevertheless, nationalism and separatism are broadly useful, if imperfect, in describing programmatic and performative differences among activists. Nationalists and separatists, to put it simply, talked about achieving collective identity through acts of exit. Whereas civil rights leaders talked about American justice as a lost ideal, revolutionaries talked about seizing the nation's reins of power and instituting a new justice. Black nationalists talked about American justice as an oxymoron. Where the moral status of white people was concerned, reformers and revolutionaries held much more in common with each other than they did with nationalists.

WHITE DEVILS AND BLACK SEPARATISTS 111

Nationalism is a multicentury story of "black discontent" in America as well as a search for Black space within or beyond their captor nation.[36] Black nationalism, in fact, is among the earliest modern expressions of nationalism, but it was sourced not in the salons of Paris but in deeply human desires for a safe home amid grinding horrors.[37]

In Boston in 1773, four enslaved people petitioned the legislature to grant them one day per week so that they might make money to buy their freedom and return to Africa.[38] "The first man in this country to die in the war for independence," Stokely Carmichael (later Kwame Ture) educated an audience in 1967, "was a black man named Crispus Attucks! A black man!" Toying with the audience's expectations, he switched course. Instead of using Attucks's story to show historic Black sacrifice in America; he called Attucks "a fool." Attucks "got shot for white folks" when "he should have gotten his brothers together to take care of natural business."[39] He died, in other words, for white nationalism rather than Black nationalism.

Carmichael gave credence to the "alienation," "differentness," and "separateness" many Black people felt during the American Revolutionary era. The Haitian revolt of 1791, the fullest expression of nationalist natural business, enchanted Frederick Douglass and nineteenth-century Black nationalists. Toussaint L'Ouverture "became a central figure in the black nationalist pantheon of heroes."[40] One African American writer in the early nineteenth century even said that when he thought about the "inimitable" Declaration of Independence, with "all its scope and strength," he thought not of Jefferson but of L'Ouverture.[41]

The epic overthrow of imperial control in Haiti captured the imaginations of early Black nationalists, but nationalist impulses were also evident in smaller, more furtive activities. Slave rebellions, for instance, of the seventeenth or eighteenth century may not look like the Haitian Revolution or later nationalists' goals to separate from "whites *qua* whites."[42] These uprisings as well as the secret settlements of free Black people, escaped enslaved persons, and Native Americans in swamps and the Sea Islands, however, definitively expressed "a desire for self-determination."[43] Other, less explicitly revolutionary Black nationalisms evident at the nation's beginning exhibited the full range of nationalist rhetorical and material resourcefulness. The first all-Black

112   WE ARE NOT ONE PEOPLE

church in America was founded in Silver Bluff, South Carolina, in the 1770s.[44] These churches—African Methodist Episcopal, African Methodist Episcopal Zion, and Abyssinian Baptist—"epitomize" early Black nationalism.[45]

In this chapter, we highlight the fulsomeness of the Black nationalist vocabulary.[46] The full nationalist rhetorical spectrum includes advocates who urged the creation of separate Black styles of dress, modes of speech, organizations, rifle clubs, schools, stores, churches, neighborhoods, cities, states, nation-states, and polities generally, all "alternatives to the oppressive social institutions" that "dominated" Black life in America.[47]

We highlight the various Black nations nationalists have imagined as both strategic goals and comforting dreams, the sheer number of individuals and organizations who concluded that America was always and forever a racist nation, and, therefore, that new possibilities for Black people required a new beginning.[48] As Robin D. G. Kelley argues, "The desire to leave Babylon, if you will, and search for a new land tells us a great deal about what people dream about, what they want, how they might want to reconstruct their lives."[49]

We have pored over influential nationalist books and speeches ranging from proto-nationalists in the antebellum period to Black power advocates in 1960s and 1970s, and we focus our claim, in particular, on how Black separatists specifically and nationalists generally consecrated physical space. As Amiri Baraka (né LeRoi Jones) said, "Can you dig it, *space*? . . . *Space* is what we're fighting for."[50]

Black nationalists concluded that white racism made American life largely unlivable and that separation was essential to safety and self-discovery. From there, nationalists entertained a pageant of possibilities. It is no exaggeration to say that millions of nationalists have thought exit to be the wise choice while disagreeing about how to leave and where to go. Their divergence on the question of how to achieve spatial separation was both tactical and philosophical. But this divergence was also introspective; there have been many different visions of Black separatism in part because there have been so many different conceptions of Black peoplehood. When we examine not any particular variant of Black nationalist discourse but many different renditions of it, what stands out is not any particular argument of Black

WHITE DEVILS AND BLACK SEPARATISTS   113

essence but instead an array, not a singular theory of Black peoplehood but a medley.

Marxist nationalists thought Black people needed land to build communal wealth. Black capitalists thought land was the building block of individual wealth. Black Christians thought land would allow the community to build on existing solidarity found in Black churches. Black Muslims thought land would stimulate the recovery of a lost faith. Nationalists of virtually every variety thought land would galvanize the rescue of a stolen culture.

Furthermore, a whole host of advocates who might be called existentialist nationalists held that for African Americans, since so much African heritage had been taken during the Middle Passage and so much American heritage had been forced during slavery, separation was necessary to work out Black peoplehood, to explore it. As the scholar Yohuru Williams notes, "The very prerequisite for classical nationalism—identification with a specific place tied to a distinct history and culture—was already in that sense absent from Black nationalism."[51] Land was the beginning of Black nationalism, not its endpoint. One activist wrote in 1970, "America is not our home and never will be. We have no country. Only each other. Among ourselves, we have created a sense of nationhood, but without land a nation does not exist."[52] That is, Black space preceded Black essence, not the other way around. "We are about to have a new life—a risen life—a life of knowing ourselves," Marcus Garvey predicted during an Easter speech in 1922.[53]

Black advocates of self-determination have also disagreed consistently about the location of their promised land. To wit, they envisioned homelands in current Black communities, some in new American communities, some on the long-denied forty acres of land somewhere in America, some southern, some in American states like Kansas or Oklahoma, some in upstart, Black-run "Soul Cities," even a federated constellation of non-contiguous "Ghetto States," some in but not of America, some not in but of Africa, some actually in Africa, maybe a New Africa in America, some Caribbean, one in Cyprus, and one in Baja, California.

Endorsing a sentiment of "anywhere but here," others have been rather lax about the location of this new national sanctuary.[54] All told,

114 WE ARE NOT ONE PEOPLE

nationalists celebrated land, and solidarity as a collective people on that land, while disagreeing energetically about the ideal conduct and organization of a Black nation on Black soil, regardless of locale. They coveted space to express Black distinctiveness and cultural solidarity in virtually every way possible: linguistically, religiously, culturally, politically, economically, and artistically.

Emphasizing this diversity of nationalist paeans to space is not to say that no common discourse about space existed. For nationalists, land may have been a vessel to celebrate many different values, but nationalists hewed to shared terms to describe their Zion. First, it was theirs. The land was Black land; it was not shared. The land was owned and operated by a free people descended from those who were themselves property and forced to labor on someone else's property. Ownership of land meant the possibility of riches, but it also meant the possibility of solitude, the chance to be left alone as a people. Land meant safety and solidarity. Black nationalists have "had to adopt the revolutionary axiom which held that land is the basis of a people's independence."[55]

Second, land meant space and opportunity. Whereas enslaved people were denied every opportunity to make choices for themselves, their families, and their communities, land ownership afforded seemingly endless choices. Whereas enslaved people were denied mobility, space enabled uncontrolled movement. Land meant, to borrow Erich Fromm's phrasing, "freedom from" and "freedom to" at the same time.[56] Finally, land meant a consistent, permanent home. For a kidnapped people, for a people subjected to bondage then peonage, for a people possessing what W. E. B. Du Bois called a "double consciousness" of an insider and an outsider, a home meant material, psychological, and spiritual stability. Symbolically, nationalists depicted land as the means of secular and spiritual deliverance; it could give them what the end of the Civil War, Reconstruction, several constitutional amendments, and a variety of anti-discrimination acts could not: true independence from white supremacy. A brutal war, the end of slavery, and many legislative acts could not solve white racism, but land could remove white control.[57] "What time is it?" Amiri Baraka would ask rhetorically at nationalist rallies. "It's Nation time! The land is gonna change hands."[58]

Black nationalists have pressed these claims for space using Pan-African, anti-colonial, Marxist, Christian, and many other rhetorical resources, but they have also used texts about which they were profoundly ambivalent, especially the core texts of American politics: the Declaration of Independence and the Constitution.[59] These texts were source materials for slavers, but two centuries of nationalists have found rhetorical power in figuring the Black freedom struggle in America as somewhat akin to the American colonists' fight against England.

Nationalists "justified their calls for dramatic, even violent action using similar concepts to those employed by George Mason and Thomas Jefferson."[60] They sardonically saluted Jefferson and other founding American slave owners.[61] They cited the founders to escape the founders and their heirs. They declared independence from the Declaration of Independence. David Ruggles, a conductor of the Underground Railroad who died in 1849, couched a defense of "exclusive" Black-only activism in the notion that all nations rise and fall by following the principles of equality "as taught by the Revolutionary Father of our country in the Declaration of Independence."[62]

Such references to American civic hallmarks were so frequent that Bindley C. Cyrus, a Chicago-based leader of the 49th State movement, an effort to create an all-Black American state, was questioning this rhetorical strategy by the mid-1930s. "Calling down maledictions," he wrote, "upon the heads of the dominant majority" and "invoking the sacred clauses of the Declaration of Independence and the United States Constitution" was going nowhere.[63] In much of the cardinal Black nationalist literature, America necessitated, justified, and prevented Black separatism all at the same time.

Snakes and Lusting Devils

Since the early eighteenth century, Black nationalists of all stripes have asserted that white racism made the peaceful coexistence of the races impossible. They have argued, both explicitly and by implication, that white people were racist, murderous, imperious, exploitative, petty, crafty, and deceitful psychopaths. Their nature was, in a word, immutable; white people were irredeemable.

116 WE ARE NOT ONE PEOPLE

Charging white people with racism, of course, was not unique to Black separatists. What separated their particular charges of essential racism from integrationists and revolutionaries was the notion that racist violence was inevitable; white people could not help themselves. As one historian asked, "What was whitey *really* like? . . . It was possible that whites weren't even fully human. If they were, ice water filled their veins."[64]

If white people were always untrustworthy as strangers or neighbors, if their promises of justice or reform were always made with crossed fingers, then separation was the only realistic hope. Fighting for civil rights in a white world was a fool's errand; a full-bore, Black-led revolution would be crushed by a wealthy white majority in control of military machinery, would be riven by infighting provoked by woke white joiners, or, even if somehow successful in altering the form of government, would still inevitably flounder if white people could settle in the post-revolutionary nation. That is, both civil rights leaders and Black revolutionaries had at least some faith in the possibility of white redemption; separatists did not.

The stories Black separatists told about white America differed in this one fundamental way from those of later revolutionaries like Newton, Angela Davis, or Assata Shakur or civil rights leaders like King or Bayard Rustin.[65] Fannie Lou Hamer, for instance, affirmed that both Black and white people were entitled to citizenship and that the latter had "souls that could be saved" with the aid of the former. She called out white supremacy antagonistically, but "even Hamer's most confrontational speeches included a glimpse of hope."[66] Separatists thought white people were born racists; any attempt to parse white audiences into a more complicated body, any attempt to find some hopeful trend in American history, was delusional. Even the most broad-minded, well-meaning white people could not be counted on. "If blacks wait for radical whites to get themselves together so that there can be a revolution," one writer worried in *Ebony* in 1970, "we may just end up as nothing more than a memory in world history, with white folks sitting around playing old Ray Charles records and remembering what it was like when there were niggers around."[67] White racism was a static American evil.

As much as King and other civil rights leaders employed a religious language of forgiveness, one that figured moral suasion as a vital tool to

WHITE DEVILS AND BLACK SEPARATISTS 117

aid white America's recalibration of its conscience, Black nationalists told religious stories to posit white essence. These stories, mainstays of Black nationalist discourse, were populated by Black angels and white devils.

Among the earliest uses of this imagery appears in David Walker's *Appeal to the Coloured Citizens of the World* (1829). Walker's *Appeal* was a protest assemblage; powerful, even revolutionary, rebukes of white behavior mixed with rallying cries aimed at the Black community, rehearsals of Thomas Paine, lines from the Declaration of Independence, and a satirical take on the Constitution.[68] Walker was unsparing in his description of race in America; Black people, he argued, were treated worse than Israelites had been in ancient Egypt. At least Egyptians did not call Jews "Monkeys or Orang-Outangs." Suggesting long-standing white villainy, Walker went on to cite far-reaching historical examples of white conquest including Greece, Rome, Gaul, Spain, and Great Britain.[69] "The whites," Walker declared, "have always been an unjust, jealous, unmerciful, avaricious and blood-thirsty set of beings, always seeking after power and authority." They were "more like devils than accountable men."[70]

Walker's *Appeal* is plausibly considered an early "black nationalist text in the sense of calling for, and seeking to create unity, self-respect, and self-help among all people of African descent." Paradoxically, however, Walker also, like Douglass and unlike most later nationalists, criticized colonization and pushed these white devils to accept Black equality.[71] Many of Walker's acolytes who took up the language of white evil fit neatly within the separatist tradition.

The roster of luminaries of many nationalist movements, Black and otherwise, is often male dominated. Maria Stewart, a lecturer and key contributor to Garrison's *The Liberator* in the 1830s, is an important correction to that reductive narrative. Stewart leaned on Walker explicitly as she took some of his precepts about white behavior to their logical conclusion. Walker impugned white evil but then urged Black equality alongside devils. Stewart, instead, encouraged "African Americans to prepare for literal battle."[72] She thought America was a modern Babylon, and Black people would have to fight their way out.[73] Ironically, within Garrison's otherwise pacifist magazine, Stewart urged a violent solution to slavery based on the mutual understanding and empathy that free and enslaved Black people might feel for one

118   WE ARE NOT ONE PEOPLE

another. She hoped, in other words, that Black people might "love each other enough to go to war" as a unified people.[74]

Henry Highland Garnet, a Presbyterian minister to a white congregation who was also influenced by Walker, is another figure who has been read as condoning, if not encouraging, violence against white slave owners. He reprinted Walker's *Appeal* along with his own nationalist broadside, an "Address to the Slaves" (1843), employing similarly stark imagery of good and evil.[75] Garnet attempted to rally slaves against masters who committed "the highest crime against God and man." Slavers were "cursed" torturers and rapists, and slaves under their boot faced the "unbridled lusts" of these "incarnate devils."[76]

He did not, however, explicitly call for revolutionary violence. He urged, in the words of one scholar, a "general strike" and "redemption through martyrdom." He charted a "middle course" between "submission" and "revolutionary violence," a path traveled by some American Revolutionaries and Protestant reformers like Martin Luther and William Tyndale.[77]

Nationalist activists saw the collapse of Reconstruction as evidence that white people were incapable of reform, and proposals to revive colonization or move Black people out West were legion in the decades following the Civil War. But it was Marcus Garvey who converted these various nineteenth-century nationalist traditions into a mass movement, a movement some argue is among the largest in American history.[78] Garvey, the Jamaican-born self-styled potentate who spearheaded what was certainly the largest nationalist movement of the twentieth century, the United Negro Improvement Association (UNIA), occasionally voiced an origin story featuring a Black Adam and Eve in which Cain's descendants were afflicted with eternal whiteness as punishment for Abel's death.[79]

Then again, Garvey's rhetoric of absolute racial differences could take surprising turns; he construed insular self-protection and even domination of other peoples as the typical behaviors of all races, not just white people. Accordingly, when Garvey spoke about meeting with representatives of the Ku Klux Klan in 1922, he emphasized common interests, not human commonality: "Whilst the Ku Klux Klan desires to make America absolutely a white man's country, the Universal Negro Improvement Association wants to make Africa absolutely a

WHITE DEVILS AND BLACK SEPARATISTS   119

black man's country."[80] Both Garvey and the Klan's Imperial Wizard desired an ethnostate. That Garvey shared some racial vision with white racists did not mean that he saw some future for Black people in white America. Garvey applied his conclusions about the Klan to the nation as a whole: "The Ku Klux Klan represents the spirit, the feeling, the attitude of every white man in the United States of America." The organization was "really the invisible government of the United States of America."[81]

The rhetorical resources of these descriptions of white malice were not solely Christian. King once asked the Nation of Islam's Elijah Muhammad if he sincerely believed that all white people were evil. Muhammad replied with a homespun analogy built on a transcendent symbol that King knew well. He and King, Muhammad communed, were both raised in Georgia; both had seen harmless king snakes and venomous rattlesnakes. "But they are both snakes," Muhammad surmised.[82]

For much of his career in the Nation of Islam, Malcolm X, Muhammad's protégé, developed a similar line of racial reasoning. After his mid-1960s break with Muhammad and the Nation of Islam (NOI), however, he was famously inspired by the possibility of multiracial coexistence during his pilgrimage to Mecca in 1964. He began to depersonalize racism, emphasizing that white evil was not inherent but, instead, a social product of "America's racist society."[83] In short, his views on race were evolving just before his death.[84] Muhammad's reptilian metaphor, nevertheless, was still evident in the post-epiphany speeches Malcolm delivered shortly before his assassination. "We've got to give the [white] man a chance," he said in 1965. "He probably won't take it, the snake. But we've got to give him a chance."[85]

Muhammad's clever snake analogy did not explain how white people came to be snakes. Muhammad popularized an inventive origin myth that did, however. His story of human origins centered on Yacub, a defiant creator deity who annoyed Allah. The first humans Yacub created were Black. Yacub then fashioned humans of various other colors as well. After six hundred years of experimentation, in his final rebuke of Allah, he devised a mutant white race, people devoid of all pigmentation.[86] When he told audiences the story of Yacub, Malcolm called this new breed of white humans "a weak tribe, a wicked tribe, a devilish

120 WE ARE NOT ONE PEOPLE

tribe, a diabolical tribe, a tribe that is devilish by nature."[87] These pale people were a separate, sinful species. They could no sooner become virtuous than they could transform into a different species of animal.[88]

What the story of Yacub lacked in narrative complexity, it made up for in metaphoric explanatory power. Muhammad's narrative explained white racism parsimoniously: "white people oppressed nonwhites because of genetic programming."[89] It was Black Muslims' answer to the curse of Ham, a biblical interpretation of Black inferiority. According to James Baldwin, Muhammad did not need to spend much time on theological explication anyway; Black audiences in places like Harlem welcomed this reversal of cosmic racial heritage. Whether assembled in meeting halls or street corners, "they were," Baldwin argued, "merely glad to have, at last, divine corroboration of their experience, to hear—and it was a tremendous thing to hear—that they had been lied to for all these years and generations, and that their captivity was ending, for God was black."[90]

Nationalists did not only reach for grandiose descriptors or characterize white menace as supernatural sin. They made sense of white danger by employing imminent, recent, recognizable human horrors as well. Nazis may not have been literal monsters or mutant devil beings, but they were the salient face of human evil after World War II. Plus, Black accusations that white Americans were Nazis cut against any national boast about besting the Third Reich in World War II. America was the South, and the South was Germany.

Speaking after he broke with Muhammad and the NOI in 1964, Malcolm said America's treatment of Black people was "worse than some of the things that they practiced in Germany against the Jews."[91] Pursuing a similar line in *Die Nigger Die!* (1969), H. Rap Brown envisioned "america" as "the Fourth Reich," called Lyndon Johnson "Hitler's illegitimate child" and J. Edgar Hoover "his half-sister," and thundered that Black people would not "play Jews" if white people wanted "to play Nazis."[92] To Amiri Baraka, these were not epithets but plain facts. White people's "evil," he wrote, is "based on empiricism," on millions of firsthand accounts of "the lynching and oppression and enslavement of black people by Europeans."[93]

In the foundational militant book *Negroes with Guns* (1962), Robert F. Williams abjured direct accusations about all white people. He

WHITE DEVILS AND BLACK SEPARATISTS   121

substituted argumentative theses for vivid narratives about specific characters from Monroe, his hometown in North Carolina. Williams's book inspired a generation of Black nationalists, but it did so largely by implication.[94] Monroe became a stand-in for American cities under the boot of white racists. Williams wrote with a keen eye for developing white character traits as well. The white Monroe community he rendered did not regret; they did not apologize. White characters in *Negroes with Guns* had one desire: Black blood.

Williams developed visceral narratives of injustice, like one in which a white man who attempted to rape a pregnant Black woman was acquitted by an all-white jury in five minutes. The jury apparently shared the defense attorney's incredulity that the alleged attacker, who was married to a white woman, a "pure flower of life," would even want to touch the victim, a woman the attorney called "that."[95]

The Black citizens of Monroe generally faced white mobs hunting Freedom Riders, white men tearfully fretting that "niggers have got guns," a white couple driving through a Black neighborhood with an "Open Season on Coons" sign affixed to their car, white women accompanying "Klan raids" just in case "anything develops into a fight it will appear that the Negro attacked a woman and the Klansman will of course be her protector," white pilots bombing Black neighborhoods from small airplanes, white prison guards beating a "seventeen-year-old Negro girl" to death "because she complained about the bad prison food," police chiefs promising to hang Black citizens "in the courthouse square," and elected officials, including the state governor, who looked the other way. The wider white Monroe community was a racist Greek chorus in these scenes. They gathered in public squares or along roadsides and screamed, "Kill the niggers! Kill the niggers!"[96]

"A Nation Within a Nation"

For Black separatists, white devils brought Africans to America, brutalized them, and robbed them of collective self-knowledge. As the historian William Van Deburg writes, "Incapable of generating compassion for others, the 'rhythmless hearts' and hate-dulled minds of these pale-skinned creatures were said to harbor only thoughts of

122   WE ARE NOT ONE PEOPLE

death and destruction."[97] Separating from these snakes and devils was as much about the necessity of refuge as it was an opportunity for self-reflection. The nationalist argument for Black separatism has been a relatively straightforward if-then statement. If white people were devilish racists, then anyone of African descent was endangered in a white-dominated country.

Since 1776, however, untold multitudes of African Americans have dreamed about, planned for, talked about, actively sought, and, importantly, achieved new national beginnings outside the reach of white Americans. The motives and methods of Black people designing new nations have differed widely and wildly, but whether they were Muslims or Marxists, nearly all of these would-be nation-builders said that a designated landmass would allow Black people to avoid white danger and, for the first time since the first slave ships arrived in the New World in 1607, achieve their own destiny.[98]

Upon entering Howard University, which he dubbed "The Mecca" of Black knowledge, Ta-Nehisi Coates recalled his "working theory" of Black people in America: "a nation of original men severed from our original names and our majestic Nubian culture."[99] When Martin Delany, in 1859, called Black people "a nation within a nation" like "Hungarians" in Austria, he was remarking on both the territorial boundaries of nation-states and the notion that nations were built on more visceral shared characteristics. He linked race to nation; "racecraft" was statecraft.[100]

In this section, we use three case studies to illustrate three different types of nationalist theories of potential homelands for African Americans. For Marcus Garvey, land was connected to racial origins. Every ethnic group had a natural homeland, an origin point of their heritage. Since Africans were taken from their native lands, they should eventually return. For Malcolm X, land was a pragmatic opening of possibilities. It did not matter much where the land was or what it looked like. What mattered was that a people had the power to occupy and self-determine on some land. For the Republic of New Africa, homelands were established by occupancy and labor. People who put in time and effort to work some bit of land had the right to that land. As such, African Americans should establish a home country, a Republic of New Africa, in the separated states of the former Confederacy.

African Territorialism

Land, for separatists, was essential to the life of a people; exercising dominion over land was an innate drive. Self-rule without land on which to make collective decisions was purely fictional. Land was a material requirement of any Black collective achievement, and those adopting this point of view claimed to see "independence" from white America in "the clearest of political terms," that is, "the sovereign exercise of complete political authority and economic control over a contiguous mass of land."[101] Moreover, among strict territorial nationalists, such land was not a collection of individually held properties or the amalgam of Black neighborhoods or towns; land meant a sovereign nation with defensible borders. Everything else was, at best, a temporary haven.

Likely engaging more than one million African Americans, Marcus Garvey's United Negro Improvement Association (UNIA) was certainly the largest single Black nationalist organization in American history.[102] (He claimed an official organization membership total of two million by 1919 in addition to "millions of followers all over the world.")[103] Bedecked in a suit that was equal parts martial and monarchic, Garvey and his Harlem-based movement captured enormous national attention in the late 1910s and early 1920s. With his first wife, Amy Ashwood, he co-founded the UNIA in 1914 "with the program of uniting all the Negro peoples of the world into one great body to establish a country and government absolutely their own."[104]

Garvey told audiences that he had traveled the Americas, the Caribbean, and Europe as a young man and saw that Black people were outcasts everywhere. After reading Booker T. Washington's endorsement of industrial uplift for African Americans, Garvey thought, "'Where is the Black man's Government?' 'Where is his King and his kingdom?' . . . I could not find them, and then I declared, 'I will help to make them.'" Garvey said that the world was "selfish, heartless." Black people should rid themselves of any naiveté about racial cooperation, cohabitation, or charity. The natural order of things was for each race to fight "for its own interests" or for "its own domain." Garvey abided by a racial nationalist theory of human behavior and, as such, basic human organization boiled down to the representatives of "England," "Italy," or "Japan" following the "principle of self-interest."[105]

124   WE ARE NOT ONE PEOPLE

Garvey's plea for separation was premised on a prediction: an American race war was inevitable. Black people would not just lose but be eradicated: "The white man can get rid of every Negro in the United States of American in three months. . . . Instead of 15,000,000 Negroes you will have 15,000,000 coffins, and the epitaph will be: 'Died from starvation.' "[106] A terrible racial conflict was coming "in another 50 to 100 years." The race war's causes would be skin color and resources; the conflict would be an intergroup "fight for bread and position." A full and formal racial separation with "the founding of a Negro nation in Africa" was, therefore, preservative. It would, moreover, benefit Black people by affording "the fullest opportunity to develop politically, socially and industrially" while removing the jealous, interracial "eyeing" that was a harbinger of genocide.[107] Separation was nature's peace.

At points, Garvey was just as critical of the "old leadership" of the Black community as he was of white supremacy. White people, according to his theory of racial behavior, could not help it. Even Klan members were "better friends to my race for telling us what they are, and what they mean, than all the hypocrites put together," he argued.[108] Unlike white people, inadequate Black leaders could be educated. "We have been camouflaged into believing that we were made free by Abraham Lincoln," Garvey declared.[109] Black elected officials were not enough; Black voting rights were not enough; Black schools and businesses were not enough; Jesus was not enough. Garvey's "new Negro" wanted all of that and more: "We want parliament houses, houses of Congress, national museums, national art galleries, great institutions of learning of our own."[110]

Limited communal and local nationalism, the establishment of safe, prosperous enclaves in America, were essential parts of Garvey's message, which was not, as is sometimes claimed, an inflexible "back-to-Africa" program.[111] "Garvey's intellectual program was a pastiche," one of his biographers concludes, "a derivative compilation of greatest hits from nineteenth-century black intellectuals, updated to reflect the new currents of world anticolonial activism and racialism."[112] He combined "economic boosterism, Pan-Africanism, and social Darwinism" into a "militantly pro-black rhetoric."[113]

Many separatists channeled Montesquieu in supporting a small nation that faithfully represented its relatively homogeneous inhabitants.

WHITE DEVILS AND BLACK SEPARATISTS 125

Garvey, however, reversed Montesquieu; his ultimate plan was simple and sweeping. He aimed to "reawaken the scattered peoples of Africa to their natural solidarity, refocus their gaze on racial cooperation and progress, and by doing so hasten the day when the African continent would be returned to its proper owners."[114] The UNIA would commission a fleet, the Black Star Line, a "new ark" in his phrasing, that would transport selected Black people to Africa.[115]

Once a limited population of pilgrims was resettled in Africa, four hundred million Black people around the world, a strength-in-numbers appeal Garvey employed frequently, could band together and rid Africa of European oppression and unite the continent into a single, magnificent country, a "superstate" where the global diaspora might claim residency.[116] In this plan, all people of African descent might not live on the continent, but "Africa" would be "for the Africans."[117] It is telling that the first biography of Garvey, written in the 1950s, was called *Black Moses*.[118]

The idea of a continental homeland, Garvey knew, was brassy. Enemies, Garvey warned his audience, would try to equate its audacity with impossibility. They might lampoon the notion of a "free and redeemed Africa," but, he urged, citing the American experience as a precedent to depart from America, "I want you to take as your argument the thirteen colonies of America that once owed their sovereignty to Great Britain, that sovereignty has been destroyed to make a United States of America." Every Black person in Garvey's audience, he enthused, could be a "George Washington." If he could "make a free America, we too can make a free Africa."[119] So, when doubters "scorn," "spurn us," or "say that we are on the wrong side of life," he told followers to invoke the pursuit of natural rights "just the way all peoples who are free" have, and espouse the uncompromising spirit of "Liberty or Death."[120]

Garvey's message captivated significant numbers of people. Twenty-five thousand people packed Madison Square Garden for the UNIA's First International Convention of Negroes in 1920.[121] The multiple-day affair saw the ratification of a "Declaration of the Rights of the Negro Peoples of the World," which included straightforward defenses of community control within the United States and Black people electing "their own representatives." The Declaration also

126 WE ARE NOT ONE PEOPLE

relieved Black people of paying taxes and of trials by all-white juries. But these were piecemeal nationalist reforms to preserve Black dignity until the Black Star Line was fully functional. "We believe," the Declaration asserted, "in the inherent right of the Negro to possess himself of Africa, and that his possession of same shall not be regarded as an infringement on any claim or purchase made by any race or nation." The conventioneers installed Garvey as the first provisional president of Africa.[122]

"Of Our Own"

Some scholars have called Garvey the first and most popular Black separatist visionary.[123] After his arrest on flimsy mail fraud charges and subsequent exile, the UNIA flamed out. It would be three decades before another vision of Black separatism would achieve a similar cultural purchase. Garvey may have been gone, but Garveyism continued in many forms.

In 1928, the Communist International, based in part on Garvey's trailblazing, recognized "black belt" African Americans in the South as a distinct and oppressed nation with the right to self-determination. The Communist Party never fully endorsed the measure and abandoned self-determination as an international revolutionary strategy in favor of the popular front by 1935.[124]

Aside from Black separatist movements with linkages abroad, in this interim between Garvey and the nationalist hothouse of the 1960s, "small, sect-like separatist groups" proliferated, and many of Garvey's followers founded them or flocked to them.[125] Many members of Noble Drew Ali's Moorish Science Temple, for example, were Garveyites.[126] Mittie Maude Lena Gordon, a former UNIA member, founded the Peace Movement of Ethiopia in Chicago in 1932. The organization delivered a 400,000-signature petition to Franklin Roosevelt soliciting federal aid to relocate Black Americans to Africa.[127] Out of this separatist milieu would emerge calls for a nation of Black Muslims from Wallace Fard, Elijah Muhammad, Malcolm X, and the Nation of Islam.[128] Muhammad had been a Garveyite, and so had Malcolm's parents.[129]

Malcolm promoted a racial-religious nationalism throughout his Nation of Islam career. His 1950s Harlem street meetings linked "the NOI's beliefs more closely to Garveyite traditions of interest in Africa."[130] But, unlike Garvey's conception of Africa as an ancestral homeland, the NOI's interest in Africa included the reclamation of African cultural traditions and Islamic practice. The NOI wanted Africans to be of Africa without consistently proposing any back-to-Africa program; Garvey wanted Africans in Africa without much emphasis on what it meant to be African. In fact, many Nation of Islam references to future Black territory were "couched in eschatological language or hidden in cryptic references."[131] The amount of land, the location of that land, and reparations to be paid by the U.S. government in addition to any land cessions varied quite broadly even among NOI spokespeople. Malcolm sometimes invoked an African homeland; he also joked that he just hoped to end up somewhere warm.[132]

Malcolm's nationalism was, however, remarkably consistent and humorless in a few important ways. First, despite his reputation for rhetorical fireworks, he discussed the NOI's national goal in plain, sensible, even restrained language. In many of his early speeches, he said the NOI merely sought "some land of our own."[133] It was a self-evidently reasonable refrain, purposefully understated and fit for a culture well versed in the virtues of personal ownership and private property. Audiences encountered the idea of a new Black nation in two disarming terms: "some land."

Malcolm, moreover, presented this goal not as a request, or even as a demand, but as a trade that might, as Garvey had suggested decades before, forestall racial violence. He styled this transaction in the if-then form in which the initial, more palatable premise invited audiences to consider a far more radical conclusion: "If we are part of America, then part of what she is worth belongs to us. We will take our share and depart, then this white country can have peace."[134] Any other solution guaranteed "violence and bloodshed."[135] Malcolm dressed up a radical political proposal, the mass exodus of African Americans into a new Black nation, in the simple language of a safe, smart swap.

Whereas Garvey and other nationalists linked particular lands to racial nations, Africa to Black people and so forth, Malcolm developed a less heritage-based and more material case that the ownership of land,

128   WE ARE NOT ONE PEOPLE

any resource-rich land, underpinned all self-determination. Acquiring "some land" was essential, not this or that land. With "some land that we can call our own," he told a Berkeley crowd in 1963, Black people could exercise total independence "instead of waiting on the American white man to solve our problems for us." On this land, Black people would develop agriculture, grow food, raise cattle, make bricks, log forests, build homes, and generally prosper "among our own people." More than any other factor, he concluded, "land" meant "economic security," was "essential to freedom, justice, and equality," and allowed "true independence."[136]

Theorizing a truly independent Black nation was political goal-setting; it was also Malcolm's cultural cudgel. His militant separatism was designed to disabuse "black listeners of their hope in liberalism" and spark their "interest in black nationalism as an alternative site to imagine political agency."[137] Support for Black nationalism was the basic difference between, in Malcolm's infamous dichotomy, the "house Negro" and the "field Negro." The former begged to be accepted by white people in white lands; the latter was "not interested in being around you." The former identified with white people and white heroes; the latter thought as a Black person and venerated Black heroes. The former found forebearers among white Pilgrims at Plymouth Rock; the latter knew their ancestors had survived slave ships. The former loved Uncle Sam; the latter knew he was a criminal. The former spoke the white man's language; the latter spoke a language of Black solidarity. The former married white women; the latter practiced racial purity. The "house Negro" wanted a white world; the "field Negro" wanted "something of his own."[138] Whereas the "house Negro," as one scholar put it, "embodied the subservience and internalized oppression that obscured black relationality to the diaspora," the "field Negro" "dreamed of freedom, of escape."[139]

Malcolm built this material case for territorial self-determination in part by reinterpreting American cultural commonplaces as justifications for Black nationalism. The master's treasured tales countenanced Black departure from the master's house. Helping audiences see, for the first time, familiar fables as separatist psalms, Malcolm framed his role as that of a visionary.

Like many American separatists, he compared modern African Americans and ancient Jews. Moses's people, he said during a Howard University debate with Bayard Rustin in 1960, "were probably the closest parallel to the problems confronting the so-called Negro."[140] He told a Queens audience that same year that ancient "integration" actually caused "disintegration." Racial proximity caused racial violence. God's plan was the opposite; God separated enslaved people from masters and liberated strangers from strange lands.

Moses, too, was a divinely inspired separatist helping end "the enslavement of the Hebrews in the land of Egypt under Pharaoh."[141] Malcolm told Yale students in 1962 that neither Moses nor Jesus taught integration.[142] Citing an unnamed biblical lesson, presumably one found in Deuteronomy, Malcolm preached that former slave masters should give former enslaved persons "something to help him get started on his own."[143] Unsurprisingly, Malcolm expressed kindred affinity with modern Zionists who "got their own state, their own country."[144]

Beyond holy stories adapted for American audiences deeply familiar with biblical passages, Malcolm also turned to American civil religion to make the case for separation. He issued his own declaration of independence in a 1964 speech after his split from the NOI.[145] He cited "Ol' Patrick Henry" to an Oxford audience as proof that "liberty or death" only seemed extreme when a Black person said it.[146]

These examples were part of a larger strategic maneuver of Malcolm's to prove that uprisings to control land, nationalist revolutions, were the common sense of the modern world. "Look at the American Revolution in 1776," he implored in 1963. "That revolution was for what? For land. Why did they want land? Independence. How was it carried out? Bloodshed." The French Revolution, he continued, pitted "the land-less against the landlord."[147] The Russians also practiced revolutionary "white nationalism."[148] The history of modern conflict was, he implied, the history of nationalist land claims. It should surprise no one that African Americans were making one too.

Many American audiences saw themselves as heirs to a democratic revolution and deified those separatist revolutionaries as the original American patriots. Malcolm spelled this link out in, again, a

130   WE ARE NOT ONE PEOPLE

straightforward if-then proposition where the self-evident obviousness of the opening camouflaged a daring gambit: "If Patrick Henry and all of the Founding Fathers of this country were willing to lay down their lives to get what you are enjoying today, then it's time for you to realize that a large, ever-increasing number of Black people in this country are willing to die for what we know is due us by birth."[149] Black people, in his appeals, wanted only what white people, commemorated in daily acts of flag-waving and anthem-singing, had achieved when they bucked England. Black people may have had a different lineage, one descended from Nat Turner, Hannibal, L'Ouverture, and grandmothers who "rocked the cradle of civilization," but they were similarly entitled to the "inalienable right" of everyone to control their "own destiny."[150]

New Africans

Malcolm X's broad appeal to Black activists as a herald of Black liberation, his cachet as a preacher of Black pride, and his mystique as a truth-teller to the white power structure were amplified by his death in 1965.[151] He was, in one historian's estimation, "the avatar of a new movement for black liberation, one anchored in the quest for self-determination epitomized by Garveyism and its many variations that would come to be known as Black Power."[152] Ta-Nehisi Coates remembered coming to college as a Malcolm devotee, but the Howard history department had seen "so many Malcolmites before and were ready."[153]

Malcolm's ghost "loomed large" for many groups preaching separatism: formal nationalists, piecemeal nationalists who worked to build on existing racial separation, cultural nationalists looking to create an authentic everyday Blackness.[154] One journalist said Malcolm's dream of a Black nation was "dreamed quite regularly" among "the black intelligentsia," with most disputes moving easily past the obvious "desirability of separation" to the "means" as well as "the geographic area to be demanded of whitey."[155]

Few organizations were as dedicated to Malcolm's memory as clearly as the Republic of New Africa (RNA).[156] Richard and Milton Henry (later Imari and Gaidi Obadele) were pallbearers at Malcolm's funeral; they worked with Betty Shabazz, his widow, to create the RNA. Milton, who lost a congressional campaign to John Conyers in 1964, experienced a nationalist conversion when he accompanied Malcolm to Africa. Meetings with Black government officials in West African nations eroded whatever early skepticism he possessed about a separate, sovereign, self-governing Black nation.[157] Although they followed what Richard termed the "Malcolm X doctrine" of "land, self-defense, and internationalization," their land goals were far more specific than the NOI's.[158] They wanted a formal Black nation in the Deep South.[159]

Garvey had identified Africa in total as the land of milk and honey; Malcolm called for "some land"; the Henry brothers staked their claim to militancy on inhabiting the former Confederacy. They chose symbolically powerful lands, white America's secession epicenter, but they were relentlessly practical about this radical goal. Speaking, for instance, about a New African electricity grid, Milton noted that even "remote rural areas of Mississippi, Louisiana, Alabama, Georgia, and South Carolina" had "electrical and telephone wires and radio and television towers," infrastructure that would accelerate their new nation's modernization.[160]

Developed ports in Charleston and New Orleans would aid international trade as well as national defense efforts. In terms of national aesthetics, however, Milton was remiss not to expand the proposed Deep South boundaries, South Carolina to Louisiana, to include North Carolina's "beautiful weather and fragrant pines, mountains, and coastal beaches."[161] RNA publications throughout the 1970s routinely concluded with a demand to "free the land!"[162]

The Republic of New Africa was an organization name and a state. In May 1969, Imari even traveled to Washington to initiate bilateral negotiations between the RNA and America. He delivered a document demanding the territorial cession of South Carolina, Georgia, Alabama, Mississippi, and Louisiana as well as the sum of $200 billion—the figure would later climb to $800 billion—to what he thought were assistants to Dean Rusk, the secretary of state. The recipients were not, however, State Department officials; they were police officers. When asked what they had done with the demand for territory and treasure, one vaguely remembered turning it over to "the bureau of African affairs, I believe, because they call themselves 'New Africa.'"[163]

132 WE ARE NOT ONE PEOPLE

A provisional government of the Republic of New Africa was, in fact, elected at a Detroit convention in 1968.[164] Robert F. Williams, then in voluntary exile in China, was named the first president. RNA offices were put to regular votes, sometimes in "national black elections" like those held in 1975 and 1978 in which thousands participated.[165] Although the role of main spokesperson for the RNA would shift from Milton to Imari in 1970 because of a tactical and relational fallout, the RNA's vision of an inchoate Black nation held captive in America stayed constant. Africans, the brothers argued in books, articles, and pamphlets for over a decade, had been brought to America as slaves, not citizens. As Imari wrote in an open letter to Jimmy Carter in 1978, the Constitution's "fugitive slave provision" in Article IV "was in essence a federal declaration of war against the freedom of the Afrikan slave, against the New Afrikan nation, *within* the United States."[166]

Given that municipal governments began distinguishing enslaved people and white laborers from one another as early as 1660, the North American war against the African predated the American one.[167] Two hundred years later, the Thirteenth and Fourteenth Amendments should have accounted for this separate multicentury legal status. Instead, the post–Civil War amendments foisted citizenship on a foreign, captive people; in lieu of forced citizenship, the just outcome would have been to extend an offer of citizenship and then hold a decisive vote among Black people about whether to accept.

Roughly four different outcomes would have been possible in that hypothetical post–Civil War vote: Black people agreeing to become American citizens, opting to go back to Africa, joining another nation (or many others), or establishing an "independent nation." None of these was possible because citizenship was forced. The "imposition" of citizenship was an act of conspiracy "with the kidnappers and illegal transporters" to "wipe out the free man's newly acquired freedom."[168] It was, to Imari, a "single, unilateral choice *for*" Black people.[169] It was a second mass American sin after slavery, the original white sin.

According to the RNA's working theory of Black nationality, when the first Black captives were forced onto American shores, they were not yet part of a New African nation. That nation, a kidnapped people, was forged in American slavery. Imari distinguished between "bandit" and "civilized" rules of law regarding a people's nationhood. America

WHITE DEVILS AND BLACK SEPARATISTS   133

operated under the bandit rule; what land and labor a people stole was theirs so long as they kept it for a long time. "White folks simply stole" America, and in possessing it for many decades they acquired some right to it. But "bandit rule" was not "civilized rule," wherein a people had a legitimate claim if they had, as a people, "worked and developed" the land. This rule, he insisted, was enshrined in "international law." Land became linked to a people not through heritage, birth, or theft but, instead, through labor. A people acquired land rights through collective labor over time. Black people, Imari argued, "have lived for over 300 years in the so-called Black Belt," worked that land tirelessly, and battled slavers, Klan members, and night riders to stay on the land.[170] Through occupation, cultivation, and defense, Black people had, in short, built themselves a southern nation. This was their traditional homeland, their "Israel."[171]

New Africans had proven more than the abstract right to nationhood; they had, for a brief moment during Reconstruction, practiced it. "The first governments of the New African nation in North America," Imari wrote, were formed in the South Carolina and Georgia Sea Islands and other Black-majority counties around the South after 1865. These self-governing Black enclaves may have grown into "black states" within America or evolved "into independent New African States." Regardless, this New African nation had been achieved in "the Holy Trinity of nationhood: people, land, and government."[172] Backed by Andrew Johnson, however, ex-Confederates violently suppressed this brief spell of Black self-determination.[173]

Nevertheless, utilizing Malcolm's master's rhetorical tools argument, if the Declaration of Independence had force when "arraigning King George for suppressing the political forms of the new white nation in the colonies," then these same ideas "meant something, and the *same* something, for the Black Nation" in the 1860s and the 1960s. A people's nationhood was perpetual; it outlived both its own self-determined governments and the conquests of its oppressors.[174] Nationality was inalienable.

The RNA's combination of bold separatist vision and a robust historical and legal theory of Black sovereignty inspired a devoted following. The RNA's step-by-step secession plan, spelled out in great detail in publications like *Black World* and *The Black Scholar*, was methodical.

134   WE ARE NOT ONE PEOPLE

The strategy they adopted has been endorsed elsewhere by libertarian separatists: move mass numbers of people to a certain area and democratically drum up separatist sentiments through plebiscites.[175]

The plan was rooted in an essentially democratic logic; if democracy is based on popular rule, then it would be difficult for any democrat to deny the will of a majority of a particular territory who wanted to rule themselves.[176] "Like the Jews moving into Israel," Milton explained in an *Esquire* interview, "we will start to organize along the lines of cooperative and collective farms."[177] The national plan, in broad terms, began with local offices. Once a critical mass of Black sheriffs and city council members had been elected in majority-Black counties, they could organize a local sovereignty vote; that is, they could attempt to change a city or county's sovereignty via referendum. Assuming some successful sovereignty switches, other Black people would be encouraged to move to adjacent counties across the South, where the sovereignty switch strategy would begin again.

Neither Henry brother expected to turn larger economic centers into cities in the Republic of New Africa painlessly. Where nations were concerned, "nothing is really peaceful," Milton said; political change for Black people would not be a false choice of ballots or bullets.[178] These sovereignty-switch votes would be contentious; voters would have to be protected from reactionary white violence.

Even if violence was inevitable as New Africans attempted to achieve formal nationhood, there were thorny philosophical and tactical questions about its timing: whether bloodshed was provoked or anticipated, whether killing was offensive or defensive. That is, changing the sovereignty of hundreds of counties over five states via democratic direct action with Black people turning out to vote, Black militia protecting voters' safety, and Black officeholders ensuring that votes were properly tallied was not the same thing as a bloody guerilla war meant to force the U.S. government to cede territory at the negotiating table.

Milton, a Yale-trained lawyer who owned two AR-15 assault rifles, initially said he was ready for either option: the ballot or the bullet.[179] He would not rule out taking land "by the same right that you took my ancestors from their homeland."[180] Flanked by two uniformed paramilitary guards, he told William F. Buckley as much on *Firing Line*'s

WHITE DEVILS AND BLACK SEPARATISTS   135

stage in 1968. A peaceful, multiracial civilization had never existed on earth, he said. Buckley cited Hawaii; Milton scoffed.[181] " 'Sovereignty,' " Milton explained elsewhere, channeling Mao Zedong's observation on guns and power, "is solely a matter of who has the sharpest and most powerful sword."[182] Imari even depicted a future in which New African army confrontations with the American military down south might be counterbalanced by Black guerillas in the urban North bringing "devastation to the American industrial heartland." These urban guerillas would be the RNA's "second strike capability" and could make Detroit or Watts look like Stalingrad.[183]

Milton's military game theory became prophecy shortly after that interview. A violent police raid of a Detroit church where the RNA celebrated the First New African Nation Day in 1969 foreshadowed later crackdowns on the organization. The raid and subsequent shootout left one police officer dead and four RNA members wounded and ended with 142 arrests.[184] The crackdown, and the tactical and personal questions it posed, divided the brothers. Imari favored moving the RNA operations southward and embarking on the county-by-county strategy of southern nation-building alongside simultaneous efforts to build an RNA military capable of a defensive war against the United States; Milton was rethinking provocative militancy entirely. Amid the brothers' schism, Imari assumed control of the organization.[185] Afterward, Milton, as the *New York Times* noted in his 2006 obituary, did not "renounce the separatist path; he simply ceased to travel it, finding other means."[186]

In 1971, under Imari's direction, RNA leaders purchased twenty acres in Hinds County, Mississippi, and attempted to build the first RNA colony; the capital city was christened El Malik, honoring Malcolm X.[187] This separatist experiment, as Milton feared, ended in tragedy. The Mississippi attorney general proclaimed that white residents were "justifiably disturbed over the fact that a group of people can proclaim to the United States government and to the world that they have withdrawn from that government and are going to create a new nation carved out of our state." There would be, he declared without a trace of irony, "no separate nation set up on the soil of Mississippi."[188] (Mississippi, meanwhile, would not ratify the Thirteenth Amendment for another twenty-five years.)[189] State officials and the FBI would,

136 WE ARE NOT ONE PEOPLE

after another deadly shootout in 1971 in Jackson, foil El Malik with a litany of charges, warrants, and arrests, including nullifying the initial land deal on which the new city was to be built.[190]

The RNA soldiered on after the El Malik crackdown. Imari, in and out of jail and fearing assassination during this period, continued his focus on liberating "the subjugated Black Nation." He had in mind another base of operations for his incremental nationalism strategy, a land he called Kush, an "unspoiled" tract of "15,000 square miles" primarily located in northwest Mississippi.[191] New Africans could build "factories and giant farms" there and practice the collective ownership and cultural solidarity of Ujamaa, Black socialism inspired by Tanzania.[192] The RNA held elections to determine Kush's provisional government, which their minister of information likened "to the 1776 assembly of a few hundred white nationalists in Philadelphia."[193]

Importantly, Kush was already a Black-majority territory.[194] If a majority of the captive Black Kush population, who had traditionally occupied and worked a land the size of Holland, supported Kush's partition, then Imari could make an international appeal for a new nation. Self-rule was the common sense of democracy, Imari thought: "Hardly anyone would question that the absence of consent would make the government of a U.S. political subdivision illegal: too much arguable support for this proposition can be found in the U.S. Constitution itself, not to mention the Declaration of Independence."[195] These were America's founding ideas; he merely quoted historical truths to present occupiers.

American officials, both federal and state, were, to put it mildly, unreceptive. Imari wrote, "It is time to do as Brother Malcolm urged; to stop going into the criminal's court seeking redress and instead, take the criminal to court."[196] If, he reasoned, he could prove his empirically grounded theory of Black citizenship to the United Nations, perhaps the organization would monitor a plebiscite. From there, "New Communities," cooperatively owned towns each consisting of five hundred families and complete with housing, industry, daycare, and "centers for communications and visual arts," could be launched both inside and outside Kush's boundaries; the goal of a larger New African nation in the former Confederacy could be revived.[197]

WHITE DEVILS AND BLACK SEPARATISTS   137

The UN in the late 1970s, however, proved no more supportive of a Republic of New Africa than the State Department had in the late 1960s. After serving a prison sentence for assaulting a federal officer, Imari switched paths, earned a Ph.D. in political science, and spent his remaining days teaching at Prairie View A&M. When he died in 2010, the *New York Times* noted that his "commitment to black empowerment fired a militant, sometimes violent effort to win reparations for descendants of slaves and to carve out, however quixotically, an African-American republic in the Deep South."[198]

Conclusion

For centuries, Black nationalists in America have portrayed themselves as apart, as removed, as beyond white America. Among the many divisions among them was a practical question of how to "build on the separatism that already exists" among races in America.[199] They affirmed the general value of a Black nation regardless of its location; they formulated practical blueprints for secession; they developed general plans to move en masse back to Africa; they also prepared separatist plots that stopped short of fully realized nations. In pluralist sentiments like Nina Simone's demand that "equality" would not force white people to "live next to me" or put forth as a clean break from whiteness entirely in Afro-futurist songs about "chocolate cities" like Detroit and motherships swinging low to carry Black people into the dark depths of outer space, nationalists equated freedom with Black exit.[200]

Although we have highlighted the dreams of a new national belonging among activists that have been variously referred to as "territorial," "classical," or "strong nationalists," the full nationalist spectrum includes expressions of "cultural nationalism" in which the pursuit of a specific homeland was secondary.[201] Put differently, Black activists have plotted their American escape by any means necessary; the establishment of a proper nation was only one of those.[202] A whole host of Black activists since the nation's founding have, some secretly, others brazenly, founded or sought parallel communities, distinct settlements

138 WE ARE NOT ONE PEOPLE

composed exclusively or mostly of Black people with semi-sovereign status either by law or by default.

Some sixty thousand "exodusters" followed George "Pap" Singleton, Edwin P. McCabe, and others out of the Reconstruction-era South to Kansas and Oklahoma and founded roughly fifty towns, small-town "bastions of black nationalism," some of which passed restrictive covenants against white settlers;[203] a related movement, the short-lived 49th State movement urging the admission of a new all-Black state, arose in the 1930s.[204]

From the Sea Islands of South Carolina to the once-busy Black stock markets of Tulsa, Oklahoma; from the massive "maroon" encampments of ex-slaves in the Great Dismal Swamp in North Carolina to Black worlds-unto-themselves towns like Rosewood, Florida, or Blackdom, New Mexico, or Freedmen's Town, Texas, or New Philadelphia, Illinois, or Colfax, Louisiana, some of which were scenes of American pogroms; from segregated Black schools to segregated Black neighborhoods all over the country, Black people have banded together on school boards and in grocery stores, practiced self-reliance, rebuked white America as treacherous, and conveyed, in Stokely Carmichael's words, "the revolutionary idea—and it is a revolutionary idea—that black people are able to do things themselves."[205]

"Black power," which Carmichael initially figured "to build a sense of community," to "define their own goals, to lead their own organizations, and to support those organizations," is plausibly read as a push for Black control of Black areas.[206] Such notions of Black communal solidarity have often been linked to left-wing critiques of colonialism or capitalism, but they have right-wing applications as well. Clarence Thomas, one scholar argues, saw himself as practicing Black nationalism from the Supreme Court bench: "On the Court, Thomas continues to believe—and to argue, in opinion after opinion—that race matters; that racism is a constant, ineradicable feature of American life; and that the only hope for black people lies within themselves, not as individuals but as a separate community with separate institutions, apart from white people."[207]

Black people did not have to wait for Canaan or Kush to practice authentic Blackness. Separate space could be found in personal habits

WHITE DEVILS AND BLACK SEPARATISTS   139

and everyday interactions. Nationalists figured Black separatism as a daily state of being. What these activists have urged is a nationalism of the psyche, a total mental divestment from American national identity and a total investment in Blackness in both psychological orientation and cultural practice.

Maulana Karenga, the founder of the illustratively named organization Us (not them), was a prime example. He envisioned Black culture as a place where language, philosophy, values, customs, dress, ritual, history, and holidays could all be modes of intracultural exchange and mutual affirmation. Such cultural nationalism has not been limited to celebrants of Kwanzaa, speakers of Swahili, or practitioners of the Nguzo Saba principles.[208] Withdrawing from wider American culture into a separate Black state of being began with a mental revolution, a "daring to be pro-black, to look, feel, be, and *do* black."[209]

Pro-Black sentiments like Henry McNeal Turner's 1895 declaration that God was Black or Carmichael's exhortation to achieve Black power implied future religious and political commitments, perhaps even engaging in electoral politics, but each was also an immediate rhetorical refusal of white power the very moment these words were spoken or written.[210] That is not to claim that saying the words "Black power" automatically achieved cultural autonomy, but it is to assert that saying the words was a Black power deed; saying "Black power" was an essential part of achieving Black power.

When H. Rap Brown bragged of wearing a "Fuck Your Mama" button to his draft board hearing, when he bragged of telling draft board officers that if they armed him he would "shoot Ladybird," he told audiences a heroic tale of a Black individual refusing to let his white colonizers' desires dictate his in-the-moment conduct.[211] In fact, the opposite was the case. Unwilling to obey white rules or observe white norms, he dressed and conducted himself to give offense; his colonizers were the foil by which he showed audiences how to militate and separate simultaneously. He instructed, "If white folks say gray suits are fashionable, you go buy a pink one. If they say america is great, you say america ain't shit."[212] Performances like Brown's were designed to invoke "the danger of violence" and "provoke" Black audiences to "imagine freedom apart from white people."[213] Separation could be achieved, in part, in "spite."[214]

140 WE ARE NOT ONE PEOPLE

By this expanded reading, Black nationalism was far more than a land revolution; it was behavioral. But even these interpersonal invocations of performative Black activism were also linked to land and space. These local acts of Black defiance still made a claim to an area, to owning space, to reorganizing territory, to privileging Black voices. The very tone of Malcolm X's voice, one rhetorical scholar argues, "provided a rhetorical shock therapy for black listeners (and whites as well) because it was a radical departure from black Christian proselytizing that introduced new political feelings designed to change how they communicated with and about white people." Even Malcolm's body, his upright, formal "physicality," was a "gestural refusal of white nationalism."[215] These provocations denied white power, reversed it, demarcated a space for self-definition separate from white voices, white desires, the pearl-clutching of aghast white audiences. As Carmichael wrote, "I know black power is good because so many white folks came out against it."[216]

5

"Dykes First"

Lesbian Separatism in America

Chichén Itzá tourists may have noticed a curious set of fellow visitors in early 1979. Four vans full of women from the United States had arrived, and they learned enough Spanish to say "Chinga su padre" (Go fuck your father), inverting the common insult "Chinga su madre" (Go fuck your mother). Their language substitutions were not the only thing distinguishing these vulgar van travelers from other Yucatán hikers. These women sported shaved heads, and they did not speak to men. In fact, aside from incidental contact with, say, male waiters or mechanics, these women did not acknowledge the existence of men. Atop an altar above one set of ruins, one of the group's founders, Lamar Van Dyke, experienced a deeply troubling realization about Chichén Itzá's ancient inhabitants. The women made the trek hoping to find an ancient "Dyke Heaven." Instead, she announced to her cohort, ancient women had been burned on the altar where she stood. They got back in their vans and drove away.[1]

These provocateurs, a mobile lesbian separatist group, aptly named the Van Dykes, were not always so dejected. Members adopted the name Van Dyke as both a personal surname and a collective label for their crisscrossing, caravanning organization; they were individual Van Dykes of the collective Van Dykes. Their Mexican adventure aside, they lived life on American highways as they traveled from one lesbian separatist community to another. What they found in Mexico was what they had found in America; the Eden they sought could not exist within a society in which men and women lived together. In mixed-sex societies, women were sacrificed, literally and figuratively, for some fatherland, to some male deity, in service of some perverse patriarchal good.

We Are Not One People. Michael J. Lee and R. Jarrod Atchison, Oxford University Press. © Oxford University Press 2022. DOI: 10.1093/oso/9780190876500.003.0006

142   WE ARE NOT ONE PEOPLE

Instead of trying to fit in a mixed nation, they chose a transient life moving from one women's community to the next. Lamar Van Dyke remembered her group being "everywhere." She recalled the excitement of finding "Women's Land" in "North Carolina, Florida, Texas, Arkansas, New Mexico, Arizona, a lot of Women's Land in California and Oregon." Many communities, separatist and otherwise, have a fixed relationship with their homeland. Lamar Van Dyke saw her community much differently: "You could actually go all around the country from Women's Land to Women's Land and you met all these other women who were doing the same thing. You would run into people in New Mexico that you had seen in Texas." Theirs was a world apart, or, more accurately, many worlds apart, a kind of lesbian archipelago.[23] Movement within and between this constellation of networked communes was a definitive feature of lesbian separatism of the 1970s, a "fecund moment," as one scholar puts it, when "lesbian separatism as a theory, ideology, political, social, and economic practice was in use across the country."[4]

These loosely connected organizations and communes created what one writer labeled "a shadow society devoted to living in an alternate, penisless reality."[5] Three lesbian separatist pioneers, Bev Jo, Linda Strega, and Ruston, co-writers of the seminal *Dykes-Loving-Dykes: Dyke Separatist Politics for Lesbians Only* (1990), reflected on the early 1970s as a time that "felt like a new beginning." They found "other Lesbians for the first time" in their lives, and "Dyke communities" were forming and growing. They began to experience, they remembered warmly, "a sense of caring, loving, and self-love among us as Lesbians."[6]

The Van Dykes were joined by the Gutter Dykes, the Gorgons, the Furies, the Separatists Enraged Proud and Strong (SEPS), the Radicalesbians, the Consensual Liberation through Intimate Tactics (or CLIT) Collective, and many others."[7] Cell 16 was one of the first. In 1968, they characterized their founding purpose as women's liberation through the methods of dissociation: "This is a call for separatism, for radical women to dissociate themselves from male-oriented, male-dominated radical organizations and join together in Women's Liberation groups as the most effective way to achieve their own independent identity and the liberation of all women, and to bring

"DYKES FIRST" 143

about the truly total revolution—the establishment of a radical society without oppression."[8] Revolution required a commitment to radical politics, and radical politics required separatism; but separatism required "groups," not a single organization helmed by iconoclasts who vied for control of the revolution.

For some separatist communities like the Van Dykes, separation meant migration, the practice of an alternative citizenship of mobility, a rebuke of American patriarchy from the road. For others, separatism meant a return to the land. In these intentional communities, separatists practiced sustainability, built their own facilities, maintained their own food supplies, and generally rejected commercialism.

The Oregon Women's Land Trust (OWLT), one of several women's communities "scattered along I-5 between Eugene and Grants Pass," was established in 1975.[9] Huntington Open Women's Land (HOWL), a thirty-minute drive from Waterbury, Vermont, "was designated a place for women and women only by a private donor in 1986."[10] Hallomas, started in 1977, was a community of thirteen members living in Northern California practicing "consensus decision-making," calling for equal workloads, and conducting all meetings according to "feminist" processes."[11]

Communities such as these trace their roots to the "womyn's land movement, who began founding rural lesbian utopias in the 1960s." There were as many as 150 intentional communities during the peak years in the late 1970s and early 1980s.[12] These communities, however, were not only located in wild places adjacent to active countercultures. Alapine occupied 100 hilly acres in Mentone, Alabama, and Camp Sister Spirit was located in Ovett, Mississippi.[13] Remoteness was essential. According to one anthropologist, "The spiritual importance of land is manifest in wilderness; for example, women who follow a feminist-Goddess tradition explicitly revere the earth and worship outdoors when possible. The land itself is often seen in these contexts as female or feminine, and also as divine."[14]

Others saw separation as an urban endeavor. Labyris was a feminist bookstore that dabbled in separatist politics in Greenwich Village in the 1970s.[15] In Durham, North Carolina, separatists started restaurants, clubs, coffee shops, and neighborhoods where they could sustain a

144 WE ARE NOT ONE PEOPLE

functional, women-only community despite their proximity to typical, mixed-sex living.[16] In 1971, the Furies Collective was founded and began publishing a prominent lesbian newspaper in a Capitol Hill neighborhood in Washington, D.C.[17] In San Francisco, Bev Jo describes her experiences with finding a flourishing lesbian community in 1970: "We had meetings, parties, dances, concerts, plays, poetry readings, support groups and bars. Something was happening at least once a week—all female-only."[18]

Women's communities emphasized multiplicity, not just geographical differences. Some women's lands prohibited all men from entry, including male children; some taught martial arts and practiced strength training to fend off violent males; some practiced celibacy; some embraced sadomasochism; some framed lesbianism as a separatist political choice, not a sexual preference. This separatist community, moreover, broadly included distinct but overlapping nodes of "women's lands," residential communities restricted to women occupants; "lesbian lands," populated by "self-identified lesbians or landdykes"; and looser urban concentrations of women living by, with, and for other women.[19] Regardless of terminology and actual practice, this dispersed community of separatists was a "highly mobile population" moving "from one community to another."[20]

But describing lesbian separatists as dispersed is not to say that they were disconnected. These communities and the women who traversed them were united in a shared belief in the progressive relationship of separation, self-determination, and self-actualization. Long before the internet, women's separatist communities became linked not just by travelers but also by a dense rhetorical network of communally produced and consumed literature.

Separatist communities produced pamphlets, newspapers, poetry, journals, and fiction, and the idea of the lesbian separatist as a political subject position was generated in canonical texts from the 1970s, including the Radicalesbians' "The Woman-Identified Woman" (1970), the Revolutionary Lesbians' "How to Stop Choking to Death, or: Separatism" (1971), the Furies' newspaper and "Lesbians in Revolt" (1972), and Alice's "Lesbian Separatism: An Amazon Analysis" (1973).[21]

"DYKES FIRST" 145

In powerful works of political theory and cultural criticism, in daily practices in, around, and between bucolic hideaways and urban enclaves, these separatists were engaged in acts of self-protection, but also rhetorical acts of self-discovery and world-making. As Jo, Strega, and Ruston emphasized, "*In a world that reviles Lesbians, it's a deeply courageous and loving choice to be a Separatist, to dare to say, 'We put Dykes first at all times. No one else cares for or loves Dykes, but we do.'* In a male supremacist world that destroys Lesbians, Separatism is survival."[22]

Separatism Without Secession

Lesbian separatists have not been a part of mainstream feminist movements in the United States. "Many of the women," one radical accused, "who fight for any given set of reforms are dishonest with the people who they are trying to 'organize.'"[23] Separatists were not pushing for personal, political, or structural reforms anyway. The problem of patriarchy, they thought, was far more fundamental; it was built into the "basic nature of this society."[24] Betty Friedan, the activist icon of the National Organization for Women, dubbed these lesbians the "Lavender Menace" (a name that was later adopted by an informal group of radicals).[25] One separatist scholar bemoaned the frequency of "feminist criticisms of separatism that amount to not much more than stereotyping it as man-hating, rigid, vegetarian, nonsmoking, children-hating, and hostile."[26]

Friedan and other feminists might have been sure of what to call these radicals, but they often were not sure what to call themselves. An anthropologist who interviewed dozens of women's land denizens found that few of them "identified as separatist."[27] Another activist, however, remembered calling herself "a separatist because I was 'separating' like crazy."[28] Even though Kathy Rudy was so "captivated by the ideals of separatist lesbian feminism" that she moved to Durham to live in its lesbian community in 1980, she notes that her cohort chose a different term of identity. They did not prefer "lesbian feminism" or "lesbian separatism" but, instead, chose "radical feminism" to describe their political project.[29] Some prominent feminist theorists

146 WE ARE NOT ONE PEOPLE

opted for "lesbian connectionism" as a positive alternative to "lesbian separatism."[30]

The physical act of separating from men, the philosophy of separation from patriarchy, and the symbolic act of exiting the nation were, nevertheless, far from ancillary to the feminist cause. In fact, as Marilyn Frye, philosopher and pathbreaking radical feminist theorist, argues, they expanded on a core feminist theme: "Most feminists, probably all, practice some separation from males and male-dominated institutions. A separatist practices separation consciously, systematically, and probably more generally than the others, and advocates thorough and 'broadspectrum' separation as part of the conscious strategy of liberation."[31] What she called broadspectrum separation obviously included the distinctive geographic separation of women's lands and lesbian separatist communities but also pop-up spaces like separate music festivals or conferences, social and protest activities, bookstores and bakeries, and larger organizations.

"Lesbians do not have much space in the world that is our own," scholar and activist Jackie Anderson maintained, "so I am suspicious of men who are unable to respect the small amount that we have been able to organize for ourselves, even if they feel somehow castrated." To her, the pursuit of "social justice" was continued, not jeopardized, by the "common and accepted practice respected by most women that there will be times when groups will choose to gather with those who are like themselves, such as women-of-color gatherings." Social justice, as she saw it, just did not require that she "interact with men" or prohibit her "desire for a context that will be free of male presence.[32]

The influential feminist theology scholar Mary Daly also theorized broadspectrum separation where each incremental step away from patriarchal culture allowed for more and more profound changes. "When women take positive steps to move out of patriarchal space and time, there is a new surge of life," she argued.[33] A fervent believer in the generative possibilities of secure spaces for women, Daly, much to the consternation of Boston College's administration, did not admit men into her seminars between 1973 and a legal challenge in the late 1990s. She thought, as the *New York Times* reported in 1999, that "women can only realize the truths of feminism among themselves."[34]

"DYKES FIRST" 147

Exclusive seminars, however, were just one part of Daly's touchstone philosophy of separation, what she called "boundary living," a way of "being in and out of 'the system'" simultaneously.[35] There was "a female reality deeper than that created by men," and life on the boundary of patriarchy was where a search for that reality could start. If men were the greatest threat to women, then, as one activist who studied Daly's work remembered, "the greatest political action that could be conceived was to separate from all men," seek safety on the boundary, "and put our energies solely into women."[36]

In this chapter, we explore the alternative, boundary-dwelling communities built by lesbian separatists in the late 1960s and throughout the 1970s. We examine their acidic criticisms of mixed-sex societies, their hope for multiple yet homogeneous communities of lesbians, and the strategies they used to recruit, build, and sustain collectives beyond the patriarchal United States.

Like other separatists, they framed categories of identity—sex and sexuality in their case—as reasons to separate. Unlike the other separatist movements we have explored, lesbian separatists did not seek to build a new nation. Other separatists wanted to leave their American prison and retreat into a national fortress; lesbian separatists envisioned a far more formless, scattered alternative. Other separatist discourses were stocked with singular ideals of a national homeland. They may have disagreed about where their homeland was or what to do once they got there, but they knew it was out there somewhere. Lesbian separatist discourse was, on the whole, nearly totally devoid of positive references to nations, nationality, or nationalism generally. As the feminist theorist Bette Tallen summarizes, "Lesbian separatism, unlike some other separatist movements, is not about the establishment of an independent state; it is about the development of an autonomous self-identity and the creation of a strong solid lesbian community."[37]

The few exceptions actually prove the rule. When Jill Johnston republished her influential *Village Voice* essays in *Lesbian Nation: The Feminist Solution* (1973), she extolled the virtues of separating without recommending that lesbians organize themselves as a sovereign state.[38] The language of nationhood had rhetorical power as a catchy book title, but hers was not a nationalist political program.

148   WE ARE NOT ONE PEOPLE

In fact, many lesbian separatists linked sovereignty to patriarchy. As philosopher Sarah Lucia Hoagland wrote, "Separatists tend to have more anarchist sensibilities—distrusting institutional power of any kind, wanting new value to emerge from small groups engaged in creating new ways of being, and realizing that the means determine the end—that is, how we behave toward each other is the value we enact."[39] Lesbian separatists wanted to ditch the nation specifically but also nationalism generally. Theirs was a politics of separation that refused the possibility of secession. Lesbian separatism was an appeal to safety, a quest for solidarity, and a wholesale critique of nationalism simultaneously. Flawed nations would not be replaced by more nations.

Separatism and secession can be sexist discourses. Many separatists framed their persecution in America as emasculation and saw the acquisition of a new nation as the redemption of their people's masculinity. The Confederacy was steeped in the languages of southern "manhood" and protecting the "virtues" of southern white women.[40] Many southern secessionists were "absolutely convinced that the fate of white southern womanhood was hanging in the balance in the wake of Lincoln's election."[41]

Similar tropes were evident in some Black nationalist discourse. Nat Turner "believed that white supremacy generated black self-hatred and that no black man could achieve manhood unless blacks could protect and govern themselves," and although the UNIA featured women in prominent positions of power, Marcus Garvey "embraced the prevailing notion that African redemption equaled manhood redemption."[42] As Malcolm X told an Oxford audience in 1964: "I have to point out that I am an American Negro. And I live in a society whose social system is based upon the castration of the black man, whose political system is based upon the castration of the black man, and whose economy is based upon the castration of the black man."[43] "The strength of the nation" was, in sum, "a measure of manhood," Robin D. G. Kelley observes.[44]

Lesbian separatists wanted to protect women, to be sure, but the notion that all lesbians or all women had a single homeland, should congregate as a collective in that homeland, and should behave according to predetermined rules in that homeland struck separatists as deeply patriarchal. They sought space to challenge patriarchal relations that had been a part of nations for centuries. Each of the values they embraced, mobility, multiplicity, and modesty, was a withdrawal from nationalism. As philosopher Claudia Card put it, "Feminist separatism has similarities to the labor union movement. Both are resistance movements. Neither is a nationalism. Each aims to empower an oppressed majority."[45] These experiments with reformulating leadership and reconsidering sovereignty as a patchwork of small communities were standout markers of the lesbian separatist tradition and unique among separatist discourses. True radicalism meant embracing communal difference, even profligacy.

Lesbian separatists did not fetishize a place; separatists accepted and celebrated a diversity of perspectives on life during and after separation.[46] They separated from patriarchy to go everywhere, not to a singular nation where they might risk recreating the patriarchal norms of existing nation-states. Insisting on uniformity, on a single nation, smacked of patriarchal control. As one radical feminist wrote, "There's no reason why a society consisting of rational beings capable of empathizing with each other, complete and having no natural reason to compete, should have a government, laws or leaders."[47]

The Scum of the Earth

The opening lines of Valerie Solanas's SCUM (Society for Cutting Up Men) Manifesto showed that she was no ordinary second-wave feminist. "Life in this society," she wrote, "being, at best, an utter bore and no aspect of society being at all relevant to women, there remains to civic-minded, responsible, thrill-seeking females only to overthrow the government, eliminate the money system, institute complete automation and destroy the male sex."[48] Although there was some debate about whether or not the manifesto was satire, the people who encountered Solanas on the streets of Greenwich Village in 1967 found a "dead serious" woman committed to challenging patriarchy.[49]

She was blunt about men: "Every man, deep down, knows he's a worthless piece of shit," she declared, and "Every male's deep-seated, secret, most hideous fear is of being discovered to be not a female, but a male, a subhuman animal."[50] When selling the manifesto on the street,

150   WE ARE NOT ONE PEOPLE

Solanas charged men a higher price than women. Solanas lived the pressures and struggles of a life of radicalism.

Solanas even asked Andy Warhol to produce her play *Up Your Ass*. Warhol agreed to read it, but then dismissed the play as so incendiary that he thought it might be a police entrapment plot to have him arrested on an obscenity charge. On June 4, 1968, Solanas went to The Factory and shot Warhol and art critic Mario Amaya, and was trying to shoot Warhol's manager, Fred Hughes, when her gun jammed. Within a matter of hours, Solanas turned herself in. One year later, she was declared fit to stand trial and pled guilty to reckless assault with the intent to harm. She served one year of her three-year sentence. The shooting and the SCUM Manifesto propelled Solanas to the center of feminist debate over radicalism. Ti-Grace Atkinson, president of the New York chapter of the National Organization for Women, referred to Solanas as "a heroine of the feminist movement."[51] Norman Mailer named her the "Robespierre of feminism."[52] Robert Marmorstein took her violence as the direct expression of her writing, noting that her purpose was the elimination of "every single male from the face of the earth."[53]

The SCUM Manifesto was just one of the many radical discourses of the late 1960s and early 1970s that figured men, white men in particular, as the root of all evil. They could not be rehabilitated. Thousands of years of global history showed that men were the enemy and must be treated as such. Roxanne Dunbar, one of the Cell 16 founders, summarized men's status this way: "Who, then, is Woman's enemy? All Men? Yes, all men who identify with the Master class are our enemy."[54]

Separatists reached for scientific evidence, specifically biology and evolutionary biology, to prove that men were inferior and dangerous beasts. Writing in the Cell 16–produced journal *No More Fun and Games: A Journal of Female Liberation*, Betsy Warrior described men's villainy as a verifiable fact. "Today," she argued, "science has found ways to alleviate famine, conquer germs that cause plagues, and check the size of the population itself. One germ hasn't been identified and destroyed; the germ that causes wars and destruction. That germ is man."[55] The disease metaphor was revealing: germs were inhuman; germs must be wiped out; germs killed millions; germs served no obvious function; germs threatened thriving organisms. Warrior also described men as having surpassed their evolutionary function: "The built-in obsolescence of his physical and emotional nature is now apparent. The aggressive, destructive drives of man lack proper reasonable outlets. He is being phased out by technology."[56] Men had been replaced by machines. Whatever limited feats of strength men once offered to build civilizations were now archaic.

For Warrior, men might have been necessary at some point, but their continued existence was costly for the entire species; men disrupted the ongoing evolutionary process. Warrior compared men to one of the most infamous incarnations of violence: "Like the tyrannosaurus, man is blocking evolution and sustaining his life at the expense of other better life forms. Until he gives up existence, either voluntarily or by force, there will be no relief from suffering nor any moral progress on this planet."[57] Solanas did not even allow men a function on the food chain, asserting that they were genetic mistakes: "The male is a biological accident: the Y (male) gene is an incomplete X (female) gene, that is, it has an incomplete set of chromosomes. In other words, the male is an incomplete female, a walking abortion, aborted at the gene stage."[58] As one historian summarized, "Maleness and heterosexuality were both declared mutant."[59]

Beyond biology and evolution, prominent separatist texts also condemned men's psychology. Men needed to be violent because their fragile masculinity was tied to a deep-seated jealousy of women. Men needed to hurt women to feel like men. They were, as one scholar vividly phrased it, "death-dealing necrophiliacs draining female energy, both figuratively and literally, in order to stay alive."[60] Frye framed male violence as rejuvenating. Violence made men feel good because it gave them power over something superior.

The usurious nature of the relationship went beyond violence, however. Frye explained, "The ministrations of women, be they willing or unwilling, free or paid for, are what restore in men the strength, will and confidence to go on with what they call living."[61] Men's violence was pure ego satisfaction. Drained and depleted "by living on their own," men "are revived and refreshed, re-created, by going home and being served dinner, changing to clean clothes, having sex with the wife; or by dropping by the apartment of a woman friend to be served coffee or a drink and stroked in one way or another; or by picking up

152   WE ARE NOT ONE PEOPLE

a prostitute for a quicky or for a dip in favorite sexual escape fantasies; or by raping refugees from their wars (foreign and domestic)."[62] Men used women to fill an existential, infinite void.

Solanas, who started a graduate program in psychology, did not agree that men were striking out in order to stroke their egos. It was worse than that: "It's not ego satisfaction; that doesn't explain screwing corpses and babies." Instead, she argued, men suffered from an acute awareness of their inferiority and their status as non-women, and this awareness produced a psychological compulsion to gratuitous violence. Violence, she argued, was a psychological spasm: "The male is eaten up with tension, with frustration at not being female, at not being capable of ever achieving satisfaction or pleasure of any kind; eaten up with hate—not rational hate that is directed at those who abuse or insult you—but irrational, indiscriminate hate." For her, men's hatred was projection, a transference of their distaste for their "own worthless" selves.[63] Violence, she concluded, was an outlet for self-hate.

In terms of both evolutionary science and psychology, the character of the enemy was becoming clearer. The third lens separatists utilized emphasized men's historical villainy. Men occupied positions of power and used their authority to keep everyone else subservient.

For many feminist theorists, like Mary Ann Weathers, it was important to keep race near the front of this historical analysis of male oppression because of the clear racialized differences in power. She wrote, "Any time the White man admits to something you know he is trying to cover something else up. We are all being exploited, even the white middle class, by the few people in control over this entire world. And to keep the real issue clouded, he keeps us at one another's throats with this racism jive."[64] Where Solanas and others saw men as dumb, "half-dead" brutes, Weathers saw them as crafty plotters who knew that women, especially women of color, were a threat, and so they would make strategic concessions to muddy the waters or co-opt potential resisters.

Others adopted a similar suspicion of anything that looked like a voluntary reform. Men would not give up power voluntarily. Even when they appeared to grant concessions, they were engaged in a cynical, self-serving ploy: "As long as we have male supremacy women are going to be kept helpless and oppressed and they will be given 'privileges' only when it is to the man's advantage. . . . So: no more fun and games."[65]

What, if any, role was there for men as allies? These radical discourses shunned cooperation outright. According to Dunbar, men were simply not in a position to help: "How can men liberate anyone, when they are not themselves liberated? They are not free. They too are bound by their need to own another."[66] The totalizing description of the enemy did not provide space for trying to parse out which men were genuine feminists. The safest assumption was that they were all suspect.

Dana Densmore, one of the original members of Cell 16, said it was very simple: just follow men's incentives. "It will do no good to ask males to admit females into their species and their world, to ask them for new, human roles," she said. "They have been the oppressors for all time; it is vain to think they would give it up now. Moreover, they're comfortable." History showed men to be obsessed with power; they would never give it up. Densmore asserted, "They've set things up this way because this is the way they like things. Woman the inessential, does the inessential work, assuring the continuation of the species, while man goes about the essential work, living and developing himself as an individual."[67]

Men who proclaimed radical ideals were, of course, no exceptions. "Liberal" men were a constant source of frustration. "No thanks, Mr. Smug Liberal," Densmore protested, "I've tried your delicious masochistic sex and it nauseates me to think about it. I'm a person, not a delectable little screwing machine equipped with subroutines for cocktail-mixing and souffle-making and listening enchanted to all the pompous drivel you want to pour out to impress me."[68] Solanas surveyed radical movements and concluded that "the male 'rebel' is a farce."[69]

Writing about revolutionary male icons like Che Guevara, Warrior outlined how even the men ostensibly most committed to social justice inevitably fell short because they were essentially oppressors. She wrote, "As depressing as it is these men are not above cynically taking advantage of the servile mentality created in women, by the inferior role they're forced to play. In this respect they're defeating their own ends. If their ends are to establish a completely rational humane

154   WE ARE NOT ONE PEOPLE

society, where every individual is allowed to live up to his or her full potential."[70] Dunbar made sure to include American revolutionaries in this critique of the double-talking male radical as oxymoron: "We have lived scores of centuries of scorn ruled by crippled mangled souls, whose birthright makes right. That is finished. We say No. All are equal. That is what the forefather revolutionaries said, but they meant it in a different way."[71]

Womanhood

The scathing reviews of men in early separatist discourses rallied, inspired, and challenged women to fully invest in the cause of women. These were unifying rebukes. Every charge against men named something that women could use to explain their own experiences and raise the consciousness of others. A few separatists pursued a softer line of argument about men, but the broader swath of radical women's discourse from the era held a clear consensus: men were the scum of the earth. The next step, however, was a real challenge.

In Cell 16's first publication, Marilyn Terry noted the difficulty of both escaping men in a man's world and galvanizing women. "Organizing for liberation," she wrote, "is a uniquely difficult problem for women." They were a massive, manifold population. Women lacked "the common religious consciousness or cultural background of the persecuted Jews, the conspicuous 'racial' characteristics of the oppressed Blacks, and the common skills and trades of the working class."[72] Identification on the basis of sex and/or gender and sexuality was not simple. Unity could easily become strained when the topic turned to more affirmative bases of organization for liberation: the status of "women," "womyn," "womon," or "wimmin," their "history" or "herstory," and their relationship to lesbianism. Some separatist groups drew firm lines around womanhood, while others saw advantages in a more inclusive approach.

Part of the reason that the debates over womanhood were so fraught was that so much was at stake. They were building new boundary worlds for women; moreover, they were defining women anew. The Radicalesbians, a separatist group in New York City, summarized the power of definition this way: "We are authentic, legitimate, real to the extent that we are the property of some man whose name we bear. To be a woman who belongs to no man is to be invisible, pathetic, inauthentic, unreal." The notions of authenticity and legitimacy were central to the question of naming. They distinguished between a public womanhood performed for men's approval and an individual woman's real personhood. They explained, "He confirms his image of us—of what we have to be in order to be acceptable by him—but not our real selves; he confirms our womanhood—as he defines it, in relation to him—but cannot confirm our personhood, our own selves as absolutes."[73] The freedom that the Radicalesbians called for required women to be in the position to define womanhood.

According to the Radicalesbians, women had internalized male desires about what women should be, how they should look, dress, act, talk, and relate. Womanhood was a concept in need of full revision. The internalization of men's desires for women produced a "self-hate" that made it difficult for women to work together toward a new understanding of themselves. This self-loathing "may be experienced as discomfort with her role, as feeling empty, as numbness, as restlessness, as a paralyzing anxiety at the center." Or, perhaps, "it may be expressed in shrill defensiveness of the glory and destiny of her role." Regardless, it poisoned "her existence, keeping her alienated from herself, her own needs, and rendering her a stranger to other women."[74]

The solution was confrontation wherein individual women addressed their own sense of identity. The stronger the fights over the definition of womanhood, the more important it became for women to recover and embody the ethos of a defiant womanhood, of refusing to compromise for a male-dominated world. These theories often touched down in the experiences of separatists living in women's communities. As OWLT woman said, "But by crossing over to be a separatist, you're saying to men, 'I will not smile at you. I will not perform the behaviors that accord your acceptance.' "[75]

Several themes developed in this community-wide conversation over authentic womanhood. One central theme linked women's suffering under patriarchy to physical and psychological trauma. Dunbar argued that it was impossible to set aside the question of who women were without examining what oppression wrought. She argued, "We are damaged—we women . . . There are very few who are not damaged, and they rule. The reason they see their kind of world, their system as the best of all possible worlds is that it is utopian for them, and they plan to keep it."[76]

For Densmore, recognizing the true depth and breadth of women's oppression, the enormous and personal horror of their subjugation, was essential to a new collective consciousness. Trauma was the starting position for a new theory of womanhood: "Women must realize the magnitude and horror of this systematic mutilation of humanity, the unthinkable atrocity of the castration of billions of women over millions of years in denying them the right to realize their potential as human beings . . . forcing upon them a role and even a self-image which is sub-human."[77] In a real sense, women's access to their own humanity had been precluded. Their oppression was so powerful, so engrained in parasitic relationships, that it was impossible for them to find fulfillment without a fundamental rupture: "She lives, a parasite, in a world he built. She is dependent on him for the expression of her own humanity: she lives only through him. She is told to find fulfillment through her biological processes: the fulfillment men find by conquering nature she is asked to find in submitting to nature."[78]

Without opportunities to express their individual humanity, women were "sub-human," mere hosts to "biological processes." These basic acts of exclusion and dehumanization were experienced differently by women across a variety of locations, but realizing the common experience of oppression had potential unifying power. "*All* women," Weathers emphasized, "suffer oppression, even white women, particularly poor white women, and especially Indian, Mexican, Puerto Rican, Oriental, and Black American women whose oppression is tripled by any of the above mentioned. But we do have female's oppression in common."[79] Establishing the commonality of women's oppression meant "that we can begin to talk to other women with this common factor and start building links with them and thereby build and transform the revolutionary force we are now beginning to amass."[80] One Oregon separatist put it similarly: "Around here we are all in agreement: we don't want to live with men and we don't want to sleep with men. My life here is totally dedicated to women. I surround my life with women."[81]

But such a recognition of common oppression was bound to be hard-won. It meant, at the very least, that women would have to acknowledge millennia of oppression, to confront lifetimes of victimhood. As one Cell 16 contributor assessed, "Since Adam's rib we have been secondary; the other half that complements the whole, which is man. We stand by HIS side. We look up to HIM. Our duty has always been to support him; husband, father, son, lover, brother, whichever category HE falls into."[82] Dunbar, similarly, took a longer view of history: "Women have never ruled. 'Matriarchy' has never existed in the terms usually meant."[83] Women's menial roles stayed the same even as hunter-gatherer societies transitioned to stable settlements: "The women continue to have two functions: reproduce the race and work. All women are 'breeders.'"[84]

A new, resonant vision of womanhood would have to emerge as women faced a further hard truth about their subjugation: they were slaves. The radical writers of the 1960s and 1970s were keenly aware that they were agitating for a stronger consciousness around women's issues during the same period when there was a growing consciousness about racial oppression.[85] Radical feminists struggled with their relationship to race. Nevertheless, the invocation of women's slavery appeared throughout the era's radical literature. Their enslavement pre-dated and was reinforced by the American founding. As Dunbar claimed, "All are equal. That is what the forefather revolutionaries said, but they meant it in a different way." Washington and the rest were "power patriots" who correctly linked "liberty" to "Whiteness and Maleness and possession of property." As Dunbar saw it, 1968 was no different from 1776: "This is the land where a White Man can be free. Actually only the rich white man can be free, but the poor sucker can fantasize with *Playboy*."[86]

Dunbar also theorized women's slavery not as a specific, historically located institution but as an ahistorical state of mind: "We identify with those who have been held in Slavery, and all oppressed people. We believe we must be in the vanguard of a revolutionary society, because we have been perpetually in bondage. We are not historical beings; we cannot be subjected to historical analysis."[87]

Awakening women to their slavery was a tough task, especially when it came to those who thought they had already achieved some measure

158 WE ARE NOT ONE PEOPLE

of liberation. As Dunbar argued, "The most 'liberated' woman, the professional or activist woman, is often the least conscious of her function as a Slave. She is a Rich Master's companion. . . . Once there, you are a slave-driver, an overseer, not a Master."[88]

Even supposedly "radical" women were not truly liberated because men dominated and defined radical activism. "Although radical women," Maureen Davidica lamented, "appear liberated (they are usually freed from the trappings of the middle class female—girdles, stockings, makeup, uncomfortable clothing), they are still expected to look pretty, i.e., look feminine, to act feminine, i.e., like fags, and ugly women are scarce because they are actively discouraged." Davidica isolated the problem of public performance for radical women in an effort to reaffirm the need for separation. Radicalism was just another male institution, like "politics," "the draft," or the Vietnam War.[89] Liberation was another useful fiction to preserve male dominance.

Dunbar and others also understood that some women would inevitably resist the slavery label. Rather than addressing such an objection, she cited it as further evidence of women's psychological torture. She argued, "The first essential step is to come to the realization that one is a Slave. No one identifies with a Slave, especially not a Slave."[90] Dunbar understood that she was asking women to leave situations wherein their relative degree of economic or social power made it difficult for them to accept the label and all its attendant racial and historical connotations. She did not accept nuance; instead, she claimed, "Just because a woman does not feel oppressed does not mean she is not. One is potentially oppressed if any of one's kind is oppressed. . . . Life is very short for a Slave."[91] Resistance was denial; if a woman doubted the label, it meant that she was blind to the reality of other women's oppression.

Although much discussion around women's slavery was ahistorical, there were some specific attempts to reconcile this recognition with the historical institution of American slavery. There were two lines of argument. First, they claimed, rather boldly, that women's oppression was simply a bigger issue that spanned a longer time than American slavery. Dunbar reasoned, "African slavery lasted only four centuries. It is an historical problem, delineated by time." Women, on the other hand, "have been enslaved universally and eternally."[92]

Second, women's oppression was the root cause of other kinds of slavery: "The sexual split is the very basis of the development of Racism." Women were "chattel" first, and then "institutionalized Slavery and Enserfment and Peonage (Capitalist developments) put the male slave in the Female role, and the Slave was deprived of all rights to his body, as women always had been."[93] The institution of slavery was the outgrowth of a deeper patriarchal system of capitalist accumulation and property ownership. African slavery was temporary and only subjected a comparatively small group of men to the same set of experiences that all women dealt with for all time.

Dunbar went so far as to make a direct comparison between women and Black men in modern America: "The myth has persisted that the American Woman is free. She is about as free as the descendants of the African slaves, soon to be less free than the male Afro-American."[94]

If the male/female hierarchy was the true cause of all social oppression, even racism, then solving women's oppression was a precondition to any broader struggle for Black liberation. Dunbar and others acknowledged the contemporary struggle for Black liberation but did not embrace the movement as allies. Instead, they saw the struggle for Black liberation as inspirational but problematic. "We have," Dunbar insisted, "learned from Black Liberation analysis that we should work on the liberation of our own people. Our people are oppressed throughout the world, even within the Black Liberation Movement. Our people are women."[95] Each deserved liberation, but each group was responsible for its own exodus.

Defying the Patriarchy

Women have long contemplated societies without men. "American women's lands" were, in fact, "presaged by the Women's Commonwealth" in late nineteenth century Texas. The "Sanctified Sisters," as joiners of the commune were called, "claimed their rights" to own property communally, to divorce their husbands, and to practice celibacy.[96]

Women-only worlds have been common tropes in fiction as well. In Charlotte Perkins Gilman's novel *Herland* (1915), women lived alone in a conflict-free society.[97] Utopian novels like Sally Miller Gearhart's

160   WE ARE NOT ONE PEOPLE

The Wanderground (1979) were based on personal experiences living in lesbian separatist communities.[98] Volumes of poetry, short stories, and films explored the possibilities of women-only worlds. The question was how to get there. Some radical feminists advocated revolutionary murder, genocide really, to achieve this ideal. Women-only societies could be achieved by purification, not extrication.[99] Lesbian separatism, however, was prudent by comparison. Women needed separate space to think, to create, to theorize, to share, to heal.

Lesbian separatists saw women-only spaces as essential to definition, defiance, and survival. The space within separatist communities enabled robust discussions of lesbianism and womanhood. Separatist groups developed nuanced explanations of the relationship between womanhood and lesbianism. Separation, for Frye, was a crucial act of intercultural insubordination and intracommunal definition: "When women separate (withdraw, break out, regroup, transcend, shove aside, step outside, migrate, say *no*), we are simultaneously controlling access and defining. We are doubly insubordinate, since neither of these is permitted. And access and definition are fundamental ingredients in the alchemy of power, so we are doubly, and radically, insubordinate."[100] That daring power could not be achieved through traditional reform efforts in which women were forced to look and act a certain way. Feminism with "an aspect of separatism" reversed historical power dynamics. "The slave" rebuffed "the master" and, in so doing, "declares herself not a slave."[101]

For many separatists, lesbianism was liberation, the practice and politics of prioritizing women in daily life. As Ann Japenga writes, "When asked about the boy-and-man-hating, a resident of OWLT farm remarked that she hadn't given a thought to men in months. That's not rancor, it's oblivion."[102] Lesbian politics were, of course, based in desire, but not exclusively.[103] Ginny Berson, a notable lesbian activist of the era, defined "Lesbianism" as a "political choice which every woman must make if she is to become woman-identified and thereby end male supremacy."[104] Lesbianism was not about sex, or at least not just about sex. She saw lesbians as "outcasts from every culture but their own," and they "have the most to gain by ending race, class, and national supremacy within their own ranks."[105] Berson argued that lesbianism should serve as a defining litmus test for any

"DYKES FIRST" 161

attempts at coalescing with other women: "Lesbians must get out of the straight women's movement and form their own movement in order to be taken seriously, to stop straight women from oppressing us, and to force straight women to deal with their own Lesbianism."[106]

Lesbianism was the essential tool for forming an alliance of radical women. To the Radicalesbians, lesbianism was an explosive "rage." The lesbian, they wrote, "is the woman who, often beginning at an extremely early age, acts in accordance with her inner compulsion to be a more complete and freer human being than her society—perhaps then, but certainly later—cares to allow her."[107] For women, lesbianism represented the possibility for humanity denied by men throughout history. It was a double move, a complete jettisoning of every aspect of men's being and a simultaneous embrace of women exclusively, of a women's life lived for herself and other women.[108] "I don't have curtains," one separatist said. "I don't have to worry about someone watching me dress or undress. There's also a sense of community, a sense of supporting each other."[109]

But lesbian separatism was not the creation of a monolithic nation. Each separatist group could self-define and then practice their particular version of lesbian womanhood. Definition and daily practice were redemptive processes. As Frye argues, "Women generally are not the people who do the defining, and we cannot from our isolation and powerlessness simply commence saying different things than others say and make it stick. There is a humpty-dumpty problem in that. But we are able to arrogate definition to ourselves when we repattern access."[110] Repatterning access meant eliminating men's voices, men's participation. These "new boundaries" and "new roles and relationships" made for unpredictable processes. It could cause "some strain, puzzlement and hostility," and it could vary considerably from group to group, even from person to person.[111]

Separating was also a galvanizing act of defiance, and separatists understood that social and political withdrawal would produce backlash. Frye writes, "It is our experience in the movement generally that the defensiveness, nastiness, violence, hostility and irrationality of the reaction to feminism tends to correlate with the blatancy of the element of separation in the strategy or project which triggers the reaction."[112] The threat or act of women's withdrawal triggered

162 WE ARE NOT ONE PEOPLE

the strongest social reactions. She notes, "The separations involved in women leaving homes, marriages and boyfriends, separations from fetuses, and the separation of lesbianism are all pretty dramatic. That is, they are dramatic and blatant when perceived from within the framework provided by the patriarchal world view and male parasitism."[113] Frye acknowledged that from the perspective of men and male dominance, separatism was deeply threatening; for many women, that was appealing.

According to Frye, the act of parting was genuinely revolutionary. Adopting the Christian language of original sin, she explained the social importance of separation: "The original sin is the separation... and it is that, not our art or philosophy, not our speechmaking, nor our 'sexual acts' (or abstinences), for which we will be persecuted, when worse comes to worst."[114] Separation was the original sin because it denied bodily access. Women's bodies were men's; they were children's; they were public displays; they were corporate billboards.

Access to women, for Frye, was social control. If women denied men access by separating, that would enrage men far more than anything lesbians otherwise wrote or said. As Frye, sounding like Stokely Carmichael and H. Rap Brown, summarizes, "The separatist lives with the added burden of being assumed by many to be a morally depraved man-hating bigot. But there is a clue here: if you are doing something that is so strictly forbidden by the patriarchs, you must be doing something right."[115]

Separation also enabled women's survival. In separatist communities, women could find physical, mental, emotional, and spiritual connections apart from the constant threat of patriarchy. As Marilyn Terry theorizes, separatist communes were constructed in clear stages. First, women came for sanctuary: "Here women can relax from involvement in their bodies as objects, forget the image mirrored in the eyes of others, go naked of makeup and women-clothes."[116] Lesbian communities were beyond the "slave spheres" where women were "brutally deprived of individual consciousness by their socially induced man-hunt mentality, or their radical dependence on husband and children for a sense of purpose, of human worth."[117] The initial stage, refuge, provided space for women to develop introspective self-knowledge.

Put differently, communes made possible what philosopher Jeffner Allen called a "philosophy of evacuation." For women to truly escape social restrictions and expectations, they had to collectively remove themselves from the manifold ways the dominant culture forces itself on their bodies. This need for evacuation was especially true where motherhood was concerned. "Our bodies," Allen argues, "are not resources to be used by men to reproduce men and the world of men while, at the same time, giving death to ourselves."[118]

In many separatist groups, there was a renewed interest in forgoing patriarchal beauty standards and for supporting new aesthetics—for instance, supporting women who wanted to pursue bodybuilding or master a martial art. Celebrating different types of beauty was itself a separation from dominant culture. As Densmore explains, women should not be tempted by the false rewards that accompany looking conventionally pretty: "That beautiful object is just an object, a work of art, to look at, not to know, total appearance, bearing no personality or will. To the extent that one is caught up in the beauty of it, one perceives object and not person."[119] There was no real liberation if women lived apart from men while reproducing patriarchy on their bodies, in their actions, and during their relationships. "The more that Lesbians looked and acted like Dykes," Bev Jo claimed, "and not the ways men and heterosexual women wanted us to be, the more Lesbian our community became."[120]

In the second stage of liberation in lesbian communes, a woman transitioned from her own individual consciousness toward a group consciousness. This process was built on education programming wherein "the commune's therapeutic environment is not simply an extension of backyard fence rapping about personal misery, but an opportunity to relate individual experience to the common oppression of women."[121] The curriculum "encourages talk across class, age, race divisions and the discovery of a new allegiance, not to the black man or the white man, not to the father or the employer, but to other women." Women became acquainted "with their slave history based on biological differentiation and cultural myth," and they stripped away "male-oriented psychology imposed on them."[122]

This second stage helped women come together to develop a collective identity and allegiance built around their relationships with

164 WE ARE NOT ONE PEOPLE

other women; it was experiential and existential. The Radicalesbians described a similar process: "It is the primacy of women relating to women, of women creating a new consciousness of and with each other, which is at the heart of women's liberation, and the basis for the cultural revolution. Together we must find, reinforce, and validate our authentic selves."[123] Survival, therefore, was not limited to helping women escape abusive relationships with men. Survival meant finding a path for women as a whole to survive, escape, and triumph over patriarchy.

Conclusion

Separatism was proactively defiant. It was a refusal to participate in all parts of a male-dominated society, including national women's organizations. It was a refusal to participate in the other movements for civil rights that were inclusive of, and often led by, men. In the end, thousands of women came out, picked up, left their homes, and joined separatist organizations throughout the nation. Whether the communities were in rural Oregon or in urban centers like New York City, separatist women used the malleable language of separation to evade male institutions and patriarchal ideas of nationalism and to build a diverse and diffuse archipelago of lesbian communities. Their separatist discourse demonstrated that separatist movements do not need a promised land; they can separate from the nation and critique the domineering ideal of a promised land at the same time.

In her 2016 presidential campaign, Hillary Clinton invoked the phrase "The future is female" to mobilize supporters to elect the first woman to the nation's highest office. The phrase was not hers; it originated at Labyris, a separatist bookstore in Greenwich Village, where the phrase was coined as an advertising slogan in the 1970s.[124] Four decades after its original coinage, a woman poised to lead the nation employed a slogan of separatists who would exit that very nation.

But the slogan was revealing beyond the irony of its reappropriation. Radical women separatists also informed, within and beyond national politics, modern feminism. According to historian Estelle Freedman, early separatist organizations were essential in the political gains made by first-wave feminists in the late nineteenth and early twentieth centuries: "When women tried to assimilate into male-dominated institutions, without securing feminist social, economic, or political bases, they lost the momentum and the networks which had made the suffrage movement possible."[125]

The revolutionary power of lesbian separatism was not measurable only in its impact on feminism or the wider culture. It was revolutionary in and of itself. To Sarah Lucia Hoagland, separating was not just a negative response to men, a "no-saying," but an insurgent act to create new meanings, a "yes-saying" to a new community.[126]

In Hoagland's understanding of political dispute, both reformist and revolutionary movements actually concede power to existing patriarchal orders; in making demands, they affirm existing power structures and "play by dominant rules." However, when women broke off from men, they simultaneously took power that men "would otherwise have had" and, by departing, created power "for ourselves" in new ways that were occluded by patriarchy. The belief that fighting or otherwise directly engaging patriarchy was the only way to change patriarchy was, to Hoagland, self-serving for men, a way to "keep us believing that patriarchy is the only reality." "Thus," she explains, "while separatism doesn't redistribute power, it alters, sometimes radically, the over-all distribution of power."[127]

The revolutionary power of separation was something many residents of women's lands and separatist communities felt everyday. Winnie Adams, for instance, called herself a "radical feminist separatist lesbian." Before her move to the Alapine women's community in northeast Alabama, Adams was an information systems consultant who was married to a man with whom she had two kids. She felt liberated once she left, under great stress, her previous life for a land community. "To me, this is the real world," she told the *New York Times* in 2009, "and it's a very peaceful world. I don't hear anything except the leaves falling. I get up in the morning, I go out on my front deck and I dance and I say, 'It's another glorious day on the mountain.' Men are violent. The minute a man walks in the dynamics change immediately, so I choose not to be around those dynamics."[128]

In Elana Dykewomon's estimation, lesbian separatism allowed so many women like Adams to refigure their lives in ways that

166 WE ARE NOT ONE PEOPLE

mainstream, mixed-sex society could not. "Without homeland, without a national food, with only sexual affinity, a glimmer of a shared sense of humor and a few common points of outrage, lesbians have managed whole lifetimes of support, interconnection, politics, ethics, art," she argues.[129] Similarly, Anna Lee, a prominent Black lesbian separatist, reflected that it was only "within the context of lesbian separatism" that "we have created spaces to know each other," "developed an analysis which unitizes lesbians as the basis," "created economic lesbian networks," and "developed lesbian skills in carpentry, music, production, printing, selling, and so forth." Such abilities only "flourished in a lesbian context" where "we have surpassed our wildest dreams."[130]

The symbolic and pragmatic success of lesbian separatism was the achievement of a "feminist process, a method for living in the world," rather than a "rigid ideology." Lesbian separatism was transformative; it enabled an entirely new "field of the possible," a chance to realize "utopian possibilities."[131]

Of course, separatism was not universally accepted or celebrated by women, including other radical women. The Combahee River Collective Statement was one of the most well-known critiques of lesbian separatism. Produced by a collective of Black feminists, the statement refused the call to privilege womanhood over everything else. The statement declared: "We reject the stance of Lesbian separatism because it is not a viable political analysis or strategy for us. It leaves out far too much and far too many people, particularly Black men, women, and children."[132]

The Collective renounced the separatists' attempt to foreground women's oppression over racial oppression. The statement also refused the separatists' biological explanation of oppressive male behavior. "As Black women," they warned, "we find any type of biological determinism a particularly dangerous and reactionary basis upon which to build a politic." Separatism based on sex, furthermore, "so completely denies any but the sexual sources of women's oppression, negating the facts of class and race."[133] But the dispute was not so simple as a divide between broad-minded Black feminists on one side and parochial white separatist lesbians on the other. As the Black separatist Anna Lee wrote, "To all my sisters who perceive separatism as a white ideology, I reject that notion. We have been defined by those who have power over us."[134] Despite the efforts of activists like Lee, the critique that the lesbian separatist groups were white stuck.[135]

Racism was only one way in which separatism was characterized as regressive by other feminists. For some, separatism was also transphobic.[136] The fate of the once-thriving Michigan Womyn's Festival was telling. Begun in 1976 as a "big party for women only," it became much more than that, "something more like a state of mind, a community, a dream come true, a Brigadoon appearing and fading away each summer for the last 28 years, built by women's hands for women to enjoy."[137] Sacred though it was, it ended in 2015 after becoming embroiled in controversy "because of its exclusion of transgender women, with many artists and organizations deciding to boycott."[138]

Some found that the ideal of a "women-only" space recreated the very acts of discrimination they were supposed to oppose. The anthropologist Keridwen Luis reports that while she encountered "some personally shocking incidences of transphobia" in her research on and immersion in women's lands, "transphobia was not uniform across all women's lands or among all land-women, made up a relatively minor aspect of my research, and must be considered in the light of women's lands that explicitly welcome—or are created for the use of—trans women." The transphobia charge, however, stuck as well; when Luis discussed her project with friends and colleagues, transphobia was the first topic many broached.[139]

Separatists did not just face the criticisms of outsiders. They faced jeremiads from founders as well. Whereas separatist communities were once egalitarian spaces in which all members contributed to separatist advocacy, Bev Jo thought they had devolved into elitist, corporate organizations that included males and farmed out advocacy to academics. The "radical ideas have almost been completely abandoned," she sighed.[140]

Separatism had its purist critics, but it also had its reformers, those who pushed separatists to see withdrawal as a process, a temporary strategy, not a final destination. As Bernice Johnson Reagon argued, "We've pretty much come to the end of a time when you can have a space that is 'ours only'—just for the people you want to be there." To her, total separation was a flat-out fantasy: "There is no hiding place.

168   WE ARE NOT ONE PEOPLE

There is nowhere you can go and only be with people who are like you. It's over. Give it up."[141]

Reagon's call for separatists to "give it up" was prescient. By the 2000s, many lesbian separatist communities had done just that. Between 1970 and 2010, the total number of separatist communities had declined by at least a third, and some surviving communities struggled to find members, especially younger ones.[142] Lani Ravin, a land-use planner who oversaw Vermont's HOWL, framed this decline as simple cause and effect. As the wider world became a little more tolerant of feminism and lesbianism, a radical feminist lesbian retreat was harder to sell. She said in 2019, "Thirty-five years ago, this was a place to escape the patriarchy—and it still can be, but honestly, in Burlington, the patriarchy has a lower volume."[143]

Another HOWL member, Michele Grimm, thought that different tactics might help reach the youth market. "We need to take more photographs," she said. "For younger people, it's all about Instagram, Facebook. They want to see what's going on here and they want a window into it before they commit to coming out here."[144]

Other women's communities faced similar recruiting and publicity problems, but they had also long nurtured a cautious secrecy that they did not feel comfortable sacrificing in catchy social media posts.[145] Alapine was an example. One of its founders, Morgana MacVicar, worried about the dangers that came with publicity: "We just don't announce our lesbianism. . . . People know who we are. We don't want somebody who's making a political statement here." Alapine's property manager, Barbara Lieu, saw the numbers problem the community faced but did not think there was a way out; the culture had shifted too much. "I don't have a fantasy that young lesbians will want to come here," she said. "They have enough freedoms in the world that we never had. And they're transitioning in all kinds of ways."[146] Alapine even considered selling plots of land to men.[147] Andrea Gibbs-Henson, who directed Camp Sister Spirit in Mississippi, said that she had seen community after community "go belly up." In a time of such scarcity, even feminist utopias had to adapt. "We would not survive here if all we did was cater to lesbian separatists," she said.[148]

6

Secession in Exodus

Achieving God's Terrestrial Kingdom

Catherine Cottam Romney celebrated her thirty-second birthday at her parents' home in St. George, Utah, on January 7, 1887. She gathered her six children and set out to a new life in Mexico that same day. She traveled by train from St. George to Salt Lake City, then to Denver, then south to Deming, New Mexico. Once there, Catherine met the guides who would take her family on a multiple-day wagon trip into the Mexican backcountry, where her husband, Miles P. Romney, was waiting for her.[1]

Back in Utah, Miles had been a public man, a police chief and a newspaper editor, but he had also been a good son by following in his father's footsteps as a builder. He put an addition onto Brigham Young's winter home.[2] But in early 1887, he hoped Catherine and their children would arrive safely to join him in Chihuahua.

He was not waiting alone. Annie, Romney's fourth wife, already lived with him at the Mexican homestead. Hannah, his first wife, would arrive shortly after Catherine, the third woman Romney married. (He married five women in his life.) The many Romneys lived modestly on the banks of the Piedras Verdes, a substantial improvement over the initial shelter Miles had initially built in Mexico by "driving four posts into the ground and covering two sides with burlap sacks sewn together."[3] Whether their accommodations were posh or shoddy, Mexico was a refuge for the Romneys. They were not there for Chihuahua's natural splendor, and they were not chasing some high desert dream. The Romneys were on the lam, having relocated to avoid the law.

Mexico was the Romneys' first stint as fugitives, but it was not their first family move. At Brigham Young's request, Miles had previously relocated the family to St. John's, Arizona. Hoping to secure a larger

We Are Not One People. Michael J. Lee and R. Jarrod Atchison, Oxford University Press. © Oxford University Press 2022. DOI: 10.1093/oso/9780190876500.003.0007

170   WE ARE NOT ONE PEOPLE

western footprint, Young thought big families of Latter-day Saint pioneers would expand Church visibility and increase its influence. But the area was hostile to the Latter-day Saints. Miles was arrested on a suspicious perjury charge related to his homestead application, skipped out on a bond, and subsequently fled to Mexico to avoid jail.[4] He had good reason to fear imprisonment; if he went back to Arizona, he faced not just this charge but also, very likely, a polygamy charge. In 1884, he watched three of his friends who had been convicted of illegal cohabitation get shipped off to a Detroit prison.[5]

Romney's run from the law was supported by the president of the Church of the Latter-day Saints, John Taylor, Young's successor. A strong polygamy proponent, Taylor also worried that losing his congregation to faraway jail cells would unravel the community. Taylor, who later spent his last years avoiding a federal polygamy charge, sent an emissary to Romney to urge an escape to Mexico, where they could live with co-religionists.[6]

The Church bought twenty thousand acres of Mexican land to support six polygamous communities in Chihuahua and nearby Sonora, and they employed a network of border guides to facilitate the difficult crossing.[7] Church-affiliated authors even wrote detailed instructions on how to make the trip. "We would recommend," one guide read, "persons intending to settle in Mexico to visit the country and become familiar with its advantages and disadvantages."[8] Aided by a convincing disguise, Romney made it to Mexico, but the border crossing did not ease his mind. He fretted that American marshals would track him down.[9] As Romney admitted in a letter to his brother-in-law, "If the Marshals come here I do not know whether I will fight or not. If I can dodge I will. If I cannot time alone will tell what I may do."[10]

Romney's indecision over fighting against or continuing to flee from federal marshals was a scaled-down version of Latter-day Saints history. The Latter-day Saints wrestled with the choice to obey, defy, or separate from American laws and cultural customs since Joseph Smith's revelations. The struggle was both intergroup and intragroup. The Latter-day Saints were historically and theologically American. They emerged following Smith in upstate New York in the 1820s, and they believed that Christ would come back to earth in Independence, Missouri.

SECESSION IN EXODUS 171

But the Latter-day Saints were separated by belief and behavior from American Christians. Forty years before Romney's departure, Smith and a group of Church leaders practiced polygamy in secret for fear of incensing the wider community in Nauvoo, Illinois. Smith may have sealed himself to as many as forty wives, including Vilate Murray Kimball, who was fourteen when they wed.[11] Smith tested his male followers by asking them to present their wives to him for marriage. John Taylor agreed to allow Smith to wed one of his wives only to see Smith decline the opportunity. Smith was confirming Taylor's loyalty. But Smith gave others the same test, and when they agreed, he went ahead with the marriages.[12] As stories of the community's polygamist practices and Smith's chicanery leaked out, Smith adopted a strategic double posture; he spoke against polygamy in public while privately encouraging Church leaders to continue the practice.[13]

When the weary Latter-day Saints arrived at the Great Salt Lake in 1847, they were in the northernmost tip of Mexico. That changed quickly. They traveled thirteen hundred miles to leave America's confines only for Utah to become an American territory one year later as part of the Mexican Cession. Regardless, for a time, the Saints generated tremendous distances between them and any hostile community or legal authority. Once the Saints made it to the relative freedom of the territories, the need for secrecy vanished, and polygamy became a central feature of Church life. Within two years of Smith's death, "the number of plural marriages expanded five-fold, involving up to 10 percent of all Latter-day Saints."[14] As one researcher of Mormon history speculates, "The Saints must have rejoiced in the freedom they encountered moving across the plains, outside the confines of the United States. There, living in the territories where polygamy was not illegal, they could talk more freely among themselves about plural marriage."[15]

When Miles Romney died in 1904, Colonia Juárez, their adopted Mexican home, was a thriving community. Six years later, the Mexican Revolution threatened their secluded existence. Revolutionaries increasingly targeted Americans over the next two years. Forty-two thousand people, including most members of the Mexican Mormon colonies, left their homes to seek safety in the United States.[16] In 1912, Catherine Cottam Romney once again fled her home. Her daughter Lula recorded the experience, noting that in their rushed exit they "left

172   WE ARE NOT ONE PEOPLE

cake and chicken in the oven and started out with less than a dollar."[17] As for the trip itself, Lula noted, "We rode all day squeezed into the train like cattle without a drop of water to drink until about 3 a.m. when we reached El Paso, Texas."[18] Twenty-five years after she left St. George to join her husband and his other wives in Mexico, Catherine arrived back in the United States to avoid persecution. She spent the last six years of her life with her children before dying in Salt Lake City in 1918.[19]

A Higher Law

In what follows, we analyze discourses of American religious separatists, one group in particular, for whom terrestrial political allegiance had divine implications, for whom civic belonging was linked to celestial admission. They had to get out to get clean; they had to get clean to get in. The utopian movements of the eighteenth and nineteenth centuries were built on the idea that earthly life is bookended by bliss: "All human existence—is just the hard distance between these two utopias, a long but finite exile from paradise."[20] Members of many experimental communities in the nineteenth century believed that "New Jerusalem was coming" but that it had to "be built from the ground up, by planners and engineers."[21]

Few of these groups agreed on exactly the sort of New Jerusalem they were building, but they all knew it had to be built beyond American civilization, cut off from American culture, outside of American religious institutions, and spatially apart from most other Americans. A widely varied group of nineteenth-century utopian communities—Shakers, Fourierists, Icarians, and residents of Oneida and New Harmony— were inspired by Thomas More's *Utopia* (1516). Ann Lee, a Manchester blacksmith's daughter who founded Shakerism, was regarded by "thousands of Americans" of the era "as the Second Coming of Christ." "Mother Ann" offered at least twenty thousand Americans a compelling vision of a "New World Zion," "an austere, celibate, communistic paradise."[22]

Religious exit is a distinct point on the horizon of separatist activity. For religious communities, separation has been both a method to protect a religious order that was under assault and a tool to create the

SECESSION IN EXODUS   173

material conditions necessary for a spiritual ideal, a godly kingdom on earth, beyond the bounds of a sinful America. Separatist religious appeals have a special place in America. Rhode Island, Pennsylvania, and Massachusetts were all founded in the image of the divine. The nation itself could perhaps be called a "utopian experiment."[23]

Few historical cases, nevertheless, represent the full spectrum of American religious separatism like the Latter-day Saints.[24] Harold Bloom notes that the Mormon Church was, on the one hand, "American to the core," but, on the other hand, the Saints were "a religion that became a people."[25] They had been of and apart from America simultaneously; the Church had faced tremendous pressure to assimilate into and separate from American culture throughout its history and, in a sense, opted to do both. In Bloom's estimation, "No other American religious movement is so ambitious, and no rival even remotely approaches the spiritual audacity that drives endlessly towards accomplishing a titanic design."[26] Brigham Young displayed such spiritual audacity when he declared in 1845, "When we go from here we dont calculate to go under any government but the government of God."[27] The Latter-day Saints' experience over the next century, in which the Saints and Utah integrated into America as a distinct religious group in a distinctly religious nation showed that Young's declaration was premised on a false choice.

Although the story of the Church's separation from and integration into the nation has been a public one, key parts of that story only became public after 2016. Since then, scholars have had access to previously concealed internal Church records of high-level debates about separation and secession in the 1840s. In this chapter, we examine these deliberations, meetings of what was called the Council of Fifty. Charged with finding "some place where we can go and establish a Theocracy either in Texas or Oregon or somewhere in California," the Council of Fifty was commissioned in 1844, in the final months of Smith's life, and plotted the community's potential exit up until the westward trek to Utah began in 1846.[28] (The Council was suspended in 1851 after Utah became a territory and, after a brief resurgence in the early 1880s, was permanently disbanded in 1884.)

These Council texts along with the public and private communication of early Church leaders reveal that the decision to move beyond

174 WE ARE NOT ONE PEOPLE

national boundaries was grounded in their own unique interpretation of American history. The nation was a divinely ordained staging ground for a future Mormon theocracy. Separating, therefore, was a sanctified act.

Early Latter-day Saints history, according to one historian, should be "considered alongside other protest movements born out of alienation from the American state—such as the American Indian Movement and various black nationalist groups, including the Nation of Islam and Black Panthers."[29] The difference, of course, is that the Latter-day Saints were overwhelmingly white and their religious alienation was not accelerated by racial alienation. Moreover, they seceded at a time when it was possible to move across the continent, as difficult as that was, and escape American oversight for a time.

The combination of divine and political justifications enabled religious separatists to envision sovereignty in different ways than other separatists. Many separatists rooted their exit in earthly concerns. Some separatists cited democratic principles to justify withdrawal. Others cited absolute differences between groups to justify living apart. Religious separatists like the Saints claimed to follow a higher law. Their God's commandments superseded any laws written by sinful, imperfect people. For the Mormons, that belief, whether threatening or fringe, was both quintessentially American and protected by the time-honored American principle of religious freedom. As the religion scholar R. Laurence Moore argues, "Mormons followed a lesson already by their time well established in American experience, that one way of becoming American was to invent oneself out of a sense of opposition." By defining themselves against the American "mainstream," the Latter-day Saints laid a "claim to it." By adopting the role of "outsiders," they actually moved closer to the American "center."[30]

Inaugurated in Oppression

In the spring of 1820, fourteen-year-old Joseph Smith walked into a New York forest to pray. With the Second Great Awakening swirling around him, he sought God's guidance on which church to join. According to the Mormon Church's official history, he received a message far more powerful than a simple inclination one way or another. He was visited by God and Jesus Christ. Jesus commanded, "Join none of them." Modern churches, Jesus instructed, "teach for doctrines the commandments of men, having a form of Godliness, but they deny the power thereof." Jesus told Smith that modern churches were, in essence, idolaters: "They have turned aside from the gospel and keep not my commandments."[31]

Stunned by his vision of God and Jesus, Smith returned home and eventually sought out a local religious leader who had been deeply involved in area revivals. Angered by Smith's story of revelation, the preacher judged the story the devil's work.[32] Smith quickly found that no one else believed him either; the mere mention of his vision sparked backlash. Smith wondered why he was berated "for telling the truth," why "the world" would deny "what I have actually seen."[33]

Much of the early history of the Latter-day Saints reads like popular narratives of the Pilgrims: a pious people striving for religious freedom while the world rejects and oppresses them. For decades, the Church moved from community to community seeking a place to dwell in peace. They traveled from Fayette, New York, to Kirtland, Ohio, to Far West, Missouri, to Nauvoo, Illinois, and, finally, to the Great Salt Lake.

In 1833, the Church felt the full wrath of communal rejection in Missouri. As historian Richard Turley summarizes, "Religious, cultural, economic, and political tensions exploded after the Church's newspaper in Missouri ran an article advising free blacks coming into the state how to avoid encountering trouble with Missouri's law."[34] An inflamed local posse rallied against the Saints. Lyman Wright, an early Church leader and ordained member of the Quorum of the Twelve Apostles, testified that "some time towards the last of the summer of 1833, they commenced their operations of mobocracy," including breaking windows, doors, burning fences, and generally terrorizing Latter-day Saints.[35] A senior Church leader, Bishop Edward Partridge, was tarred and feathered.[36] Although a local judge ruled in his favor in the case that followed, Partridge was awarded only "a penny and a peppercorn" for his damages.[37]

The conflict in Missouri escalated to a "Mormon War" by 1838, wherein mob attacks were so devastating that the Church leadership appealed directly to the governor for help. The governor replied that

176 WE ARE NOT ONE PEOPLE

the "quarrel was between the Mormons and the mob" and refused to intervene.[38] In August 1838, the mob attempted to stop Church members from voting, and the Mormon War escalated. The governor sent a militia to stop the fighting, but there was no pretense of protecting the Church. A militia captain even kidnapped three Church members. When members of the Church attacked a militia camp to free their people, more fighting broke out. One militiaman died.

The governor, in retaliation, issued an "extermination order" calling the Latter-day Saints "enemies" who "must be exterminated or driven from the State if necessary, for the public peace."[39] Three days later, a mob executed the governor's order. Seventeen Church members were killed at Hawn's Mill. Turley describes the graphic violence: "Before blowing off the head of a young boy found hiding under the bellows in the blacksmith shop, one vigilante uttered the slogan used for generations by bigots to justify killing the children of minorities, 'Nits will make lice.' "[40]

Evading further violence, the Latter-day Saints evacuated Missouri and purchased and settled a small town in Illinois that Smith named Nauvoo.[41] They started construction on a temple and hoped their sheer numbers and tight communal organization would empower them to control local government. Initially, the plan worked. According to Turley, "Mormons were the majority, and Joseph Smith became the leader of the city, the court, and the militia. The city grew and prospered, aided by an influx of immigrant converts, and Joseph continued to seek equality and justice for his people."[42] By 1844, Nauvoo rivaled Chicago's size at 12,000 people.[43] They had achieved local power, but that did not solve the continued persecution of the Church by state powers, and it could not protect Smith.

In many ways, Smith and the leadership of the Church tried every political and legal remedy available to them to try to stop the harassment of their members. They used the courts, appealed to governors, and bought their own land. Smith even went to Washington to make a direct appeal to President Martin Van Buren. The president expressed his sympathy but had practical and political considerations to worry about. Van Buren did not think the federal government had a reason to intervene in the matter, and he did not want to lose support in Missouri or Illinois.[44]

In 1843, Smith queried the presidential candidates about what they would do to protect the Latter-day Saints, and when he found their answers unacceptable, he decided to run for the office. "Smith," one historian suggests, "was more than a protest candidate." He and the Church truly believed that he could win.[45]

As Smith pursued every legal and political option available to them, they began exploring options outside of America. The Council of Fifty deliberations, in particular, show how seriously Smith and his followers considered separation as both a pragmatic remedy and a divine prophecy. The Council of Fifty, both a separatist task force and an all-powerful advisory commission, was a group of men that Smith handpicked to help him plan a new government, an American Zion, beyond America's borders. Religion scholars Joseph McConkie and Robert Millet explain the theological difference of the Mormon conception of Zion: "In an Old Testament setting, Zion usually has reference to the holy mount or, by extension, to the city of Jerusalem." But in the Book of Mormon, "Zion seems to represent the gathering place of the believers, the society of the pure in heart, the setting for the Saints."[46] Zion was where the Saints were. The mobility of Zion was, therefore, essential for Smith because the community faced torment at every turn. If all of his efforts at reforming government failed, he would need a clean escape.

Another group of Church leaders, the Quorum of Twelve Apostles, already worked in public "to act as special witnesses of Christ, baptizing in His name and gathering converts to Zion and its branches."[47] The Council of Fifty, on the other hand, was secretive and focused on strengthening the Latter-day Saints' political power.[48] In Smith's assessment, the Council "was designed to be got up for the safety and salvation of the saints by protecting them in their religious rights and worship."[49] Council members were sworn to secrecy. Council deliberations, though carefully guarded, were also carefully recorded; the entire minutes of previous meetings were read aloud to commence subsequent sessions.

Smith so feared that these sensitive discussions of separation could be characterized as sedition that he ordered the Council secretary, William Clayton, to hide the records. (Clayton dutifully buried them in his garden, but he later dug them up and recopied them.) The group,

178   WE ARE NOT ONE PEOPLE

after all, was developing plans to protect themselves through the fulfillment of Smith's vision of what he termed a "theodemocracy." As the
historian Richard Bushman writes, members of the Council of Fifty
"insisted on confidentiality" because what they were plotting was potentially traitorous, in the same vein "as Samuel Adams and the Boston
patriots." The Council was laying the groundwork "to declare the
Mormons' independence from the United States."[50]

Scholars have had a few hints about the Council's existence even
without the garden minutes. Since the Church restricted access to
the records, "the minutes had become a sort of 'holy grail' of early
Mormon documents."[51] In 2013, the Church of Latter-day Saints
agreed to grant access to these crucial documents, and in 2016,
it published the first official volume of the Council's deliberations,
spanning some six hundred pages. Matthew Grow, the managing di-
rector of the Church's history department, and Eric Smith, editor of
the Joseph Smith papers, argue, "The era between March 1844 and
January 1846—or, roughly, between Joseph Smith's murder and the
Mormon exodus from Illinois—is a particularly important time of
transition in Mormon history." "The minutes," they explain, show
the group's larger "determination to find a place of safety and refuge
in western North America where they could build their kingdom in
peace."[52] While Smith was publicly advocating for legal and political
protections to foster integration, the Council worked the opposite
strategy; they diligently pursued a separate future for the Church
outside the United States.

The Kingdom of God Beyond America

The Council of Fifty thoroughly sketched the theology, organization, and daily practices of a separate Latter-day Saints theocracy.
According to historian Patrick Mason, "Indeed, theocracy was built
into the council's DNA from the beginning. Sidney Rigdon, Brigham
Young, and other council members stood ready to ditch *demos* in
favor of *theos* and the political rule of God's appointed servant, Joseph
Smith."[53] Brigham Young said, "No line can be drawn between the
church and other governments, of the spiritual and temporal affairs

of the church. Revelations must govern. The voice of God, shall be the voice of the people."[54]

Rigdon, a powerful member of the Council who was later excommunicated after he asserted control of the Church when Smith was killed, believed that the Council might "form a Theocracy according to the will of Heaven."[55] As John Taylor, also a member of the Council of Fifty, said, "Was the kingdom that the Prophets talked about, that should be set up in the latter times, going to be a Church? Yes. And a state? Yes, it was going to be both Church and State."[56] In fact, Joseph Smith sometimes referred to the Council of Fifty itself as the kingdom of God because "the council was considered as the nucleus of God's future government on earth."[57] Smith wrote in his testament in the Book of Mormon that the angel Moroni commanded him to refuse any "motive" other "than that of building his kingdom."[58]

Designing a new government that mirrored and fulfilled God's will was no easy task. The Council of Fifty members researched, deliberated, and reported on how to address pragmatic concerns, Church members' basic needs for food, water, and shelter, as well as grander visions of an international political system with "two great centers of world government—the city of Zion on our Western continent, and Jerusalem."[59]

Throughout their discussions, one theme persisted: the "kingdom of God" included a *political* institution that protected the Church. Government, in other words, must protect the Church and its believers. Smith and the Church leadership tried to use existing American political institutions at the local, state, and national levels to grow and protect their Church, but their continued persecution demonstrated that Americans only paid lip service to religious freedom; the only path to a true kingdom was their own theocracy.

As violent as Americans had been, Church discourse of the era paid homage to the design of the United States federal government and its founding. 1776 was both historically and theologically significant for the Latter-day Saints. Church leaders and the Council of Fifty depicted separation as God's plan for America, and America was a necessary condition in God's plan for the Mormon Church. As Hyrum Andrus, curator of the Church's documents at Brigham Young University, observes, "The establishment of the Constitution of the United States

180 WE ARE NOT ONE PEOPLE

was looked upon as a preparatory development necessary to the later establishment of the Kingdom of God."[60] In other words, America was chosen by God as the birthplace of his kingdom. God sent his only son to die in the Middle East; he would return in the West.

The Church preached American exceptionalism, but only as a prelude to the Saints' exceptionalism. Orson Pratt, a member of the Council and an original member of the Quorum of the Twelve Apostles, exclaimed, "O America! How art thou favored above all lands! O happy Republic, how exalted above all nations! Within thee is the Kingdom of God! Thou wast chosen to prepare its ways![61] Americans have long seen themselves as a chosen people, but for Pratt, America's divine role was in facilitating Smith's creation of a godly nation with a worldwide mission: "It was for this purpose, then, that a republic was organized upon this continent, to prepare the way for a kingdom which shall have dominion over all the earth to the ends thereof."[62] America, like John the Baptist, was essential for future deliverance, but it was not deliverance itself. Bloom summarizes, "The entire burden of Joseph Smith's prophecy was that the Kingdom of God was destined to be set up in America and that only a Chosen People could rely upon themselves enough to be able to organize the Kingdom."[63]

Although the Council of Fifty raged at Americans and the failure of American institutions to protect the Church, for Pratt and others, America's founding was the first step in God's plan; it was up to them to follow his commandment to bring forth yet another nation, a more perfect theocracy. Following that commandment meant building on America's founding documents, not replacing them wholesale.

The Council's rhetorical and doctrinal commitments show the depth of their connection to the founding, especially the preamble to the Constitution. The Latter-day Saints would build an even "more perfect" nation; the Constitution was "a stepping stone to a form of government infinitely greater and more perfect—a government founded upon Divine laws, and officers appointed by the God of heaven."[64] The Constitution began by stating that "We, the People" commission a new government to promote "Justice" and "Tranquility," "provide for the common defense," "promote the general welfare, and "secure the blessings of Liberty." As the Council saw it, secular democracy was fundamentally flawed. God established perfect governments through

SECESSION IN EXODUS   181

people; people did not erect perfect governments without God. The divine, moreover, was nowhere to be found in the Preamble's list of the goals of a just government.

America's imperfection foretold its demise and necessitated the Latter-day Saints' departure. As Pratt put it, "But will the government of the United States continue forever? No, it is not sufficiently perfect; and, notwithstanding it has been sanctioned by the Lord at a time when it was suited to the circumstances of the people."[65] As one scholar describes their aim, "It was held that the Kingdom of God would restore the true concept of government as envisioned by the Founding Fathers in 1787."[66]

Young went to great lengths to cast the nation's founding as God's will: "The signers of the Declaration of Independence and the framers of the Constitution were inspired from on high to do that work." The founders "laid the foundation"; it was, nevertheless, "for aftergenerations to rear the superstructure upon it."[67] God, then, used the secular Enlightenment philosophy that underscored America's founding to show the Latter-day Saints, through Smith's revelations, the insufficiency of godless government. The defects of America's separation helped God reveal to Smith what a true kingdom of God looked like. For Pratt, the divine die had been cast, and now that Joseph Smith had set God's plan in motion, the kingdom of God would eventually supplant the need for America. The kingdom of God "must increase," and America "shalt decrease!"[68]

Correcting for America's founding indulgence in the secular, the new kingdom would govern via the sacred; political institutions would be guided by an inspired priesthood and govern a pious citizenry. John Taylor explained the political chain of command: "The proper mode of government is this—God first speaks, and then the people have their action. . . . We have our voice and agency, and act with the most perfect freedom; still we believe there is a correct order—some wisdom and knowledge proceeds from God through the medium of the Holy Priesthood."[69] For a polity to be truly reflective of the divine, the Council stipulated a direct line between the Church and government. Taylor concluded, "We believe that no man or set of men, of their own wisdom and by their own talents, are capable of governing the human family aright."[70] Human political judgment alone was insufficiently reflective of God's will.

182   WE ARE NOT ONE PEOPLE

The Council designed an active role for the priesthood in daily government, but they reached somewhat of an impasse over what other democratic principles to model. For example, Smith asked the Council to write a constitution for their new government. They came back frustrated. The ensuing debate over the document centered on two questions: was there a difference between the kingdom of God and the Church of God, and would the founding documents of governance be treated as binding in the same way scripture was?

The Council met and debated these questions for hours without a clear resolution.[71] Finally, Smith said he experienced a revelation directing him to end the debate. The proposed constitution would be left "alone." One Council member said, "He would tell us the whole matter about the constitution as follows—Verily thus saith the Lord, ye are my constitution, and I am your God, and ye are my spokesmen. From henceforth do as I shall command you."[72] Parley Pratt, an author of the scrapped constitution, said that he "'burnt [his] scribbling' as soon as 'a ray of light shewed' that the council was to be the constitution itself. The voice of God's chosen people was the voice of God."[73] The political controversy was settled via revelation. Smith would head the theocracy; the Council of Fifty was the only governing body that Smith needed to foster the kingdom.

Rather than attempting to recreate the machinery of government from scratch, the Council of Fifty modeled much of their new government on the United States; they claimed to have perfected the original vision of the founders, so there was no need to scrap the entirety of the nation's organization. The kingdom of God was to be a full-scale representative democracy modeled on federal, state, and local governments. According to Brigham Young, "Few, if any, understand what a theocratic government is. In every sense of the word, it is a republican government, and differs but little in form from our National, State, and Territorial Governments; but its subjects will recognize the will and dictation of the Almighty." America, though deficient, was near the mark. According to Young, "The Constitution and laws of the United States resemble a theocracy more closely than any government now on earth. . . . Even now the form of the Government of the United States differs but little from the Kingdom of God."[74] The new kingdom of God grounded government in the Mormon faith, but its operations,

SECESSION IN EXODUS   183

Young hoped, would be somewhat recognizable to anyone leaving the United States of America.

The core operational difference between America's government and the kingdom's proposed government was the priesthood; the priesthood would drive the governing agenda. According to the Council, the newly developed relationship between church and state best represented God's vision. Church leaders and the Council, nevertheless, drew some lines between the political functions of the kingdom and the Church itself. George Q. Cannon, a member of both the Council and the Quorum of the Twelve Apostles, explained, "The Kingdom of God is a separate organization from the Church of God. There may be men acting as officers in the Kingdom of God who will not be members of the Church of Jesus Christ of Latter-day Saints."[75] The two organizations, the kingdom and the Church, would work in concert, but the members would be elected for different purposes.

Although they were explicitly planning a theocracy inspired by divine revelation outside of a nation they found insufficiently protective of their religious practices, the need for the new kingdom to protect religious freedom was voiced consistently in Council deliberations. Contradictory though it may appear, the Saints' investment in religious freedom reflected their criticism of America's founding and the experience with violent Americans. After all, the Saints would not need to leave to establish their kingdom if Americans practiced what they preached where religious freedom was concerned. They did not want to risk yet another political threat to the Church by empowering the new kingdom to legislate religious morality explicitly.

The tension between a theocracy and a government that stayed out of religious belief was evident between Council members and sometimes appeared to trouble individual Council members. For instance, Cannon interpreted Smith as allowing political officials in the kingdom to come from outside the auspices of the Church. "The Kingdom of God," Cannon held, "when established will not be for the protection of the Church of Jesus Christ alone, but for the protection of all men, whatever their religious views or opinions may be."[76] Brigham Young concurred; legislators may pass laws and still "not belong to the Church of Jesus Christ at all."[77]

184 WE ARE NOT ONE PEOPLE

Despite their openness to men from outside the Church, Young was still concerned with the moral character of their elected officials. How could they guarantee the morality of legislators who were not Church-affiliated? After all, he did not want elected officials "who would let the nation sink for a can of oysters and a lewd woman."[78] The priesthood provided the ultimate check. Elected officials, whether Church grandees or not, were expected to, at the very least, honor the priesthood and listen to its recommendations if not actually serve as the instrument of its visions.

It is clear that the failure to put an a priori emphasis on religious freedom was, for Pratt, Young, and other Council members, an essential American failure. For Smith and the Council of Fifty, the emptiness of religious freedom in America was an existential threat that could only be remedied through separation. They felt that political protection was pivotal to the Church's continued survival.

When Smith described his initial decision in February 1844 to send a group to investigate inhabitable lands out West, he emphasized protection as the essential telos of secession: "I instructed the Twelve Apostles to send out a delegation and investigate the locations of California and Oregon, and hunt out a good location, where we can build a city in a day, and have a government of our own, get up into the mountains, where the devil cannot dig us out."[79] It would be much easier to practice religious freedom in a remote mountain theocracy of their own.

For Young and the other members of the Council of Fifty, the search for religious freedom was yet another way in which the Latter-day Saints were a continuation, not a repudiation, of the nation they were departing. Religious freedom, per Church history, compelled America's separation from England, so it was only just that the Latter-day Saints would follow suit in forming their own divine government. According to Young, "We consider that the men in the Revolution were inspired by the Almighty, to throw off the shackles of the mother government, with her established religion. For this cause were Adams, Jefferson, Franklin, Washington, and a host of others inspired to deeds of resistance to the acts of the King of Great Britain."[80] The emphasis on deeds of resistance took on an entirely new meaning just months after

Smith created the Council of Fifty. An Illinois mob murdered Joseph Smith him and his brother, Hyrum, on June 27, 1844.

Murder and Fear: An Elixir of Secession

The murder of the Smith brothers shook the Latter-day Saints. Joseph was their seer and their governor. Just three months before the killings, Church leaders envisioned that Smith would either become the next president of the United States or lead the creation of a new Latter-day Saints theocracy. "Mormon history is Joseph Smith," Bloom argues, "and his continued effect upon the Saints."[81]

One of Smith's last acts had been surrendering to Illinois authorities who alleged that he violated a law when he ordered the closure of a printing press. As Smith mounted his horse to turn himself over in Carthage, he reportedly said to his wife, "I am going like a lamb to the slaughter, but I am calm as a summer's morning."[82] After the Carthage violence, the Smith brothers became founding Saint martyrs, and their deaths led the Council to move from theoretical conversations about the kingdom of God to the very practical need for safety far away at high altitudes.

Church leaders begged members to forswear revenge after the Smith brothers' deaths. Some elders called for the community to have faith in the legal system—"Trust in the law for redress"—while others encouraged the community to seek justice in the eternal: "Leave vengeance to the Lord."[83] Young, ascendant after Smith's death, assured everyone that Smith had already bestowed upon them the necessary resources to survive and thrive without him. "Be of good cheer," he said. "When God sends a man to do a work, all the devils in hell cannot kill him until he gets through."[84] Young testified that the Saints had everything they needed to carry on; Smith had given Church leadership the "keys of the priesthood" before his death.[85] Privately in the Council, Young and others saw the murders as a clear sign that to save the Church they had to depart the nation entirely.

The secret Council deliberations highlight that Church leaders knew that the murders were foundational moments for their people. As Bushman writes, "Prophecy told them an independent kingdom

186   WE ARE NOT ONE PEOPLE

would be established before the Second Coming, and this was the moment."[86] The Council of Fifty would have to decide how to proceed with their vision of theocracy right away.

Young assumed control over the Council of Fifty and vented his anger in the private meetings. In March 1845, Young said, "Let the damned scoundrels be killed, let them be swept off from the earth, and then we can go and be baptized for them, easier than we can convert them."[87] The nation's founding and organization were frequently praised in Council meetings, but the moral status of its contemporary citizens and leadership was abysmal. The nation as a whole, not just an Illinois mob, killed the Smiths. America was, to Taylor, "as far fallen and degenerate as any nation under heaven."[88] The nation, another Council member said, was "gone, gone to hell."[89] Council member Amasa Lyman, an ordained member of the Quorum of Twelve, characterized the Church's antipathy viscerally. Lyman "believes we shall just have as much protection wherever we be, as we can raise ourselves." The federal government was "a damned wrotten thing—, full of lice, moth eaten, corrupt," a purveyor of "the blackest perfidy and murder." The government and its laws belonged "in hell."[90]

Just as Edmund Ruffin saw his beleaguered southern people in 1865 as Jews under Roman occupation, to Young the Saints were the same: "The gentiles have rejected the gospel; they have killed the prophets, and those who have not taken an active part in the murder all rejoice in it and say amen to it, and that is saying that they are willing the blood of the prophet should be shed."[91]

Young pined for a place where the community could be safe, but also for a base from which a retaliatory war could begin: "As to the suffering any more of the oppression and tyranny of the gentiles . . . just as soon as we can secure our women and children and put them where they will be safe, we will put our warriors into the field and never cease our operations until we have swept the scoundrels from the face of the earth."[92] The Church's members, to Young, were both messengers of the divine and administrators of God's justice. Whatever salvation was possible on earth was possible within the confines of the community; similarly, whatever punishment needed to be meted out could be done by the Church. As Young said in 1845, "If when a man comes here who is guilty of murder—we would cut off his head, it would be a million times better for him, than it would be to let him live."[93]

Council sessions after the murders were scenes of raw anger, but they also included key movements as the pendulum swung away from strategies for American integration and toward full separation. Notably, in the same meeting where Young suggested wiping the gentiles from the face of the earth, he said that he did not "care about preaching to the gentiles any longer."[94] The Saints could not live safely alongside gentiles; they should not preach to them either. According to Bushman, "The minutes reveal how desperate and angry the leaders were and how far they were willing to go." Their language, both castigating their abusers and lamenting government protections from violence, "boils to the surface time and again." Some of the vitriol in these minutes was certainly "froth, not hard policy." Nevertheless, whether they were fuming or not, the Council of Fifty voiced repeated, passionate appeals to separate from the nation.[95] They were "ready to abandon the United States."[96]

Salvific Independence

After Smith's murder, Young came to believe that the very survival of the Church of Jesus Christ of Latter-day Saints rested on getting far into the western hinterlands, to a place where American law and culture had not yet been fully established. Whatever affections that his community had shared with fellow American citizens had been broken through violent conflict: "The time has come when we must seek out a location. The yoke of the gentiles is broke, their doom is sealed, there is not the least fiber can possibly be discovered that binds us to the gentile world." Founding the kingdom of God was first a matter of immediate safety, of refuge. Founding the kingdom of God was also, however, a matter of congregation, of fellowship: "It is for us to take care of ourselves and go and pick out a place where we can go and dwell in peace after we have finished the houses and got our endowment, not but that the Lord can give it to us in the wilderness, but I have no doubt we shall get it here. But we want a home where we can gather by thousands and dwell in peace."[97]

Rather than staying in the United States in a doomed effort to convert their enemies, Church members must realize that American "gentiles" were unreachable. Staying put with them was both unsafe and unholy: "The gentiles have rejected the gospel, and where shall we

188   WE ARE NOT ONE PEOPLE

go to preach. We cannot go any where but to the house of Israel. We can't get any salvation without it."[98] The Saints declared independence.

Exodus, then, was their path to righteousness. Councilor Orson Spencer, who had been elected mayor of Nauvoo but never had a chance to serve before the city charter was revoked by the governor of Illinois, supported the western relocation strategy. Perhaps the Church could even ally with Indigenous Peoples to build a military. Indeed, they had a common enemy: America. If united, they might pose a threat to these gentiles: "Our salvation is the destruction of the gentiles and their destruction will be our salvation."[99] Other Council members agreed that the flesh-and-blood members of the community needed safety and security but that their faith was essentially moribund as long as the community was hemmed in by Americans. Amasa Lyman argued, "We never enjoyed any liberty untill we cut the cords that bound us to them and looked to ourselves for protection."[100]

Achieving "liberty" in the faith depended on generating a new set of laws consistent with the kingdom of God. John Taylor, for instance, reasoned that distance was essential to liberty and liberty was essential to theocratic lawmaking. "If we got together here," he said, referring to existing Church settlements in America, "and established the kingdom we should be in the same situation we are in now." The key was to "cut off" the "transgressors" from "the kingdom of God." He opted for an exploratory expedition to find a suitable place in the western beyond: "I go in for a company being sent out to find a place where we can establish the kingdom, erect the standard and dwell in peace, and have our own laws."[101] Young agreed. Any settlement in America was merely piecemeal, "rent from the gentiles," he called it. "We will soon," he predicted, "be where we can make our own laws and publish them to the world."[102]

Some community leaders had mulled over a move to the West since at least 1834, but the discussion of potential locations for a new Mormon Shangri-La consumed the Council of Fifty throughout the mid-1840s. There were suggestions for specific locations based on the travels of some of the councilors, while others relied on testimonies from friends and family that had seen the West's far reaches. Some suggested upper California. Some advised Mexico. Others proposed Oregon or Texas. (Texas was "scratched" after its admission into the Union, confirming that the early Church clearly wanted space outside the nation.)[103]

SECESSION IN EXODUS 189

Young emphasized the theological importance of a separate space as well the strategic utility of ocean access. Missions across the world required ports. But strategic thinking meant finding land the community could defend, a location with a topography fit for defensive military operations. "We want to get some mountains," he declared, "where we can fortify ourselves, and erect the standard of liberty on one of the highest mountains we can find."[104] The Council, of course, also desired rich land, a place with gold, silver, and precious stones along with fertile soil. The Council stressed the need for beautiful, plentiful land that simultaneously provided worldly access for mission trips but still remained distant from the Americans.

The Council, however, did not let the desire to find the perfect land become an excuse to delay. Council minutes show that while there was little direct knowledge of locations, early discussions centered on getting outside of the United States as soon as possible. Young argued, "When we start we will move in a solid body untill we get beyond the limits of the United States so that we could protect ourselves after that we would divide off Into companies of, say, twenty wagons in each company."[105] Young put the marker of safety at "one hundred miles beyond the jurisdiction of the United States."[106]

By January 1846, Young settled on the area just beyond the Rocky Mountains as the ideal location for an initial settlement. According to the official Church history, "After fasting and praying daily in the temple, Brigham had seen a vision of Joseph pointing to a mountaintop with a flag flying atop it as an ensign." Young said that Smith instructed him "to build a city under the shadow of that mountain."[107] The area certainly had some of the advantages they craved, but, more importantly, it was not in America, and it was not a place many Americans wanted to go. According to Young, the reason the Church would have to take the treacherous route through the Rocky Mountains rather than stopping short was strategic distance: "If we stop this side the mountains there will be complaints which will reach us. If it is a cold country, and a hard country to live in we wont be envied, but if we go to a good country before we are able to defend it we would be troubled by mobs as we are here."[108] Taylor agreed, adding, "We would also be free from jealousies of any government."[109]

Young thought America would "have no business to come there." If they did, he promised, "will treat them as enemies" and would "make

190   WE ARE NOT ONE PEOPLE

a stand somewhere on the vallies of the Bear River."[110] In the end, the new kingdom of God was selected because it was beyond the reach of the United States, it was difficult to access, it was a hard place to live, and it was defensible.

Young gave the order to begin the departure in February 1846. Thousands of Church members from across the United States joined a mass exodus. Some traveled via a six-month sea voyage from the East Coast, while most set out as "Handcart Pioneers," moving across the plains pulling rickshaws stacked with limited provisions, including one hundred pounds of flour.[111] Many died during brutal winter travel over harsh terrain. Young arrived in the area that would become Salt Lake City on July 24, 1847. He was sick with mountain fever, but when he saw the valley below, he declared, "It is enough. This is the right place."[112]

Separation and Integration

Young and the Council of Fifty's fear that the Americans would find them were prescient. The Church "presented the US government with a geopolitical challenge, as they sought to establish settlements beyond the boundaries of the United States."[113] There had been initial signs of federal cooperation after the Saints' arrival; Millard Fillmore made Brigham Young the governor of the Utah Territory after it was acquired in the Mexican Cession.

The discovery of gold at Sutter's Mill in California in 1848 propelled thousands of other Americans along the same path that Church members had traveled, however. The gentiles were coming. The increased contact led to conflicts such as the "Mountain Meadows Massacre," wherein members of the Church's militia, the Nauvoo Legion, slaughtered a group of settlers making their way to California. President James Buchanan dispatched federal troops to Utah to notify Young that he was no longer governor. The deployment of troops to the territory led to a series of skirmishes in 1857 and 1858 labeled the "Utah War." The Church used its geographic know-how to cut off federal supply lines. Back east, the short conflict—there were no major battles and few casualties—became "Buchanan's blunder" because it was so poorly managed. But there were consequences for the Church

SECESSION IN EXODUS   191

as well. Young agreed to step down as governor; the area was under military occupation until the Civil War broke out; Saints' settlements were destroyed, and crop fields failed.

By one measure, the Church of Jesus Christ of Latter-day Saints' attempt to secede went wrong. They sought to create the kingdom of God as a separate theocratic government and ended up right back in America. By other measures, however, theirs was a successful separation, if not an instance of formal secession. As political scientists Lee Trepanier and Lynita K. Newswander explain, "In the isolation of the West, the Mormons established a new form of Government mandated directly by God."[114] In 1849, two years after arriving in Zion, Young submitted the paperwork representing the first of many attempts at achieving statehood. Although the Saints may not have escaped the United States, they would accumulate vast wealth, religious influence, and control of a massive, remote area whose government they designed and dominated and whose social structure they heavily influenced. They got, in short, their own state.

Saints make up more than 60 percent of Utah's entire population. They hold virtually every important political office in the state, ranging from the lowest levels of town governance to the governor's office. They account for 90 percent of the state legislature and 75 percent of the state judiciary.[115] "The fact is," the former editor of the *Salt Lake Tribune* told Lawrence Wright, "we live in a quasi theocracy." He explained, "Eighty percent of officeholders are of a single party, ninety percent of a single religion, ninety-nine percent of a single race, and eighty-five percent of one gender."[116] The Saints may not have secured a separate kingdom or an independent nation, but they got awfully close.

They also built the staging ground of a worldwide recruitment operation. Beyond Utah, an estimated sixteen million people worldwide are Latter-day Saints.[117] The financial strength of the Church has been the subject of public discussion, with some estimates putting their holdings at over \$100 billion.[118] Between the growth of the Church and the control of a state government, the Latter-day Saints ended up achieving much of what they originally wanted by collaborating "with the government" on their terms.[119]

Strategic integration was essential to the survival and growth of the Mormon Church. Under the "pragmatic" leadership of people like

192   WE ARE NOT ONE PEOPLE

Wilford Woodruff, who succeeded John Taylor as Church president in 1889, the Latter-day Saints in Utah made a shrewd bargain. The massive rise in polygamy that happened as soon as the Saints made it out West had not gone unnoticed in Washington, D.C.

In 1856, the Republican Party platform prohibited "those twin relics of barbarism—Polygamy, and Slavery" in the territories. In 1862, Congress passed the Morrill Anti-Bigamy Act even though it was largely unenforceable due to the Civil War.[120] The 1882 Edmunds Act and the subsequent 1887 Edmunds-Tucker Act were both tailored to punish more than individual polygamists. Law enforcement was empowered to "confiscate all Church property (except chapels) in excess of $50,000 and to dissolve the Church as a corporate entity."[121]

The enforcement of these acts led to the arrest of thousands of Saints, wives being compelled to testify against husbands, and the dissolution of the Nauvoo Legion. Under Woodruff's leadership, the Church issued its first dissociative writ in 1890 and then again under the leadership of Joseph F. Smith in 1904 as the Church officially gave up the religious practice most antithetical to Washington. "In the end," one scholar concludes, "the Saints gave way to the government."[122]

But the Saints did not succumb or even fully assimilate. As the turn-of-the-century Saints publicly disavowed polygamy, they gained a functional homeland, and "their hostile countrymen were not allowed to grind the Saints into the dust." After the Civil War, the Latter-day Saints "merged into the American political system, including the participation in the competing political parties." They agreed to "play by American rules." Their strategic integration was complete when "the Saints themselves acted the part of hyper patriots, declaring their utter loyalty to the government and enlisting enthusiastically in the armed services during World War I."[123] The Saints "were forced to flee the United States—to become emigrants—before they became accommodated and accepted."[124]

The Romney family's story is emblematic of this larger Saint movement from separation to strategic integration with a prosperous enclave of their own. Mitt Romney (a bishop of his ward) secured the Republican Party's nomination for the 2012 presidential election 127 years after Miles P. Romney, his great-grandfather, fled to Mexico to avoid the laws of the United States. The same party whose

SECESSION IN EXODUS   193

platform once prohibited polygamy in the territories gave the heir of Miles P. Romney, a fugitive of that prohibition, its highest political responsibility.

Some religious groups, like Christian Exodus and many others, claimed to follow a higher law to escape an immoral society.[125] Some groups, like the Shakers or Oneida in the nineteenth century, withdrew to create a model that might inspire others to change their ways. The early Latter-day Saints faced persecution at every turn. They were beaten and murdered for their religious beliefs. Separation gave them space to grow, land to control, and ultimately enough political power to protect their people. Their westward expansion, however, had a natural limit. Moreover, once back within American boundaries and faced with swarms of gentile settlers, the Church leadership had to choose between a state of ongoing conflict with the federal government and a negotiated peace by which they maintained local control.

There was, however, an internal cost to this peace agreement: schism. As the Latter-day Saints gained the benefits of integration, breakaway Saints who did not want to sacrifice their cherished religious practices, like polygamy, cited early Church leaders as justifications to form new Mormon churches. The Fundamentalist Church of Jesus Christ of Latter-Day Saints (FLDS) was established after the official LDS Church began excommunicating polygamists after issuing its second anti-polygamy diktat in 1904. After these excommunications, polygamous community leaders like those of the FLDS followed the precedent set by the Church's first three presidents, Smith, Young, and Taylor, and found outlying areas where they could practice polygamy and dress traditionally with little oversight. The exodus of Saints began again.

Zion had been a mobile concept for Smith and Young as they moved the Church from location to location. This mobility has made it easier for any purist alleging that integration sacrificed the core principles to justify separation again and again. The separatist precepts of Smith, Young, Taylor, and others have presented a paradox for the Latter-day Saints. Separation following higher law was the basis of communal identity but left them open to fundamentalist challenges.

Citing a direct line of communication with God, men like Rulon and Warren Jeffs have recreated the righteous rhetoric of the early Saints leaders, an enduring rhetorical playbook, to assert themselves

194   WE ARE NOT ONE PEOPLE

as "President and Prophet, Seer and Revelator" as well as "President of the Priesthood" of these splinter groups, resistant areas, and remote compounds. Short Creek, for example, became a thriving polygamous community straddling the border between Utah and Arizona, which allowed polygamist denizens to crisscross state lines to complicate any attempt at law enforcement.[126] Some estimates put FLDS membership at ten thousand people, mostly in Utah, but also in sprawling compounds in Texas, South Dakota, Colorado, Nevada, British Columbia, and Mexico.[127] More broadly, an estimated thirty thousand people live in polygamous communities in Utah.[128] Smaller polygamous communities still operate in Mexico.[129]

Despite what might appear to be the full Americanization of the official Latter-day Saints Church leadership, some historians caution against assuming that they changed their positions on separation completely: "If prudence required cooperation, we cannot believe that the passion of the Council of Fifty died away immediately. That separatist urge, that rage against injustice, that despair of ever finding security under the federal government must have lived on in many hearts."[130] In the end, mainstream Latter-day Saints have become "dedicated to monogamy" and "strenuously" insist on an ordinary identity as run-of-the-mill American Christians, but Smith and Young's messages were no pious affirmations of "Western monogamy" or venerations of "American democracy."[131]

The Church may have cracked down on polygamy in the early twentieth century and may have alienated polygamists in Short Creek and elsewhere since, but the founding Saints were, quite literally, separatist polygamist theocrats, and that legacy has never been far away from the centers of Church power in Salt Lake City. "For Mormons," one historian stresses, "the events of the nineteenth century are sacred history, the inauguration of the 'dispensation of the fulness of times,' years filled with sacred heroes whose actions and words still shape the contemporary church."[132] From that angle, it was unsurprising when, after so much time and infighting, the governor of Utah signed a law effectively decriminalizing polygamy by reducing "the crime of bigamy among consenting adults to an infraction—on par with a traffic ticket" in 2020.[133]

7

Conclusion

We Are Not One People has told an American story through the words of those who, one way or another, tried to leave America. We have attempted to rethink a concept, separatism—one that is not unique to America but has a unique importance in America—by exploring how five varied groups have talked about it, argued for it, practiced it, pursued it, and organized themselves around it. These groups' grievances and goals took many forms, points we have plotted along a horizon of separatist symbolic activity, from focused and limited acts of refusal to geographic separation, to de facto secession through legal instruments like interposition and nullification, all the way to de jure secession.

We chose groups of disunionists scattered across American history to demonstrate both the variety of separatist claimants and claims. In pursuit of different destinies, each group, nevertheless, spoke a similar political language, one that is not harnessed to any era, region, demographic, or ideology but arises out of American political identity, democratic theory, and group attachments.

That separatism is not the ideological property of any particular group of believers does not, however, mean that the political language is unideological; the patterns of words and the lines of argument employed across diverse groups are politically consequential. Separatists may not share many beliefs, but each group creates and perpetuates an atomistic world. These disparate separatists share a static view of the political world and, often, an unforgiving view of other people. Separatism is a language of enemies too big to eliminate and too dangerous to live with.

More specifically, separatism is a syllogistic political language; regardless of how the speaker felt about Thomas Jefferson, that syllogism is most famously modeled in the Declaration of Independence. A "people," the major premise stipulated, may "alter or abolish" governments that imperil basic human rights. King George, in Jefferson's minor premise,

We Are Not One People. Michael J. Lee and R. Jarrod Atchison, Oxford University Press. © Oxford University Press 2022. DOI: 10.1093/oso/9780190876500.003.0008

196   WE ARE NOT ONE PEOPLE

threatened the rights of American colonists. The colonists, therefore, were justified in breaking away to form a government that respected those rights.[1] Although all separatists parrot Jefferson's syllogism to some degree, we chose these five groups of separatists because they exemplified particular variants of the language, assertions of different "rights" in the major premise, different allegations and amplifications of a "long train of abuses" in the minor premise, and declarations of different kinds of government in the conclusion.[2]

To some extent, all separatist appeals are rooted in a vaguely libertarian, don't-tread-on-me ethos. Libertarian separatists, however, show that sovereign, autonomous citizens are the logical extreme of individual freedom. More broadly, libertarians demonstrate how the commitment to a singular idea, individual liberty in their case, can motivate secessionist activity. For them, dissolving bands between peoples actually affirmed the innate separation of individuals from one another; their separation was a refusal to be a part of a people. Even libertarian nationalists wanted to create new, ruleless societies where virtually anything, except collective action, went.

Libertarian arguments for separation have been seized by a motley collection of American advocates from different social stations with different goals, including anarchists, counterculture activists, advocates of states' rights, enslavers, abolitionists, populists, identitarians, and, most consistently, the wealthy. In a world where no one gets to tell anyone what to do, regulate others' behavior, tax others' money, or make demands on behalf of the public, those with vast means are untouchable.

Southern secessionists are, by some measures, the paradigmatic case of separation in American history. Theirs was certainly the most consequential act of separation, both in terms of provoking the Civil War and in terms of their attempt to preserve a violent, exploitative racial caste system. By another measure, however, the southern case for secession was odd. Unlike later white separatists who claimed to want racial solitude, southern separatists before and after the Civil War wanted to preserve a "way of life," a hierarchical relationship, and practices of domination. Confederates and later southern nationalists generally thwarted any national attempt at racial justice, including but not limited to the regulation of slavery.

CONCLUSION   197

Southern secessionists illustrate how separatist appeals can be grounded in a group's desire to set aside a practice, a set of behaviors, even a particular relationship between groups of people from governance or cultural judgment. Additionally, many groups take to separatist causes as an alternative to their down-power status; separatism is often the language of the oppressed. There are too few of them to form an electoral majority; they are not wealthy enough to buy political influence or military power. The southerners who seceded in 1860 claimed victimhood, but they were, in fact, the opposite. Even the southerners who lost the Civil War continued their separatist ways through demands for federalism, states' rights, interposition, and nullification, and continued enjoying enormous political privileges all the same.

Black nationalism is a quintessential example of a few types of separatist claims. Black nationalists' fight for mass escape from American captivity illustrates how identity, some presumably immutable group characteristic, some stipulated group essence, can be the fundamental basis of an argument for Balkanization. Black nationalism symbolizes the power of difference as the fundamental rationale for departure, of racial identity as the foundation of a new nation.

Nationalists argued from a position of marginalization since before the country's founding. Up against the Slave Power, Jim Crow, segregation, economic as well as social and political discrimination, and both individual and institutional racism, many Black people turned to separatist causes as the only viable course of political action. Black nationalism may bear some similarities to other racial nationalisms, but it is far from uncomplicated. Black nationalism varied quite radically both in terms of land-based goals and in terms of the imagined Black nation that nationalists claimed to redeem.

Lesbian separatists, on the whole, also affirmed group difference as a reason for group departure. They claimed membership in a distinct peoplehood based on sex, gender, and sexuality. They also had been socially relegated, and they turned to acts of exit as a recourse. Lesbian separatists prove that exit is not necessarily tied to a typical vision of nationalism. That is, lesbian separatists certainly envisioned themselves as a people, but they resisted as patriarchal the nationalist notion that they must inhabit the same named, controlled, bordered space.

198   WE ARE NOT ONE PEOPLE

Beyond building an argument for exit on several categories of group identity, what distinguished lesbian separatists was this total disinvestment in the nation and nationalism. Every other group covered in *We Are Not One People*, including libertarians, featured prominent advocates pushing for every point on the separatist spectrum. Every other group featured vocal advocates demanding their own contiguous nation-state, their own identifiable homeland under their control. Celebrating life on the boundaries, a politics of evacuation, and mobility between small, diverse enclaves, lesbian separatists wanted no part of that patriarchal project. Lesbian separatism was far more a critique of nationalism itself than it was a reassertion of the sovereignty of nation-states.

Latter-day Saints separatists figured their New Jerusalem as a refuge from American persecution, as an earthly embodiment of the divine, as a way to extricate their citizenship from national sin, and as a gateway to heaven. In terms of the wider separatist political language, Latter-day Saints highlight the separatist appeal to a higher law to deny the sovereignty of a sinful nation and affirm the sovereignty of a kingdom of God.

The Saints' separation was premised on movement in several senses. Although they ended up in a geographically distanced mountain homeland, they held that the kingdom of God followed the pious. They were entitled to follow God's law wherever they worshipped. But as they became secure in their new promised land, they moved up in social and political power in the sinful nation their founders tried to leave. For a century, they engaged in acts of strategic reintegration by trading some distinctiveness in order to enjoy the benefits of national citizenship while maintaining fundamental control over a homeland that was largely organized around their religion and largely populated by their co-religionists.

All told, separatist discourse is, quite ironically, an essential performance of American political identity. That is to say, separation has an American chic, and therefore some performances of American political identity negate the possibility of a nation. Put differently, individuals and groups rehearse a resonant rendition of American political identity when they give centralized authority the finger and go their own way. As a practical matter, when senses of civic duty or the desire

CONCLUSION 199

for, as communication scholar Leslie Hahner terms it, "American belonging" compete for collective psychic space with refusals of the very possibility of shared national identity, fractiousness can flourish.[3] The country can be even more difficult to govern.

Rebuke has been celebrated as a quintessentially American act, one that links lawbreakers, norm-defilers, and all manner of outsiders and misfits who, as warranted by a public memory of the nation's sublime separatist origins, followed their own compass. In 2020, one protestor scrawled in Sharpie these telling words on a posterboard sign that she displayed from the deck of an expensive boat cruising Charleston harbor: "If we always followed rules, we'd still be British."[4] Paradoxically, she hoped to show support for Donald Trump's reelection campaign, but her classic national rationale applied widely to countless causes in hers and many other American eras as well. Separatism is a national inheritance.

Separatism and American Democracy

It would be rather easy to lazily prophesy that these and other forms of the political language of separation would proliferate in the nation's future; in a political world of rising partisanship, polarization, and gerrymandering, an online world where more and more citizens retreat into digital silos, a warming world growing increasingly unpredictable and uninhabitable, it is far more difficult to predict who will take to this language and to what end.

That is the thing about American separatism; it has been a rhetorical tool available for any group to use. National identities, moreover, are complicated. To be an American means both encountering and likely speaking many different political languages simultaneously.[5] Separation is not the only political language spoken in America. This centrifugal language competes with centripetal American political languages. As political theorist Benjamin Barber writes, "American national identity has from the start been a remarkable mixture of cosmopolitanism and parochialism. The colonists and later the founders understood themselves to be engaged in a novel process of uprooting and rerooting."[6]

200   WE ARE NOT ONE PEOPLE

In classrooms and at holiday festivities, sporting events, civic meetings, and campaign rallies, Americans celebrate national togetherness, and they call forth the sacred texts of the holy saints of intra-American affections: George Washington, Abraham Lincoln, Martin Luther King, and many others.[7] Americans of the nineteenth century used to know Washington's Farewell Address, in which the first president warned Americans to "properly estimate the immense value of your national union," to "cherish a cordial, habitual, and immovable attachment to it," the way more contemporary citizens might be familiar with other bonding texts: the pledge of allegiance, the Gettysburg Address, or King's "I Have a Dream" speech.[8]

America's centrifugal language emphasizes commonality despite difference, identification over division. Two Civil War historians explain the fusing force of American emblems. Americans lacked "the bonds" that a singular shared religion, heritage, or place might provide, but they "found communal bonds in ideas, images, myths, and symbols that reflected a shared belief and agreed-upon values in what they called republican society."[9] This fusion of American identity is importantly a nationalist language that, as Herbert Croly said in 1909, linked "the democratic idea" and the "national principle."[10]

To be sure, there are far more bellicose, nativist, exceptionalist, love-it-or-leave-it versions of American nationalism, but this egalitarian version of unionism is a discourse of mutuality, of association, of community, of interdependence, of charity, of grace, of flux, of fluidity, of forgiveness, of love. This unionist discourse holds "difference" as "a fact of life to which divisiveness is only one response." Another response to difference is inclusivity, "not just tolerating but celebrating difference, fighting for the rights of all, not just the few."[11] Or, as political theorist Danielle Allen argues, a "people" does not have to be "one" to be "whole."[12]

This is a language that unionists, like Barbara Jordan in 1976, have used to warn one another of the dangers of coddling cynicism about other citizens. Speaking in measured tones, she wondered about the civic risks of the long separatist tradition in America: "Are we to be one people bound together by common spirit, sharing in a common endeavor; or will we become a divided nation? For all of its uncertainty, we cannot flee the future. We must not become the 'New Puritans' and

CONCLUSION   201

reject our society. We must address and master the future together. It can be done if we restore the belief that we share a sense of national community, that we share a common national endeavor."[13] Unionists of various political leanings have called forth this language in local and national debates with separatists in their midst. In 1977, Black feminists of the Combahee River Collective, for instance, endorsed collective action through vibrant pluralism, not rigid particularity: "Although we are feminists and Lesbians, we feel solidarity with progressive Black men and do not advocate the fractionalization that white women who are separatists demand."[14]

But the more alienating political language of separatism has proven durably appealing; it has its holy writs and gutsy heroes as well. The nation's separatist origins, its philosophical heritage in the disaggregating democratic principles of the Enlightenment, its lionization of rebellious individuals and isolated communities, and its often brutal acts of oppression have produced, in a sense, ideal laboratory conditions for groups to appeal to separation again and again. Separatists make for strange bedfellows because there is always some hallowed American tale of individualism or communal self-determination to which the aggrieved can appeal, an endless supply of stories about beloved bandits or likable outlaws, more pious Pilgrims, more plucky pioneers, more Confederates, more pathfinders living by their own rules, more trailblazers evading or eschewing national norms.

Unionists and disunionists mine the same reserve of American history for different resources. The disunionist vein, as one writer explains, has been particularly rich: "From the accidental discovery of this entire landmass in the 15th century to the pioneering Puritans who fled their native country to pursue religious worship on their terms, the Transcendentalists and their environmental spirituality, and New Age back-to-the-landers . . . America has always been driven by a particular brand of utopianism, the idea that at any time, in any context, it is always possible to start a new life and create an intentional society ruled by the beliefs of its participants."[15] Americans have been afforded a language of self-government but also a repertoire of rupture.

In some ways, many citizens have been committed in practice to the visionary revamping project that Thomas Paine announced in *Common Sense*. Paine declared, "We have it in our power to begin

202   WE ARE NOT ONE PEOPLE

the world over again."[16] But it was not just revolutionary thinkers and American utopians who have celebrated radical reinvention; presidents have too. Ronald Reagan was particularly fond of Paine's notion that the present world was impermanent. Demonstrating the broad appeal of this idea, Reagan closed his 1983 address to the National Association of Evangelicals, more commonly called the "evil empire" speech, by quoting Paine's line.[17] Separation becomes imminently thinkable, even logical, in a national environment where pioneers and presidents glorify leaving the nation behind to start over.

Separation is both American and un-American, and it is also both democratic and undemocratic. Separation, at least the legitimate threat of it, is a vital element of any democratic public sphere. Only in a totalitarian society is the desire to withdraw from the collective will classified as a criminal act. The actual prospect of withdrawal is a necessary test of a person's or a people's consent to be governed. Separation has often been a response to segregation and discrimination, an attempt to achieve greater safety for and connections within a beleaguered community.[18]

Opponents of separatism have derided it as retreatism dressed up like revolution, as a flight into a mythical sphere. They have worried that separatists disarm effective political advocacy by turning away from the political world, by taking leave rather than taking action. The cost of such a pursuit of "authenticity" may be a fundamental "disengagement from this-worldly ways of thinking."[19] Theirs was a fool's errand into the wilderness.

The poet Adrienne Rich said that separatists pursuing exit as an "end in itself" were engaged in an "inner emigration" into a fanciful world rather than the world that was.[20] Ralph Ellison made a similar point in 1969: "For all their talk of black separatism—really another version of secessionism, an old American illusion which arises whenever groups reach an explosive point of frustration—and for all their stance of alienation they are really acting out a state of despair."[21]

The separatist quest will always be open to charges of evasion and infeasibility, but many acts on the separatist spectrum, like exclusive coffee shops, bookstores, clubs, concerts, and collective spaces, do not have to trade off with confrontational politics, and they can be generative, world-building acts all their own.[22] In many contexts, there is no

CONCLUSION 203

more democratic word than "no," no more democratic act than exit. The lesbian separatist philosopher Sarah Lucia Hoagland likened engaging a corrupt, discriminatory system to debating racists. Sure, well-meaning people could generate a "raft of arguments" to dispute some racist claim, "but in so doing, they are tacitly agreeing that the claim is intelligible and debatable." Separatists find more power in refusing to give the racist attention, oxygen, and credit, in disengaging by treating "the claim as nonsense" that "makes no sense." Separating can present a wholesale challenge to "what counts as a fact"; separating is an attempt at fashioning a world governed by new rules and new groups, perhaps "the beginning of the creation of new value."[23] Opting out is the sharp edge of self-determination.

Separation is an unavoidably democratic idea for other reasons as well. Separatist arguments are assertions of different democratic rights claims. They come from majoritarian precepts. The advocate who claims to represent a majority of a given population asserts that the will of a majority of people has been consistently denied, and therefore seeks to create a new nation.

Secessionist arguments come from minority-rights precepts as well. The advocate claims to represent a downtrodden people of a particular region and asserts that only a rehabilitated home rule or even a new nation can protect this group's way of life. In the end, for both majorities and minorities, separation is an essential safeguard of self-government. One libertarian writer captured this sentiment with the classic metaphor of the citizenry in terms of a personal relationship. Countries are like marriages, and separation is just a simple matter of breaking up: "Why do we need to submit to people and ideas that go against our own convictions? Sometimes you just need to say, 'Hey, you're a good person and I wish you the best, but I just feel like I need to go my own way. It's not you, it's me.'"[24]

Democracy may imply, perhaps necessitate, the right of separation or secession, but when pursued dogmatically, seeking to separate or secede can negate democracy for a few reasons. Some vestige of democracy is always employed by separatists because they invariably locate sovereign authority in the people, even if the people may then choose to express that authority in regular referenda or vest that authority in an undemocratic polis.

204　WE ARE NOT ONE PEOPLE

On the other hand, democracies count votes and determine winners. For all its advantages, democracy requires two discomfiting practices: gambling on the decisions of strangers and living with losses. As the potential language of individuals opting out of every deal but the best ones, separation does not cultivate neighborly trust or long-term viability. "The principle" of secession, Lincoln argued on July 4, 1861, "is one of disintegration, and upon which no government can possibly endure."[25]

Separation is the full form of several different drives—for self-government, for independence, for isolation, for privacy, for group solidarity, for populist power, for "ur-identity."[26] When this democratic separatist impulse becomes a staid screed by which one people, figured as fixed, blameless heroes, cuts ties with another, figured as irredeemable villains, separation is hard to square with anything approaching the cooperative vision of a hand-holding citizen choir that King, standing before the national shrine to Lincoln, conceived in his "I Have a Dream" speech.

Lincoln, too, invoked the metaphor of a citizen chorus in his first inaugural address, but he also continued Jefferson's metaphor of peoples bound together. "We are not enemies, but friends," he pleaded in early 1861. "We must not be enemies. Though passion may have strained, it must not break our bonds of affection."[27] Lincoln knew well that the promise of liberty was fraught with the peril of disunion. Liberty and equality must be coequal national ideals; democracy requires both.[28] A politics that slips too far in one direction puts self-government in real jeopardy.

Separatism can enable the practice of freedom, enable a greater degree of local and personal choice, and promote diversity within and between communities, but separatist absolutism can pull democracy apart. Separatists pushing the blood-and-soil concerns of "real Americans," separatists who view other groups of people, even those groups who have perpetrated real abuses against them, as forever cursed, imperil any sort of pluralist politics of collaboration or forgiveness.[29] The advocate who claims to represent a sacred, chosen group and says that they can only achieve their destiny as a people with their own space to live alone has walled their group off from democratic life. The separatist who says that whole groups of people,

CONCLUSION   205

the enemy, are irredeemably mean or dumb or both and, therefore, a noble, chosen people should not have to live alongside them has eliminated other groups from being worthy or capable of democratic participation.

James Baldwin heard a version of this concretized conclusion about white people from the Nation of Islam's Harlem street preachers. White people were the mutant products of nefarious experiments conducted by an impish demigod. "There is thus," Baldwin wrote, "by definition, no virtue in white people, and since they are another creation entirely and can no more, by breeding, become black than a cat, by breeding, can become a horse, there is no hope for them."[30]

Separation is not necessarily a language of paranoia, but it lends itself to paranoid indulgences. Many of the groups we analyzed cited all-too-real acts of oppression against them as cause for departure. But some separatists take partial, temporary, or bridgeable differences between people and transmogrify them into total, perpetual deviances.

Separatists can encourage a dire view of the nature of others in which out-group members are unpersuadable and incorrigible. This harsh view of political enemies is what some scholars call "motive attribution asymmetry," where the actions of others are attributed not to honest mistakes, understandable errors, or human failings but, instead, to a rotten core.[31] It is a "tragic frame," among the most tragic of all political frames, where the worst of other people is assumed.[32] Baldwin noticed this systematic descent into a dark myopia: "Most Negroes cannot risk assuming that the humanity of white people is more real to them than their color. And this leads, imperceptibly but inevitably, to a state of mind in which, having long ago learned to expect the worst, one finds it very easy to believe the worst."[33]

Separatists do not have to cloister, and separatism does not have to be "inimical to coalition."[34] Separatists can control their visibility, vulnerability, and "accessibility" without lapsing into hermitic misanthropy.[35] As Bernice Johnson Reagon, a Black feminist lesbian separatist, said, "Now every once in awhile there is a need for people to try to clean out corners and bar the doors and check everybody who comes in the door, and check what they carry in and say, 'Humph, inside this place the only thing we are going to deal with is X or Y or Z.' And so only the X's or Y's or Z's get to come in." To her, that hypothetical room

206   WE ARE NOT ONE PEOPLE

"can then become a nurturing place," or, if the community pretends that the "room is a world," it can become a "very destructive place."[36]

Whereas separatism springs from democratic ideals and has vital democratic usefulness, when it is based in absolute difference and the perpetual wickedness of others, it is destructive to cosmopolitan democracies, to a politics of "allegiance to the worldwide community of human beings."[37] Others have called this idea "democratic humanism." As political scientist Amy Gutmann writes, "All children—regardless of ethnicity, religion, gender, race, or class—should be educated to deliberate together as free and equal citizens in a democracy that is dedicated to furthering social justice for all individuals, not just members of their own society."[38] Where some democratic theorists have encouraged citizens to "stretch our concern outward from the narrowest personal confines toward the needs of outsiders, strangers, all of humanity, and sometimes also of animals," fundamentalist separatists go in the other direction.[39] They encourage citizens to care about the likeminded, people who look like them, people who act like them, people of shared space, ancestry, heritage, and location.

Separatists reply, of course, that they are merely doing to others what has been done to them. Their group has been excluded, oppressed; they aim to create an exclusive space free of historical oppressors. Baldwin called this attempt "to do to others what has been done to them" a "spiritual wasteland."[40] The identification and dismissal of whole classes of people is a failure of imagination, and not just democratic imagination.

Democracy requires freedom of consent, of self-determination, but it also requires doubt, about ourselves, about our opponents, about our nation. What if the people I oppose and those that oppose me are capable of good, at least some of the time? What if my judgments of others are wrong? Ta-Nehisi Coates shared such democratic doubts when he realized that his own suffering did not preclude him from causing suffering: "I am black, and have been plundered and have lost my body. But perhaps I too had the capacity for plunder, maybe I would take another human's body to confirm myself in a community. Perhaps I already had. Hate gives identity. The nigger, the fag, the bitch illuminate the border, illuminate what we ostensibly are not, illuminate the Dream of being white, of being a Man. We name the hated strangers and are thus confirmed in the tribe."[41] The more monstrous

CONCLUSION 207

the stranger, the greater the need to depart from them or exterminate them. "The human capacity to injure other people," literature scholar Elaine Scarry explains, "is very great precisely because our capacity to imagine other people is very small."[42]

By casting others as incorrigible, some separatist discourse violates the spirit of a coequal democratic citizenry.[43] Such intense "distrust" of one another "paralyzes democracy" because "citizens no longer think it sensible, or feel secure enough, to place their fates in the hands of democratic strangers."[44] The obstinate separatist alternative, a new, univocal space of civic belonging, risks a similar violation.[45] As legal scholar Cass Sunstein explains, "One of the key goals of democracy's constitution is to solve the problem of enduring disagreement—by promoting exposure to multiple perspectives, by proliferating the points of access to government, and by finding productive courses of action when disagreements cannot be solved."[46] Separatists hope for a space outside of argument, beyond democratic contestation, where debate is unnecessary because all the key questions have been answered.

One historian's conclusion about southern fire-eaters is broadly illustrative: "Faced with the challenge of Garrison and others opposed to slavery, the fire-eaters refused to remain in a nation where theirs was not the only interpretation of the Constitution and the only vision of America."[47] Separatist dogmatists posit a world of essences, of fixity, not a world of argument, of different takes, a deeply rhetorical world, a world where questions long settled have to be answered again and people muddle through political life, but they muddle together.

This stance against separatist rhetorics of irredeemability does not require the removal of sharp critique from politics. Pointed arguments can also reject parochialism. In her influential 1973 "Letter to My People," which she composed in a New Jersey prison, Assata Shakur of the Black Liberation Army identified as a "black revolutionary" and attacked the "pigs," "the rich," lying "politicians," their "heartless robots," and "amerikkka" generally. She said that "black people should, and, inevitably must, determine our destinies." She did not, however, decry white people or dismiss the possibility of coalitions.[48]

Similarly, philosopher Claudia Card argues that separation can be depersonalized: "It may be possible to separate with respect to many kinds of oppression if, instead of focusing on 'from whom?' we think

208   WE ARE NOT ONE PEOPLE

more about 'from what kinds of connections?' and 'why?,' 'with what aims in view?'"[49] Warranted suspicion of some social connections because of historical persecution need not result in total seclusion. It need not prohibit contact, whether incidental, social, or strategic.

One lesbian separatist, for instance, "puts her separatism aside when her neighbor—a 70-year-old Mormon man—needs help fixing a fence or repairing the roof," and others welcomed the father of a separatist community member so they could bond over heavy-metal music together.[50] For Jean Mountaingrove, a lesbian separatist in Oregon, "separatism is not an absolute position." Giving some strategic ground here and there was not the same thing as submissively assimilating, sacrificing safety, or abandoning identity. Separatism, she defined, was "a move toward recovery, not isolation," a "conscious setting of boundaries, both psychological and physical."[51] Those boundaries were not high walls.

If democracy is going to nurture doubt, it must also nurture debate. Even if they succeed in leaving, either partially or totally, separatists pushing to create a homogeneous space risk recreating the exclusive world they left.[52] As poet Robert Pinsky puts it, "Insofar as the chauvinist refers to any human group or making as a static purity, the chauvinist elevates an illusion." "Cultures," in his view, "are motion."[53] They are inevitably syncretic, inevitably cantankerous, inevitably combustible, even if their inhabitants have traveled great distances and erected high walls to live harmoniously in separation. As political scientist Bryan Garsten argues, "Even if we hope to draw citizens into deliberating reasonably with one another, we cannot help but begin by appealing to them as we find them—opinionated, self-interested, sentimental, partial to their friends and family, and often unreasonable." "The rhetorical moment," in other words, wherein citizens encounter others who look or act differently, is unavoidable.[54]

Although he was friendly to secession for much of his life, authored some of the founding verses of American separatism, and, simultaneously, marred the cause of individual and group freedom as the owner of 607 enslaved persons over his lifetime, Thomas Jefferson occasionally recognized that the inevitability of political dispute did not necessitate political division or portend political domination.[55] He famously voiced such a view in his first inaugural address: "But every difference of opinion is not a difference of principle. We have called by different names brethren of the same principle. We are all Republicans, we are all Federalists. If there be any among us who would wish to dissolve this Union or to change its republican form, let them stand undisturbed as monuments of the safety with which error of opinion may be tolerated where reason is left free to combat it."[56]

But Jefferson, as he wrote to John Taylor in 1798, also thought that seceding to stifle dissent or achieve unquestioned power was a doomed project. There was no space outside of dispute, no ether of pure agreement. Jefferson was then out of power, and he lamented Hamilton's influence over the country generally and President Washington specifically. Nevertheless, he explained, "Seeing, therefore, that an association of men who will not quarrel with one another is a thing which never yet existed, from the greatest confederacy of nations down to a town meeting or a vestry; seeing that we must have somebody to quarrel with, I had rather keep our New England associates for that purpose, than to see our bickerings transferred to others." Since bickering was inexorable, "evils of a scission," were, Jefferson reasoned, inscrutable in the worst way: "When & where would they end?" For him, it may have been a prudent strategy in the moment to "have patience, till luck turns, & then we shall have an opportunity of winning back the principles we have lost," but, in hindsight, his assumption that people and countries could change was democracy in action.[57]

Notes

Introduction

1. Ron Chernow, *Alexander Hamilton* (New York: Penguin Press, 2004), 478. See also Ron Chernow, *Washington: A Life* (London: Penguin Books, 2010), 722.
2. William Hogeland, *The Whiskey Rebellion: George Washington, Alexander Hamilton, and the Frontier Rebels Who Challenged America's Newfound Sovereignty* (New York: Scribner, 2006), 66, 68–70.
3. Hogeland, *The Whiskey Rebellion*, 68–70.
4. Chernow, *Washington*, 719.
5. Chernow, *Alexander Hamilton*, 468.
6. Alexander Hamilton, *Federalist* 12, November 27, 1787, in *The Federalist with Letters of "Brutus,"* ed. Terence Ball (Cambridge: Cambridge University Press, 2003), 56.
7. George Washington to Charles Mynn Thruston, August 10, 1794, available via https://founders.archives.gov/documents/Washington/05-16-02-0376.
8. Chernow, *Alexander Hamilton*, 473.
9. Chernow, *Alexander Hamilton*, 470.
10. Chernow, *Washington*, 724.
11. Chernow, *Alexander Hamilton*, 474.
12. Chernow, *Washington*, 726.
13. Chernow, *Alexander Hamilton*, 476. See also Alexander Hamilton, *Federalist* 15, in *The Federalist with the Letters of "Brutus,"* ed. T. Ball (Cambridge: Cambridge University Press, 2003), 68.
14. Hogeland, *The Whiskey Rebellion*, 217.
15. Chernow, *Washington*, 725.
16. Chernow, *Alexander Hamilton*, 477.
17. Chernow, *Alexander Hamilton*, 98.
18. Chernow, *Alexander Hamilton*, 98, 672, 678, 697, 708.
19. Paul C. Nagel, *The Lees of Virginia: Seven Generations of an American Family* (New York: Oxford University Press, 1990), 161–162.

212 NOTES

20. Robert M. Poole, "Light Horse Harry Lee: Overreaching Hero of the Revolution," *American History 47* (2012): 35.
21. Nagel, *The Lees of Virginia*, 162.
22. Nagel, *The Lees of Virginia*, 169–170.
23. Poole, "Light Horse Harry Lee," 35.
24. Nagel, *The Lees of Virginia*, 175–176.
25. Nagel, *The Lees of Virginia*, 176.
26. Poole, "Light Horse Harry Lee," 37.
27. Poole, "Light Horse Harry Lee," 37–38. See also J. Anderson Thomson and Carlos Michael Santos, "The Mystery in the Coffin: Another View of Lee's Visit to His Father's Grave," *The Virginia Magazine of History and Biography 103* (1995): 75–94.
28. Neil H. Cogan, "Introduction," in *Union and States' Rights: A History and Interpretation of Interposition, Nullification, and Secession 150 Years After Sumter*, ed. N. H. Cogan (Akron, OH: University of Akron Press, 2014), 2.
29. James Madison, *Federalist 14*, in *The Federalist with the Letters of "Brutus,"* ed. T Ball (Cambridge: Cambridge University Press, 2003), 35.
30. Joanna Sweet and Martha F. Lee, "Christian Exodus: A Modern American Millenarian Movement," *Journal for the Study of Radicalism* 4, no. 1 (2010): 1–23; Anand Giridharadas, "Silicon Valley Roused by Secession Call," *New York Times*, October 28, 2013, available via https://www.nytimes.com/2013/10/29/us/silicon-valley-roused-by-secession-call.html.
31. C. Brian Smith, "Why Do These Straight Men Want Nothing to Do with Women?," *Narratively*, October 18, 2016, available via https://narratively.com/why-do-these-straight-men-want-nothing-to-do-with-women/; Nellie Bowles, "How to Prepare Now for the Complete End of the World," *New York Times*, March 5, 2020, available via https://www.nytimes.com/2020/03/05/style/rewilding-stone-age-bushcraft.html.
32. Rafia Zakaria, "A Feminist Thoreau," *Lithub*, November 30, 2016, available via https://lithub.com/a-feminist-thoreau/.
33. William Kittredge, "'Blood Orchid: An Unnatural History of America' by Charles Bowden," *Los Angeles Times*, August 20, 1995, available via http://www.latimes.com/la-bk-william-kittredge-1995-08-20-story.html.
34. Adam Harris, "The New Secession," *The Atlantic*, May 20, 2019, available via https://www.theatlantic.com/education/archive/2019/05/resegregation-baton-rouge-public-schools/589381/; Lauren Camera, "The Quiet Wave of School District Secessions," *US News and World Report*, May 5, 2017, available via https://www.usnews.com/news/education-news/articles/2017-05-05/the-quiet-wave-of-school-district-secessions.

NOTES 213

35. Kevin Kruse, *White Flight: Atlanta and the Making of Modern Conservatism* (Princeton, NJ: Princeton University Press, 2005), 247.

36. Dana Goldstein, "Liberals, Don't Homeschool Your Kids," *Slate*, February 16, 2012, available via https://slate.com/human-interest/2012/02/homeschooling-and-unschooling-among-liberals-and-progressives.html.

37. Jason Sorens, *Secessionism: Identity, Interest, and Strategy* (Montreal: McGill-Queen's University Press, 2012), 5. See also Ilya Somin, *Free to Move: Foot Voting, Migration, and Political Freedom* (New York: Oxford University Press, 2020).

38. Robert L. Tsai, *America's Forgotten Constitutions: Defiant Visions of Power and Community* (Cambridge, MA: Harvard University Press, 2014), 300.

39. Robert Reich, "The Secession of the Successful," *New York Times Magazine*, January 20, 1991, available via https://www.nytimes.com/1991/01/20/magazine/secession-of-the-successful.html.

40. Jeff Deist, "Secession Begins at Home," *Mises* Daily Articles, January 30, 2015, available via https://mises.org/library/secession-begins-home-0.

41. John Perry Barlow, "*A Declaration of the Independence of Cyberspace,*" Electronic Frontier Foundation, February 8, 1996, available via https://www.eff.org/cyberspace-independence.

42. William L. Van Deburg, "Introduction," in *Modern Black Nationalism: From Marcus Garvey to Louis Farrakhan*, ed. W. L. Van Deburg (New York: New York University Press, 1997), 14.

43. LeRoi Jones, *Home: Social Essays* (New York: Akashic Books, 2009), 104.

44. James Poulos, "America's Slumbering Secession Obsession," *TheDailyBeast*, September 23, 2014, available via https://www.thedailybeast.com/americas-slumbering-secession-obsession; Glenn Harlan Reynolds, "Across the Country, Rural Communities Want to Secede from their States. Here's Why," *USA Today*, February 26, 2020, available via https://www.usatoday.com/story/opinion/2020/02/26/across-country-rural-communities-secede-states-why-column/4851817002/; Jay Winik, *April 1865: The Month That Saved America* (New York: HarperCollins, 2001), 16; Albert O. Hirschman, *Exit, Voice, and Loyalty: Responses to Decline in Firms, Organizations, and States* (Cambridge, MA: Harvard University Press, 1970), 106.

45. Richard Kreitner, *Break It Up: Secession, Division, and the Secret History of America's Imperfect Union* (New York: Little, Brown, 2020), 6.

46. Nathaniel Philbrick, *Mayflower: A Story of Courage, Community, and War* (New York: Penguin, 2007); Nelson D. Lankford, *Cry Havoc! The Crooked Road to Civil War, 1861* (New York: Viking, 2007); William A. Link, *Roots of Secession: Slavery and Politics in Antebellum Virginia* (Chapel

214 NOTES

Hill: University of North Carolina Press, 2003); Daniel Wait Howe, *Political History of Secession: To the Beginning of the American Civil War* (New York: Negro Universities Press, 1914).

47. Daniel W. Hamilton, "Still Too Close to Call? Rethinking Stampp's 'The Concept of a Perpetual Union,'" in *Union and States' Rights: A History and Interpretation of Interposition, Nullification, and Secession 150 Years After Sumter*, ed. N. H. Cogan (Akron, OH: University of Akron Press, 2014), 86.

48. Akhil Reed Amar, "An Open Letter to Professors Paulsen and Powell," *The Yale Law Journal* 115 (2006): 2105; see also Sanford Levinson, "Perpetual Union, Free Love, and Secession: On the Limits to the Consent of the Governed," *Tulsa Law Review 39* (2005): 461–462.

49. Ira Glass, "*Ira Glass's Commencement Speech at the Columbia Journalism School Graduation,*" May 17, 2018, available via https://www.thisamericanlife.org/about/announcements/ira-glass-commencement-speech.

50. Daniel T. Rodgers, *Age of Fracture* (Cambridge, MA: Harvard University Press, 2011); Tsai, *America's Forgotten Constitutions*; Amy Chua, *Political Tribes: Group Instinct and the Fate of Nations* (New York: Penguin Press, 2018); Steven Levitsky and Daniel Ziblatt, *How Democracies Die* (New York: Crown, 2018); Lilliana Mason, *Uncivil Agreement: How Politics Became Our Identity* (Chicago: University of Chicago Press, 2018); Yascha Mounk, *The People vs. Democracy: Why Our Freedom Is in Danger and How to Save It* (Cambridge, MA: Harvard University Press, 2018); Andreas Wimmer, *Why Some Countries Come Together While Others Fall Apart* (Princeton, NJ: Princeton University Press, 2018); Sam Rosenfeld, *The Polarizers: Postwar Architects of Our Partisan Era* (Chicago: University of Chicago Press, 2018).

51. James H. Read and Neal Allen, "Living, Dead, and Undead: Nullification Past and Present," in *Nullification and Secession in Modern Constitutional Thought*, ed. S. Levinson (Lawrence: University Press of Kansas, 2016), 119.

52. Abraham Lincoln, "*The Perpetuation of Our Political Institutions: Address Before the Young Men's Lyceum of Springfield, Illinois,*" January 27, 1838, available via http://www.abrahamlincolnonline.org/lincoln/speeches/lyceum.htm.

53. George Washington, "*Farewell Address,*" September 1796, available via https://www.senate.gov/artandhistory/history/resources/pdf/Washingtons_Farewell_Address.pdf.

54. This scale also includes some acts of local roadblocking, heel-dragging, outright dissent, and subtle noncompliance with federal law consistent with what scholars have called "uncooperative federalism" or instances of

NOTES 215

"vetocracy" in action. See Jessica Bulman-Pozen and Heather K. Green, "Uncooperative Federalism," *The Yale Law Journal* 118 (2009): 1258–1307; Francis Fukuyama, "The Decay of American Political Institutions," *The American Interest*, December 8, 2012, available via https://www.the-american-interest.com/2013/12/08/the-decay-of-american-political-institutions/.

55. Kreitner, *Break It Up*, 291.

56. Ethan J. Kytle and Blain Roberts, *Denmark Vesey's Garden: Slavery and Memory in the Cradle of the Confederacy* (New York: New Press, 2019); Nicholas Lemann, *Redemption: The Last Battle of the Civil War* (New York: Farrar, Straus, & Giroux, 2007); Heather Cox Richardson, *West from Appomattox: The Reconstruction of America After the Civil War* (New Haven, CT: Yale University Press, 2007); A. J. Langguth, *After Lincoln: How the North Won the Civil War and Lost the Peace* (New York: Simon and Schuster, 2014).

57. Bette Tallen, "Lesbian Separatism: A Historical and Comparative Perspective," in *For Lesbians Only*, ed. S. L. Hoagland and J. Penelope (London: Onlywomen Press, 1988), 140.

58. Josh Levin, "How Is America Going to End?," *Slate*, August 5, 2009, available via http://www.slate.com/articles/news_and_politics/the_end_of_america/2009/08/how_is_america_going_to_end_3.single.html. See also Sanford Levinson, "The 21st Century Rediscovery of Nullification and Secession in American Political Rhetoric," in *Nullification and Secession in Modern Constitutional Thought*, ed. S. Levinson (Lawrence: University Press of Kansas, 2016), 33.

59. Jan-Werner Muller, *What Is Populism?* (Philadelphia: University of Pennsylvania Press, 2016); see also Edward Schiappa, *Defining Reality: Definitions and the Politics of Meaning* (Carbondale: Southern Illinois University Press, 2003).

60. Maurice Charland, "Constitutive Rhetoric: The Case of the *Peuple Quebecois*," *Quarterly Journal of Speech 73* (1987): 138.

61. Charland, "Constitutive Rhetoric," 141.

62. James C. Cobb, *Away Down South: A History of Southern Identity* (New York: Oxford University Press, 2005), 3.

63. Susan-Mary Grant, *North over South: Northern Nationalism and American Identity in the Antebellum Era* (Lawrence: University Press of Kansas, 2000);

64. Allen Buchanan, *Secession: The Morality of Political Divorce from Fort Sumter to Lithuania and Quebec* (Boulder, CO: Westview Press, 1991), 49.

216 NOTES

65. Michael Seymour, "Internal Self-Determination and Secession," in *The Ashgate Research Companion to Secession*, ed. A. Pavkovic and P. Radan (Burlington, VT: Ashgate, 2011), 387.

66. Ronda Kaysen, "Some Said They'd Flee Trump's America. These People Actually Did," *New York Times*, April 14, 2018, available via https://www.nytimes.com/2018/04/14/style/moving-to-canada-jk-traveling-until-2020.html; Rebecca Mead, "A New Citizen Decides to Leave the Tumult of Trump's America," *New Yorker*, August 20, 2018, available via https://www.newyorker.com/magazine/2018/08/20/a-new-citizen-decides-to-leave-the-tumult-of-trumps-america.

67. Alexis de Tocqueville, *Democracy in America* (Indianapolis, IN: Liberty Fund, 2012), 1:92.

Chapter 1

1. Aleksandar Pavkovic and Peter Radan, "Introduction: What Is Secession?," in *The Ashgate Research Companion to Secession*, ed. A. Pavkovic and P. Radan (Burlington, VT: Ashgate, 2011), 3; Tom Hillard, "The First Secessions," in *On the Way to Statehood: Secession and Globalisation*, ed. A. Pavkovic and P. Radan (Burlington, VT: Ashgate, 2008), 163–174.

2. Don H. Doyle, "Introduction: Union and Secession in the Family of Nations," in *Secession as an International Phenomenon: From America's Civil War to Contemporary Separatist Movements*, ed. D. H. Doyle (Athens: University of Georgia Press, 2010), 1.

3. Donald W. Livingston, "Secession: A Specifically American Principle," Mises Daily Articles, January 15, 2013, available via https://mises.org/library/secession-specifically-american-principle. See also Laura Rominger Porter, "Church Government and the Body Politic: The Religious Logic of Secession in Tennessee," *Tennessee Historical Quarterly* 70 (2011): 126–141.

4. Percy B. Lehning, "Theories of Secession: An Introduction," in *Theories of Secession*, ed. P. B. Lehning (London: Routledge, 1998), 14.

5. Sean Wilentz, *The Rise of American Democracy* (New York: W. W. Norton, 2005), 4–5.

6. James Mayall, "Secession and International Order," in *The Ashgate Research Companion to Secession*, ed. A. Pavkovic and P. Radan (Burlington, VT: Ashgate, 2011), 11–12.

NOTES   217

7. Bridget L. Coggins, "The History of Secession: An Overview," in *The Ashgate Research Companion to Secession*, ed. A. Pavkovic and P. Radan (Burlington, VT: Ashgate, 2011), 24. See also Timothy William Waters, *Boxing Pandora: Rethinking Borders, States, and Secession in a Democratic World* (New Haven, CT: Yale University Press, 2020), 15–16.

8. Wendy Brown, *Undoing the Demos: Neoliberalism's Stealth Revolution* (New York: Zone Books, 2015), 19.

9. Michael Freeman, "The Priority of Function over Structure," in *Theories of Secession*, ed. P. B. Lehning (London: Routledge, 1998), 13–16.

10. Donald L. Horowitz, "A Right to Secede?," in *Secession and Self-Determination*, ed. S. Macedo and A. Buchanan (New York: New York University Press, 2003), 51.

11. The philosophical debate over the definition of secession is robust. See Aleksandar Pavkovic, "Secession: A Much Contested Concept," in *Territorial Separatism in Global Politics: Causes, Outcomes, and Resolution* (New York: Routledge, 2015), 15; Peter Radan, "Secession: A Word in Search of a Meaning," in *On the Way to Statehood: Secession and Globalisation*, ed. A. Pavkovic and P. Radan (Burlington, VT: Ashgate, 2008), 17; Aleksandar Pavkovic and Peter Radan, *Creating New States: Theory and Practice of Secession* (Burlington, VT: Ashgate, 2007), 6; Christopher Heath Wellman, *A Theory of Secession: The Case for Political Self-Determination* (Cambridge: Cambridge University Press, 2005), 67–85; Allen Buchanan, *Secession: The Morality of Political Divorce from Fort Sumter to Lithuania and Quebec* (Boulder, CO: Westview Press, 1991), 48; Harry Beran, "A Liberal Theory of Secession," *Political Studies* 32 (1984): 21–31. Definitions of secession vary in the means of withdrawal, the effects of withdrawal on the original state, and the legal and political effect on the withdrawing state. Secession can be subdivided variously to include unilateral secession, consensual secession, devolutionary secession, and dissolving secession. Secession can also be subdivided by three different theoretical premises. Remedial, or just cause, theories of secession require the withdrawing group to show substantial evidence of oppression and the impossibility of redress. Primary, or choice or plebiscitary, theories of secession hold that if a majority of citizens in a particular area of a nation-state want to secede, then their choice should be considered just with or without an accompanying claim of oppression. National self-determination theories of secession hold that secession is a right possessed by groups with distinct identities, nations bounded by language, culture, or belief. See Lee Ward, "Thomas Hobbes and John Locke on a Liberal Right of Secession," *Political Research Quarterly* 70 (2017): 878; Allen Buchanan, "Democracy

218 NOTES

and Secession," in *National Self-Determination and Secession*, ed. M. Moore (Oxford: Oxford University Press, 1998), 14–30; Allen Buchanan, "Theories of Secession," *Philosophy and Public Affairs* 26 (1997): 31–61; David Copp, "Democracy and Communal Self-Determination," in *The Morality of Nationalism*, ed. J. McMahon and R. McKim (New York: Oxford University Press, 1997), 296; Daniel Philpott, "In Defense of Self-Determination," *Ethics* 105 (1995): 360–361; David Gauthier, "Breaking Up: An Essay on Secession," *Canadian Journal of Philosophy* 24 (1994): 371. As a concept, secession can be defined broadly to include several forms of national withdrawal, including decolonization, suzerainty, and irredentism. See Glen Anderson, "Secession in International Law: What Are We Talking About?," *Loyola of Los Angeles International and Comparative Law Journal* 35 (2013): 343–389. Conversely, it can also be defined narrowly and only denote the explicit withdrawal of one people from another that includes a change of jurisdiction over specified territory. See James R. Crawford, *The Creation of States in International Law* (Oxford: Oxford University Press, 2006). We have opted for an expansive definition of not just secession but separatism generally because we are exploring linkages between lots of separatist strategies throughout American history and the ways in which each refuses shared citizenship and mutual obligation.

12. Pavkovic and Radan, "Introduction: What Is Secession?," 3.

13. Don H. Doyle, "An Attempt at Secession from an Early Nation-State: The Confederate States of America," in *The Ashgate Research Companion to Secession*, ed. A. Pavkovic and P. Radan (Burlington, VT: Ashgate, 2011), 103.

14. Jay Winik, *April 1865: The Month That Saved America* (New York: HarperCollins, 2001), 13.

15. Robert L. Tsai, *America's Forgotten Constitutions: Defiant Visions of Power and Community* (Cambridge, MA: Harvard University Press, 2014), 9–10.

16. Terence Ball, "'A Republic—If You Can Keep It,'" in *Conceptual Change and the Constitution*, ed. T. Ball and J. G. A. Pocock (Lawrence: University Press of Kansas, 1988), 137.

17. James E. Lewis Jr., *The Burr Conspiracy: Uncovering the Story of an Early American Crisis* (Princeton, NJ: Princeton University Press, 2017), 6.

18. H. W. Brands, *The Heartbreak of Aaron Burr* (New York: Anchor Books, 2012), 97.

19. Brutus, October 18, 1787, available via https://www.constitution.org/afp/brutus01.txt.

20. Alexis de Tocqueville, *Democracy in America* (Indianapolis, IN: Liberty Fund, 2012), 1:98; Ball, "'A Republic—If You Can Keep It,'" 141.

NOTES 219

21. Elvin T. Lim, *The Lovers' Quarrel: The Two Foundings and American Political Development* (New York: Oxford University Press, 2014), 2.

22. Andrew Delbanco, *The War Before the War: Fugitive Slaves and the Struggle for America's Soul from the Revolution to the Civil War* (New York: Penguin Press, 2018), 221.

23. Winik, *April 1865*, 14–15.

24. Jack N. Rakove, "'A Real Nondescript': James Madison's Thoughts on States' Rights and Federalism," in *Union and States' Rights: A History and Interpretation of Interposition, Nullification, and Secession 150 Years After Sumter*, ed. N. H. Cogan (Akron, OH: University of Akron Press, 2014), 16.

25. Alexander Hamilton, *Federalist 8*, in *The Federalist with the Letters of "Brutus,"* ed. T. Ball (Cambridge: Cambridge University Press, 2003), 35.

26. Alexander Hamilton, *Federalist 9*, in *The Federalist with the Letters of "Brutus,"* ed. T. Ball (Cambridge: Cambridge University Press, 2003), 37.

27. Thomas Jefferson to Peregrine Fitzhugh, February 23, 1798, available via https://founders.archives.gov/documents/Jefferson/01-30-02-0089.

28. Brian Steele, "Thomas Jefferson, Coercion, and the Limits of Harmonious Union," *The Journal of Southern History* 74 (2008): 853.

29. Lincoln makes the same infinite regress argument. Abraham Lincoln, "First Inaugural Address," March 4, 1861, available via https://avalon.law.yale.edu/19th_century/lincoln1.asp. See also Brian Steele, "Thomas Jefferson, Coercion, and the Limits of Harmonious Union," *The Journal of Southern History* 74 (2008): 832–833; Christopher Heath Wellman, *A Theory of Secession: The Case for Political Self-Determination* (Cambridge: Cambridge University Press, 2005), 71–73; Radan, "A Liberal Theory of Secession," 21–31.

30. Thomas Jefferson to John Taylor, June 4, 1798, available via https://founders.archives.gov/documents/Jefferson/01-30-02-0280.

31. Steele, "Thomas Jefferson," 854.

32. Joseph Ellis, "Remarks on the Founding Fathers," June 21, 2010, available via https://www.c-span.org/video/?294168-1/joseph-ellis-remarks-founding-fathers.

33. Thomas Jefferson to James Madison, August 23, 1799, available via https://founders.archives.gov/documents/Jefferson/01-31-02-0145.

34. Thomas Jefferson to John Breckenridge, August 12, 1803, available via https://founders.archives.gov/documents/Jefferson/01-41-02-0139.

35. Thomas Jefferson to William H. Crawford, June 20, 1816, available via https://founders.archives.gov/documents/Jefferson/03-10-02-0101.

36. Rakove, "'A Real Nondescript,'" 26, 24.

220 NOTES

37. Benjamin E. Park, "The Angel of Nullification: Imagining Disunion in an Era Before Secession," *Journal of the Early Republic* 37 (2017): 513.

38. James Madison to Mathew Carey, July 27, 1831, available via https://www.loc.gov/item/mjm020986/.

39. James Madison to Henry Clay, October 9, 1830, available via https://www.loc.gov/item/mjm020812/.

40. Rakove, "'A Real Nondescript,'" 25. See also James Madison to Nicholas P. Trist, December 23, 1832, available via http://www.loc.gov/resource/mjm.23_1158_1160.

41. James Madison to Edward Coles, 1834, available via https://www.loc.gov/item/mjm021486/.

42. Alison L. LaCroix, *The Ideological Origins of American Federalism* (Cambridge, MA: Harvard University Press, 2010), 6.

43. James Madison, *Federalist* no. 39, available via https://avalon.law.yale.edu/18th_century/fed39.asp.

44. John C. Calhoun, *Exposition and Protest* (Columbia, SC: D. W. Sims, 1829).

45. Christian G. Fritz, "Interposition: An Overlooked Tool of American Constitutionalism," in *Union and States' Rights: A History and Interpretation of Interposition, Nullification, and Secession 150 Years After Sumter*, ed. N. H. Cogan (Akron, OH: University of Akron Press, 2014), 177, 184. See also Lee J. Strang, "Originalism's Limits: Interposition, Nullification, and Secession," in *Union and States' Rights: A History and Interpretation of Interposition, Nullification, and Secession 150 Years After Sumter*, ed. N. H. Cogan (Akron, OH: University of Akron Press, 2014), 206.

46. Fritz, "Interposition," 177.

47. Christian G. Fritz, *American Sovereigns: The People and America's Constitutional Tradition Before the Civil War* (Cambridge: Cambridge University Press, 2008), 218–223; Rakove, "'A Real Nondescript,'" 27; Sanford V. Levinson, "Union and States' Rights 150 Years After Sumter: Some Reflections on a Tangled Political and Constitutional Conundrum," in *Union and States' Rights: A History and Interpretation of Interposition, Nullification, and Secession 150 Years After Sumter*, ed. N. H. Cogan (Akron, OH: University of Akron Press, 2014), 249–250.

48. Kenneth M. Stampp, "The Concept of a Perpetual Union," *The Journal of American History* 65 (1978): 31.

49. Shearer Davis Bowman, *At the Precipice: Americans North and South During the Secession Crisis* (Chapel Hill: University of North Carolina Press, 2010), 36–37. See also Daniel Wait Howe, *Political History of Secession to the Beginning of the American Civil War* (New York: G. P. Putnam's Sons, 1914).

NOTES 221

50. Rakove, "'A Real Nondescript,'" 15.

51. Eric Foner, *Politics and Ideology in the Age of the Civil War* (New York: Oxford University Press, 1980), 53. See also James McPherson, *The War That Forged a Nation: Why the Civil War Still Matters* (New York: Oxford University Press, 2015).

52. Garry Wills, *Lincoln at Gettysburg* (New York: Simon & Schuster, 1992), 145.

53. Winik, *April 1865*, 19.

54. Waters, *Boxing Pandora*, 20.

55. Eric Turkewitz, "Scalia: 'There is No Right to Secede,'" February 16, 2010, available via http://www.newyorkpersonalinjuryattorneyblog.com/2010/02/scalia-there-is-no-right-to-secede.html.

56. Akhil Reed Amar, "An Open Letter to Professors Paulsen and Powell," *The Yale Law Journal* 115, no. 8 (2006): 2105.

57. Cass R. Sunstein, *Designing Democracy: What Constitutions Do* (New York: Oxford University Press, 2001), 95.

58. Richard Kreitner, *Break It Up: Secession, Division, and the Secret History of America's Imperfect Union* (New York: Little, Brown, 2020), 291–293.

59. Daniel A. Farber, "The 14th Amendment and the Unconstitutionality of Secession," in *Union and States' Rights: A History and Interpretation of Interposition, Nullification, and Secession 150 Years After Sumter*, ed. N. H. Cogan (Akron, OH: University of Akron Press, 2014), 141; Delbanco, *The War Before the War*, 221.

60. Stampp, "The Concept of a Perpetual Union," 5–33; Daniel Farber, *Lincoln's Constitution* (Chicago: University of Chicago Press, 2003).

61. Cynthia Nicoletti, "The American Civil War as a Trial by Battle," *Law and History Review* 28 (2010): 76. See also Strang, "Originalism's Limits," 217.

62. Herman Belz, "Secession, Revolution and Social Contract Theory in American Political Thought," *The Good Society* 6 (1996): 14.

63. Sanford Levinson, "The 21st Century Rediscovery of Nullification and Secession in American Political Rhetoric," in *Nullification and Secession in Modern Constitutional Thought*, ed. S. Levinson (Lawrence: University Press of Kansas, 2016), 38.

64. H. Jefferson Powell, "William Rawle and Secession: Legal Rights and Political Wrongs," in *Union and States' Rights: A History and Interpretation of Interposition, Nullification, and Secession 150 Years After Sumter*, ed. N. H. Cogan (Akron, OH: University of Akron Press, 2014), 111. The quotation is attributed to professor Charles L. Black.

222 NOTES

65. David Blight, "The Civil War Isn't Over," *The Atlantic*, April 8, 2015, available via https://www.theatlantic.com/politics/archive/2015/04/the-civil-war-isnt-over/389847/.

66. Strang, "Originalism's Limits," 215.

67. Belz, "Secession, Revolution and Social Contract Theory," 11.

68. Nicoletti, *Secession on Trial*, 66–67. See also R. Jarrod Atchison, *A War of Words: The Rhetorical Leadership of Jefferson Davis* (Tuscaloosa: University of Alabama Press, 2017).

69. Salmon P. Chase, Opinion, *Texas v. White* 74 U.S. 700.

70. Mark E. Brandon, "Secession, Constitutionalism, and American Experience," in *Secession and Self-Determination*, ed. S. Macedo and A. Buchanan (New York: New York University Press, 2003), 306; Richard Striner, "A Brief History of Secession," *The American Scholar*, March 6, 2017, available via https://theamericanscholar.org/a-brief-history-of-secession/#.Xlgkh5NKh0t.

71. Mark R. Killenbeck, "Political Facts, Legal Fictions," in *Nullification and Secession in Modern Constitutional Thought*, ed. S. Levinson (Lawrence: University Press of Kansas, 2016), 237.

72. Winik, *April 1865*, 22.

73. William Hogeland, *The Whiskey Rebellion: George Washington, Alexander Hamilton, and the Frontier Rebels Who Challenged America's Newfound Sovereignty* (New York: Simon & Schuster, 2010).

74. Daniel Nasaw, "Who, What, Why: How Many Soldiers Died in the US Civil War?," BBC, April 4, 2012, available via http://www.bbc.com/news/magazine-17604991.

75. In Lewis, *The Burr Conspiracy*, 133.

76. H. W. Brands, *The Heartbreak of Aaron Burr* (New York: Anchor Books, 2012), 86, 97.

77. Thomas DiLorenzo, "Yankee Confederates: New England Secession Movements Prior to the War Between the States," in *Secession, State and Liberty*, ed. D. Gordon (Piscataway, NJ: Transaction, 1998), 135.

78. Brandon, "Secession, Constitutionalism, and American Experience," 287–288; James H. Read and Neal Allen, "Living, Dead, and Undead: Nullification Past and Present," in *Nullification and Secession in Modern Constitutional Thought*, ed. S. Levinson (Lawrence: University Press of Kansas, 2016), 108.

79. In Paul C. Nagel, *One Nation Indivisible: The Union in American Thought, 1776–1861* (New York: Oxford University Press, 1964), 19; Kevin M. Gannon, "Escaping 'Mr. Jefferson's Plan of Destruction': New England Federalists and the Idea of a Northern Confederacy, 1803–1804," *Journal*

NOTES   223

of the Early Republic 21 (2001): 435. It was not Pickering's first flirtation with separatism. See Fritz, *American Sovereigns*, 49.

80. Delbanco, *The War Before the War*, 91–92.

81. Rakove, "'A Real Nondescript," 69.

82. Delbanco, *The War Before the War*, 169–179.

83. Delbanco, *The War Before the War*, 235.

84. Elizabeth R. Varon, *Disunion! The Coming of the American Civil War, 1789–1859* (Chapel Hill: University of North Carolina Press, 2008), 195, 154.

85. Brandon, "Secession, Constitutionalism, and American Experience," 288.

86. Delbanco, *The War Before the War*, 219.

87. William Lloyd Garrison, "Disunion: The American Union," *The Liberator*, January 10, 1845, 1. See also William Lloyd Garrison, "The Right of Secession," *The Liberator*, April 12, 1861, 1.

88. Delbanco, *The War Before the War*, 250.

89. Garrison, "Disunion," 1.

90. Fritz, *American Sovereigns*, 452–453.

91. Varon, *Disunion!*, 154.

92. Henry Mayer, *All on Fire: William Lloyd Garrison and the Abolition of Slavery* (New York: St. Martin's Griffin, 1998), 313.

93. Varon, *Disunion!*, 153–154.

94. Fritz, *American Sovereigns*, 314.

95. Brandon, "Secession, Constitutionalism, and American Experience," 288.

96. In Varon, *Disunion!*, 150.

97. Richard Kreitner, "When the North Almost Seceded," *Boston Globe*, October 28, 2016, available via https://www.bostonglobe.com/ideas/2016/10/28/when-north-almost-seceded/GlhxrYBNijl830cWtViVtK/story.html.

98. Varon, *Disunion!*, 326–328.

99. Varon, *Disunion!*, 326. Nat Turner may have been headed to hide out in the Great Dismal Swamp before he and his band were defeated by a white militia. See Wilentz, *The Rise of American Democracy*, 339.

100. Kyle Chayka, "America Is a Utopia Experiment—And Always Has Been," *Pacific Standard*, June 14, 2017, available via https://psmag.com/social-justice/america-utopian-experiment-always-73410.

101. Delbanco, *The War Before the War*, 221.

102. Winik, *April 1865*, 22.

103. Levinson, "The 21st Century Rediscovery of Nullification and Secession in American Political Rhetoric," 31.

104. *Cooper v. Aaron*, 358 U.S. 1 (1958).

224 NOTES

105. Ari Berman, "The New Nullification Movement," *The Nation*, October 23, 2013, available via https://www.thenation.com/article/archive/new-nullification-movement/; David A. Graham, "Can States Ignore the Supreme Court on Gay Marriage?," *The Atlantic*, July 1, 2015, available via https://www.theatlantic.com/politics/archive/2015/07/nullification-again/397373/; Caroline Kelly, "Republicans Ramp Up Efforts to Restrict Abortion in 2020," CNN, January 4, 2020, available via https://www.cnn.com/2020/01/04/politics/abortion-policy-changes-2020/index.html; Kevin Mahnken, "Red States' Legally Dubious Strategy to Destroy Obamacare," *The New Republic*, January 28, 2014, available via https://newrepublic.com/article/116373/red-states-wage-legally-dubious-war-nullify-obamacare; Lois Beckett, "Virginia Democrats Won an Election. Gun Owners Are Talking Civil War," *The Guardian*, January 10, 2020, available via https://www.theguardian.com/us-news/2020/jan/09/virginia-gun-control-second-amendment-civil-war. See also Read and Allen, "Living, Dead, and Undead: Nullification Past and Present," 91–93.

106. Thomas B. Edsall, "When the Mask You're Wearing Tastes Like Socialism," *New York Times*, May 20, 2020, available via https://www.nytimes.com/2020/05/20/opinion/coronavirus-trump-partisanship.html.

107. Sam Tanenhaus, "Original Sin," *The New Republic*, February 10, 2013, available via https://newrepublic.com/article/112365/why-republicans-are-party-white-people.

108. Jared A. Goldstein, "To Kill and Die for the Constitution: Nullification and Insurrectionary Violence," in *Nullification and Secession in Modern Constitutional Thought*, ed. S. Levinson (Lawrence: University Press of Kansas, 2016), 182. See also Michael Gerson, "Trump Wants Parts of the Country to Secede—At Least in Their Minds," *Washington Post*, October 22, 2020, available via https://www.washingtonpost.com/opinions/trump-wants-parts-of-the-country-to-secede—at-least-in-their-minds/2020/10/22/7f4bc048-148f-11eb-ad6f-36c93e6e94fb_story.html; David Frum, "Trump Is a Secessionist from the Top," *The Atlantic*, August 28, 2020, available via https://www.theatlantic.com/ideas/archive/2020/08/trump-secessionist-top/615847/.

109. Michael J. Lee, *Creating Conservatism: Postwar Words That Made an American Movement* (East Lansing: Michigan State University Press, 2014), 39–74.

110. Rebecca Solnit, "Easy Chair: The Ideology of Isolation," *Harper's*, July 2016, 4.

NOTES 225

111. Douglas MacKinnon, *The Secessionist States of America: The Blueprint for Creating a Traditional Values Country . . . Now* (New York: Skyhorse, 2014), 10, 199–200.

112. MacKinnon, *The Secessionist States of America*, 10, 199–200.

113. F. H. Buckley, "How to Avoid America's Coming Secession Crisis," *New York Post*, January 24, 2020, available via https://nypost.com/2020/01/24/how-to-avoid-americas-coming-secession-crisis/. See also F. H. Buckley, *American Secession: The Looming Threat of a National Breakup* (New York: Encounter Books, 2020).

114. David French, *Divided We Fall: America's Secession Threat and How to Restore Our Nation* (New York: St. Martin's Press, 2020), 27.

115. Strang, "Originalism's Limits," 209.

116. "The Seattle Secessionists," editorial, *Wall Street Journal*, June 11, 2020, available via https://www.wsj.com/articles/the-seattle-secessionists-11591919047; Judd Gregg, "The South May Now Secede," *The Hill*, June 22, 2020, available via https://thehill.com/opinion/civil-rights/503825-judd-gregg-the-south-may-now-secede; Victor Davis Hanson, "Are Sanctuary Cities the New Confederates?" *National Review*, October 15, 2015, available via https://www.nationalreview.com/2015/10/sanctuary-cities-illegal-immigration-confederates-nullification/; Heather Gerken, "We're About to See States' Rights Used Defensively Against Trump," Vox, January 20, 2017, available via https://www.vox.com/the-big-idea/2016/12/12/13915990/federalism-trump-progressive-uncooperative.

117. Sanford Levinson, "Introduction: Zombie (or Dinosaur) Constitutionalism? The Revival of Nullification and Secession," in *Nullification and Secession in Modern Constitutional Thought*, ed. S. Levinson (Lawrence: University Press of Kansas, 2016), 10.

118. Jeremy Zogby, "Secessionist Sentiment Remains a Plurality Among Likely Voters," August 10, 2018, available via https://johnzogbystrategies.com/secessionist-sentiment-remains-a-plurality-among-likely-voters/.

119. Jim Gaines, "One in Four Americans Want Their State to Secede from the U.S., but Why?," Reuters, September 19, 2014, available via http://blogs.reuters.com/jamesrgaines/2014/09/19/one-in-four-americans-want-their-state-to-secede-from-the-u-s-but-why/.

120. "Southern Secessionists Welcome Yankees to Convention," Fox News, October 3, 2007, available via http://www.foxnews.com/story/2007/10/03/southern-secessionists-welcome-yankees-to-convention.html.

121. Paul Farhi, "Secession? Rush Limbaugh Floats a Startling Notion—Then Quickly Backs Off," *Washington Post*, December 10, 2020, available via

226 NOTES

https://www.washingtonpost.com/lifestyle/media/rush-limbaugh-trump-secession-election/2020/12/10/8889397a-3b0d-11eb-bc68-96af0daae728_story.html; Casey Michel, "What All the Secession Talk Really Means," Politico, December 21, 2020, available via https://www.politico.com/news/magazine/2020/12/21/secession-donald-trump-449348; Kenya Evelyn, "Texas Republicans Endorse Legislation to Allow Vote on Secession from US," *The Guardian*, February 5, 2021, available via https://www.theguardian.com/us-news/2021/feb/05/texas-republicans-endorse-legislation-vote-secession; Matt Ford, "We Regret to Inform You That Republicans Are Talking About Secession Again," *The New Republic*, January 22, 2021, available via https://newrepublic.com/article/161023/republicans-secede-texas-wyoming-brexit.

122. Craig M. Burnett, "Kalikow School Poll at Hofstra University," September 29, 2020, available via https://www.hofstra.edu/pdf/academics/colleges/hclas/gov-policy-international/kalikow-poll-0920.pdf.

123. Sheera Frenkel, "Facebook Bans a Page Used to Coordinate Pro-Trump Protests After Calls for Violence," *New York Times*, January 6, 2021, available via https://www.nytimes.com/2021/01/06/us/politics/facebook-bans-a-page-used-to-coordinate-pro-trump-protests-after-calls-for-violence.html.

124. Nathan Newman, "The Case for Blue-State Secession," *The Nation*, February 20, 2021, available via https://www.thenation.com/article/politics/secession-constitution-elections-senate/.

125. Jordan Ball, "#Calexit: Is It Possible for California to Secede," *USA Today*, November 10, 2016, available via https://www.usatoday.com/story/news/nation-now/2016/11/10/calexit-possible-california-secede-us/93581688/. See also James Ronald Kennedy, "Could 'Calexit' Create a Left-Right Confederacy?," *The Abbeville Blog*, October 22, 2018, available via https://www.abbevilleinstitute.org/blog/could-calexit-create-a-left-right-confederacy/; Donald Livingston, "A Red and Blue Coalition?," *The Abbeville Blog*, October 15, 2018, available via https://www.abbevilleinstitute.org/blog/a-red-and-blue-coalition/; David Siders, "Jerry Brown, President of the Independent Republic of California," Politico, November 11, 2017, available via https://www.politico.com/magazine/story/2017/11/11/jerry-brown-california-profile-215812; Adam Goodheart, *1861: The Civil War Awakening* (New York: Alfred A. Knopf, 2011), 228.

126. Kevin Baker, "It's Time for a Bluexit," *The New Republic*, March 9, 2017, available via https://newrepublic.com/article/140948/bluexit-blue-states-exit-trump-red-america. See also Jesse Kelly, "It's Time for the

United States to Divorce Before Things Get Dangerous," The Federalist, April 10, 2018, available via http://thefederalist.com/2018/04/10/time-united-states-divorce-things-get-dangerous/.

127. Neal Caren, Ali Eshraghi, Sarah Gaby, Brandon Gorman, Michael Good, Jonathan Horowitz, Ali Kadivar, Rachel Ramsay, Charles Seguin, and Didem Turkoglu, "The New Secessionists: Plotting Whitehouse. gov Secession Petitions," November 24, 2012, available via https://badhessian.org/2012/11/the-new-secessionists/.

128. Thomas H. Naylor, *Secession: How Vermont and All the Other States Can Save Themselves from the Empire* (Port Townsend, WA: Feral House, 2008), 24.

129. Peter Applebome, "If at First You Don't Secede . . . ," *New York Times*, November 27, 2000, available via https://archive.nytimes.com/www.nytimes.com/learning/teachers/featured_articles/20001127monday. html. See also Michelle Goldberg, "If at First You Don't Secede," *Salon*, November 16, 2004, available via https://www.salon.com/2004/11/17/states_2/.

130. Farber, "The 14th Amendment and the Unconstitutionality of Secession," 132; Striner, "A Brief History of Secession"; Peter Applebome, "A Vision of the Nation No Longer in the U.S.," *New York Times*, October 18, 2007, available via https://www.nytimes.com/2007/10/18/nyregion/18towns.html.

131. Delbanco, *The War Before the War*, 220.

132. Ward, "Thomas Hobbes and John Locke on a Liberal Right of Secession," 877.

133. Bill McKibben, *Radio Free Vermont: A Fable of Resistance* (New York: Blue Rider Press, 2017), 177.

134. Jessie Walker, "Delaware's Odd, Beautiful, Contentious, Private Utopia," *Reason*, November 2017, available via https://reason.com/2017/10/14/delawares-odd-beautiful-conten.

135. Christopher Kilbourn, "An Oral History of the West African Village That Has Been in South Carolina for Decades," *Vice*, July 30, 2015, available via https://www.vice.com/en_us/article/5gj973/an-oral-history-of-the-west-african-village-that-has-been-in-south-carolina-for-four-decades-729.

136. No Author, "The Republic of Molossia," *Atlas Obscura*, https://www.atlasobscura.com/places/the-republic-of-molossia-dayton-nevada.

137. Kristy Totten, "Nevada Is Home to a Micronation—But Don't Tell the Micronation That," KNPR, May 31, 2016, available via https://knpr.org/knpr/2016-05/nevada-home-micronation-dont-tell-micronation.

228 NOTES

138. Ralph Ellison, *Going to the Territory* (New York: Random House, 1995), 21.

139. Christopher Ketcham, "Long Live Secession!," *Salon*, January 26, 2005, available via https://www.salon.com/2005/01/26/secession_2/. See also Thomas Naylor, *The Vermont Manifesto* (Bloomington, IN: Xlibris, 2003).

140. Mindy Fetterman, "Despite Secession Talk, Breaking Up Is Hard to Do," *Pew*, May 4, 2017, available via http://www.pewtrusts.org/en/research-and-analysis/blogs/stateline/2017/05/04/despite-secession-talk-breaking-up-is-hard-to-do. See also Kirkpatrick Sale, "Texas Secession?," *The Abbeville Blog*, available via https://www.abbevilleinstitute.org/blog/texas-secession/.

141. Anne Hull, "Randy Weaver's Return from Ruby Ridge," *Washington Post*, April 30, 2001, available via https://www.washingtonpost.com/archive/politics/2001/04/30/randy-weavers-return-from-ruby-ridge/946b58c3-2d46-4df0-9b06-f5ca7c562d09/?utm_term=.91772107ed4e.

142. Russell Means, "UN Listening Session Is US Smokescreen," March 18, 2010, available via http://www.russellmeansfreedom.com/tag/republic-of-lakotah/.

143. Kevin Sullivan, "A Fortress Against Fear," *Washington Post*, August 27, 2016, available via https://www.washingtonpost.com/sf/national/2016/08/27/a-fortress-against-fear/?utm_term=.ec3499720fe4.

144. Sandy Ikeda, "Secession: New York City as Polis," *New York Sun*, January 31, 2008, available via https://www.nysun.com/blogs/culture-of-congestion/2008/01/secession-new-york-city-as-polis.html.

145. Daniel Robison, "N.Y. Town Still Uncertain Why It Left the Union," NPR, October 14, 2011, available via https://www.npr.org/2011/10/14/141362876/n-y-town-still-uncertain-why-it-left-the-union. See also Christopher Klein, "This New York Village Seceded from the Union . . . for 85 Years," *History*, October 18, 2018, available via https://www.history.com/news/civil-war-secession-new-york-town. Another example is Rough and Ready, California, a small town that seceded for a few months in 1850 to avoid mining taxes. See Rick Paulas, "A Brief History of the Town That Seceded 'til It Ran Out of Booze," *Vice*, December 12, 2016, available via https://www.vice.com/en_us/article/ypvqvw/a-brief-history-of-the-california-town-that-seceded-til-it-ran-out-of-booze.

146. Allen Buchanan, "Introduction," in *Secession and Self-Determination*, ed. S. Macedo and A. Buchanan (New York: New York University Press, 2003), 1.

NOTES 229

147. Anna Ella Carroll, "John C. Calhoun A Secessionist," *New York Times*, July 23, 1861, available via https://www.nytimes.com/1861/07/23/archives/john-c-calhoun-a-secessionist.html.

148. Brandon, "Secession, Constitutionalism, and American Experience," 279.

149. Allen Buchanan, *Justice, Legitimacy, and Self-Determination* (New York: Oxford University Press, 2004), 332.

150. Jason Sorens, *Secessionism: Identity, Interest, and Strategy* (Montreal: McGill-Queen's University Press, 2012), 5.

151. Blight, "The Civil War Isn't Over."

152. Ian Millhiser, "The Supreme Court Will Hear 2 Major Cases About When Religious Schools Can Ignore Civil Rights Laws," *Vox*, December 19, 2019, available via https://www.vox.com/policy-and-politics/2019/12/19/21028094/supreme-court-religious-schools-ministerial-exception.

153. Hogeland, *The Whiskey Rebellion*, 239.

154. J. G. A. Pocock, "Texts as Events: Reflections on the History of Political Thought," in *Politics of Discourse: The Literature and History of Seventeenth-Century England*, ed. Kevin Sharp and Steven N. Zwicker (Berkeley: University of California Press, 1987); J. G. A. Pocock, "The Reconstruction of Discourse: Towards the Historiography of Political Thought," *MLN* 96 (1981); J. G. A. Pocock, "Verbalizing a Political Act: Toward a Politics of Speech," *Political Theory* 1 (1973); J. G. A. Pocock, *Politics, Language, and Time: The Transformation of the Study of Political Thought* (New York: Atheneum, 1971), 28.

155. See also Richard Weaver, *The Ethics of Rhetoric* (Chicago: Henry Regnery, 1953), 212–214. For a book-length example, see Manisha Sinha, *The Counter-revolution of Slavery: Politics and Ideology in Antebellum South Carolina* (Chapel Hill: University of North Carolina Press, 2000).

156. Doyle, "An Attempt at Secession from an Early Nation-State," 103.

157. Albert O. Hirschman, *Exit, Voice, and Loyalty: Responses to Decline in Firms, Organizations, and States* (Cambridge, MA: Harvard University Press, 1970), 107, 108.

158. Benedict Anderson, *Imagined Communities: Reflections on the Origin and Spread of Nationalism*, rev. ed. (London: Verso, 1991), 191.

159. Donald W. Livingston, "The Secession Tradition in America," in *Secession, State, and Liberty*, ed. D. Gordon (New Brunswick, NJ: Transaction, 1998), 5.

160. Louis Hartz, *The Liberal Tradition in America: An Interpretation of American Political Thought Since the Revolution* (New York: Harcourt Brace Jovanovich, 1955), 64–65.

161. Winik, *April 1865*, 16.

230 NOTES

162. Chayka, "America Is a Utopia Experiment—And Always Has Been"; Kreitner, *Break It Up*, 21–23.

163. Wilentz, *The Rise of American Democracy*, 5–6.

164. G. Jeffrey MacDonald, "A Surge in Secessionist Theology," *The Christian Century*, November 29, 2012, available via https://www.christiancentury.org/article/2012-11/secession-theology-runs-deep-american-religious-political-history.

165. Robert J. Cook, "The Shadow of the Past: Collective Memory and the Coming of the American Civil War," in *Secession Winter: When the Union Fell Apart*, ed. R. J. Cook, W. L. Barney, and E. R. Varon (Baltimore: Johns Hopkins University Press, 2013), 70.

166. Eric Walther, *The Fire-Eaters* (Baton Rouge: Louisiana State University Press, 1992), 64–65.

167. John McCardell, *The Idea of a Southern Nation: Southern Nationalists and Southern Nationalism, 1830–1860* (New York: W. W. Norton, 1979), 14.

168. Tsai, *America's Forgotten Constitutions*, 2.

169. Fritz, "Interposition," 185.

170. Fritz, *American Sovereigns*, 49.

171. Fritz, *American Sovereigns*, 55, 62.

172. David Gordon, "Introduction," in *Secession, State, and Liberty*, ed. D. Gordon (New Brunswick, NJ: Transaction, 1998), ix.

173. William W. Freehling, *The Road to Disunion*, vol. II, *Secessionists Triumphant, 1854–1861* (New York: Oxford University Press, 2007), 18.

174. Doyle, "Introduction: Union and Secession in the Family of Nations," 1.

175. John C. Calhoun, "Speech on the General State of the Union," March 4, 1850, in *Union and Liberty: The Political Philosophy of John C. Calhoun*, ed. R. M. Lence (Indianapolis, IN: Liberty Fund, 1992), 591.

176. Bowman, *At the Precipice*, 13–14; Cook, "The Shadow of the Past," 67.

177. Levinson, "The 21st Century Rediscovery of Nullification and Secession in American Political Rhetoric," 46. See also Wayne Norman, "Domesticating Secession," in *Secession and Self-Determination*, ed. S. Macedo and A. Buchanan (New York: NYU Press, 2003), 198; Sunstein, *Designing Democracy*, 106–111; Coggins, "The History of Secession: An Overview," 25.

178. Garry Wills, *Inventing America: Jefferson's Declaration of Independence* (Garden City, NY: Doubleday, 1978), 290–292.

179. Doyle, "Introduction: Union and Secession in the Family of Nations," 8.

180. Naylor, *Secession*, 24.

181. Sunstein, *Designing Democracy*, 101–102.

182. Wilentz, *The Rise of American Democracy*, 9.

NOTES 231

183. Beran, "A Liberal Theory of Secession," 21–31; Stephen C. Neff, "Secession and the Breach of Compact: The Law of Nature Meets the United States Constitution," in *Union and States' Rights: A History and Interpretation of Interposition, Nullification, and Secession 150 Years After Sumter*, ed. N. H. Cogan (Akron, OH: University of Akron Press, 2014), 97–98.

184. Thomas Paine, "The Rights of Man," in *Thomas Paine: Political Writings*, ed. B. Kuklick (Cambridge: Cambridge University Press, 2000), 88.

185. Buchanan, *Secession*, 4.

186. Daniel Philpott, "In Defense of Self-Determination," *Ethics* 105 (1995): 353; David Copp, "Democracy and Communal Self-Determination," in *The Morality of Nationalism*, ed. J. McMahon and R. McKim (New York: Oxford University Press, 1997), 296.

187. Abraham Lincoln, "Speech in the United States House of Representatives: The War with Mexico," January 12, 1848, available via https://quod.lib.umich.edu/l/lincoln/lincoln1/1:444?rgn=div1;view=fulltext.

188. David Gauthier, "Breaking Up: An Essay on Secession," *Canadian Journal of Philosophy* 24 (1994): 371. See also Christopher Caldwell, *The Age of Entitlement: America Since the Sixties* (New York: Simon & Schuster, 2020), 14–23.

189. Tsai, *America's Forgotten Constitutions*, 17.

190. John Stuart Mill, *On Liberty* (Mineola, NY: Dover, 2002), 10. See also John Stuart Mill, "The Contest in America," *Fraser's Magazine for Town and Country* 35 (1862): 265.

191. Wills, *Inventing America*, 303.

192. Alexander Hamilton, *Federalist 15*, in *The Federalist with the Letters of "Brutus,"* ed. T. Ball (Cambridge: Cambridge University Press, 2003), 64. See also Alexander Hamilton, *Federalist 85*, in *The Federalist with the Letters of "Brutus,"* ed. T. Ball (Cambridge: Cambridge University Press, 2003), 426.

193. Abraham Lincoln, "Speech at Indianapolis, Indiana," February 11, 1861, in *Abraham Lincoln: Political Writings and Speeches*, ed. T. Ball (Cambridge: Cambridge University Press, 2013), 114. A young John Quincy Adams offered a similar metaphor but came to a remarkably different conclusion in an 1801 letter: "I love the Union as I love my wife. But if my wife should ask for and insist upon a separation, she should have it though it broke my heart." In Goldstein, "To Kill and Die for the Constitution," 34.

194. Foner, *Politics and Ideology in the Age of the Civil War*, 25.

195. Francis Lieber, *What Is Our Constitution: League, Pact, or Government?* (Sydney: Wentworth Press, 2019), 45.

196. Aleksandar Pavkovic and Peter Radan, *Creating New States: Theory and Practice of Secession* (Burlington, VT: Ashgate, 2007), 15.

232 NOTES

197. Thomas Jefferson, rough draft of the Declaration of Independence, available via https://www.loc.gov/exhibits/declara/ruffdrft.html.
198. Henry Wiencek, "The Dark Side of Thomas Jefferson," *Smithsonian Magazine*, October 2012, available via https://www.smithsonianmag.com/history/the-dark-side-of-thomas-jefferson-35976004/.
199. Delbanco, *The War Before the War*, 46.
200. Bowman, *At the Precipice*, 29; Doyle, "An Attempt at Secession from an Early Nation-State," 103.
201. Ibram X. Kendi, *Stamped from the Beginning: The Definitive History of Racist Ideas in America* (New York: Bold Type Books, 2017), 109–110.
202. Wills, *Inventing America*, 306.
203. Wills, *Inventing America*, 304.
204. Casey Ryan Kelly, "'We Are Not Free': The Meaning of <Freedom> in American Indian Resistance to President Johnson's War on Poverty," *Communication Quarterly* 62 (2014): 455–473.
205. Tsai, *America's Forgotten Constitutions*, 3.
206. Ralph Waldo Emerson, "Self-Reliance," 1841, available via https://archive.vcu.edu/english/engweb/transcendentalism/authors/emerson/essays/selfreliance.html.
207. Robert N. Bellah, Richard Madsen, William M. Sullivan, Ann Swidler, and Steven M. Tipton, *Habits of the Heart: Individualism and Commitment in American Life* (Berkeley: University of California Press, 2008), 55.
208. Solnit, "Easy Chair," 4.
209. See Grace Elizabeth Hale, *A Nation of Outsiders: How the White Middle Class Fell in Love with Rebellion in Postwar America* (New York: Oxford University Press, 2011), 6; Charles Bowden, *Blood Orchid: An Unnatural History of America* (New York: North Point Press, 2002).
210. Hunter S. Thompson, *Hell's Angels: A Strange and Terrible Saga* (New York: Ballantine Books, 1996), n.p.

Chapter 2

1. Lynn Kinsky and Robert W. Poole Jr., "Abaco: Birth of a New Country," *Reason*, October 1974, available via http://reason.com/archives/1974/10/01/abaco; John L. Snare, "The National Builders' Struggle," *Reason*, December 1972, available via http://reason.com/archives/1972/12/01/the-nation-builders-struggle/1.

NOTES 233

2. Nancy Faber and Ross H. Munro, "Spears and a Nevada Businessman Help a South Pacific Island Proclaim Itself a New Country," *People*, July 21, 1980, available via https://people.com/archive/spears-and-a-nevada-businessman-help-a-south-pacific-island-proclaim-itself-a-new-country-vol-14-no-3/.

3. "Designing a Free Country: An Interview with Mike Oliver," *Reason*, December 1972, available via http://reason.com/archives/1972/12/01/designing-a-free-country/.

4. "Designing a Free Country."

5. Harry Blutstein, "A Libertarian Utopia Was Actually Tried Here—and It Failed Miserably," History News Network, October 16, 2017, available via https://www.rawstory.com/2017/10/a-libertarian-utopia-was-actually-tried-here-and-it-failed-miserably/.

6. "Designing a Free Country."

7. Blutstein, "A Libertarian Utopia Was Actually Tried Here—and It Failed Miserably." See also Katherine Mangu-Ward, "Artifact: Hope Floats," *Reason*, August/September 2008, available via http://reason.com/archives/2008/08/01/artifact-hope-floats.

8. Kinsky and Poole, "Abaco: Birth of a New Country."

9. John Hospers, "A New Constitution for a New Country," *Reason*, December 1975, available via http://reason.com/archives/1975/12/01/a-new-constitution-for-a-new-c.

10. Kenneth Bain, "Obituary: Jimmy Stevens," *Independent*, March 4, 1994, available via https://www.independent.co.uk/news/people/obituary-jimmy-stevens-1426905.html.

11. Bain, "Obituary: Jimmy Stevens."

12. Faber and Munro, "Spears and a Nevada Businessman Help a South Pacific Island Proclaim Itself a New Country."

13. Bain, "Obituary: Jimmy Stevens." See also Brian Doherty, *Radicals for Capitalism: A Freewheeling History of the Modern American Libertarian Movement* (New York: Public Affairs, 2007), 401–404.

14. Doherty, *Radicals for Capitalism*, 404.

15. Doherty, *Radicals for Capitalism*, 400.

16. Harry Cheadle, "Atlas Mugged: How a Libertarian Paradise in Chile Fell Apart," Vice, September 22, 2014, available via https://www.vice.com/en_us/article/bn53b3/atlas-mugged-922-v21n10. See also Adam Weinstein, "Ayn Rand's Capitalist Paradise Is Now a Greedy Land-Grabbing Shitstorm," Gawker, August 28, 2014, available via http://gawker.com/ayn-rands-capitalist-paradise-is-now-a-greedy-land-grab-1627574870.

234 NOTES

17. Doherty, *Radicals for Capitalism*, 473–477. See also Thomas Frank, "To Galt's Gulch They Go," *The Baffler*, April 2013, available via https://thebaffler.com/salvos/to-galts-gulch-they-go.

18. Rachel Riederer, "Libertarians Seek a Home on the High Seas," *The New Republic*, May 29, 2017, available via https://newrepublic.com/article/142381/libertarians-seek-home-high-seas. See also Rahim Taghizadegan, "The Politics of Seasteading," in *Seasteads: Opportunities and Challenges for Small New Societies*, ed. V. Tiberius (Zurich: VDF Hochschulverlag, 2017), 75.

19. Peter Thiel, "The Education of a Libertarian," Cato Unbound, April 13, 2009, available via https://www.cato-unbound.org/2009/04/13/peter-thiel/education-libertarian; Albert Jay Nock, *Our Enemy, the State* (New York: Arno Press, 1972), 19.

20. Pam Belluck, "Libertarians Pursue New Political Goal: State of Their Own," *New York Times*, October 27, 2003, available via https://www.nytimes.com/2003/10/27/us/libertarians-pursue-new-political-goal-state-of-their-own.html.

21. Nathan Brooker, "The Homebuyers Aiming to Make New Hampshire a Libertarian Utopia," *Financial Times*, November 1, 2016, available via https://www.ft.com/content/73cb867a-9c31-11e6-8324-be63473ce146.

22. Livia Gershon, "I Went to a Convention for Libertarian Revolutionaries Trying to Take Over New Hampshire," Vice, March 12, 2015, available via https://www.vice.com/en_us/article/qbegjp/i-went-to-convention-for-free-state-libertarians-trying-to-take-over-new-hampshire-312.

23. Brian Doherty, "New Hampshire Now Has Third Sitting Libertarian Party Legislator," *Reason*, June 29, 2017, available via http://reason.com/blog/2017/06/29/new-hampshire-now-has-third-sitting-libe; Kevin Townsend, "How a Libertarian Carpetbagger Helped Steal a Senate Seat for Democrats," *Slate*, November 30, 2016, available via http://www.slate.com/articles/news_and_politics/politics/2016/11/how_new_hampshire_s_libertarian_utopian_movement_helped_steal_a_senate_seat.html.

24. Townsend, "How a Libertarian Carpetbagger"; Michael F. Cannon, "Illegal Manicure in the 'Live Free or Die' State," Cato at Liberty, July 26, 2007, available via https://www.cato.org/blog/illegal-manicure-live-free-or-die-state.

25. Townsend, "How a Libertarian Carpetbagger."

26. Townsend, "How a Libertarian Carpetbagger."

27. Belluck, "Libertarians Pursue New Political Goal: State of their Own."

28. Jason Sorens, "Announcement: The Free State Project," *The Libertarian Enterprise*, July 23, 2001, available via http://www.ncc-1776.org/tle2001/libe131-20010723-03.html.

NOTES 235

29. Townsend, "How a Libertarian Carpetbagger."
30. Other libertarians describe this off-the-beaten-path lifestyle as "vonuism." See Erwin Strauss, *How to Start Your Own Country* (Port Townsend, WA: Loompanics Unlimited, 1984), 26; Rayo, *Vonu: The Search for Personal Freedom*, Jon Fisher, ed. (Port Townsend, WA: Loompanics Unlimited, 1983).
31. Gershon, "I Went to a Convention for Libertarian Revolutionaries Trying to Take Over New Hampshire."
32. Elizabeth Gilbert, "The Last American Man," *GQ*, August 8, 2010, available via https://www.gq.com/story/elizabeth-gilbert-gq-february-1998-last-american-man-eustace-conway-turtle-island. See also Valerie Bauerlein, "Ah, Wilderness! Mountain Man vs. the Building Inspector," *Wall Street Journal*, March 14, 2013, available via https://www.wsj.com/articles/SB10001424127887324178904578340850547093268.
33. Gilbert, "The Last American Man."
34. Ira Glass, "Adventures in the Simple Life," *This American Life*, September 11, 1998, available via https://www.thisamericanlife.org/111/adventures-in-the-simple-life. For more on the sheer variety of libertarians, see Jerome Tuccille, *It Usually Begins with Ayn Rand* (New York: Stein & Day, 1971), 106.
35. Doherty, *Radicals for Capitalism*, 248–249.
36. Benjamin Tucker, "The Relation of the State to the Individual," in *The Individualist Anarchists: An Anthology of Liberty (1881–1908)*, ed. F. H. Brooks (New Brunswick, NJ: Transaction, 1996), 24.
37. See James Arnt Aune, *Selling the Free Market: The Rhetoric of Economic Correctness* (New York: Guilford, 2002).
38. Jeff Deist, "Secession Begins at Home," Mises Daily Articles, January 30, 2015, available via https://mises.org/library/secession-begins-home-0.
39. Harry Beran, "A Liberal Theory of Secession," *Political Studies* 32 (1984): 22. See also Linda Bishai, "Altered States: Secession and the Problems of Liberal Theory," in *Theories of Secession*, ed. P. B. Lehning (London: Routledge, 1998), 92; David Copp, "Democracy and Communal Self-Determination," in *The Morality of Nationalism*, ed. J. McMahon and R. McKim (New York: Oxford University Press, 1997), 296; Daniel Philpott, "In Defense of Self-Determination," *Ethics* 105 (1995): 360–361; David Gauthier, "Breaking Up: An Essay on Secession," *Canadian Journal of Philosophy* 24 (1994): 371; Lee C. Buchheit, *Secession: The Legitimacy of Self-Determination* (New Haven, CT: Yale University Press, 1978).
40. George H. Nash, *The Conservative Intellectual Movement in America Since 1945* (Wilmington, DE: ISI Books, 1998), 296–297.

236 NOTES

41. Friedrich A. Hayek, *The Road to Serfdom*, 50th anniv. ed. (Chicago: University of Chicago Press, 1984). See also Ludwig von Mises, *Liberalism: In the Classical Tradition* (Irvington, NY: Foundation for Economic Education, 1985).

42. Charles Murray, *What It Means to Be a Libertarian* (New York: Broadway Books, 1997), xii.

43. Murray Rothbard, *For a New Liberty* (New York: Macmillan, 1973), 202. See also Nash, *The Conservative Intellectual Movement in America Since 1945*, 7–9.

44. David Friedman, *The Machinery of Freedom: Guide to Radical Capitalism*, 2nd ed. (LaSalle, IL: Open Court, 1989), 55, 72.

45. Hospers, "A New Constitution for a New Country."

46. Stephan Kinsella, "Randy Barnett's Proposed 'Federalism Amendment,'" *Mises Wire*, April 23, 2009, available via https://mises.org/wire/randy-barnetts-proposed-federalism-amendment.

47. Wendy Brown, *Undoing the Demos: Neoliberalism's Stealth Revolution* (New York: Zone Books, 2015), 19.

48. Deist, "Secession Begins at Home." See also William O. Reichert, *Partisans of Freedom: A Study in American Anarchism* (Bowling Green, KY: Bowling Green University Popular Press, 1976), 4.

49. Quinn Slobodian, *Globalists: The End of Empire and the Birth of Neocolonialism* (Cambridge, MA: Harvard University Press, 2018), 31.

50. Rothbard, *For a New Liberty*, 25–26.

51. Rothbard, *For a New Liberty*, 26–27.

52. Murray, *What It Means to Be a Libertarian*, 6.

53. Isabel Paterson, *The God of the Machine* (Freeport, NY: Books for Libraries Press, 1972), 121. See also David Boaz, *The Libertarian Mind: A Manifesto for Freedom* (New York: Simon & Schuster, 2015), 79, 81.

54. Doherty, *Radicals for Capitalism*, 35.

55. Herbert Spencer, *Social Statics* (London: John Chapman, 1851), 103.

56. John Locke, *Two Treatises on Government*, ch. 5, sec. 27, available via https://www.gutenberg.org/files/7370/7370-h/7370-h.htm. See also Stephen L. Newman, *Liberalism at Wit's End: The Libertarian Revolt Against the Modern State* (Ithaca, NY: Cornell University Press, 1984), 16–17.

57. Spencer, *Social Statics*, 207.

58. See for example, George C. Leef, "Secession, State, and Liberty," Foundation for Economic Education, June 1, 1999, available via https://fee.org/articles/secession-state-liberty/; Murray Rothbard, "The Laissez-Faire Radical: A Quest for the Historical Mises," *The Journal of*

NOTES 237

Libertarian Studies 5 (1981): 251; Albert Jay Nock, *Our Enemy, the State* (New York: Arno Press, 1972), 52.

59. Rothbard, *For a New Liberty*, 8, 9, 11, 50.

60. Friedman, *The Machinery of Freedom*, xvii.

61. Friedman, *The Machinery of Freedom*, xvii.

62. Nock, *Our Enemy, the State*, 36, 49–50.

63. Nock, *Our Enemy, the State*, 11.

64. Jeffrey Addicott, "Waving the Secede Flag—How to Regain State's Rights," speech at the Abbeville Institute, December 15, 2016, available via https://www.abbevilleinstitute.org/lectures/waving-the-secede-flag-how-to-regain-states-rights/.

65. Rothbard, *For a New Liberty*, 53.

66. Reichert, *Partisans of Freedom*, 135.

67. Paterson, *The God of the Machine*, 120.

68. Ludwig von Mises, *Nation, State, and Economy* (Washington, DC: Institute for Humane Studies, 1983), 34–35.

69. Patrick Allitt, *The Conservatives: Ideas and Personalities Throughout American History* (New Haven, CT: Yale University Press, 2009), 89.

70. Mises, *Nation, State, and Economy*, 60.

71. Mises, *Nation, State, and Economy*, 60.

72. Mises, *Liberalism*, 108–109. See also Rothbard, "The Laissez-Faire Radical," 240–241.

73. Rothbard, *For a New Liberty*, 297.

74. Murray Rothbard, *Man, State, and Economy with Power and Market*, 2nd ed. (Auburn, AL: Ludwig von Mises Institute, 2009), 1282–1283.

75. Rothbard, *For a New Liberty*, 287.

76. Murray Rothbard, "A Libertarian View of Nationalism, Secession, and Ethnic Enclaves," Mises Wire, March 5, 2014, available via https://mises.org/wire/libertarian-view-nationalism-secession-and-ethnic-enclaves.

77. Murray N. Rothbard, "Nations by Consent: Decomposing the Nation-State," in *Secession, State, and Liberty*, ed. D. Gordon (New Brunswick, NJ: Transaction, 1998), 83.

78. Daniel J. Mitchell, "Is Secession a Good Idea?," Cato at Liberty, October 17, 2012, available via https://www.cato.org/blog/secession-good-idea.

79. Dan Sanchez, "Mises Never Gave In to Evil," 2016, available via https://fee.org/articles/mises-never-gave-in-to-evil-1/; Hans-Hermann Hoppe, "Mises on Secession," Mises Daily Articles, October 19, 2012, available via https://mises.org/library/mises-secession; Hans-Hermann Hoppe, "What Must Be Done," speech at a Mises Institute conference,

238 NOTES

Newport Beach, California, January 24–25, 1997, available via https://mises-media.s3.amazonaws.com/What%20Must%20Be%20Done_7.pdf?file=1&type=document.

80. Jen Maffessanti, "Secession Is Sweeping the World, and We Should Let It," Foundation for Economic Education, October 3, 2017, available via https://fee.org/articles/secession-is-sweeping-the-world-and-we-should-let-it/. See also Ryan McMaken, "Self-Determination and Secession," Mises Daily Articles, June 27, 2015, available via https://mises.org/library/self-determination-and-secession.

81. Ryan McMaken, "Anarchism and Radical Decentralization Are the Same Thing," Mises Wire, January 29, 2016, available via https://mises.org/wire/anarchism-and-radical-decentralization-are-same-thing.

82. Joseph T. Salerno, "Mises on Nationalism, the Right of Self-Determination, and the Problem of Immigration," Mises Wire, March 28, 2017, available via https://mises.org/wire/mises-nationalism-right-self-determination-and-problem-immigration.

83. Nock, *Our Enemy, The State*, 46–47. See also Donald Livingston, "The Secession Tradition in America," in *Secession, State, and Liberty*, ed. D. Gordon (New Brunswick, NJ: Transaction, 1998), 2.

84. Mises, *Liberalism*, 109.

85. Boaz, *The Libertarian Mind*, 79. Some say the first writer to adopt "libertarian" as a term of identity was Joseph Dejacque, a nineteenth-century French anarchist. See Livia Gershon, "A Libertarian Utopia," *Aeon*, April 24, 2014, available via https://aeon.co/essays/what-happens-when-libertarians-try-to-build-a-new-society.

86. Livingston, "The Secession Tradition in America," 32.

87. Clyde N. Wilson, "Secession: The Last, Best Bulwark of Our Liberties," in *Secession, State, and Liberty*, ed. D. Gordon (New Brunswick, NJ: Transaction, 1998), 89.

88. Elvin T. Lim, *The Lovers' Quarrel: The Two Foundings and American Political Development* (New York: Oxford University Press, 2014).

89. Llewellyn H. Rockwell, "The Libertarian Principle of Secession," *The Austrian* 1 (2015): 4–5, 16–17. See also Lew Rockwell, "Secession Is Libertarian," speech at the Mises Institute Conference on Secession, January 24, 2015, available via https://mises.org/files/secession-libertarian-lew-rockwell.

90. Wilson, "Secession," 89.

91. Rockwell, "The Libertarian Principle of Secession," 4–5, 16–17; Rockwell, "Secession Is Libertarian"; Brion McClanahan, "Conventions: The Voice of the People," speech at the 2016 Abbeville Scholars Conference, December

NOTES 239

15, 2016, available via https://www.abbevilleinstitute.org/lectures/
conventions-the-voice-of-the-people/. See also Donald Livingston, "What
Is an American State?," speech at the Abbeville Institute, December 15,
2016, available via https://www.abbevilleinstitute.org/lectures/what-
is-an-american-state/; John Devanny, "Zombies No More: Secession,
Nullification, and the Academy," *The Abbeville Review*, April 17, 2018, available via https://www.abbevilleinstitute.org/review/zombies-no-more-
secession-nullification-and-the-academy/; Joseph S. Johnston, "Rolling
Back Federal Judicial Tyranny: State Courts as the True Guardians of the
Constitution of the United States and of Cases and Laws Arising Pursuant
Thereto," speech at the 2016 Abbeville Scholars Conference, December 15,
2016, December 15, 2016, available via https://www.abbevilleinstitute.org/
lectures/rolling-back-federal-judicial-tyranny-state-courts-as-the-true-
guardians-of-the-constitution-of-the-united-states-and-of-cases-
and-laws-arising-pursuant-thereto/; Clarence Carson, "The Civil War
and Political Nationalization," Foundation for Economic Education,
January 1, 1982, available via https://fee.org/articles/the-civil-war-and-
political-nationalization/; Frank Chodorov, *Income Tax: The Root of All
Evil* (New York: Devin-Adair, 1954), 64–69. See also Patrick Allitt, *The
Conservatives: Ideas and Personalities Throughout American History* (New
Haven, CT: Yale University Press, 2009), 21; Chris Calton, "Why Secession
Is a Big Problem—For Politicians," Mises Wire, April 23, 2018, available
via https://mises.org/wire/why-secession-big-problem-%E2%80%94-
politicians; Neil H. Cogan, "Introduction," in *Union and States' Rights: A
History and Interpretation of Interposition, Nullification, and Secession 150
Years After Sumter*, ed. N. H. Cogan (Akron, OH: University of Akron
Press, 2014), 4.
92. Eric Walter, *The Fire-Eaters* (Baton Rouge: Louisiana State University
Press, 1992), 1.
93. Livingston, "The Secession Tradition in America," 10–11.
94. John Niven, *John C. Calhoun and the Price of Union* (Baton
Rouge: Louisiana State University Press, 1988), 188.
95. Allitt, *The Conservatives*, 33.
96. David Bernstein, "Some Dubious Claims in Nancy MacLean's
'Democracy in Chains,'" *Washington Post*, June 28, 2017, available
via https://www.washingtonpost.com/news/volokh-conspiracy/wp/
2017/06/28/some-dubious-claims-in-nancy-macleans-democracy-
in-chains/?utm_term=.1c1fea96c4b6. For a positive treatment of
Calhoun among libertarians, see Murray Rothbard, *For a New Liberty*
(New York: Macmillan, 1973), 51.

240 NOTES

97. Allitt, *The Conservatives*, 34. See also Thomas F. Schaller, "First to Secede, Last to Accede: South Carolina's Resistance to the Republic, 1780–Present," in *Nation Within a Nation: The American South and the Federal Government*, ed. G. Feldman (Gainesville: University of Florida Press, 2014), 20–63.

98. An accounting of Calhoun's conduct as a slaveowner is available via https://www.clemson.edu/about/history/bios/john-c-calhoun.html.

99. Fabio Andreotti, "Why Freedom Is Favored by Secession and Subsidiarity," Foundation for Economic Freedom, January 23, 2017, available via https://fee.org/articles/why-freedom-is-favored-by-secession-and-subsidiarity/.

100. Nock, *Our Enemy, the State*, 85.

101. See, for example, Randy E. Barnett, "Is the Constitution Libertarian?," Georgetown Public Law and Legal Theory Research Paper, 2009, available via https://scholarship.law.georgetown.edu/cgi/viewcontent.cgi?article=1839&context=facpub.

102. Nock, *Our Enemy, the State*, 159, 165–166.

103. Boaz, *The Libertarian Mind*, 153; Murray, *What It Means to Be a Libertarian*, xi.

104. Joseph Sobran, "The Right to Secede," The Imaginative Conservative, December 3, 2012, available via http://www.the-imaginativeconservative.org/2012/12/the-right-to-secede.html.

105. Addicott, "Waving the Secede Flag." See also Sobran, "The Right to Secede"; Walter E. Williams, "Parting Company Is an Option," Foundation for Economic Education, June 1, 2004, available via https://fee.org/articles/parting-company-is-an-option/; Brion McClanahan, "Is Secession Legal?," *The American Conservative*, December 7, 2012, available via http://www.theamericanconservative.com/articles/is-secession-legal/; McClanahan, "Conventions"; Kent Masterson Brown, "The Compact Theory of the Constitution," speech at the Abbeville Institute, December 15, 2016, available via https://www.abbevilleinstitute.org/lectures/the-compact-theory-of-the-constitution/; Brion McClanahan, *The Politically Incorrect Guide to the Founding Fathers* (Washington, DC: Regnery, 2009); Thomas E. Woods Jr., *The Politically Incorrect Guide to American History* (Washington, DC: Regnery, 2004); Charles Adams, *When in the Course of Human Events: Arguing the Case for Southern Secession* (Lanham, MD: Rowman & Littlefield, 2000).

106. Sobran, "The Right to Secede."

107. Boaz, *The Libertarian Mind*, 10.

108. Nock, *Our Enemy, the State*, 57.

NOTES 241

109. For a different view of Jefferson, see Garry Wills, *Inventing America: Jefferson's Declaration of Independence* (Garden City, NY: Doubleday, 1978), 292.

110. Donald W. Livingston, "Origins of the New England Secession Tradition," *The Vermont Independent*, May 25, 2007, available via http://www.vermontindependent.org/origins-of-the-new-england-secession-tradition/.

111. Brion McClanahan, "The Extreme Northern Position," *The Abbeville Blog*, November 16, 2017, available via https://www.abbevilleinstitute.org/blog/the-extreme-northern-position/.

112. Richard M. Ebeling, "They Said No to Big Government," Foundation for Economic Education, July 2, 2016, available https://fee.org/articles/they-said-no-to-big-government/.

113. Ebeling, "They Said No to Big Government."

114. Murray, *What It Means to Be a Libertarian*, 6.

115. Wills, *Inventing America*, 362.

116. Livingston, "What Is an American State?"

117. James Jasinski and Jennifer R. Mercieca, "Analyzing Constitutive Rhetorics: The Virginia and Kentucky Resolutions and the 'Principles of '98,'" in *The Handbook of Rhetoric and Public Address*, ed. S. Parry-Giles and J. M. Hogan (West Sussex, UK: Wiley-Blackwell, 2010), 313–341.

118. Boaz, *The Libertarian Mind*, 11.

119. Livingston, "What Is an American State?"

120. Thomas E. Woods Jr., "Nullification: The Jeffersonian Brake on Government," Foundation for Economic Education, March 1, 2002, available via https://fee.org/articles/nullification-the-jeffersonian-brake-on-government/. See also Brown, "The Compact Theory of the Constitution"; Thomas E. Woods, *Nullification: How to Resist Federal Tyranny in the 21st Century* (Washington, DC: Regnery, 2010).

121. Walter, *The Fire-Eaters*, 36.

122. Elizabeth R. Varon, *Disunion! The Coming of the American Civil War, 1789–1859* (Chapel Hill: University of North Carolina Press, 2008), 36.

123. Delbanco, *The War Before the War*, 46.

124. Conservatives even flirted briefly with an independent states' rights party in 1960. See Donald Critchlow, *The Conservative Ascendancy: How the GOP Right Made Political History* (Cambridge, MA: Harvard University Press, 2007), 47–48; See also William P. Hustwit, *James J. Kilpatrick: Salesman for Segregation* (Chapel Hill: University of North Carolina Press, 2013), 42–66.

242 NOTES

125. John Gross, "Should America Forgive Samuel Johnson?," *New York Times*, September 9, 1984, available via https://www.nytimes.com/1984/09/09/books/about-books-should-america-forgive-samuel-johnson.html.

126. James J. Kilpatrick, *The Sovereign States: Notes of a Citizen of Virginia* (Chicago: Henry Regnery, 1957), 174–221. See also Raoul Berger, *Government by Judiciary: The Transformation of the Fourteenth Amendment* (Cambridge, MA: Harvard University Press, 1977); Felix Morley, *The Power in the People* (Toronto: D. Van Nostrand, 1949).

127. Hustwit, *James J. Kilpatrick*, 51.

128. Hustwit, *James J. Kilpatrick*, 56, 58.

129. Hustwit, *James J. Kilpatrick*, 58.

130. Hustwit, *James J. Kilpatrick*, 55.

131. Hustwit, *James J. Kilpatrick*, 67–70.

132. Shearer Davis Bowman, *At the Precipice: Americans North and South During the Secession Crisis* (Chapel Hill: University of North Carolina Press, 2010), 28–29.

133. Nancy MacLean, *Democracy in Chains: The Deep History of the Radical Right's Stealth Plan for America* (New York: Viking, 2017).

134. Michael J. Lee, *Creating Conservatism: Postwar Words That Made an American Movement* (East Lansing: Michigan State University Press, 2014), 75–107.

135. Rockwell, "The Libertarian Principle of Secession," 4–5, 16–17. See also Rockwell, "Secession Is Libertarian."

136. McClanahan, "Is Secession Legal?"

137. Tom Mullen, "Both Lincoln and the Confederacy Were Awful," Foundation for Economic Education, August 29, 2017, available via https://fee.org/articles/both-lincoln-and-the-confederacy-were-awful/.

138. James J. Martin, *Men Against the State: The Expositors of Individualist Anarchism in America, 1827–1908* (DeKalb, IL: Adrian Allen Associates), 7; Frank H. Brooks, "Introduction," in *The Individualist Anarchists: An Anthology of Liberty (1881–1908)*, ed. F. H. Brooks (New Brunswick, NJ: Transaction, 1996), 4.

139. Doherty, *Radicals for Capitalism*, 13, 38, 51, 251–253, 359.

140. Rothbard, *For a New Liberty*, 316.

141. Jeff Riggenbach, "Henry David Thoreau: Founding Father of American Libertarian Thought," Mises Daily Articles, July 15, 2010, available via https://mises.org/library/henry-david-thoreau-founding-father-american-libertarian-thought. See also Wendy McElroy, "Henry David Thoreau's *Civil Disobedience*," n.d., available via https://www.libertarianism.org/guides/lectures/henry-david-thoreaus-civil-disobedience.

NOTES 243

142. Henry David Thoreau, "Civil Disobedience," 1849, available via http://xroads.virginia.edu/~hyper2/thoreau/civil.html.

143. Thoreau, "Civil Disobedience."

144. Reichert, *Partisans of Freedom*, 65.

145. Doherty, *Radicals for Capitalism*, 39.

146. Eunice Minette Schuster, *Native American Anarchism: A Study of Left-Wing American Individualism* (Northampton, MA: AMS Press, 1970), 96.

147. Reichert, *Partisans of Freedom*, 66–69, 74–75. See also Schuster, *Native American Anarchism*, 97–98.

148. Doherty, *Radicals for Capitalism*, 40–42.

149. Josiah Warren, "True Civilization," in *The Practical Anarchist: The Writings of Josiah Warren*, ed. C. Sartwell (New York: Fordham University Press, 2011), 177.

150. Warren, "True Civilization," 139.

151. Crispin Sartwell, "Introduction," in *The Practical Anarchist: The Writings of Josiah Warren*, ed. C. Sartwell (New York: Fordham University Press, 2011), 12, 14. Sartwell writes, "Eventually, the idea of self-sovereignty became something of a euphemism for license, and the residents of Modern Times in the 1850s were referred to with a bit of derision as 'sovereigns.'"

152. Reichert, *Partisans of Freedom*, 75.

153. Josiah Warren, "Of Our State Difficulties," in *The Practical Anarchist: The Writings of Josiah Warren*, ed. C. Sartwell (New York: Fordham University Press, 2011), 103.

154. Warren, "Of Our State Difficulties," 104.

155. Reichert, *Partisans of Freedom*, 117.

156. Reichert, *Partisans of Freedom*, 131.

157. Lysander Spooner, *An Essay on the Trial by Jury* (Boston: John Jewett, 1852), 19.

158. Reichert, *Partisans of Freedom*, 122.

159. Lysander Spooner, *No Treason: The Constitution of No Authority*, No. VI (Boston: Lysander Spooner, 1867), available via https://en.wikisource.org/wiki/No_Treason/6.

160. Lysander Spooner, *No Treason: The Constitution of No Authority*, No. I (Boston: Lysander Spooner, 1867), available via https://en.wikisource.org/wiki/No_Treason/1.

161. Spooner, *No Treason: The Constitution of No Authority*, No. I.

162. Lysander Spooner, *No Treason: The Constitution of No Authority*, No. II (Boston: Lysander Spooner, 1867), available via https://en.wikisource.org/wiki/No_Treason/2.

163. Newman, *Liberalism at Wit's End*, 24; Doherty, *Radicals for Capitalism*, 48, 631.

244 NOTES

164. Rockwell, "The Libertarian Principle of Secession," 4–5, 16–17. See also Rockwell, "Secession Is Libertarian"; Devanny, "Zombies No More"; Robert Higgs, "Do We Really Consent to Be Governed?," Foundation for Economic Education, November 30, 2017, available via https://fee.org/articles/do-we-really-consent-to-be-governed/.

165. Frank H. Brooks, "Introduction," in *The Individualist Anarchists: An Anthology of* Liberty *(1881–1908)*, ed. F. H. Brooks (New Brunswick, NJ: Transaction, 1996), 1.

166. Doherty, *Radicals for Capitalism*, 42; Reichert, *Partisans of Freedom*, 144.

167. Doherty, *Radicals for Capitalism*, 43–44.

168. Lee, *Creating Conservatism*.

169. Reichert, *Partisans of Freedom*, 155.

170. Benjamin Tucker, "Anarchism and Consent," in *The Individualist Anarchists: An Anthology of* Liberty *(1881–1908)*, ed. F. H. Brooks (New Brunswick, NJ: Transaction, 1996), 17.

171. Benjamin Tucker, "State Socialism and Anarchism: How Far They Agree, And Wherein They Differ," in *The Individualist Anarchists: An Anthology of* Liberty *(1881–1908)*, ed. F. H. Brooks (New Brunswick, NJ: Transaction, 1996), 86–87.

172. Benjamin Tucker, "On Picket Duty," in *The Individualist Anarchists: An Anthology of* Liberty *(1881–1908)*, ed. F. H. Brooks (New Brunswick, NJ: Transaction, 1996), 258–259.

173. Benjamin Tucker, "The Power of Passive Resistance," in *The Individualist Anarchists: An Anthology of* Liberty *(1881–1908)*, ed. F. H. Brooks (New Brunswick, NJ: Transaction, 1996), 266. See also Tucker, "On Picket Duty"; Victor Yarros, "Anarchy or Government," in *The Individualist Anarchists: An Anthology of* Liberty *(1881–1908)*, ed. F. H. Brooks (New Brunswick, NJ: Transaction, 1996), 30–32; J. William Lloyd, "A Poet of Nature," in *The Individualist Anarchists: An Anthology of* Liberty *(1881–1908)*, ed. F. H. Brooks (New Brunswick, NJ: Transaction, 1996), 232.

174. Livingston, "What Is an American State?"

175. David A. Fahrenthold, "Daddy Issues: Are Ron Paul's Hard-Core Stands a Problem for Son's Presidential Bid," *Washington Post*, January 25, 2015, available via https://www.washingtonpost.com/politics/daddy-issues-are-ron-pauls-hard-core-stands-a-problem-for-sons-presidential-bid/2015/01/25/e23b1cdc-a4a9-11e4-a7c2-03d37af98440_story.html?utm_term=.8a79cc379c1c.

176. Deist, "Secession Begins at Home."

177. Mike Maharrey, "Putting Nullification into Practice: Current Efforts in the States," speech at the 2016 Abbeville Scholars Conference, 2016, December

NOTES 245

15, 2016, available via https://www.abbevilleinstitute.org/lectures/putting-nullification-into-practice-current-efforts-in-the-states/. See also Cogan, "Introduction," 5. See also Bruce L. Benson, "How to Secede in Business Without Really Leaving: Evidence of the Substitution of Arbitration for Litigation," in *Secession, State, and Liberty*, ed. D. Gordon (New Brunswick, NJ: Transaction, 1998), 243.

178. Douglas Rushkoff, "Survival of the Richest: The Wealthy Are Plotting to Leave Us Behind," *One Zero*, July 5, 2018, available via https://onezero.medium.com/survival-of-the-richest-9ef6cddd0cc1. See also Mark O'Connell, "Why Silicon Valley Billionaires Are Prepping for the Apocalypse in New Zealand," *The Guardian*, February 15, 2018, available via https://www.theguardian.com/news/2018/feb/15/why-silicon-valley-billionaires-are-prepping-for-the-apocalypse-in-new-zealand.

179. Soleil Ho, "Kohanaiki: Where the Mega-Rich Hide Away on Hawai'i," *GQ*, April 20, 2018, available via https://www.gq.com/story/kohanaiki-where-the-mega-rich-hide-away-in-hawaii?mbid=synd_digghttps://www.gq.com/story/kohanaiki-where-the-mega-rich-hide-away-in-hawaii?mbid=synd_digg; Justin Farell, "Where the Very Rich Fly to Hide," *New York Times*, April 15, 2020, available via https://www.nytimes.com/2020/04/15/opinion/jackson-hole-coronavirus.html.

180. Kenneth Rapoza, "Tax Haven Cash Rising, Now Equal to at Least 10% of World GDP," *Forbes*, September 15, 2017, available via https://www.forbes.com/sites/kenrapoza/2017/09/15/tax-haven-cash-rising-now-equal-to-at-least-10-of-world-gdp/#424c82f70d6a.

181. Robert Reich, "The Secession of the Successful," *New York Times Magazine*, January 20, 1991, available via https://www.nytimes.com/1991/01/20/magazine/secession-of-the-successful.html.

182. Albert O. Hirschman, *Exit, Voice, and Loyalty: Responses to Decline in Firms, Organizations, and States* (Cambridge, MA: Harvard University Press, 1970), 108–109.

Chapter 3

1. Eric H. Walther, "The Fire-Eaters and Lincoln," *Journal of the Abraham Lincoln Association* 32 (2011): 32.

2. William Kauffman Scarborough, ed., *The Diary of Edmund Ruffin*, vol. 3, *A Dream Shattered* (Baton Rouge: Louisiana State University Press, 1989), 126–127; William K. Scarborough, "Propagandists for Secession: Edmund

246 NOTES

Ruffin of Virginia and Robert Barnwell Rhett of South Carolina," *The South Carolina Historical Magazine* 112 (2011): 129.

3. William Kauffman Scarborough, ed., *The Diary of Edmund Ruffin*, vol. 1, *Toward Independence* (Baton Rouge: Louisiana State University Press, 1972), 550.

4. Elizabeth R. Varon, *Disunion! The Coming of the American Civil War, 1789–1859* (Chapel Hill: University of North Carolina Press, 2008), 223; William C. Davis, *A Fire-Eater Remembers: The Confederate Memoir of Robert Barnwell Rhett* (Columbia: University of South Carolina Press, 2000), ix.

5. Eric H. Walther, *The Fire-Eaters* (Baton Rouge: Louisiana State University Press, 1992), 3, 231. See also Edward S. Cooper, *Louis Trezevant Wigfall: The Disintegration of the Union and Collapse of the Confederacy* (Madison, NJ: Fairleigh Dickinson University Press, 2012); Eric H. Walther, *William Lowndes Yancey and the Coming of the Civil War* (Chapel Hill: University of North Carolina Press, 2006); William C. Davis, *Rhett: The Turbulent Life and Times of a Fire-Eater* (Columbia: University of South Carolina Press, 2001).

6. Scarborough, ed., *The Diary of Edmund Ruffin*, 3:179.

7. Scarborough, ed., *The Diary of Edmund Ruffin*, 1:512.

8. Scarborough, ed., *The Diary of Edmund Ruffin*, 1:557.

9. Scarborough, ed., *The Diary of Edmund Ruffin*, 1:560.

10. Sean Wilentz, *The Rise of American Democracy: Jefferson to Lincoln* (New York: W. W. Norton, 2005), 788.

11. Scarborough, ed., *The Diary of Edmund Ruffin*, 1:588.

12. Scarborough, ed., *The Diary of Edmund Ruffin*, 3:155.

13. Scarborough, ed., *The Diary of Edmund Ruffin*, 3:189. See also Drew Gilpin Faust, *This Republic of Suffering: Death and the American Civil War* (New York: Vintage, 2009).

14. Scarborough, ed., *The Diary of Edmund Ruffin*, 3:563–564.

15. David F. Allmendinger Jr., *Ruffin: Family and Reform in the Old South* (New York: Oxford University Press, 1990), 168–169.

16. Allmendinger, *Ruffin*, 170.

17. Scarborough, ed., *The Diary of Edmund Ruffin*, 3:435.

18. Scarborough, ed., *The Diary of Edmund Ruffin*, 3:843.

19. Mitchell, *Edmund Ruffin*, 252.

20. Allmendinger, *Ruffin*, 163.

21. Scarborough, ed., *The Diary of Edmund Ruffin*, 1:179.

22. Scarborough, ed., *The Diary of Edmund Ruffin*, 3:937.

NOTES   247

23. Scarborough, ed., *The Diary of Edmund Ruffin*, 3:938.
24. Allmendinger, *Ruffin*, 152.
25. Walther, *The Fire-Eaters*, 228–231. See also Wilentz, *The Rise of American Democracy*, 790.
26. Betty L. Mitchell, *Edmund Ruffin: A Biography* (Bloomington: Indiana University Press, 1981), 254–255. See also Scarborough, ed., *The Diary of Edmund Ruffin*, 3:*xxx*.
27. Mitchell, *Edmund Ruffin*, 156.
28. The Confederate flag claim has been made since at least 1910 and perhaps earlier. See Henry G. Ellis, "Edmund Ruffin: His Life and Times," *John P. Branch Historical Papers of Randolph-Macon College* III (June 1910): 101. See also Mitchell, *Edmund Ruffin*, 287; Walther, *The Fire-Eaters*, 231.
29. William W. Freehling, *The Road to Disunion*, vol. II, *Secessionists Triumphant, 1854–1861* (New York: Oxford University Press, 2007), 292–308.
30. Varon, *Disunion!*, 3–4.
31. John C. Calhoun, "Speech on the Admission of California—and the General State of the Union," March 4, 1850, in *Union and Liberty: The Political Philosophy of John C. Calhoun*, ed. R. M. Lence (Indianapolis, IN: Liberty Fund, 1992), 575.
32. William W. Freehling, "Reviving States' Rights," in *A Political Nation: New Directions in American Political History*, ed. G. W. Gallagher and R. A. Shelden (Charlottesville: University Press of Virginia, 2012), 112–125.
33. R. Jarrod Atchison, *War of Words: The Rhetorical Leadership of Jefferson Davis* (Tuscaloosa: University of Alabama Press, 2017), 24–43.
34. William L. Harris, speech to the Georgia Secession Convention, 1861, available via http://www.civilwarcauses.org/wharris.htm.
35. Isham Garrott and Robert H. Smith, letter to North Carolina, 1861, available via http://www.civilwarcauses.org/al-nc.htm.
36. Robert Toombs, speech to the Georgia Secession Convention, November 13, 1860, in *Secession Debated: Georgia's Showdown in 1860*, ed. C. M. Simpson and W. W. Freehling (New York: Oxford University Press, 1992), 49.
37. Shearer Davis Bowman, *At the Precipice: Americans North and South During the Secession Crisis* (Chapel Hill: University of North Carolina Press, 2010), 51. See also Varon, *Disunion!*, 13.
38. Dwight. T. Pitcaithley, "Introduction," in *The U.S. Constitution and Secession: A Documentary Anthology of Slavery and White Supremacy*, ed. D. T. Pitcaithley (Lawrence: University Press of Kansas, 2018), 12.

248 NOTES

39. Arthur Bestor, "State Sovereignty and Slavery: A Reinterpretation of Proslavery Constitutional Doctrine, 1846–1860," *Journal of the Illinois State Historical Society* 54 (1961): 178.

40. Charles B. Dew, *Apostles of Disunion: Southern Secession Commissioners and the Causes of the Civil War* (Charlottesville: University of Virginia Press, 2001), 10–11.

41. Frank Towers, "The Origins of the Antimodern South: Romantic Nationalism and the Secession Movement in the American South," in *Secession as an International Phenomenon: From America's Civil War to Contemporary Separatist Movements*, ed. D. H. Doyle (Athens: University of Georgia Press, 2010), 179.

42. Walther, *The Fire-Eaters*, 300.

43. Mark Graber, *Dred Scott and the Problem of Constitutional Evil* (Cambridge: Cambridge University Press, 2006), 125.

44. Walter, *The Fire-Eaters*, 7, 300.

45. Stephen Berry, "The Future of Secession Studies: An Introduction," *Tennessee Historical Quarterly* 70 (2011): 86.

46. Thelma Jennings, *The Nashville Convention: Southern Movement for Unity, 1848–1851* (Memphis, TN: Memphis State University Press, 1980), 201–202.

47. Varon, *Disunion!*, 225.

48. Robert J. Cook, "The Shadow of the Past: Collective Memory and the Coming of the American Civil War," in *Winter: When the Union Fell Apart*, ed. R. J. Cook, W. L. Barney, and E. R. Varon (Baltimore: Johns Hopkins University Press, 2013), 64.

49. Edward E. Baptist, *This Half Has Never Been Told: Slavery and the Making of American Capitalism* (Philadelphia: Basic Books, 2014), 392. See also Robert J. Cook, William L. Barney, and Elizabeth R. Varon, "Introduction: The Secession Crisis as a Study in Conflict Resolution," in *Secession Winter: When the Union Fell Apart*, ed. R. J. Cook, W. L. Barney, and E. R. Varon (Baltimore: Johns Hopkins University Press, 2013), 5; Bowman, *At the Precipice*, 39.

50. Dew, *Apostles of Disunion*, 80.

51. Eli Saslow, *Rising Out of Hatred: The Awakening of a Former White Nationalist* (New York: Doubleday, 2018), 177.

52. William L. Barney, "Rush to Disaster: Secession and the Slaves' Revenge," in *Winter: When the Union Fell Apart*, ed. R. J. Cook, W. L. Barney, and E. R. Varon (Baltimore: Johns Hopkins University Press, 2013), 23.

53. Pitcaithley, "Introduction," 22; Eric Foner, *Politics and Ideology in the Age of the Civil War* (New York: Oxford University Press, 1980), 40–41.

NOTES   249

54. John C. Calhoun, "Slavery a Positive Good," February 6, 1837, available via https://teachingamericanhistory.org/library/document/slavery-a-positive-good/.

55. Walther, *The Fire-Eaters*, 297.

56. Richard Barry, *Mr. Rutledge of South Carolina* (Salem, NH: Ayer Company, 1971), 328.

57. David O. Stewart, *The Summer of 1787: The Men Who Invented the Constitution* (New York: Simon & Schuster, 2007), 197. See also Michael J. Klarman, *The Framers' Coup: The Making of the United States Constitution* (New York: Oxford University Press, 2016), 286; Paul Finkelman, "Making a Covenant with Death: Slavery and the Constitutional Convention," Cleveland Civil War Roundtable, 2008, available via http://clevelandcivilwarroundtable.com/articles/society/slavery_founders.htm.

58. Jack Rakove, *Original Meanings: Politics and Ideas in the Making of the Constitution* (New York: Vintage, 1997), 85, 88, 91.

59. Paul Finkelman, "States' Rights, Southern Hypocrisy, and the Crisis of the Union," in *Union and States' Rights: A History and Interpretation of Interposition, Nullification, and Secession 150 Years After Sumter*, ed. N. H. Cogan (Akron, OH: University of Akron Press, 2014), 60.

60. Rakove, *Original Meanings*, 73.

61. Klarman, *The Framers' Coup*, 274.

62. Klarman, *The Framers' Coup*, 286.

63. Klarman, *The Framers' Coup*, 287.

64. James Madison, Madison Debates, June 30, 1787, available via http://avalon.law.yale.edu/18th_century/debates_630.asp.

65. Klarman, *The Framers' Coup*, 286.

66. Klarman, *The Framers' Coup*, 303.

67. Richard Beeman, *Plain, Honest Men: The Making of the American Constitution* (New York: Random House, 2009), 332. See also Varon, *Disunion!*, 23–24.

68. Rakove, *Original Meanings*, 93.

69. Klarman, *The Framers' Coup*, 303.

70. Delbanco, *The War Before the War*, 26.

71. Klarman, *The Framers' Coup*, 303.

72. Graber, *Dred Scott*, 122.

73. James C. Cobb, *Away Down South: A History of Southern Identity* (New York: Oxford University Press, 2005), 21.

74. Baptist, *This Half Has Never Been Told*, 156.

250 NOTES

75. William C. Davis, *A Fire-Eater Remembers: The Confederate Memoir of Robert Barnwell Rhett* (Columbia: University of South Carolina Press, 2000), xii.

76. Davis, *Rhett*, 198–202. See also Mark Wahlgren Summers, *A Dangerous Stir: Fear, Paranoia, and the Making of Reconstruction* (Chapel Hill: University of North Carolina Press, 2009), 16.

77. Irving H. Bartlett, *John C. Calhoun: A Biography* (New York: W. W. Norton, 1993), 180–181.

78. Bartlett, *John C. Calhoun*, 181.

79. Wilentz, *The Rise of American Democracy*, 376–377.

80. John C. Calhoun, "The Fort Hill Address: On the Relations of the States and Federal Government," in *Union and Liberty: The Political Philosophy of John C. Calhoun*, ed. R. M. Lence (Indianapolis, IN: Liberty Fund, 1992), 371.

81. Manisha Sinha, *The Counter-Revolution of Slavery: Politics and Ideology in Antebellum South Carolina* (Chapel Hill: University of North Carolina Press, 2000), 23–24.

82. Varon, *Disunion!*, 11.

83. Bartlett, *John C. Calhoun*, 358–372.

84. John C. Calhoun, "Speech on the Resolutions on the Slave Question," in *Union and Liberty: The Political Philosophy of John C. Calhoun*, ed. R. M. Lence (Indianapolis, IN: Liberty Fund, 1992), 519, 520.

85. John C. Calhoun, "Speech at the Meeting of the Citizens of Charleston," in *Union and Liberty: The Political Philosophy of John C. Calhoun*, ed. R. M. Lence (Indianapolis, IN: Liberty Fund, 1992),

86. Bartlett, *John C. Calhoun*, 371.

87. Baptist, *This Half Has Never Been Told*, 339.

88. John C. Calhoun, "Speech on the General State of the Union," in *Union and Liberty: The Political Philosophy of John C. Calhoun*, ed. R. M. Lence (Indianapolis, IN: Liberty Fund, 1992), 599, 600, 601.

89. Paul Starobin, *Madness Rules the Hour: Charleston, 1860 and the Mania for War* (New York: Public Affairs, 2017), 36.

90. Bowman, *At the Precipice*, 7. See also Summers, *A Dangerous Stir*, 17.

91. See, for example, Bowman, *At the Precipice*, 1–2; William E. Gienapp, "The Republican Party and the Slave Power," in *A Political Nation: New Directions in American Political History*, ed. G. W. Gallagher and R. A. Shelden (Charlottesville: University Press of Virginia, 2012), 51–78.

92. Gienapp, "The Republican Party and the Slave Power," 73. See also Don H. Doyle, "An Attempt at Secession from an Early Nation-State: The Confederate States of America," in *The Ashgate Research Companion*

NOTES 251

to Secession, ed. A. Pavkovic and P. Radan (Burlington, VT: Ashgate, 2011), 107.

93. Gienapp, "The Republican Party and the Slave Power," 74.

94. Barney, "Rush to Disaster," 30.

95. Walther, *The Fire-Eaters*, 2.

96. Pitcaithley, "Introduction," 3–4; Starobin, *Madness Rules the Hour*, 131; Bowman, *At the Precipice*, 70.

97. Varon, *Disunion!*, 228.

98. "A Declaration of the Immediate Causes Which Induce and Justify Secession of the State of Mississippi from the Federal Union," 1860, available via http://avalon.law.yale.edu/19th_century/csa_missec.asp.

99. Confederate States of America—Georgia Secession, January 29, 1861, available via http://avalon.law.yale.edu/19th_century/csa_geosec.asp.

100. "A Declaration of the Causes Which Impel the State of Texas to Secede from the Federal Union," February 2, 1861, available via http://avalon.law.yale.edu/19th_century/csa_texsec.asp.

101. Virginia Secession Convention, "Resolutions," April 5, 1861, in *The Confederate and Neo-Confederate Reader: The "Great Truth" About the "Lost Cause,"* ed. J. W. Loewen and E. H. Sebesta (Jackson: University Press of Mississippi, 2010), 153.

102. Harris, speech to the Georgia Secession Convention. See also Dew, *Apostles of Disunion*, 28.

103. Thomas R. R. Cobb, speech to Georgia Secession Convention, November 12, 1860, in *Secession Debated: Georgia's Showdown in 1860*, ed. W. W. Freehling and C. M. Simpson (New York: Oxford University Press, 1992), 8, 9.

104. Henry L. Benning, "Address Delivered Before the Virginia State Convention," February 18, 1861, in *The Confederate and Neo-Confederate Reader: The "Great Truth" About the "Lost Cause,"* ed. J. W. Loewen and E. H. Sebesta (Jackson: University Press of Mississippi, 2010), 150.

105. Alexander H. Stephens, Corner Stone Speech, March 21, 1861, available via http://teachingamericanhistory.org/library/document/cornerstone-speech/.

106. Walter, *The Fire-Eaters*, 300.

107. Thomas F. Schaller, "First to Secede, Last to Accede: South Carolina's Resistance to the Republic, 1780–Present," in *Nation Within a Nation: The American South and the Federal Government*, ed. G. Feldman (Gainesville: University of Florida Press, 2014), 31.

108. Sinha, *The Counter-Revolution of Slavery*, 2–3, 7.

109. Bowman, *At the Precipice*, 29.

252 NOTES

110. Schaller, "First to Secede," 31.

111. Robin L. Einhorn, "Patrick Henry's Case Against the Constitution: The Structural Problem with Slavery," *Journal of the Early Republic* 22 (2002): 549–573.

112. Harris, speech to the Georgia Secession Convention.

113. Joseph Jones, address before the Cotton Planters Convention of Georgia, Macon, December 13, 1860, available via http://docsouth.unc.edu/imls/agriculture/agriculture.html.

114. Adam Goodheart, *1861: The Civil War Awakening* (New York: Alfred A. Knopf, 2011), 351. See also Bowman, *At the Precipice*, 13–14; Davis, *Rhett*, 200.

115. Delbanco, *The War Before the War*, 48; Schaller, "First to Secede," 20.

116. William W. Freehling, *The Road to Disunion*, vol. I, *Secessionists at Bay, 1776–1854* (New York: Oxford University Press, 1990), 3. See also Manisha Sinha, "Revolution or Counterrevolution? The Political Ideology of Secession in Antebellum South Carolina," *Civil War History* 46 (2000): 208.

117. Wilentz, *The Rise of American Democracy*, 773.

118. Samuel A. Cartwright, "Diseases and Peculiarities of the Negro Race," in *The Confederate and Neo-Confederate Reader: The "Great Truth" About the "Lost Cause,"* ed. J. W. Loewen and E. H. Sebesta (Jackson: University Press of Mississippi, 2010), 70.

119. Alexander H. Stephens, Corner Stone Speech, March 21, 1861, available via http://teachingamericanhistory.org/library/document/cornerstone-speech/.

120. John C. Calhoun, "Speech on the Oregon Bill," in *Union and Liberty: The Political Philosophy of John C. Calhoun*, ed. R. M. Lence (Indianapolis, IN: Liberty Fund, 1992), 565.

121. Calhoun, "Speech on the Oregon Bill," 566.

122. Calhoun, "Speech on the Oregon Bill," 569.

123. Calhoun, "Speech on the Oregon Bill," 570.

124. Delbanco, *The War Before the War*, 89.

125. Jacob Thompson, "Letter from Mississippi's Commissioner to North Carolina," December 22, 1860, available via http://www.civil-warcauses.org/thompson.htm.

126. Dew, *Apostles of Disunion*, 92–93.

127. Barney, "Rush to Disaster," 31.

128. Benjamin Palmer, "Thanksgiving Sermon," December 29, 1860, available via https://archive.org/stream/thanksgivingserm00lcpalm/thanks-givingserm00lcpalm_djvu.txt.

NOTES 253

129. James D. B. De Bow, "The Interest of Slavery for the Non Slaveholder," December 5, 1860, available via https://archive.org/stream/interestinslaver00indebo/interestinslaver00indebo_djvu.txt.

130. De Bow, "The Interest of Slavery for the Non Slaveholder."

131. Joseph E. Brown, public letter, December 7, 1860, in *Secession Debated: Georgia's Showdown in 1860*, ed. W. W. Freehling and C. M. Simpson (New York: Oxford University Press, 1992), 155, 156.

132. Dew, *Apostles of Disunion*, 92–93.

133. Garrott and Smith, letter to North Carolina.

134. John Townsend, "The Doom of Slavery in the Union: Its Safety Out of It," 1860, available via https://archive.org/stream/doomofslaveryinu02town/doomofslaveryinu02town_djvu.txt.

135. Townsend, "The Doom of Slavery in the Union: Its Safety Out of It." See also Barney, "Rush to Disaster," 29.

136. James Hammond, "Cotton Is King," March 4, 1858, available via https://teachingamericanhistory.org/library/document/cotton-is-king/.

137. Hammond, "Cotton Is King."

138. Baptist, *This Half Has Never Been Told*, 339.

139. Stephen Berry, "The Future of Secession Studies: An Introduction," *Tennessee Historical Quarterly* 70 (2011): 84.

140. Baptist, *This Half Has Never Been Told*, 352; Delbanco, *The War Before the War*, 26–27.

141. Hammond, "Cotton Is King."

142. Starobin, *Madness Rules the Hour*, 192.

143. Varon, *Disunion!*, 294, 324.

144. Leonidas W. Spratt, "The Philosophy of Secession: A Southern View," February 13, 1861, available via http://docsouth.unc.edu/imls/secession/secession.html.

145. Jones, address before the Cotton Planters Convention of Georgia.

146. Baptist, *This Half Has Never Been Told*, 336, 367.

147. Spratt, "The Philosophy of Secession."

148. Dew, *Apostles of Disunion*, 32.

149. Brown, public letter.

150. Toombs, speech to the Georgia Secession Convention, 49.

151. Garrott and Smith, letter to North Carolina.

152. Jones, address before the Cotton Planters Convention of Georgia. See also Bernard E. Powers Jr., "'The Worst of All Barbarism': Racial Anxiety and the Approach of Secession in the Palmetto State," *The South Carolina Historical Magazine* 112 (2011): 143.

254 NOTES

153. Benning, "Address Delivered Before the Virginia State Convention," 152. See also Baptist, *This Half Has Never Been Told*, 390–391.

154. Charles B. Dew, "Lincoln, the Collapse of Deep South Moderation, and the Triumph of Secession: A South Carolina Congressman's Moment of Truth," in *Secession as an International Phenomenon: From America's Civil War to Contemporary Separatist Movements*, ed. D. H. Doyle (Athens: University of Georgia Press, 2010), 108.

155. Stephen F. Hale, "Letter to Beriah Magoffin," December 27, 1860, available via https://teachingamericanhistory.org/library/document/stephen-f-hale-to-governor-beriah-magoffin/.

156. Harris, speech to the Georgia Secession Convention.

157. Pitcaithley, "Introduction," 51–52. See also Varon, *Disunion!*, 338.

158. Starobin, *Madness Rules the Hour*, 7. See also Cook, Barney, and Varon, *Secession Winter*, 86–87.

159. Barney, "Rush to Disaster: Secession and the Slaves' Revenge," 31.

160. See also James A. Rawley, "Review of *The Political Crisis of the 1850s*, and: *Division and Reunion: America, 1848–1877*," *Civil War History* 24 (1978): 268–270.

161. Sinha, *The Counter-Revolution of Slavery*, 254.

162. South Carolina's passage of the "Negro-Seaman's Act" in 1822 is another example of early nullification. See Walter C. Rucker, *The River Flows On: Black Resistance, Culture, and Identity Formation in Early America* (Baton Rouge: Louisiana State University Press, 2006), 178; Michael Schoeppner, "Peculiar Quarantines: The Seamen Acts and Regulatory Authority in the Antebellum South," *Law and History Review* 31 (2013): 559–586.

163. Wilentz, *The Rise of American Democracy*, 387.

164. Wilentz, *The Rise of American Democracy*, 411. See also Jennifer Mercieca, "The Culture of Honor: How Slaveholders Responded to the Abolitionist Mail Crisis of 1835," *Rhetoric and Public Affairs* 10 (2007): 51–76.

165. Kenneth M. Stampp, *The Era of Reconstruction: 1865–1877* (New York: Vintage Books, 1965), 199.

166. Andrew F. Lang, *In the Wake of the War: Military Occupation, Emancipation, and Civil War America* (Baton Rouge: Louisiana University Press, 2017), 217.

167. Eric Foner, *Reconstruction: America's Unfinished Revolution, 1863–1877* (New York: Perennial, 2014), 457–458.

168. Foner, *Reconstruction*, 459.

169. Philip Dray, *Capitol Men: The Epic Story of Reconstruction Through the Lives of the First Black Congressmen* (Boston: Houghton Mifflin, 2008), 101.

NOTES 255

170. Scott J. Varda, "Drew Ali and the Moorish Science Temple of America: A Minor Rhetoric of Black Nationalism," *Rhetoric and Public Affairs* 16 (2013): 690–691.

171. Summers, *The Ordeal of the Reunion*, 395.

172. Sarah Carr, "In Southern Towns, 'Segregation Academies' Are Still Going Strong," *The Atlantic*, December 13, 2012, available via https://www.theatlantic.com/national/archive/2012/12/in-southern-towns-segregation-academies-are-still-going-strong/266207/.

173. Valerie Strauss, "Back to the Future: A New School District Secession Movement Is Gaining Steam," *Washington Post*, May 2, 2018, available via https://www.washingtonpost.com/news/answer-sheet/wp/2018/05/02/back-to-the-future-a-new-school-district-secession-movement-is-gaining-steam/?noredirect=on&utm_term=.1a8d73734272.

174. Alvin Chang, "More Affluent Neighborhoods Are Creating Their Own School Districts," Vox, April 17, 2019, available via https://www.vox.com/2019/4/17/18307958/school-district-secession-worsening-data.

175. Adam Liptak, "Supreme Court Invalidates Key Part of Voting Rights Act," *New York Times*, June 25, 2013, available via https://www.nytimes.com/2013/06/26/us/supreme-court-ruling.html.

176. Maggie Astor, "Seven Ways Alabama Has Made It Harder to Vote," *New York Times*, June 23, 2018, available via https://www.nytimes.com/2018/06/23/us/politics/voting-rights-alabama.html.

177. Wilentz, *The Rise of American Democracy*, 774.

178. Schaller, "First to Secede," 57. See also Ben Terris, "Scholars Nostalgic for the Old South Study the Virtues of Secession, Quietly," *The Chronicle of Higher Education*, December 6, 2009, available via https://www.chronicle.com/article/Secretive-Scholars-of-the-Old/49337/.

179. See Richard Weaver, *Visions of Order: The Cultural Crisis of Our Time* (Wilmington, DE: ISI Books, 1995). See also Russell Kirk, *John Randolph of Roanoke: A Study in American Politics* (Indianapolis, IN: Liberty Fund, 1997); Jeffrey Hart, *The Making of the American Conservative Mind: National Review and Its Times* (Wilmington, DE: ISI Books, 2007), 53.

180. Fred Arthur Bailey, "Texas Philosophy, Nashville Agrarianism, Reagan Republicanism, and the Neo-Confederacy: The Influence of M. E. Bradford," in *Nation Within a Nation: The American South and the Federal Government*, ed. G. Feldman (Gainesville: University of Florida Press, 2014), 190.

181. Bailey, "Texas Philosophy," 197.

182. Daniel W. Hamilton, "Still Too Close to Call? Rethinking Stampp's 'The Concept of a Perpetual Union,'" in *Union and States' Rights: A History and Interpretation of Interposition, Nullification, and Secession 150 Years*

256 NOTES

After Sumter, ed. N. H. Cogan (Akron, OH: University of Akron Press, 2014), 86.

183. Schaller, "First to Secede," 19–20.

184. Anne J. Bailey, *War and Ruin: William T. Sherman and the Savannah Campaign* (Wilmington, DE: SR Books, 2003), 25.

185. David R. Jansson, "'The Evil Empire Within: Southern Nationalism and the Washington Problem," in *Nation Within a Nation: The American South and the Federal Government*, ed. G. Feldman (Gainesville: University of Florida Press, 2014), 223.

186. Joseph Crespino, *In Search of Another Country: Mississippi and the Conservative Counterrevolution* (Princeton, NJ: Princeton University Press, 2007). See also John Avlon, "Return of the Confederacy," *The Daily Beast*, July 14, 2017, available via https://www.thedailybeast.com/return-of-the-confederacy; Nancy MacLean, "Neo-Confederacy Versus the New Deal: The Regional Utopia of the Modern American Right," in *The Myth of Southern Exceptionalism*, ed. M. D. Lassiter and J. Crespino (New York: Oxford University Press, 2010), 309, 316.

Chapter 4

1. Waldo E. Martin Jr., *The Mind of Frederick Douglass* (Chapel Hill: University of North Carolina Press, 1984), 219.

2. Adam Goodheart, *1861: The Civil War Awakening* (New York: Alfred A. Knopf, 2011), 316–317.

3. Goodheart, *1861*, 316–317.

4. Frederick Douglass, "What to the Slave Is the Fourth of July?," in *Narrative of the Life of Frederick Douglass, an American Slave*, ed. Ira Dworkin (New York: Penguin, 2014), 144–145.

5. Frederick Douglass, "The President and His Speeches," *Douglass' Monthly*, September 1862, available via http://rbscp.lib.rochester.edu/4387.

6. Edward E. Baptist, *This Half Has Never Been Told: Slavery and the Making of American Capitalism* (Philadelphia: Basic Books, 2014), 417.

7. Black emigrationists included Prince Hall, Paul Cuffe, Edward Wilmot Blyden, Alexander Crummell, Mary Ann Shadd Cary, James T. Holly, Martin Delany, Henry Highland Garnet, and Henry McNeal Turner.

8. Robin D. G. Kelley, *Freedom Dreams: The Black Radical Imagination* (Boston: Beacon Press, 2002), 18.

NOTES 257

9. Thomas Jefferson, "Notes on the State of Virginia," in *Classical Black Nationalism*, ed. W. J. Moses (New York: New York University Press, 1996), 46.

10. Peter C. Myers, *Frederick Douglass: Race and the Rebirth of American Liberalism* (Lawrence: University Press of Kansas, 2008), 120–121. See also Garry Wills, *Inventing America: Jefferson's Declaration of Independence* (Garden City, NY: Doubleday, 1978), 306.

11. Sterling Stuckey, *Slave Culture: Nationalist Theory and the Foundations of Black America* (New York: Oxford University Press, 1987), 18–19.

12. Elizabeth R. Varon, *Disunion! The Coming of the American Civil War, 1789–1859* (Chapel Hill: University of North Carolina Press, 2008), 50. See also Monroe Fordham, "Nineteenth-Century Black Thought in the United States: Some Influences of the Santo Domingo Revolution," *Journal of Black Studies* 6 (1975): 120.

13. Paul Kendrick and Stephen Kendrick, *Douglass and Lincoln: How a Revolutionary Black Leader and a Reluctant Liberator Struggled to End Slavery and Save the Union* (New York: Walker, 2008), 79; Varon, *Disunion!*, 238.

14. Kendrick and Kendrick, *Douglass and Lincoln*, 77.

15. William S. McFeely, *Frederick Douglass* (New York: W. W. Norton, 1995), 208–211.

16. McFeely, *Frederick Douglass*, 211.

17. Robert S. Levine, *The Lives of Frederick Douglass* (Cambridge, MA: Harvard University Press, 2016), 197.

18. Kendrick and Kendrick, *Douglass and Lincoln*, 77.

19. Kendrick and Kendrick, *Douglass and Lincoln*, 75.

20. Frederick Douglass, "The Inaugural Address," *Douglass' Monthly*, April 1861.

21. Frederick Douglass, "A Trip to Hayti," *Douglass' Monthly*, May 1861, available via https://atlanticslaverydebate.stanford.edu/sites/default/.../TriptoHaytiDglss1861.doc.

22. Kendrick and Kendrick, *Douglass and Lincoln*, 78.

23. Douglass, "A Trip to Hayti."

24. Wilson Jeremiah Moses, *Afrotopia: The Roots of African American Popular History* (Cambridge: Cambridge University Press, 1998).

25. John T. McCartney, *Black Power Ideologies: An Essay in African-American Political Thought* (Philadelphia: Temple University Press, 1992).

26. William L. Van Deburg, "Introduction," in *Modern Black Nationalism: From Marcus Garvey to Louis Farrakhan*, ed. W. L. Van Deburg (New York: New York University Press, 1997), 1, 4. See also

258 NOTES

Algernon Austin, *Achieving Blackness: Race, Black Nationalism, and Afrocentrism in the Twentieth Century* (New York: New York University Press, 2008), 172; William L. Van Deburg, *New Day in Babylon: The Black Power Movement and American Culture, 1965–1975* (Chicago: University of Chicago Press, 1992), 129; Bracey, Meier, and Rudwick, "Introduction," xxvi–xxix.

27. Roy L. Brooks, *Racial Justice in the Age of Obama* (Princeton, NJ: Princeton University Press, 2009), 82.

28. William Jeremiah Moses, *Classical Black Nationalism: From the American Revolution to Marcus Garvey* (New York: New York University Press, 1996), 28–29. See also Tommie Shelby, "Two Conceptions of Black Nationalism: Martin Delany on the Meaning of Black Political Solidarity," *Political Theory* 31 (2003): 667; Roger W. Hite, "Voice of a Fugitive: Henry Bibb and Antebellum Black Separatism," *Journal of Black Studies* 4 (1974): 270.

29. Dean E. Robinson, *Black Nationalism in American Politics and Thought* (Cambridge: Cambridge University Press, 2001), 60; Bracey, Meier, and Rudwick, "Introduction," li.

30. Hugh Pearson, *The Shadow of the Panther: Huey Newton and the Rise of Black Power in America* (Cambridge, MA: Da Capo Press, 1995), 111–112.

31. Huey Newton, "To the Republic of New Africa," in *To Die for the People*, ed. T. Morrison (San Francisco: City Lights Books, 2009), 95, 96. See also Peniel E. Joseph, *Waiting 'Til the Midnight Hour: A Narrative History of Black Power in America* (New York: Henry Holt, 2006), 219–220.

32. Robert S. Browne, "Separation," *Ebony*, August 1970, 47.

33. Joseph, *Waiting 'Til the Midnight Hour*, xiii.

34. Ousmane K. Power-Greene, "U.S. Slavery and the Black Radical Tradition: The 25th Anniversary Edition of Sterling Stuckey's *Slave Culture*," *Reviews in American History* 43 (2015): 733.

35. Robert F. Williams, *Negroes with Guns* (Detroit: Wayne State University Press, 1998), 81, 82.

36. S. Jay Walker, "Foreword II," in *Black Separatism and Social Reality: Rhetoric and Reason*, ed. R. L. Hall (Elmsford, NY: Pergamon Press, 1977), xiii.

37. Stuckey, *Slave Culture*, 48–49; Moses, *Classical Black Nationalism*, 6.

38. Moses, *Classical Black Nationalism*, 7.

39. Peniel E. Joseph, *Stokely: A Life* (New York: Basic Civitas, 2014), 195. See also Robert E. Terrill, "Protest, Prophecy, and Prudence in the Rhetoric of Malcolm X," *Rhetoric and Public Affairs* 4 (2001): 28; Robert E. Terrill, *Malcolm X: Inventing Radical Judgment* (East Lansing: Michigan State University Press, 2004), 130–131.

NOTES   259

40. Moses, "Introduction," 10.
41. Monroe Fordham, "Nineteenth-Century Black Thought in the United States: Some Influences of the Santo Domingo Revolution," *Journal of Black Studies* 6 (1975):
42. Raymond L. Hall, *Black Separatism and Social Reality: Rhetoric and Reason* (Elmsford, NY: Pergamon Press, 1977), 3. See also Moses, "Introduction," 8.
43. Moses, "Introduction," 7.
44. Bracey, Meier, and Rudwick, "Introduction," xxxi.
45. Bracey, Meier, and Rudwick, "Introduction," xxxi, xxxii.
46. Hall, *Black Separatism and Social Reality*, 1–2.
47. Russell Rickford, *We Are an African People: Independent Education, Black Power, and the Radical Imagination* (New York: Oxford University Press, 2016), 3.
48. Robert L. Tsai, *America's Forgotten Constitutions: Defiant Visions of Power and Community* (Cambridge, MA: Harvard University Press, 2014), 219; Brenda Gayle Plummer, *In Search of Power: African Americans in the Era of Decolonization, 1956–1974* (New York: Cambridge University Press, 2013), 17; Austin, *Achieving Blackness*, 179.
49. Kelley, *Freedom Dreams*, 16.
50. Imamu Ameer Baraka, "A Black Value System," in *Black Separatism and Social Reality: Rhetoric and Reason*, ed. R. L. Hall (New York: Pergamon Press, 1977), 32.
51. Yohuru Williams, "Nationalism," in *Keywords for African American Studies*, ed. E. R. Edwards, R. A. Ferguson, and J. O. G. Ogbar (New York: New York University Press, 2018), 121–122.
52. Julius Lester, "The Necessity for Separation," *Ebony*, August 1970, 169. See also Malanye T. Price, *Dreaming Blackness: Black Nationalism and African American Public Opinion* (New York: New York University Press, 2009), 161.
53. Marcus Garvey, "The Resurrection of the Negro," in *Selected Writings and Speeches of Marcus Garvey*, ed. B. Blaisdell (Mineola, NY: Dover Publications, 2004), 68.
54. Bracey, Meier, and Rudwick, "Introduction," xxxvii; Van Deburg, "Introduction," 139; Christopher Strain, "Soul City, North Carolina: Black Power, Utopia, and the African American Dream," *Journal of African American History* 79 (2004): 58.
55. Van Deburg, *New Day in Babylon*, 113.
56. Erich Fromm, *Escape from Freedom* (New York: Holt, 1994).
57. Kelley, *Freedom Dreams*, 125; Malanye T. Price, *Dreaming Blackness: Black Nationalism and African American Public Opinion* (New York: New York University Press, 2009), 161.

260 NOTES

58. Van Deburg, *New Day in Babylon*, 179–180; See also Alex Poinsett, "It's Nation Time!," *Ebony*, December 1970, 104.
59. Eddie S. Glaude Jr., "Introduction," in *Is It Nation Time? Contemporary Essays on Black Power and Black Nationalism*, ed. E. S. Glaude Jr. (Chicago: University of Chicago Press, 2002), 6–8.
60. Veronica Burchard, "From James Madison to Malcolm X: Black Power and the American Founding," *OAH Magazine of History*, July 2008, 42.
61. Kelley, *Freedom Dreams*, 17; Tsai, *America's Forgotten Constitutions*, 226.
62. Robert C. Dick, "Rhetoric of Antebellum Black Separatism," *Negro History Bulletin* 34 (1971): 134.
63. David Llorens, "Black Separatism in Perspective," *Ebony*, September 1968, 94.
64. Van Deburg, *New Day in Babylon*, 260.
65. Maegan Parker Brooks, "Oppositional Ethos: Fannie Lou Hamer and the Vernacular Persona," *Rhetoric and Public Affairs* 14 (2011): 534.
66. Brooks, "Oppositional Ethos," 534.
67. Lester, "The Necessity for Separation," 168. See also Ashely D. Farmer, *Remaking Black Power: How Black Women Transformed an Era* (Chapel Hill: University of North Carolina Press, 2017), 53.
68. Ian Finseth, "David Walker, Nature's Nation, and Early African-American Separatism," *The Mississippi Quarterly* 54 (2001): 337–339.
69. Robinson, *Black Nationalism in American Politics and Thought*, 120–121.
70. David Walker, "Appeal in Four Articles," 1829, available via http://docsouth.unc.edu/nc/walker/walker.html.
71. Robinson, *Black Nationalism in American Politics and Thought*, 15–16, 79; Finseth, "David Walker, Nature's Nation, and Early African-American Separatism," 355.
72. Christina Henderson, "Sympathetic Violence: Maria Stewart's Antebellum Vision of African American Resistance," *MELUS* 38 (2013): 66.
73. Kelley, *Freedom Dreams*, 20.
74. Henderson, "Sympathetic Violence," 66. See also Lena Ampadu, "Maria W. Stewart and the Rhetoric of Black Preaching: Perspectives on Womanism and Black Nationalism," in *Black Women's Intellectual Traditions: Speaking Their Minds*, ed. K. Waters and C. Conaway (Chicago: University of Chicago Press, 2007), 38–54; E. Frances White, "Africa on My Mind: Gender, Counter Discourse, and African American Nationalism," in *Is It Nation Time? Contemporary Essays on Black Power and Black Nationalism*, ed. E. S. Glaude Jr. (Chicago: University of Chicago Press, 2002), 130–155; Patricia Hill Collins, "Learning to Think for Ourselves: Malcolm X's Black Nationalism Reconsidered," in *Malcolm X in Our Own Image*, ed. J. Wood (New York: St. Martin's Press, 1992), 59–85.

NOTES 261

75. Moses, *Classical Black Nationalism*, 69.

76. Henry Highland Garnet, "An Address to the Slaves of the United States of America," August, 21, 1843, available via http://www.pbs.org/wgbh/aia/part4/4h2937t.html.

77. James Jasinski, "Constituting Antebellum African American Identity: Resistance, Violence, and Masculinity in Henry Highland Garnet's (1843) 'Address to the Slaves,'" *Quarterly Journal of Speech* 93 (2007): 43, 44.

78. Bette Tallen, "Lesbian Separatism: A Historical and Comparative Perspective," in *For Lesbians Only*, ed. S. Hoagland and J. Penelope (London: Onlywomen Press, 1988), 133.

79. Kelley, *Freedom Dreams*, 24.

80. Marcus Garvey, "Hon. Marcus Garvey Tells of Interview with the Ku Klux Klan," in *Selected Writings and Speeches of Marcus Garvey*, ed. B. Blaisdell (Mineola, NY: Dover Publications, 2004), 75.

81. Garvey, "Hon. Marcus Garvey Tells of Interview with the Ku Klux Klan," 75.

82. Jeffrey O. G. Ogbar, *Black Power: Radical Politics and African American Identity* (Baltimore: Johns Hopkins University Press), 147.

83. Alphonso Pinkney, *Red, Black, and Green: Black Nationalism in the United States* (Cambridge: Cambridge University Press, 1979), 67.

84. Allison Keyes, "Is It Time for a Reassessment of Malcolm X?" *Smithsonian Magazine*, February 23, 2018, available via https://www.smithsonianmag.com/smithsonian-institution/it-time-reassessment-malcolm-x-180968247/.

85. Celeste Michelle Condit and John Louis Lucaites, "Malcolm X and the Limits of the Rhetoric of Revolutionary Dissent," *Journal of Black Studies* 23 (1993): 304. See also Robert E. Terrill, "Colonizing the Borderlands: Shifting Circumference in the Rhetoric of Malcolm X," *Quarterly Journal of Speech* 86 (2000): 79.

86. Hans J. Massaquoi, "Elijah Muhammad: Prophet and Architect of the Separate Nation of Islam," *Ebony*, August 1970, 86.

87. Malcolm X, "Black Man's History," December 1962, available via http://www.malcolm-x.org/speeches/spc_12__62.htm.

88. James Baldwin, "Letter from a Region in My Mind," *New Yorker*, November 17, 1962, available via https://www.newyorker.com/magazine/1962/11/17/letter-from-a-region-in-my-mind. See also Jeffrey Stout, "Theses on Black Nationalism," in *Is It Nation Time? Contemporary Essays on Black Power and Black Nationalism*, ed. E. S. Glaude Jr. (Chicago: University of Chicago Press, 2002),

89. Robinson, *Black Nationalism in American Politics and Thought*, 38–39.

262 NOTES

90. Baldwin, "Letter from a Region in My Mind."

91. Malcolm X, "Speech at the Founding Rally of the Organization of Afro-American Unity," June 28, 1964, available via https://www.blackpast.org/african-american-history/speeches-african-american-history/1964-malcolm-x-s-speech-founding-rally-organization-afro-american-unity/. See also Chokwe Lumumba, "Repression and Black Liberation," *The Black Scholar* 5 (1973): 34.

92. H. Rap Brown, *Die Nigger Die!* (Chicago: Lawrence Hill Books, 2002), 107, 137, 139 (italics and capital letters in original text).

93. Baraka, "A Black Value System," 31.

94. Robinson, *Black Nationalism in American Politics and Thought*, 61; Kelley, *Freedom Dreams*, 70.

95. Williams, *Negroes with Guns*, 24, 25.

96. Williams, *Negroes with Guns*, 10, 48, 48, 49, 67, 50, 43–44, 9–11. Williams, it should be noted, suggested that racism "warped" white minds and suggested that perhaps "some sort of institution" could find a way to make them "whole and well again." *Negroes with Guns*, 73. See also Ta-Nehisi Coates, *Between the World and Me* (New York: Spiegel & Grau, 2015), 139.

97. Van Deburg, *New Day in Babylon*, 261.

98. Lisa Rein, "Mystery of Virginia's First Slaves Unlocked 400 Years Later," *Washington Post*, September 3, 2006, available via http://www.washingtonpost.com/wp-dyn/content/article/2006/09/02/AR2006090201097.html.

99. Coates, *Between the World and Me*, 46.

100. Robinson, *Black Nationalism in American Politics and Thought*, 18; Coates, *Between the World and Me*, 56.

101. Lumumba, "Repression and Black Liberation," 38.

102. Browne, "Separation," 47; Walker, "Foreword II," 53.

103. Marcus Garvey, "The Negro's Greatest Enemy," in *Selected Writings and Speeches of Marcus Garvey*, ed. B. Blaisdell (Mineola, NY: Dover Publications, 2004), 3, 6.

104. Keisha N. Blain, "The Hidden History of Black Nationalist Women's Political Activism," The Conversation, January 30, 2018, available via https://theconversation.com/the-hidden-history-of-black-nationalist-womens-political-activism-89695.

105. Marcus Garvey, "Leadership," in *Selected Writings and Speeches of Marcus Garvey*, ed. B. Blaisdell (Mineola, NY: Dover Publications, 2004), 37–38.

106. Marcus Garvey, "The Hidden Spirit of America," in *Selected Writings and Speeches of Marcus Garvey*, ed. B. Blaisdell (Mineola, NY: Dover Publications, 2004), 64.

NOTES 263

107. Garvey, "The Negro's Greatest Enemy," 8–9.
108. Corey Robin, "Clarence Thomas's Radical Vision of Race," *New Yorker*, September 10, 2019, available via https://www.newyorker.com/culture/essay/clarence-thomass-radical-vision-of-race.
109. Marcus Garvey, "Negroes Will Stop at Nothing Short of Redemption of Motherland and Establishment of African Empire," in *Selected Writings and Speeches of Marcus Garvey*, ed. B. Blaisdell (Mineola, NY: Dover Publications, 2004), 46.
110. Marcus Garvey, "Leadership," 41.
111. Robinson, *Black Nationalism in American Politics and Thought*, 25.
112. Adam Ewing, *The Age of Garvey: How a Jamaican Activist Created a Mass Movement and Changed Global Black Politics* (Princeton, NJ: Princeton University Press, 2014), 6.
113. Robinson, *Black Nationalism in American Politics and Thought*, 28, 25.
114. Ewing, *The Age of Garvey*, 9.
115. Kelley, *Freedom Dreams*, 29.
116. Moses, "Introduction," 6.
117. Garvey, "Negroes Will Stop at Nothing Short of Redemption of Motherland and Establishment of African Empire," 45.
118. Elliott Rudwick, "Marcus Garvey's Revenge," *Reviews in American History* 5 (1977): 93.
119. Garvey, "Negroes Will Stop at Nothing Short of Redemption of Motherland and Establishment of African Empire," 46.
120. Garvey, "Negroes Will Stop at Nothing Short of Redemption of Motherland and Establishment of African Empire," 45–46.
121. Robinson, *Black Nationalism in American Politics and Thought*, 26–27.
122. Marcus Garvey, "Declaration of the Rights of the Negro Peoples of the World," in *Selected Writings and Speeches of Marcus Garvey*, ed. B. Blaisdell (Mineola, NY: Dover Publications, 2004), 19, 23.
123. Robinson, *Black Nationalism in American Politics and Thought*, 24.
124. Hall, *Black Separatism and Social Reality*, 7; Kelley, *Freedom Dreams*, 49–50.
125. Hall, *Black Separatism and Social Reality*, 7.
126. Scott J. Varda, "Drew Ali and the Moorish Science Temple of America: A Minor Rhetoric of Black Nationalism," *Rhetoric and Public Affairs* 16 (2013): 685–717.
127. Blain, "The Hidden History of Black Nationalist Women's Political Activism."
128. Robinson, *Black Nationalism in American Politics and Thought*, 35.
129. Ewing, *The Age of Garvey*, 240; Ted Vincent, "The Garveyite Parents of Malcolm X," *The Black Scholar* 20 (1989): 10–13.

264 NOTES

130. Plummer, *In Search of Power*, 41.

131. Van Deburg, *New Day in Babylon*, 141.

132. Van Deburg, *New Day in Babylon*, 141, 144.

133. Malcolm X, "Debate with Bayard Rustin," November 1960, available via http://malcolmxfiles.blogspot.ca/2013/05/bayard-rustin-debate-november-1960.html.

134. Quoted in Van Deburg, *New Day in Babylon*, 129.

135. Malcolm X. "Racial Separation," October 11, 1963, available via http://www.blackpast.org/1963-malcolm-x-racial-separation.

136. Malcolm X, "Racial Separation."

137. Lisa Corrigan, *Black Feelings: Race and Affect in the Long Sixties* (Oxford: University Press of Mississippi, 2020), 65.

138. Malcolm X, "Twenty Million Black People in a Political, Economic, and Mental Prison," January 23, 1963, available via http://malcolmxfiles.blogspot.com/2013/06/twenty-million-black-people-in.html. See also Joseph, *Waiting 'Til the Midnight Hour*, 91–92.

139. Corrigan, *Black Feelings*, 58.

140. Malcolm X, "Debate with Bayard Rustin."

141. Malcolm X, address at Queens College, May 5, 1960, available via http://malcolmxfiles.blogspot.ca/2013/05/queens-college-speech-may-5-1960.html.

142. Malcolm X, speech at Yale Law School, October 20, 1962, available via http://malcolmxfiles.blogspot.ca/2013/06/malcolm-x-at-yale-university-october-20.html.

143. Malcolm X, "Harlem Freedom Rally," 1960, available via http://malcolmxfiles.blogspot.ca/2013/05/harlem-freedom-rally-1960.html.

144. Malcolm X, "Twenty Million Black People."

145. Malcolm X, "A Declaration of Independence," March 12, 1964, available via http://malcolmxfiles.blogspot.ca/2013/06/a-declaration-of-independence-march-12.html.

146. Malcolm X, speech at Oxford University, December 3, 1964, available via http://malcolmxfiles.blogspot.com/2013/07/oxford-union-debate-december-3-1964.html.

147. Malcolm X, "Message to the Grassroots," December 10, 1963, available via https://www.blackpast.org/african-american-history/speeches-african-american-history/1963-malcolm-x-message-grassroots/.

148. Malcolm X, "Message to the Grassroots."

149. Malcolm X, "Twenty Million Black People."

150. Malcolm X, "Speech at the Founding Rally."

151. Robinson, *Black Nationalism in American Politics and Thought*, 47, 48.

NOTES 265

152. Joseph, *Stokely*, 40. See also Robinson, *Black Nationalism in American Politics and Thought*, 35.

153. Coates, *Between the World and Me*, 53–54.

154. Robinson, *Black Nationalism in American Politics and Thought*, 65.

155. Robert Sherrill, "We Want Georgia, South Carolina, Louisiana, Mississippi and Alabama—Right Now," *Esquire*, January 1969, 72.

156. Van Deburg, *New Day in Babylon*, 145.

157. Van Deburg, *New Day in Babylon*, 145.

158. Tsai, *America's Forgotten Constitutions*, 219, 223; Imari Obadele, "People's Revolt Against Poverty: An Appeal and Challenge," *The Black Scholar* 9 (1978): 39.

159. Richard Henry would largely publish under his adopted name, Imari Obadele, so that is how we refer to him. We refer to Milton Henry as such because he largely published under his original name, not Gaidi Obadele; he later favored his original name as well.

160. Milton R. Henry, "An Independent Black Republic in North America," in *Black Separatism and Social Reality: Rhetoric and Reason*, ed. R. L. Hall (New York: Pergamon Press, 1977), 37–38.

161. Henry, "An Independent Black Republic in North America," 37.

162. See, for example, Imari Obadele, "Getting Ready for the United Nations," *The Black Scholar* 8 (1977): 45.

163. Sherrill, "We Want Georgia," 72.

164. Van Deburg, *New Day in Babylon*, 145.

165. Obadele, "People's Revolt Against Poverty," 37–38.

166. Imari Obadele, "Open Letter to U.S. President Jimmy Carter from RNA President Imari Abubakari Obadele, I," *The Black Scholar* 8 (1978): 59. Some later RNA writings changed the spelling of Africa and African.

167. Imari Obadele, "National Black Elections Held by Republic of New Afrika," *The Black Scholar* 7 (1975): 29.

168. Imari Obadele, "The Struggle Is for Land," *The Black Scholar* 3 (1972): 28.

169. Imari Obadele, "The Republic of New Africa—An Independent Black Nation," *Black World* 20 (1971): 85–86.

170. Obadele, "The Struggle Is for Land," 25.

171. Obadele, "The Republic of New Africa," 82.

172. Obadele, "National Black Elections Held by Republic of New Afrika," 30.

173. Imari Obadele, "The Struggle of the Republic of New Africa," *The Black Scholar* 5 (1974): 37–38.

174. Obadele, "National Black Elections Held by Republic of New Afrika," 30.

175. Jason Sorens, *Secessionism: Identity, Interest, and Strategy* (Montreal: McGill-Queen's University Press, 2012), 155; Timothy

266 NOTES

William Waters, *Boxing Pandora: Rethinking Borders, States, and Secession in a Democratic World* (New Haven, CT: Yale University Press, 2020).

176. Allen Buchanan, "Democracy and Secession," in *National Self-Determination and Secession*, ed. M. Moore (Oxford: Oxford University Press, 1998), 15.

177. Sherrill, "We Want Georgia," 73.

178. Sherrill, "We Want Georgia, 73.

179. Sherrill, "We Want Georgia," 72.

180. Henry, "An Independent Black Republic in North America," 38. Milton plotted urban guerilla tactics since at least 1964. See also Joseph, *Waiting 'Til the Midnight Hour*, 107–108.

181. Milton Henry, *Firing Line*, November 18, 1968, available via https://digitalcollections.hoover.org/objects/6060.

182. Henry, "An Independent Black Republic in North America," 37.

183. Obadele, "The Struggle Is for Land," 34.

184. Tsai, *America's Forgotten Constitutions*, 238.

185. Tsai, *America's Forgotten Constitutions*, 238–239.

186. Francis Wilkinson, "Segregationist Dreamer," *New York Times*, December 31, 2006, available via https://www.nytimes.com/2006/12/31/magazine/31henry.t.html.

187. Obadele, "The Struggle Is for Land," 24; Tsai, *America's Forgotten Constitutions*, 242.

188. Tsai, *America's Forgotten Constitutions*, 242.

189. Stephanie Condon, "After 148 Years, Mississippi Finally Ratifies 13th Amendment, Which Bans Slavery," CBS News, February 28, 2013, available via https://www.cbsnews.com/news/after-148-years-mississippi-finally-ratifies-13th-amendment-which-banned-slavery/.

190. Tsai, *America's Forgotten Constitutions*, 243.

191. Obadele, "National Black Elections Held by Republic of New Afrika," 27.

192. Obadele, "The Struggle of the Republic of New Africa," 37; Yusufu Sonebeyatta and Joseph F. Brooks, "Ujamaa for Land and Power," *The Black Scholar* 3 (1971): 15.

193. Lumumba, "Repression and Black Liberation," 38.

194. Obadele, "National Black Elections Held by Republic of New Afrika," 38.

195. Obadele, "Getting Ready for the United Nations," 38.

196. Obadele, "National Black Elections Held by Republic of New Afrika," 35.

197. Lumumba, "Repression and Black Liberation," 39.

198. Douglas Martin, "Imari Obadele, Who Fought for Reparations, Dies at 79," *New York Times*, February 5, 2010, available via https://www.nytimes.com/2010/02/06/us/06obadele.html.

NOTES   267

199. Robert S. Browne, "A Case for Separatism," in *Black Separatism and Social Reality: Rhetoric and Reason*, ed. R. L. Hall (New York: Pergamon Press, 1977), 27.

200. Kelley, *Freedom Dreams*, 30–31, 16. See also Coates, *Between the World and Me*, 52–53.

201. Hall, *Black Separatism and Social Reality*, 1–2; Robert A. Brown and Todd C. Shaw, "Separate Nations: Two Attitudinal Dimensions of Black Nationalism," *The Journal of Politics* 64, no. 1 (2002): 23; Shelby, "Two Conceptions of Black Nationalism," 667; Williams, "Nationalism," 121–122.

202. Peniel Joseph, "The Black Power Movement: A State of the Field," *Journal of American History* 96 (2009): 754–755.

203. Arthur L. Tolson, "Black Towns of Oklahoma," *The Black Scholar* 1 (1970): 2–21; Kwame Ture and Charles V. Hamilton, *Black Power: The Politics of Liberation in America* (New York: Vintage Books, 1992), 150. See also Tsai, *America's Forgotten Constitutions*, 221; Van Deburg, "Introduction," 10; Brooks, *Racial Justice in the Age of Obama*, 70.

204. Van Deburg, *New Day in Babylon*, 36. See also Hall, *Black Separatism and Social Reality*, 7; Bracey, Meier, and Rudwick, "Introduction," xlv.

205. Ture and Hamilton, *Black Power*, 46. See also Rickford, *We Are an African People*, 74–99; Brandee Sanders, "History's Lost Black Towns," *The Root*, January 27, 2011, available via https://www.theroot.com/historys-lost-black-towns-1790868004; Kelley, *Freedom Dreams*, 16–17; Lane DeGregory, "The Last House in Rosewood," *Tampa Bay Times*, June 6, 2018, available via http://www.tampabay.com/data/2018/06/06/the-last-house-in-rosewood/; William H. Pease and Jane H. Pease, *Black Utopia: Negro Communal Experiments in America* (Madison: State Historical Society of Wisconsin, 1963).

206. Ture and Hamilton, *Black Power*, 44. See also Robinson, *Black Nationalism in American Politics and Thought*, 93.

207. Robin, "Clarence Thomas's Radical Vision of Race."

208. Robinson, *Black Nationalism in American Politics and Thought*, 57.

209. Van Deburg, "Introduction," 15.

210. Joseph, *Waiting 'Til the Midnight Hour*, 164, 200–201, 303.

211. Brown, *Die Nigger Die!*, 69, 74.

212. Brown, *Die Nigger Die!*, 55.

213. Glaude, "Introduction," 8.

214. Joseph, *Stokely*, 162.

215. Corrigan, *Black Feelings*, 48, 49. See also Lisa Corrigan, "50 Years Later: Commemorating the Life and Death of Malcolm X," *Howard Journal of Communications* 28 (2017): 153.

216. Joseph, *Stokely*, 167.

268 NOTES

Chapter 5

1. This opening anecdote is from Ariel Levy's "Lesbian Nation: When Gay Women Took to the Road," *New Yorker*, February 22, 2009, available via https://www.newyorker.com/magazine/2009/03/02/lesbian-nation.
2. Julie R. Enszer, "'How to Stop Choking to Death': Rethinking Lesbian Separatism as a Vibrant Political Theory and Feminist Practice," *Journal of Lesbian Studies* 20 (2016): 184.
3. Levy, "Lesbian Nation," 11.
4. Enszer, "'How to Stop Choking to Death,'" 184.
5. Levy, "Lesbian Nation," 1.
6. Bev Jo, Linda Strega, and Ruston, "Introduction," *Dykes-Loving-Dykes: Dyke Separatist Politics for Lesbians Only* (Oakland, CA: Battleaxe, 1990), 6.
7. Levy, "Lesbian Nation," 1.
8. Maureen Davidica, "Women and the Radical Movement," *Untitled* 1, no. 1 (1968): 43.
9. Ann Japenga, "The Separatist Revival," *Outlook* 2 (1990): 80.
10. Rebecca Bengal, "Country Women," *Vogue*, June 25, 2017, available via https://www.vogue.com/projects/13532936/pride-2017-lesbians-on-the-land-essay/; Pina Raphael, "Why Doesn't Anyone Want to Live in This Perfect Place?," *New York Times*, August 24, 2019, available via https://www.nytimes.com/2019/08/24/style/womyns-land-movement-lesbian-communities.html.
11. Lenore Ralston and Nancy Stoller, "Hallomas: Longevity in a Back-to-the-Land Women's Group in Northern California," in *Lesbian Communities: Festivals, RVs, and the Internet*, ed. P. Sablove and E. Rothblum (Philadelphia: Haworth Press, 2005), 65.
12. Raphael, "Why Doesn't Anyone Want to Live in This Perfect Place?"
13. Raphael, "Why Doesn't Anyone Want to Live in This Perfect Place?"; Sarah Kershaw, "My Sister's Keeper," *New York Times*, January 30, 2009, available via https://www.nytimes.com/2009/02/01/fashion/01womyn.html.
14. Keridwen N. Luis, *Herlands: Exploring the Women's Land Movement in the United States* (Minneapolis: University of Minnesota Press, 2018), 131.
15. Katie Mettler, "Hillary Clinton Just Said It, but 'The Future Is Female' Began as a 1970s Lesbian Separatist Slogan," *Washington Post*, February 8, 2017, available via https://www.washingtonpost.com/news/morning-mix/wp/2017/02/08/hillary-clinton-just-said-it-but-the-future-is-female-began-as-a-1970s-lesbian-separatist-slogan/.

NOTES 269

16. Kathy Rudy, "Radical Feminism, Lesbian Separatism, and Queer Theory," *Feminist Studies* 27 (2001): 191–222.

17. Luis, *Herlands*, 3.

18. Bev Jo, "Lesbian Community: From Sisterhood to Segregation," *Journal of Lesbian Studies* 9 (2005): 136.

19. Luis, *Herlands*, 12.

20. Luis, *Herlands*, 135.

21. Luis, *Herlands*, 48, 290. Many of these texts and much more have been collected and preserved at the Lesbian Herstory Archive in New York City, which "is home to the world's largest collection of materials by and about lesbians and their communities." "Welcome to the Lesbian Herstory Archives," available via http://www.lesbianherstoryarchives.org/.

22. Jo, Strega, and Ruston, "Introduction," 6.

23. Alice Gordon, "The Problems of Our Movement," in *For Lesbians Only: A Separatist Anthology*, ed. Sarah Lucia Hoagland and Julia Penelope (San Francisco: Onlywomen Press, 1992), 393.

24. Gordon, "Problems of Our Movement," 393.

25. Linda Napikoski, "Lavender Menace: The Phrase, the Group, the Controversy," ThoughtCo., March 1, 2019, available via https://www.thoughtco.com/lavender-menace-feminism-definition-3528970.

26. Jackie Anderson, "Separatism, Feminism, and the Betrayal of Reform," *Signs* 19 (1994): 438.

27. Luis, *Herlands*, 7.

28. Enszer, " 'How to Stop Choking to Death,' " 193.

29. Rudy, "Radical Feminism, Lesbian Separatism, and Queer Theory," 193.

30. Japenga, "The Separatist Revival," 80.

31. Marilyn Frye, "Some Reflections on Separatism and Power," *Sinister Wisdom* 6 (1978): 31.

32. Anderson, "Separatism, Feminism, and the Betrayal of Reform," 445–447; Tracy Baim, "PASSAGES Activist, Professor Jackie Anderson Dies," *Windy City Times*, January 8, 2018, available via http://www.windycitymediagroup.com/lgbt/PASSAGES-Activist-professor-Jackie-Anderson-dies/61537.html.

33. Mary Daly, "After the Death of God the Father," in *The Mary Daly Reader*, ed. J. Rycenga (New York: New York University Press, 2017), 90.

34. Ann Powers, "Mary, Quite Contrary," *New York Times*, November 7, 1999, available via https://www.nytimes.com/1999/11/07/education/mary-quite-contrary.html.

35. Daly, "After the Death of God the Father," 89, 90; Adrienne Rich, "That Women Be Themselves," *New York Times*, February 4, 1979, available

270   NOTES

via https://www.nytimes.com/1979/02/04/archives/that-women-be-themselves-women.html.

36. Rudy, "Radical Feminism, Lesbian Separatism, and Queer Theory," 198.

37. Bette Tallen, "Lesbian Separatism: A Historical and Comparative Perspective," in *For Lesbians Only*, ed. S. Hoagland and J. Penelope (London: Onlywomen Press, 1988), 141.

38. Jill Johnston, *Lesbian Nation: The Feminist Solution* (New York: Simon & Schuster, 1973).

39. Sarah Lucia Hoagland, "Introduction," *Sinister Wisdom* 34 (1988): 29–30, available at http://www.sinisterwisdom.org/sites/default/files/Sinister%20Wisdom%2034.pdf.

40. Elizabeth R. Varon, *Disunion! The Coming of the American Civil War, 1789–1859* (Chapel Hill: University of North Carolina Press, 2008), 291–292.

41. Charles B. Dew, "Lincoln, the Collapse of Deep South Moderation, and the Triumph of Secession: A South Carolina Congressman's Moment of Truth," in *Secession as an International Phenomenon: From America's Civil War to Contemporary Separatist Movements*, ed. D. H. Doyle (Athens: University of Georgia Press, 2010), 108.

42. Robin D. G. Kelley, *Freedom Dreams: The Black Radical Imagination* (Boston: Beacon Press, 2002), 21, 26.

43. Quoted in Stephen Tuck, *The Night Malcolm X Spoke at the Oxford Union* (Berkeley: University of California Press, 2014), 154.

44. Kelley, *Freedom Dreams*, 21, 26.

45. Claudia Card, "Pluralist Lesbian Separatism," in *Lesbian Philosophies and Cultures*, ed. J. Allen (Albany: SUNY Press, 1990), 128.

46. See examples such as Maria Lugones, "Purity, Impurity, and Separation," *Signs* 19 (1994): 458–479; Maria Luisa "Papusa" Molina, "Fragmentations: Meditations on Separatism," *Signs* 19 (1994): 449–457.

47. Valerie Solanas, *The SCUM Manifesto* (London: Matriarchal Study Group, 1983), available via https://www.ccs.neu.edu/home/shivers/rants/scum.html.

48. Solanas, *The SCUM Manifesto*.

49. James Penner, *Pinks, Pansies, and Punks: The Rhetoric of Masculinity in American Literary Culture* (Bloomington: Indiana University Press, 2011), 232–233; for more on Solanas, see Breanne Fahs, *Valerie Solans: The Defiant Life of the Woman Who Wrote SCUM* (New York: Feminist Press, 2014); Bonnie Wertheim, "Overlooked No More: Valerie Solanas, Radical Feminist Who Shot Andy Warhol," *New York Times*, June 26, 2020, available via https://www.nytimes.com/2020/06/26/obituaries/valerie-solanas-overlooked.html.

NOTES 271

50. Solanas, *The SCUM Manifesto*.
51. Thom Nickels, *Out in History: Collected Essays* (Herndon, VA: STARbooks Press, 2005), 17.
52. Nickels, *Out in History*, 17.
53. Robert Marmorstein, "A Winter Memory of Valerie Solanis [*sic*]: Scum Goddess," *The Village Voice*, June 13, 1968, 9–10, 20.
54. Dunbar, "Slavery," 3.
55. Betsy Warrior, "Man as an Obsolete Life Form," *No More Fun and Games: A Journal of Female Liberation* 2 (February 1969): 78.
56. Warrior, "Man as an Obsolete Life Form," 77.
57. Warrior, "Man as an Obsolete Life Form," 78.
58. Warrior, "Man as an Obsolete Life Form," 77.
59. Greta Rensenbrink, "Parthenogenesis and Lesbian Separatism: Regenerating Women's Community Through Virgin Birth in the United States in the 1970s and 1980s," *Journal of the History of Sexuality* 19 (2010): 302.
60. Verta Taylor and Leila J. Rupp, "Women's Culture and Lesbian Feminist Activism: A Reconsideration of Cultural Feminism," *Signs* 19 (1993): 42.
61. Frye, "Some Reflections on Separatism and Power," 30–39.
62. Frye, "Some Reflections on Separatism and Power," 30–39.
63. Solanas, *The SCUM Manifesto*.
64. Mary Ann Weathers, "An Argument for Black Women's Liberation as a Revolutionary Force," *No More Fun and Games: A Journal of Female Liberation* 2 (February 1969):70.
65. Dana Densmore, "The Slave's Stake in the Home," *No More Fun and Games: A Journal of Female Liberation* 2 (February 1969): 20.
66. Dunbar, "Slavery," 3.
67. Dana Densmore, "Our Place in the Universe," *Untitled* 1, no. 1 (1968): 71.
68. Dana Densmore, "Against Liberals," *No More Fun and Games: A Journal of Female Liberation* 2 (February 1969): 63.
69. Solanas, *The SCUM Manifesto*.
70. Betsy Warrior, "Che's Achilles Heel," *No More Fun and Games: A Journal of Female Liberation* 2 (February 1969): 71.
71. Dunbar, "Slavery," 3.
72. Marilyn Terry, "The Psychological Commune," *Untitled* 1, no. 1 (1968): 61.
73. Radicalesbians, *The Woman Identified Woman* (Pittsburgh: Know, 1970), 3.
74. Radicalesbians, *The Woman Identified Woman*, 3.
75. Quoted in Japenga, "The Separatist Revival," 81.
76. Roxanne Dunbar, "Who Is the Enemy?," *No More Fun and Games: A Journal of Female Liberation* 2 (February 1969): 55.

272 NOTES

77. Densmore, "Our Place in the Universe," 70.
78. Densmore, "Our Place in the Universe," 70.
79. Weathers, "An Argument for Black Women's Liberation as a Revolutionary Force," 70.
80. Weathers, "An Argument for Black Women's Liberation as a Revolutionary Force," 70.
81. Quoted in Japenga, "The Separatist Revival," 80.
82. Stella Kingsbury, "Women Up Against the Wall," *Untitled* 1, no. 1 (1968): 10.
83. Dunbar, "Slavery," 6.
84. Dunbar, "Slavery," 6.
85. Several women wrote about the lessons that could be learned from observing the movements for racial justice while also preserving a focus on women. Dunbar, for example, wrote, "But we should not simply imitate the rhetoric of the Black movement. It must be frustrating for Black people to see their language taken out of context and destroyed not only by society's media, but also by young white radicals, and now by women. . . . Language which is historically and socially at odds with the subject of analysis not only cheapens one's analysis, but is an insult to the absolutely necessary struggle of the Black people in this country, a struggle necessarily related to our own." Dunbar, "Who Is the Enemy?," 58.
86. Roxanne Dunbar, "Slavery," *Untitled* 1, no. 1 (1968): 3.
87. Roxanne Dunbar, "What Is to Be Done?," *Untitled* 1, no. 1 (1968): 64.
88. Dunbar, "Slavery," 6.
89. Maureen Davidica, "Women and the Radical Movement," *Untitled* 1, no. 1 (1968): 44.
90. Dunbar, "Slavery," 5–6.
91. Dunbar, "Slavery," 5–6.
92. Dunbar, "Slavery," 3.
93. Dunbar, "Slavery," 3.
94. Dunbar, "Slavery," 3.
95. Dunbar, "Slavery," 3.
96. Luis, *Herlands*, 246–248.
97. Charlotte Perkins Gilman, *Herland* (New York: Pantheon Books, 1979).
98. Sally Miller Gearhart, *The Wanderground: Stories of the Hill Women* (Boston: Alyson Publications, 1984).
99. Warrior, "Man as an Obsolete Life Form," 77.
100. Frye, "Some Reflections on Separatism and Power," 30–39.
101. Frye, "Some Reflections on Separatism and Power," 30–39.

NOTES   273

102. Japenga, "The Separatist Revival," 83.
103. Ariane Brunet and Louise Turcotte, "Separatism and Radicalism: An Analysis of the Differences and Similarities," *Lesbian Ethics* 2 (1986): 41–49.
104. Ginny Berson, "Untitled," *The Furies: Lesbian/Feminist Monthly*, January 1972, 1.
105. Berson, "Untitled," 1.
106. Berson, "Untitled," 1.
107. Radicalesbians, *The Woman Identified Woman*, 1.
108. Radicalesbians, *The Woman Identified Woman*, 1.
109. Kershaw, "My Sister's Keeper."
110. Frye, "Some Reflections on Separatism and Power," 30–39.
111. Frye, "Some Reflections on Separatism and Power," 30–39.
112. Frye, "Some Reflections on Separatism and Power," 30–39.
113. Frye, "Some Reflections on Separatism and Power," 30–39.
114. Frye, "Some Reflections on Separatism and Power," 30–39.
115. Frye, "Some Reflections on Separatism and Power," 30–39.
116. Terry, "The Psychological Commune," 61.
117. Terry, "The Psychological Commune," 61.
118. Jeffner Allen, *Sinuosities, Lesbian Poetic Politics* (Bloomington: University of Indiana Press, 1996), 43. See also Baim, "PASSAGES Activist, Professor Jackie Anderson Dies"; Anderson, "Separatism, Feminism, and the Betrayal of Reform," 446–447.
      Jeffner Allen, *Sinuosities, Lesbian Poetic Politics* (Bloomington: University of Indiana Press, 1996), 42.
119. Dana Densmore, "On the Temptation to be a Beautiful Object," *No More Fun and Games: A Journal of Female Liberation* 2 (February 1969): 44.
120. Jo, "Lesbian Community," 141.
121. Terry, "The Psychological Commune," 62.
122. Terry, "The Psychological Commune," 62.
123. Radicalesbians, *The Woman Identified Woman*, 4.
124. Mettler, "Hillary Clinton Just Said It, but 'The Future Is Female' Began as a 1970s Lesbian Separatist Slogan."
125. Estelle Freedman, "Separatism as Strategy: Female Institution Building and American Feminism, 1870–1930," *Feminist Studies* 5 (1979): 524.
126. Hoagland, "Introduction," 24–25.
127. Hoagland, "Introduction," 25, 27.
128. Kershaw, "My Sister's Keeper."
129. Elana Dykewomon, "Lesbian Quarters: On Building Space, Identity, Institutional Memory and Resources," *Journal of Lesbian Studies* 9 (2005): 39.

274 NOTES

130. Anna Lee, "For the Love of Separatism," in *Lesbian Philosophies and Cultures*, ed. J. Allen (Albany: SUNY Press, 1990), 154.

131. Enszer, "'How to Stop Choking to Death,'" 193.

132. The Combahee River Collective, "A Black Feminist Statement," in *The Second Wave: A Reader in Feminist Theory*, ed. Linda Nicholson (New York: Routledge, 1997), 63–70.

133. The Combahee River Collective, "A Black Feminist Statement," 63–70. Some separatists agreed with this critique of biology. The Gorgons, for instance, wrote, "Although many Separatists believe that men are biologically disposed to destructive behavior, we do not base our analysis on men's behavior, both historically and now. We cannot discount the effects of culture and history." Gorgons, "Response by the Gorgons," in *For Lesbians Only: A Separatist Anthology*, ed. Sarah Lucia Hoagland and Julia Penelope (San Francisco: Onlywomen Press, 1998), 396.

134. Anna Lee, "A Black Separatist," in *For Lesbians Only: A Separatist Anthology*, ed. Sarah Lucia Hoagland and Julia Penelope (San Francisco: Onlywomen Press, 1998), 91.

135. Molina, "Fragmentations: Meditations on Separatism," 451; Rudy, "Radical Feminism, Lesbian Separatism, and Queer Theory," 202; Japenga, "The Separatist Revival," 81.

136. Luis, *Herlands*, 7, 21–22.

137. Frances Wasserlein and Carolynn L. Sween, "Lesquire's Pub—An Essay on Virtual Community Building," in *Lesbian Communities: Festivals, RVs, and the Internet*, ed. P. Sablove and E. Rothblum (Philadelphia: Haworth Press, 2005), 112.

138. Trudy King, "This Year's Michigan Womyn's Music Festival Will Be the Last," *The Advocate*, April 21, 2015, available via https://www.advocate.com/michfest/2015/04/21/years-michigan-womyns-music-festival-will-be-last.

139. Luis, *Herlands*, 21–22.

140. Jo, "Lesbian Community," 138–139.

141. Bernice Johnson Reagon, "Coalition Politics: Turning the Century," in *Home Girls: A Black Feminist Anthology*, ed. B. Smith (New York: Kitchen Table Press, 1983), 357.

142. Kershaw, "My Sister's Keeper."

143. Raphael, "Why Doesn't Anyone Want to Live in This Perfect Place?"

144. Raphael, "Why Doesn't Anyone Want to Live in This Perfect Place?"

145. Raphael, "Why Doesn't Anyone Want to Live in This Perfect Place?"

146. Raphael, "Why Doesn't Anyone Want to Live in This Perfect Place?"

147. Raphael, "Why Doesn't Anyone Want to Live in This Perfect Place?"

148. Kershaw, "My Sister's Keeper."

NOTES 275

Chapter 6

1. Jennifer M. Hansen, ed., *Letters of Catharine Cottam Romney, Plural Wife* (Urbana: University of Illinois Press, 1992), 116.
2. Michael Kranish and Michael Paulson, "Mitt's LDS Roots Run Deep," *Deseret News*, July 2, 2007, available via https://www.deseret.com/2007/7/2/20027702/mitt-s-lds-roots-run-deep#mitt-romney-march-21-1969; for more on Romney's life, see Thomas Cottam Romney, *Life Story of Miles P. Romney* (Independence, MO: Zion's, 1948).
3. Hansen, ed., *Letters of Catharine Cottam Romney, Plural Wife*, 112.
4. JoAnn W. Blair and Richard L. Jensen, "Prosecution of the Mormons in Arizona Territory in the 1880s," *Arizona and the West* 19 (1977): 34.
5. Hansen, ed., *Letters of Catharine Cottam Romney, Plural Wife*, 100.
6. Hansen, ed., *Letters of Catharine Cottam Romney, Plural Wife*, 100.
7. For more on the Church's settlements in Mexico, see Estelle Webb Thomas, *Uncertain Sanctuary: A Story of Mormon Pioneering in Mexico* (Evergreen, CO: Westwater Press, 1980); F. LaMond Tullis, *Mormons in Mexico: The Dynamics of Faith and Culture* (Logan: Utah State University Press, 1987).
8. A. F. MacDonald, "The Mexican Colonies: Valuable Information to Intending Settlers and Tourists," *Correspondence of the Deseret News*, September 11, 1890, 3.
9. Thomas C. Romney, *A Divinity Shapes Our Ends as Seen in My Life Story* (Salt Lake City: Thomas C. Romney, 1953), 34.
10. Hansen, ed., *Letters of Catharine Cottam Romney, Plural Wife*, 113.
11. "Plural Marriage in Kirtland and Nauvoo," Church of Jesus Christ of Latter-day Saints, available via https://www.churchofjesuschrist.org/topics/plural-marriage-in-kirtland-and-nauvoo?lang=eng#24.
12. Brian C. Hales, *Modern Polygamy and Mormon Fundamentalism: The Generations After the Manifesto* (Salt Lake City: Greg Kofford Books, 2006), 3–4; "Plural Marriage in Kirtland and Nauvoo."
13. Hales, *Modern Polygamy and Mormon Fundamentalism*, 18.
14. Hales, *Modern Polygamy and Mormon Fundamentalism*, 18.
15. Hales, *Modern Polygamy and Mormon Fundamentalism*, 32.
16. Hansen, ed., *Letters of Catharine Cottam Romney, Plural Wife*, 261. See also Karl Egbert Young, *The Long Hot Summer of 1912: Episodes in the Flight of the Mormon Colonists from Mexico* (Provo, UT: Brigham Young University, 1967).
17. Hansen, ed., *Letters of Catharine Cottam Romney, Plural Wife*, 262.
18. Hansen, ed., *Letters of Catharine Cottam Romney, Plural Wife*, 262.
19. Hansen, ed., *Letters of Catharine Cottam Romney, Plural Wife*, 278.

276 NOTES

20. Christopher Jennings, *Paradise Now: The Story of American Utopianism* (New York: Random House, 2016), 4.

21. Jennings, *Paradise Now*, 5.

22. Jennings, *Paradise Now*, 11–12.

23. Kyle Chayka, "America Is a Utopia Experiment—And Always Has Been," *Pacific Standard*, June 14, 2017, available via https://psmag.com/social-justice/america-utopian-experiment-always-73410.

24. Although Latter-day Saints have often been referred to as "Mormons" since the nineteenth century, Russell Nelson, president of the LDS Church, said in 2019 he experienced a revelation instructing him to drop the moniker "Mormon" in favor of "Latter-day Saints." When possible, we have chosen to respect the Church's position that it should be referred to as such. See Daniel Burke, "Why the 'Mormon' Church Changed Its Name. It's About Revelation, Not Rebranding," CNN, March 22, 2019, available via https://www.cnn.com/2019/03/22/us/mormon-lds-name-change-revelation/index.html.

25. Harold Bloom, *The American Religion: The Emergence of a Post-Christian Nation* (New York: Simon & Schuster, 1992), 81–83.

26. Bloom, *The American Religion*, 94.

27. Richard L. Bushman, "The Separatist Impulse in the Nauvoo Council of Fifty," in *The Council of Fifty: What the Records Reveal About Mormon History*, ed. M. J. Grow and R. E. Smith (Provo, UT: Brigham Young University Press, 2017), 3.

28. Matthew J. Grow and R. Eric Smith, eds., *The Council of Fifty: What the Records Reveal About Mormon History* (Provo, UT: Brigham Young University Press, 2017), vii.

29. Patrick Q. Mason, "God and the People Reconsidered," in *The Council of Fifty: What the Records Reveal About Mormon History*, ed. M. J. Grow and R. E. Smith (Provo, UT: Brigham Young University Press, 2017), 39.

30. R. Laurence Moore, *Religious Outsiders and the Makings of Americans* (New York: Oxford University Press, 1986), 45–46.

31. Matthew J. Grow et al., *Saints: The Story of the Church of Jesus Christ in the Latter Days, the Standard of Truth, 1815–1846* (Salt Lake City: Church of Jesus Christ of Latter-day Saints, 2018), 1:15–16.

32. Grow et al., *Saints*, 17.

33. Grow et al., *Saints*, 17.

34. Richard Turley Jr., "Injustices Leading to the Creation of the Council of Fifty," in *The Council of Fifty What the Records Reveal about Mormon History*, ed. M. J. Grow and R. E. Smith (Provo, UT: Brigham Young University Press, 2017), 8.

NOTES 277

35. Turley, "Injustices Leading to the Creation of the Council of Fifty," 9.
36. Turley, "Injustices Leading to the Creation of the Council of Fifty," 8.
37. Turley, "Injustices Leading to the Creation of the Council of Fifty," 11–12.
38. Turley, "Injustices Leading to the Creation of the Council of Fifty," 15.
39. *Our Heritage: A Brief History of the Church of Jesus Christ of Latter-day Saints* (Salt Lake City: Church of Latter-day Saints Press, 1996), 47.
40. Turley, "Injustices Leading to the Creation of the Council of Fifty," 15.
41. Joseph Smith explained that the name "is of Hebrew origin and signifies a beautiful situation or place, carrying with it also the idea of *rest*." Grow et al., *Saints*, 417.
42. Turley, "Injustices Leading to the Creation of the Council of Fifty," 17.
43. Homer Hoyt, *One Hundred Years of Land Values in Chicago* (Chicago: University of Chicago Press, 1933), 49–50.
44. Turley, "Injustices Leading to the Creation of the Council of Fifty," 17.
45. Spencer W. McBride, "The Council of Fifty and Joseph Smith's Presidential Ambitions," in *The Council of Fifty: What the Records Reveal About Mormon History*, ed. M. J. Grow and R. E. Smith (Provo, UT: Brigham Young University Press, 2017), 21–22.
46. Joseph McConkie and Robert Millet, *Doctrinal Commentary on the Book of Mormon* (Salt Lake City: Deseret Books, 1992), 1:103.
47. Grow et al., *Saints*, 214.
48. Grow and Smith, eds., *The Council of Fifty*, vii.
49. Grow and Smith, eds., *The Council of Fifty*, vii.
50. Bushman, "The Separatist Impulse in the Nauvoo Council of Fifty," 3.
51. Grow and Smith, eds., *The Council of Fifty*, viii.
52. Grow and Smith, eds., *The Council of Fifty*, xiii.
53. Mason, "God and the People Reconsidered," 35.
54. Brigham Young, "April 5, 1844," in *The Joseph Smith Papers: Administrative Records, Council of Fifty Minutes, March 1844–January 1846*, ed. M. J. Grow, R. K. Esplin, M. Ashurst-McGee, G. J. Dirkmaat, and J. D. Mahas (Salt Lake City: Church Historian's Press, 2016), 82.
55. Mason, "God and the People Reconsidered," 35.
56. Hyrum Andrus, *Joseph Smith and World Government* (Salt Lake City: Desert Book Co., 1958), 5.
57. Andrus, *Joseph Smith and World Government*, 4.
58. Joseph Smith, "Introduction," in *The Book of Mormon: Another Testament of Jesus Christ* (Salt Lake City: Church of Jesus Christ of Latter-day Saints, 2013), x.
59. Andrus, *Joseph Smith and World Government*, 29.
60. Andrus, *Joseph Smith and World Government*, 17.

278 NOTES

61. Orson Pratt, *The Seer* (Liverpool: S. W. Richards, 1853), 149.

62. Andrus, *Joseph Smith and World Government*, 18.

63. Bloom, *The American Religion*, 89.

64. Andrus, *Joseph Smith and World Government*, 215.

65. Andrus, *Joseph Smith and World Government*, 18.

66. Andrus, *Joseph Smith and World Government*, 28.

67. Brigham Young, *Discourses of Brigham Young: Second President of the Church of Jesus Christ of Latter-day Saints*, ed. J. A. Widtsoe (Salt Lake City: Deseret Book Company, 1954), 359.

68. Pratt, *The Seer*, 149.

69. Andrus, *Joseph Smith and World Government*, 20.

70. Andrus, *Joseph Smith and World Government*, 20.

71. For an excellent summary of the debate and the implications, see Benjamin E. Park, "The Council of Fifty and the Perils of Democratic Governance," in *The Council of Fifty: What the Records Reveal About Mormon History*, ed. M. J. Grow and R. E. Smith (Provo: Brigham Young University Press, 2017), 43–54.

72. Joseph Smith, "April 25, 1844," in *The Joseph Smith Papers: Administrative Records, Council of Fifty Minutes, March 1844–January 1846*, ed. M. J. Grow, R. K. Esplin, M. Ashurst-McGee, G. J. Dirkmaat, and J. D. Mahas (Salt Lake City: Church Historian's Press, 2016), 135–137.

73. Park, "The Council of Fifty and the Perils of Democratic Governance," 51.

74. Andrus, *Joseph Smith and World Government*, 20–22.

75. Andrus, *Joseph Smith and World Government*, 9.

76. Joseph Smith, *History of the Church of Jesus Christ of Latter-day Saints*, VII (Salt Lake City: Deseret Book Company, 1948), 382.

77. Smith, *History of the Church of Jesus Christ of Latter-day Saints*, VII:382.

78. Andrus, *Joseph Smith and World Government*, 31–32.

79. Smith, *History of the Church of Jesus Christ of Latter-day Saints*, VI:222.

80. Young, *Discourses of Brigham Young*, 359–360.

81. Bloom, *The American Religion*, 95.

82. Grow et al., *Saints*, 543.

83. Grow et al., *Saints*, 555.

84. Grow et al., *Saints*, 559.

85. Grow et al., *Saints*, 559.

86. Bushman, "The Separatist Impulse in the Nauvoo Council of Fifty," 3.

87. Brigham Young, "March 11, 1845," in *The Joseph Smith Papers: Administrative Records, Council of Fifty Minutes, March 1844–January 1846*, ed. M. J. Grow, R. K. Esplin, M. Ashurst-McGee, G. J. Dirkmaat, and J. D. Mahas (Salt Lake City: Church Historian's Press, 2016), 299–300.

NOTES   279

88. John Taylor, "April 18, 1844," in *The Joseph Smith Papers: Administrative Records, Council of Fifty Minutes, March 1844–January 1846*, ed. M. J. Grow, R. K. Esplin, M. Ashurst-McGee, G. J. Dirkmaat, and J. D. Mahas (Salt Lake City: Church Historian's Press, 2016), 114.

89. William Phelps, "April 11, 1844," in *The Joseph Smith Papers: Administrative Records, Council of Fifty Minutes, March 1844–January 1846*, ed. M. J. Grow, R. K. Esplin, M. Ashurst-McGee, G. J. Dirkmaat, and J. D. Mahas (Salt Lake City: Church Historian's Press, 2016), 94.

90. Amasa Lyman, "March 18, 1845," in *The Joseph Smith Papers: Administrative Records, Council of Fifty Minutes, March 1844–January 1846*, ed. M. J. Grow, R. K. Esplin, M. Ashurst-McGee, G. J. Dirkmaat, and J. D. Mahas (Salt Lake City: Church Historian's Press, 2016), 336–337.

91. Young, "March 11, 1845," 300.

92. Young, *The Joseph Smith Papers*, 328.

93. Young, *The Joseph Smith Papers*, 351.

94. Young, *The Joseph Smith Papers*, 299.

95. Bushman, "The Separatist Impulse in the Nauvoo Council of Fifty," 1–2.

96. Bushman, "The Separatist Impulse in the Nauvoo Council of Fifty," 2.

97. Brigham Young, "March 1, 1845," in *The Joseph Smith Papers: Administrative Records, Council of Fifty Minutes, March 1844–January 1846*, ed. M. J. Grow, R. K. Esplin, M. Ashurst-McGee, G. J. Dirkmaat, and J. D. Mahas (Salt Lake City: Church Historian's Press, 2016), 257–258.

98. Young, "March 11, 1845," 300.

99. Orsen Spencer, "March 18, 1845," in *The Joseph Smith Papers: Administrative Records, Council of Fifty Minutes, March 1844–January 1846*, ed. M. J. Grow, R. K. Esplin, M. Ashurst-McGee, G. J. Dirkmaat, and J. D. Mahas (Salt Lake City: Church Historian's Press, 2016), 335.

100. Lyman, "March 18, 1845," 337.

101. John Taylor, "March 1, 1845," in *The Joseph Smith Papers: Administrative Records, Council of Fifty Minutes, March 1844–January 1846*, ed. M. J. Grow, R. K. Esplin, M. Ashurst-McGee, G. J. Dirkmaat, and J. D. Mahas (Salt Lake City: Church Historian's Press, 2016), 265.

102. Brigham Young, "March 18, 1845," in *The Joseph Smith Papers: Administrative Records, Council of Fifty Minutes, March 1844–January 1846*, ed. M. J. Grow, R. K. Esplin, M. Ashurst-McGee, G. J. Dirkmaat, and J. D. Mahas (Salt Lake City: Church Historian's Press, 2016), 338.

103. Bushman, "The Separatist Impulse in the Nauvoo Council of Fifty," 2.

280 NOTES

104. Young, "March 18, 1845," 328.
105. Young, "March 18, 1845," 331.
106. Young, "March 18, 1845," 328.
107. Grow et al., *Saints*, 581.
108. Brigham Young, "January 11, 1846," in *The Joseph Smith Papers: Administrative Records, Council of Fifty Minutes, March 1844–January 1846*, ed. M. J. Grow, R. K. Esplin, M. Ashurst-McGee, G. J. Dirkmaat, and J. D. Mahas (Salt Lake City: Church Historian's Press, 2016), 519.
109. John Taylor, "January 11, 1846," in *The Joseph Smith Papers: Administrative Records, Council of Fifty Minutes, March 1844–January 1846*, ed. M. J. Grow, R. K. Esplin, M. Ashurst-McGee, G. J. Dirkmaat, and J. D. Mahas (Salt Lake City: Church Historian's Press, 2016), 515.
110. Young, "January 11, 1846," 513.
111. *Our Heritage*, 77.
112. *Our Heritage*, 76.
113. Grow and Smith, eds., *The Council of Fifty*, xiii.
114. Lee Trepanier and Lynita K. Newswander, *LDS in the USA: Mormonism and the Making of American Culture* (Waco, TX: Baylor University Press, 2012), 103.
115. "Mormons Account for 90 Percent of the State Legislature," Associated Press, January 27, 2019, available via https://apnews.com/286983987f484cb182fba9334c52a617.
116. Lawrence Wright, "Lives of the Saints," *The New Yorker*, January 21, 2002, available via https://www.newyorker.com/magazine/2002/01/21/lives-of-the-saints.
117. "2018 Statistical Report," *April 2019 General Conference News and Announcements for The Church of Jesus Christ of Latter-day Saints*, April 7, 2019, available via https://newsroom.churchofjesuschrist.org/article/april-2019-general-conference-news-summary?imageView=GC1.jpeg.
118. Ian Lovett and Rachael Levy, "The Mormon Church Amassed $100 Billion. It Was the Best-Kept Secret in the Investment World," *Wall Street Journal*, February 8, 2020, available via https://www.wsj.com/articles/the-mormon-church-amassed-100-billion-it-was-the-best-kept-secret-in-the-investment-world-11581138011.
119. Bushman, "The Separatist Impulse in the Nauvoo Council of Fifty," 3.
120. Randall Guynn and Gene Schaerr, "The Mormon Polygamy Cases," *Sunstone* 11 (September 1987): 9.
121. Hales, *Modern Polygamy and Mormon Fundamentalism*, 40.
122. Bushman, "The Separatist Impulse in the Nauvoo Council of Fifty," 3.
123. Bushman, "The Separatist Impulse in the Nauvoo Council of Fifty," 4.
124. Trepanier and Newswander, *LDS in the USA*, 2.

NOTES 281

125. Cory Burnell, "2006 Year in Review," *Christian Exodus* 1 (2007): 1.
126. John Dougherty, "Polygamy's Odyssey," *Phoenix New Times,* March 12, 2003, available at https://www.phoenixnewtimes.com/news/polygamys-odyssey-6409120.
127. "Fundamentalist Church of Jesus Christ of Latter-day Saints Fast Facts," CNN, August 14, 2019, available via https://www.cnn.com/2013/10/31/us/fundamentalist-church-of-jesus-christ-of-latter-day-saints-fast-facts/index.html.
128. "Utah Senate Supports Bill Decriminalising Polygamy," BBC News, February 19, 2020, available via https://www.bbc.com/news/world-us-canada-51562737.
129. Patrick Mason, "The History of Mormons in Mexico," National Public Radio, November 9, 2019, available via https://www.npr.org/2019/11/09/777957221/the-history-of-mormons-in-mexico.
130. Bushman, "The Separatist Impulse in the Nauvoo Council of Fifty," 3.
131. Bloom, *The American Religion*, 90–91.
132. John G. Turner, "All the Truth Does Not Always Need to Be Told," in *Out of Obscurity: Mormonism Since 1945*, ed. P. Q. Mason and J. G. Turner (New York: Oxford University Press, 2016), 320.
133. Ben Winslow, "Polygamy Is Essentially Decriminalized in Utah Under a Bill Signed into Law," Fox 13 News, May 13, 2020, available via https://www.foxnews.com/us/utah-polygamy-essentially-decriminalized.

Chapter 7

1. Timothy Ferris, *The Science of Liberty: Democracy, Reason, and the Laws of Nature* (New York: Harper, 2010), 93.
2. Philip Abbott, "The Lincoln Propositions and the Spirit of Secession," in *Theories of Secession*, ed. P. B. Lehning (London: Routledge, 1998), 183.
3. Leslie A. Hahner, *To Become an American: Immigrants and Americanization Campaigns of the Early Twentieth Century* (East Lansing: Michigan State University Press, 2017), xix.
4. Aris Folley, "Hundreds Participate In, Watch South Carolina Boat Parade in Support of Trump," *The Hill*, May 25, 2020, available via https://thehill.com/blogs/blog-briefing-room/news/499443-hundreds-participate-in-watch-south-carolina-boat-parade-in.
5. Shawn J. Parry-Giles and David S. Kaufer, *Memories of Lincoln and the Splintering of American Political Thought* (University Park: Pennsylvania State University Press, 2017), 5–10.

282 NOTES

6. Benjamin R. Barber, "Constitutional Faith," in *For Love of Country?*, ed. J. Cohen (Boston: Beacon Press, 1996), 31.

7. Barber, "Constitutional Faith," 32–33.

8. George Washington, "Farewell Address," 1796, available via https://avalon.law.yale.edu/18th_century/washing.asp. See also Scott Bomboy, "Five Lessons We Can Learn from George Washington's Farewell Address," *Constitution Daily*, September 19, 2018, available via https://constitutioncenter.org/blog/five-lessons-we-can-learn-from-george-washingtons-farewell-address.

9. Lorman A. Ratner and Dwight L. Teeter Jr., *Fanatics and Fire-eaters: Newspapers and the Coming of the Civil War* (Urbana: University of Illinois Press, 2003), 117.

10. Nathan Pippenger, "Secession: Still a Bad Idea," *Democracy: A Journal of Ideas*, March 16, 2017, available via https://democracyjournal.org/alcove/secession-still-a-bad-idea/.

11. Sarah Churchwell, "America's Original Identity Politics," *New York Review of Books*, February 7, 2019, available via https://www.nybooks.com/daily/2019/02/07/americas-original-identity-politics/.

12. Danielle Allen, *Talking to Strangers: Anxieties of Citizenship Since Brown v. Board of Education* (Chicago: University of Chicago Press, 2004), 17.

13. Barbara Jordan, 1976 Democratic National Convention keynote address, July 12, 1976, available via https://www.americanrhetoric.com/speeches/barbarajordan1976dnc.html.

14. Combahee River Collective Statement, 1973, available via https://americanstudies.yale.edu/sites/default/files/files/Keyword%20Coalition_Readings.pdf.

15. Kyle Chayka, "America Is a Utopia Experiment—And Always Has Been," *Pacific Standard*, June 14, 2017, available via https://psmag.com/social-justice/america-utopian-experiment-always-73410.

16. Thomas Paine, "Common Sense," in *Paine: Political Writings*, ed. B. Kuklick (Cambridge: Cambridge University Press, 1997), 44.

17. Ronald Reagan, "Remarks at the Annual Convention of the National Association of Evangelicals," March 8, 1983, available via https://americanrhetoric.com/speeches/ronaldreaganevilempire.htm.

18. Ian Barnard, "Toward a Postmodern Understanding of Separatism," *Women's Studies* 27 (1998): 620–621.

19. Celeste Michelle Condit and John Louis Lucaites, "Malcolm X and the Limits of the Rhetoric of Revolutionary Dissent," *Journal of Black Studies* 23 (1993): 297.

NOTES   283

20. Adrienne Rich, "Review: Living the Revolution," *The Women's Review of Books* 3 (1986): 3. See also Alice Echols, *Daring to Be Bad: Radical Feminism in America, 1967–1975* (Minneapolis: University of Minnesota Press, 1989), 5.

21. Ralph Ellison, "Haverford Statement," May 31, 1969, available via https://teachingamericanhistory.org/library/document/haverford-statement/.

22. Barnard, "Toward a Postmodern Understanding of Separatism," 626.

23. Sarah Lucia Hoagland, "Introduction," *Sinister Wisdom* 34 (1988): 23, 24.

24. Ryan Miller, "Secession Is a Solution for Deep Political Division," Foundation for Economic Education, November 9, 2016, available via https://fee.org/articles/secession-is-a-solution-for-deep-political-division/.

25. Abraham Lincoln, "July 4th Message to Congress," July 4, 1861, available via https://millercenter.org/the-presidency/presidential-speeches/july-4-1861-july-4th-message-congress.

26. Churchwell, "America's Original Identity Politics."

27. Abraham Lincoln, First Inaugural Address, March 4, 1861, available via https://avalon.law.yale.edu/19th_century/lincoln1.asp. See also David Zarefsky, "Philosophy and Rhetoric in Lincoln's First Inaugural Address," *Philosophy and Rhetoric* 45 (2012): 165–188.

28. Danielle Allen, *Our Declaration: A Reading of the Declaration of Independence in Defense of Equality* (New York: Liveright, 2014), 21.

29. Maria Lugones, "Purity, Impurity, and Separation," *Signs* 19 (1994): 476.

30. James Baldwin, "Letter from a Region in My Mind," *New Yorker*, November 17, 1962, available via https://www.newyorker.com/magazine/1962/11/17/letter-from-a-region-in-my-mind.

31. Adam Waytz, Liane L. Young, and Jeremy Ginges, "Motive Attribution Asymmetry for Love vs. Hate Drives Intractable Conflict," *Proceedings of the National Academy of Sciences of the United States of America* 111 (2014): 15687–15692.

32. Celeste Condit, "Framing Kenneth Burke: Sad Tragedy or Comic Dance?," *Quarterly Journal of Speech* 80 (1994): 77–82.

33. Baldwin, "Letter from a Region in My Mind."

34. Barnard, "Toward a Postmodern Understanding of Separatism," 627. See also Darrel Wanzer-Serrano, *The New York Young Lords and the Struggle for Liberation* (Philadelphia: Temple University Press, 2015), 68, 87.

35. Claudia Card, "Pluralist Lesbian Separatism," in *Lesbian Philosophies and Cultures*, ed. J. Allen (Albany: SUNY Press, 1990), 136.

284 NOTES

36. Bernice Johnson Reagon, "Coalition Politics: Turning the Century," in *Home Girls: A Black Feminist Anthology*, ed. B. Smith (New York: Kitchen Table Press, 1983), 357–358.

37. Martha C. Nussbaum, "Patriotism and Cosmopolitanism," in *For Love of Country?*, ed. J. Cohen (Boston: Beacon Press, 1996), 4.

38. Amy Gutmann, "Democratic Citizenship," in *For Love of Country?*, ed. J. Cohen (Boston: Beacon Press, 1996), 67.

39. Sissela Bok, "From Part to Whole," in *For Love of Country?*, ed. J. Cohen (Boston: Beacon Press, 1996), 39.

40. James Baldwin, "Letter from a Region in My Mind."

41. Ta-Nehisi Coates, *Between the World and Me* (New York: Spiegel & Grau, 2015), 60.

42. Elaine Scarry, "The Difficulty of Imagining Other People," in *For Love of Country?*, ed. J. Cohen (Boston: Beacon Press, 1996), 103.

43. Jeremy Engels, "Friend or Foe? Naming the Enemy," *Rhetoric and Public Affairs* 12 (2009): 57.

44. Allen, *Talking to Strangers*, xvi.

45. Lugones, "Purity, Impurity, and Separation," 460, 464, 476.

46. Cass R. Sunstein, *Designing Democracy: What Constitutions Do* (New York: Oxford University Press, 2001), 9.

47. Eric Walther, *The Fire-Eaters* (Baton Rouge: Louisiana State University Press, 1992), 301.

48. Assata Shakur, "To My People," *Women's Studies Quarterly* 46 (2018): 217–221.

49. Card, "Pluralist Lesbian Separatism," 136.

50. Ann Japenga, "The Separatist Revival," *Outlook* 2 (1990): 82.

51. Japenga, "The Separatist Revival," 83.

52. Allen Buchanan, "Democracy and Secession," in *National Self-Determination and Secession*, ed. M. Moore (New York: Oxford University Press, 1998), 14–30.

53. Robert Pinsky, "Eros Against Esperanto," in *For Love of Country?*, ed. J. Cohen (Boston: Beacon Press, 1996), 86.

54. Bryan Garsten, *Saving Persuasion: A Defense of Rhetoric and Judgment* (Cambridge, MA: Harvard University Press, 2006), 4–5.

55. Karen Grigsby Bates, "Life at Jefferson's Monticello, as His Slaves Saw It," NPR, March 11, 2012, available via https://www.npr.org/2012/03/11/148305319/life-at-jeffersons-monticello-as-his-slaves-saw-it.

56. Thomas Jefferson, First Inaugural Address, March 4, 1801, available via https://avalon.law.yale.edu/19th_century/jefinau1.asp.

57. Thomas Jefferson to John Taylor, June 4, 1798, available via https://founders.archives.gov/documents/Jefferson/01-30-02-0280.

Index

For the benefit of digital users, indexed terms that span two pages (e.g., 52–53) may, on occasion, appear on only one of those pages.

abolitionism, 26, 27, 68, 70–71, 75, 78–79, 81, 82, 85–86, 88–89, 95, 98, 100, 106–7, 196
Adams, John Quincy, 27, 84
Africa, 48–49, 96, 106, 109, 111, 113, 118, 122, 124–28, 130–31, 132, 137
Alleghenies, 1, 3
American experiment, 2
American Revolution, 1, 35–36, 37, 38, 41, 43, 45, 65–66, 71–72, 81, 89, 91, 108, 111, 118, 129, 153. *See* Revolutionary War
anarchism, 51, 53–54, 68, 69–70, 71–73
anarchy, 4–5, 43, 95
Anderson, Jackie, 146
anti–federalism, 4, 5, 17–18, 53, 60–61
Appomattox (end of the Civil War), 6, 52–22, 60–61, 77
Articles of Confederation, 17–18, 61, 63

Baldwin, James, 120, 204–5, 206
Baraka, Amiri, 112, 114, 120
Berson, Ginny, 160–61
Black nationalism, 110–15
Black Panthers, 109–10
Black power, 109–10, 112, 130, 138, 139, 140
Bloom, Harold, 170, 185
Brown, H. Rap, 120, 139
Brown, John, 27–28, 32, 76, 86, 88–89
Brown v. Board, 101, 102
Burr, Aaron, 4, 24

Calhoun, John C., 5–6, 19–21, 23–24, 39–40, 61–63, 66–67, 78, 80–82, 84–86, 87, 92, 97–98, 99–100, 102–3

California, 30–31, 73, 78, 85–86
Carmichael, Stokely (Ture, Kwame), 111, 138, 139, 140
Chisholm v. Georgia, 23–24
citizenship, 8, 15, 23, 30–31, 116, 132, 136, 143, 198, 217–18n.11
Civil War (1861–65), 6, 10, 19, 21–24, 27–28, 67, 76, 79–81, 86, 87, 96, 99–101, 109, 114, 118, 132, 190, 191–92, 196
Clay, Henry, 19–20, 25, 106
Clayton, William, 177
Clinton, Hillary, 164
Coates, Ta-Nehisi, 122, 130, 206
colonization, 106, 107, 110, 117, 118
Combahee River Collective, 166, 200
Confederacy, 19, 23, 32, 39–40, 76, 79, 89, 90–91, 92–93, 97–98, 100, 131, 136, 148
conservatives, 28–30, 66–67, 71–72, 102–3
Constitutional Convention, 26, 63, 80–81, 82–83, 97–98, 99–100
Cooper v. Aaron, 102
currency, 1, 31

Daly, Mary, 146
Davis, Angela, 116
Davis, Jefferson, 23, 66–67, 78, 102–3
De Bow, J.D.B., 93, 94, 96
De Bow's Review, 87, 91
Declaration of Independence, 10–11, 15, 16, 17–18, 36–37, 39–40, 63–64, 90–92, 99–100, 105, 110, 111, 115, 116–17, 129, 133, 136, 181, 195
Delany, Martin, 109–10, 122

286 INDEX

democracy, 6–7, 8–9, 16, 23, 31, 36–37, 42, 45, 54–55, 57–58, 72, 89–90, 96, 107, 133–34, 136, 182–83, 194, 203–7, 208–9

Densmore, Dana, 153, 155–56, 163

disunion, 3, 8, 18, 23, 27, 65, 99–100, 195, 204

Douglass, Frederick, 105, 106–7, 108–9, 111, 117

Dred Scott v. Sandford, 79, 86

Du Bois, W.E.B., 114

Dunbar, Roxanne, 150, 153, 155–56, 157–59

Dykewomon, Elana, 165–66

emancipation, 106–7

Emerson, Ralph Waldo, 10–11, 45

emigration, 106–7

Enlightenment era, 15, 41, 60, 89–90

e pluribus unum, 6

federal authority, 1, 2, 27–28, 34, 87–88

federal government, 5, 17–18, 19–21, 23, 38, 50, 63, 70, 73–74, 78–79, 102, 103, 176, 179–80, 185–86, 193, 194

federalism, 2, 4, 10–11, 20, 29, 54, 196, 214–15n.54

Federalist Papers, 2, 18, 20–21, 29

Federalist Party, 5, 17–18, 24–25, 61, 65

feminism, 145–46, 150, 160, 161–62, 164–65, 168
    lesbian, 145–46

Fifteenth Amendment, 101

fire-eaters, 75, 78–79, 80–82, 85, 86–88, 94, 96, 97–99

Fort Sumter, 23–24, 76, 77, 79, 80, 108

Fourteenth Amendment, 23, 132

France, 2, 78–79, 95–96

Friedan, Betty, 145

Frye, Marilyn, 146, 151, 161–62

Garnet, Henry Highland, 118

Garrison, William Lloyd, 34, 83, 117

Garvey, Marcus, 113, 118, 122, 123–28, 131, 148

George, Henry, 31

Georgia, 5–6, 8–9, 78–79, 83–84, 87–88, 90–91, 119, 131, 133

Haiti, 106–8, 111–12

Hamer, Fannie Lou, 116

Hamilton, Alexander, 1, 2–5, 18, 23, 43, 53, 60–61, 208–9

Hammond, James, 95–96

Hayek, Friedrich, 54, 68

Henry, Milton (Gaidi Obadele), 130–31, 133–35

Henry, Patrick, 89–90

Henry, Richard (Imari Obadele), 130–31, 132, 133, 134, 135–36

Hoagland, Sarah Lucia, 147, 202

Houston, Sam, 99

individualism, 29, 43–44, 65–66, 68, 69, 72–73, 74, 201

indivisibility, 6, 101

interposition, 9–10, 20, 25, 28, 33, 61

Jackson, Andrew, 61–62, 68, 70, 100

Jefferson, Thomas, 1, 4, 16, 18–20, 23, 24, 39–41, 43, 44, 53, 60–61, 63–67, 68, 71, 72, 78, 83, 84, 90, 91–92, 102–3, 106, 111, 115, 184–85, 195, 208–9

Jo, Bev, 142, 143–44, 167

Johnston, Jill, 147

Karenga, Maulana, 138–39

Kilpatrick, James J., 66–67

King, Martin Luther King, Jr., 109, 116–17, 119, 200, 204

Knox, Henry, 2–3

Ku Klux Klan, 100, 118, 121, 124, 132–33

Lane, Rose Wilder, 55

Latter–Day Saints, 11–12, 50, 169–71, 173, 174, 175–76, 177–81, 185, 187, 191–92, 193, 194, 198

Lee, Anna, 165–66

Lee III, Henry, 2–6

lesbian separatism, 141–42, 144, 145–46, 147, 148–49, 159, 161, 165–66, 168, 197, 202, 205–6, 207

Libertarian party, 54

libertarianism, 50, 52–60, 62–64, 67–70, 73

liberty, 2, 4–5, 9–11, 16, 19, 25–26, 33–35, 37, 40–41, 51, 52, 54–55, 57–58,

59–60, 64, 65–67, 69–70, 71–73, 78–
79, 89–90, 91, 92, 107–8, 125, 129,
157, 180, 188, 196, 204
Lieber, Francis, 43
Lincoln, Abraham, 9–10, 21–22, 23–24,
42, 43, 53, 61, 64, 67, 71–72, 76, 80,
88–89, 106–7, 124, 200, 203–4
Locke, John, 55–56, 64, 92
Lost Cause, 65–66, 102–3
Lyman, Amasa, 185–86, 188

Madison, James, 6–7, 18, 19–21, 83,
92–93, 106
Maine, 2–3, 21–22, 37–38
Malcolm X, 119, 122, 126–31, 135–
36, 148
Manifest Destiny, 10–11, 45
Marshall, John, 53, 61, 65
Massachusetts, 4, 24–25, 27, 37–38, 68,
70, 71–72, 172–73
Mexico, 37–38, 42, 97–98, 141, 169–70,
171–72, 188, 192–94
Mill, John Stuart, 42–43
minority groups, 38
minority rights, 2, 42, 53, 54–56, 203
Mississippi, 80, 87–88, 100, 136
Missouri, 84, 85–86, 99–100
von Mises, Ludwig, 47, 54, 58, 59–61
Montesquieu, 124–25
Mormonism, 177, 178–79
Book of—, 177, 178–79
Church, 173, 174–76, 179–80, 182–83,
191–92, 193
theocracy, 173
War, 175–76
Muhammad, Elijah, 119–20, 126

national identity, 10, 11–12, 13, 16–17, 51,
92–93, 105, 138–39, 198–200
nationalism, 16, 35, 41, 54, 58, 62, 109,
110–11, 113, 124, 127, 136, 147,
148–49, 164, 197, 200
Black, 109, 110–12, 113, 128, 138–39,
140, 197
cultural, 137–39
libertarian, 52
southern, 31, 67–68, 75, 103
white, 129, 140

natural rights, 41, 53, 54, 55–56, 57, 58–
59, 89–90, 91, 125
New England, 4, 24–25, 32, 36–37, 208–9
New Hampshire, 49–51
New Orleans, 1, 24, 93, 131
New York, 25, 32, 37–38, 61, 170, 174–75
New York City, 23–24, 61, 154–55, 164
Newton, Huey P., 109–10, 116
Nock, Albert Jay, 49, 57, 60, 62–63
Nozick, Robert, 51
nullification, 9–10, 15, 19–21, 23–24, 25,
28–30, 33, 52, 61–63, 64–67, 70, 73,
78–79, 84–86, 99–100, 196

Obama, Barack, 29–30
Ohio River, 2, 69
Oliver, Mike, 47–49
Owen, Robert, 69

Paine, Thomas, 41, 60–61, 68, 116–
17, 201
Patterson, Isabel, 55, 57–58
Pennsylvania, 1–3, 5–6, 25, 173
Petigru, James, 99–100
Philadelphia, 2–4, 25, 136, 138
Pilgrims, 8, 36–37
Pinckney, Charles, 82–83
Pinckney, Charles Cotesworth, 82–84
pluralism, 200–1
polarization, 8–9, 45, 199
political language, 8, 34–35, 36–37, 195,
198, 199, 201, 203–4
popular rule, 2, 133–34
Pratt, Orson, 179–80, 181, 184
presidential power, 2
Prigg v. Pennsylvania, 79
protest, 2, 20–21, 77, 116–17, 146, 174

racism, 66–68, 107, 119, 138, 152, 158–59,
167, 197
white, 112, 114, 115, 116, 120
Rand, Ayn, 47, 49, 50, 55, 68
Randolph, John, 75
Reagon, Bernice Johnson, 167–68
Reconstruction, 101
"religious liberty," 33–34
religious oppression, 10–11, 36–37
Republic of New Africa, 113, 122, 130–36

288 INDEX

Revolutionary War, 1, 4–5, 37, 38
Rhett, Robert Barnwell, 75, 78, 80, 82–83, 84, 87, 96
Rhode Island, 36–37, 61
Rigdon, Sidney, 178–79
Romney, Catherine Cottam, 169, 171–72
Romney, Miles P., 169–70, 171–72
Romney, Mitt, 192–93
Rothbard, Murray, 55, 57–59, 60, 68
Ruffin, Edmund, 75–78, 80, 82–83, 87, 108
rule of law, 2, 100
rum, 1
Rustin, Bayard, 116, 128
Ruston, 142, 144
Rutledge, John, 82–83

Scalia, Antonin, 21–22
seasteading, 47–49
secession, 4, 6–10, 15–16, 18, 21–34, 41, 50, 53, 73–74, 81–82, 109–10, 131, 133–34, 137, 196, 203
self–determination, 2, 15–16, 33, 42–43, 44, 58, 59, 77, 107, 108–9, 110, 111–12, 113, 126, 127–28, 133, 144, 201, 202
separatism, 6, 10–11, 13, 21, 32, 33, 34–44, 73–74, 81, 82–83, 89–91, 110–11, 195–99, 203, 204, 205–6
Shakur, Assata, 116, 207
Shelby Co. v. Holder, 102
Sherman, William Tecumseh, 76, 103
Silicone Valley, 74
slavery, 4, 11–12, 25, 27, 29–30, 31, 44, 57–58, 62, 67–68, 70–72, 79–80, 81, 82–84, 85, 88–89, 90, 92–94, 95, 96, 97–100, 101, 102–3, 105, 106–8, 113, 114, 117, 132–33, 158, 191–92, 196, 207
African—, 81–82, 87–88, 94, 96, 158
anti–slavery, 25, 27, 44, 83–84, 88–89, 100
chattel—, 89–90, 91
pro–slavery laws, 78–79
southern—, 26–27, 81–82
women—, 157–58
Smith, Joseph, 170, 174–75, 176–79, 181, 182, 183–85, 189, 193, 194

Solanas, Valerie, 149–50, 151, 152
South Carolina, 7–8, 19–20, 23–24, 25, 31–32, 43, 61–62, 70, 80, 82–84, 89–91, 95, 98, 99–100, 102–3, 109–10, 111–12, 131, 133, 138
sovereignty, 2, 13–14, 15, 37–38, 41, 42–43, 45, 48, 64, 73–74, 125, 134–35, 147, 148–49, 174, 197–98
Black, 133–34
individual, 69–70, 71–72
national, 23, 73
personal, 69–70
popular, 37–38, 41
state, 20–21, 29, 65, 78, 89–90
Spencer, Herbert, 55–57
Spencer, Orson, 188
Spooner, Lysander, 68, 70–72
Spratt, Leonidas, 96–98
states' rights, 10–11, 19, 25, 33–34, 60, 61, 65–66, 75, 79, 196
Stephens, Alexander, 85–86, 87, 89, 91, 102–3
Stewart, Maria, 117
Story, Joseph, 53, 61, 71
Strega, Linda, 142, 144
subsidiarity, 61, 62–63

taxes, 1, 31, 50, 52, 73–74, 196
avoidance, 74
collector, 1–2, 72–73
and excise, 1, 2
and whiskey, 2, 34
Taylor, John, 75, 170, 178–79, 185–86, 188
Tenth Amendment, 17–18, 61, 63, 73–74
Tertium Quids, 27–28, 61, 65–66, 75
Texas, 23, 32, 38, 87–88, 98
Texas v. White, 23
Thirteenth Amendment, 132, 135–36
Thomas, Clarence, 138
Thoreau, Henry David, 10–11, 68
transphobia, 167
Tucker, Benjamin, 68, 71–73
Turner, Nat, 148
tyranny, 4–5, 37, 41, 55–56, 186

United States Congress, 19–20, 27, 28, 62, 64–65, 79–80, 85, 92, 99–100, 109–10, 124, 130–31, 191–92

INDEX 289

United States Constitution (1787),
2–3, 17–18, 19–22, 23, 26–27, 28,
36–37, 43, 53, 61, 63–64, 70–71,
78–80, 82–84, 85, 88–89, 90, 92–93,
97–98, 115, 116–17, 136, 179–81,
182–83, 207
and ratification, 5, 17–18, 19–20, 53,
61, 70–71, 83–84

Van Dykes, 141, 142–43
Vermont, 30–31, 37–38
Vesey, Denmark, 106
Virginia, 2–3, 5–6, 18, 88–89, 90
Virginia Resolution, 19–21, 64

Walker, David, 116–17
Warren, Josiah, 68, 69–70, 71–72
Warrior, Betsy, 150–51

Washington, George, 2–5, 9–10, 38–40,
73, 90, 125, 131, 157, 184–85,
200, 208–9
Weathers, Mary Ann, 152, 156
Webster, Daniel, 23, 53, 61, 65, 70, 71, 106
whiskey, 1, 2
Whiskey Rebellion, 1, 3, 5, 34
and Whiskey Rebels, 2, 24
white supremacy, 44, 88, 92–93, 99, 101,
108–9, 114, 116, 124, 148
Wigfall, Louis, 75
Williams, Robert, 110, 120–21, 132
Woodruff, Wilford, 191–92
Worcester v. Georgia, 23–24
Wright, Lyman, 175

Yancey, William Lowndes, 76, 79–80, 96
Young, Brigham, 173, 178–79, 182–83, 190